THE WORK OF JESUS CHRIST IN ANABAPTIST PERSPECTIVE

*Published in association with
Bluffton University,
Bluffton, Ohio*

THE WORK OF JESUS CHRIST IN ANABAPTIST PERSPECTIVE

ESSAYS IN
HONOR OF
J. DENNY WEAVER

EDITED BY
ALAIN EPP WEAVER & GERALD J. MAST

Cascadia
Publishing House
Telford, Pennsylvania

copublished with
Herald Press
Scottdale, Pennsylvania

Cascadia Publishing House orders, information, reprint permissions:
contact@CascadiaPublishingHouse.com
1-215-723-9125
126 Klingerman Road, Telford PA 18969
www.CascadiaPublishingHouse.com

The Work of Jesus Christ in Anabaptist Perspective
Copyright © 2008 by Cascadia Publishing House,
Telford, PA 18969
All rights reserved.
Copublished with Herald Press, Scottdale, PA
ISBN 13: 978-1-931038-49-2; ISBN 10: 1-931038-49-X
Library of Congress Catalog Number: 2008010450
Book design by Cascadia Publishing House
Cover design by Dawn Ranck

The paper used in this publication is recycled and meets the
minimum requirements of American National Standard for Information Sciences—Permanence of Paper for Printed Library Materials, ANSI Z39.48-1984.

Except when loose translations or paraphrases are offered, Bible quotations are used by permission, all rights reserved, and unless otherwise noted are from *The New Revised Standard Version of the Bible*, copyright 1989, by the Division of Christian Education of the National; Council of the Churches of Christ in the USA; scripture marked NIV taken from the Holy Bible, *New International Version®*. Copyright © 1973, 1978, 1984 International Bible Society. All rights reserved throughout the world. Used by permission of International Bible Society; KJV from the *King James Version of the Bible*; Burton H. Throckmorton Jr. from *The Gospels and Letters of Paul: An Inclusive Language Edition* (Cleveland. Pilgrim Press, 1992)

Library of Congress Cataloguing-in-Publication Data
The work of Jesus Christ in Anabaptist perspective : essays in honor of J. Denny Weaver / edited by Alain Epp Weaver and Gerald J. Mast ; foreword by Myron S. Augsburger.
  p. cm.
"Bibliography of the published works of J. Denny Weaver"--P.
Includes bibliographical references and index.
ISBN-13: 978-1-931038-49-2 (6 x 9" trade pbk. : alk. paper)
ISBN-10: 1-931038-49-X (6 x 9" trade pbk. : alk. paper)
 1. Jesus Christ--Person and offices. 2. Anabaptists--Doctrines. 3. Mennonites--Doctrines. I. Weaver, J. Denny, 1941- II. Weaver, Alain Epp. III. Biesecker-Mast, Gerald, 1965- IV. Title. V. Series.

BT203.W67 2008
232.088'2843--dc22

2008010450

16 15 14 13 12 11 10 09 08   10 9 8 7 6 5 4 3 2 1

To J. Denny Weaver
scholar, teacher, friend

CONTENTS

Foreword by Myron S. Augsburger   10
Introduction by Gerald J. Mast   13

PART 1: THE WORK OF JESUS IN THE LIFE AND THEOLOGY OF J. DENNY WEAVER

1 J. Denny Weaver: A Biased Appreciation • 21
   Alain Epp Weaver

2 A Fresh Riff on J. Denny Weaver's A-Theology or Prolegomenon to a Stewardship Rhetoric • 29
   Susan L. Biesecker and Jason R. Moyer

PART 2: THE WORK OF JESUS IN THE SCRIPTURES

3 Historical Reconstruction and Theological Construction in Tension in the Work of J. Denny Weaver • 63
   Ray F. Person Jr.

4 The Violence of God and the Hermeneutics of Paul • 74
   Christopher D. Marshall

5 Imitation as Participation: Discipleship in Paul's Letters • 106
   Laura L. Brenneman

6 Atonement and Sacrifice in the Book of Revelation • 124
   Loren L. Johns

PART 3: THE WORK OF JESUS IN ANABAPTISM

7 Retrieving Historical Anabaptist Christology for Contemporary Anabaptist Theology • 149
   Thomas N. Finger

8 Jesus' Flesh and the Faithful Church in the
  Theological Rhetoric of Menno Simons • 173
  Gerald J. Mast

9 The Canons of Anabaptism: Which Anabaptism?
  Whose Canon? • 191
  Ray Gingerich

PART 4: THE WORK OF JESUS ON THE CROSS

10 Atonement: Being Remembered • 225
   Harry J. Huebner

11 "Who Durst Defy the Omnipotent to Arms?"
   The Nonviolent Atonement and a Non-Competitive
   Doctrine of God • 246
   J. Alexander Sider

12 Needles Not Nails: Marginal Methodologies and
   Mennonite Theology • 263
   Malinda Elizabeth Berry

13 Notes for a Nonviolent Eschatology • 282
   Jane Thorley Roeschley

PART 5: THE WORK OF JESUS IN THE CHURCH

14 "The Tongue is a Fire": On the Dangerous Missiological
   Vocation of the Theologian • 309
   Alain Epp Weaver

15 An Anabaptist Theology of Youth Ministry • 323
   Randy Keeler

16 Taking Up Our Harps, Hanging Up Our Harps:
   Worship in the "Already, But Not Yet" Church • 337
   Janeen Bertsche Johnson

PART 6: THE WORK OF JESUS IN THE WORLD

17 The Gift of Creation and Interpretation • 345
   Trevor George Hunsberger Bechtel

18 "Truth Did Not Come Into the World Naked": Some Images, Some Stories, and an Immodest Proposal • 371
   Jeff Gundy
19 Christus Victor and the Preoccupation With the Concrete in the Work of Christian Peacemaker Teams • 386
   Kathleen Kern

Bibliography of the Published Works of J. Denny Weaver   401
Index   417
The Contributors   427

Foreword

"**B**ut God forbid that I should glory, save in the cross of our Lord Jesus Christ, by whom the world is crucified unto me and I unto the world" (KJV). This is not only Paul's declaration but that of many persons in the Anabaptist tradition. To paraphrase similar words central to Anabaptist faith from Ephesians 2:14-16: "He is our peace who has made both one new humanity, so making peace, and in this one body to reconcile both to God through the cross."

Reading this amazing festchrift with its diverse chapters, I have been impressed first with the references to the person and emphases of J. Denny Weaver. This volume makes me wish to have had opportunity to know Denny as more than an acquaintance. But it is good to come to know him more fully in these pages. I thank God for his keen mind and his deliberate challenge to theologians to seek consistency with the "truth as it is in Jesus."

Given the vigor of Weaver's thought as well as the diversity with which his perspectives are engaged in this volume, it is likely inevitable that any commentator will find areas both of affirmation and creative tension. The value of this book is not in offering unassailable theology but in plunging us into vigorous engagement with important issues, whether or not we always agree. Let me offer examples.

Weaver's interpretation of theology from the perspective of nonviolence is a commitment to God's plan of peace, a conviction I share. In scores of evangelistic missions in presenting the message of Christ, I have related the gospel and its call to nonviolence.

As to the atonement, frequently addressed by Weaver and in these pages, with Weaver I have long rejected the perspective of a violent God pouring out judgment on his son. However, I have interpreted "satisfaction" more relationally. When Paul writes, "God was in Christ reconciling the world to himself," this says to me that God was suffering in and with Jesus in paying the price of forgiveness. He did so with the integrity that defeats all enemies forever.

Much of what Denny Weaver teaches on Christ and nonviolence could, and in fact I think should, be shared on the basis of an interpretation of the incarnation—God's expression of true humanness in the life of Jesus. Here we have the word and will of God personified, nonviolence being expressed through his life and teaching, ultimately on the cross in bearing the full intensity of human hostility.

A basic division of theories of atonement is whether its meaning is objective or subjective. For St. Anselm, the atonement is primarily objective; its effect is primarily on God. Meanwhile in Abelard, the atonement is primarily subjective; its effect is primarily on us. But as H. E. W. Turner says of these approaches in *The Meaning of the Cross* (Mowbray, 1959), "Both are needed for any interpretation of the atonement. The objective view maintains that 'He did it for me,' while the subjective theories assure that 'He died to make us good'" (7).

Several chapter writers who deal with Anabaptist history and thought do not emphasize any one view of the atonement but rather the new community. From my studies under John Howard Yoder and Harold S. Bender, especially in my own theological work, I see the central focus of the Anabaptists to be, in fact, on our being new creatures in Christ. Emphasizing transforming grace, the Anabaptists then called people to a new life of discipleship shaped in love, freedom, justice, and nonviolence. There are numerous references to the subjective meanings of being crucified with Christ to be found in Anabaptist writings, often in letters from prison. In the 1527 Schleitheim confession and in the thought of early Anabaptist Michael Sattler, the emphasis is on the new life in covenant of those who are reconciled citizens of the kingdom, called into a community of faith as a presence for Christ in society.

Various chapters, perhaps especially those of Huebner and Marshall, express the dynamics of grace in the salvific work of Christ as basic to the meaning of at-one-ment in the cross. I affirm Marshall's point that as there was no violence in creation, so we should see this as significant in our interpretation of the new creation. Meanwhile Marshall's expression of a hermeneutic relating Old Testament and New Testament as "promise to fulfillment" presents God as meeting people at their level of understanding. This suggests answers to concerns with the use of law and the presence of war in the Old Testament order. Further we need to distinguish between the descriptive and the prescriptive in biblical passages to discern what God is ordering. For those who fail to see this progress of revelation, I would point to the doctrine of resurrection, regarding which we have only limited Old Testament statements so need to turn to Christ for the fuller word.

There are references in these pages to the sovereignty of God and his justice in relation to the problem of our sin. I believe sovereignty is best understood as God's self-determination: God always acts consistently with himself. Therefore in his love God will not violate the human person but in sovereign patience respects our choices. God judges sin by exposing it in the cross for what it is even while being sovereignly present in love.

As we turn to the judgment passages in the book of the Revelation, it seems we are shown that evil self-destructs, that its future is the nothingness of the "bottomless pit" in which evil moves farther and farther from God forever. This deserves to be placed in conversation with the perspective of at least one author whose treatment of nonviolent eschatology can be read as a restatement of universalism. Further, the last chapters, in section V, leave me wanting to pursue more clarity regarding how we present the "Good News" as a transforming power that can in turn call persons to the experience of salvation, discipleship, and the way of nonviolence.

In viewing the cross and thinking of the atonement, with all of the mystery of its meaning so evident in these pages, we become aware that here is the center of our being reconciled to God. This reconciliation, this forgiveness in self-giving, is central to our redemption. As my friend J. Lawrence Burkholder commented to me at a conference on Christology, "Some want a Christology for ethics, but I still need a savior." Good people need a savior because merely being "good" is not enough; being good or religious does not in itself earn God's acceptance. The basic need is for relationship with the Lord himself.

In simple faith response to the gospel, we recognize that we cannot explain all of this mystery but can still find at the cross God's amazing grace. I thank all involved with this book for inviting us to think about that cross. There is risk here of shrouding the cross in abstraction and contention. There is also the possibility of hearing God anew. Thank God for the cross!

—Myron S. Augsburger
 President Emeritus, Eastern Mennonite University
 Harrisonburg, Virginia

INTRODUCTION

Gerald J. Mast

*I*n Matthew's Gospel, Jesus teaches that the difference between true and false prophets is shown by the fruit they produce: "every good tree bears good fruit, but a bad tree bears bad fruit" (Matt. 7:17 NIV). In this volume of Anabaptist perspectives on the work of Jesus Christ, the prophetic teaching and writing of J. Denny Weaver bears good fruit. This does not mean that all the essays in the book conform to Denny's viewpoint. Indeed, many of the authors take issue with positions Denny advances throughout his work. But all of the chapters are concerned with the question which J. Denny Weaver urges his friends, colleagues, and fellow church members to address with seriousness: how can the life, teaching, death, and resurrection of Jesus Christ become the indispensable performative script for the practices of God's people?

Denny typically answers this question by highlighting the nonviolent character of God as revealed in Jesus Christ and by critiquing all forms of *Heilsgeschichte* (salvation history) that feature a violent God who demands bloody sacrifices, whether that be the sacrifice of the enemy in warfare or the sacrifice of God's child as an atonement for human sin. Denny's vigorous challenge both to just war doctrines and to substitutionary atonement theology can be understood best from the standpoint of his conviction that the acceptance of the latter was one cause of the church's pagan accommodation to the former. For Denny, an angry and violent God who demands just recompense for offenses to his honor is the sort of God easily invoked by people who are prepared to kill in the name of ideology, nation, or empire.

Furthermore, the willingness of such a God to sacrifice his beloved son as a substitute for the payment/punishment owed by the disobedient human race is simply confirmation of a logic of justice based on reciprocity: eye for eye, tooth for tooth, life for life. For Denny, the good news of the gospel is not that God sent his son Jesus to pay the price for our sin, but rather that God's son Jesus accomplished a nonviolent victory over sin that makes true freedom possible by breaking the cycles of reciprocity and retaliation in which people are enslaved. The God of Jesus Christ is the God who seeks to "loose the chains of injustice and untie the cords of the yoke, to set the oppressed free and break every yoke" (Isa. 58:6 NIV).

Denny has been tireless in proclaiming the visibility of this nonviolent liberating God in the work of Jesus Christ and in the life of Jesus' body—the faithful church throughout the ages, whenever and wherever it has proclaimed the gospel of peace through word and deed. Of course, Denny's insistence precisely on the lordship of the Prince of Peace—the one who came preaching peace—over against any form of Christian allegiance to a vaguer or more general deity has often annoyed and provoked those who wish to reproduce the safe marginality to which Ernst Troeltsch and the brothers Niehbur had consigned those Christians historically known as the peace churches. For if Denny has insisted on anything, it is that the God of peace to which peace churches give their allegiance is the same God of Jesus Christ served by all who claim to be Christian.

The first two essays in the book seek to account for this sometimes annoying argumentativeness that characterizes Denny's theological posture. Alain Epp Weaver offers a biographical sketch of key moments and contexts that have shaped Denny's perspective on the world. Sue Biesecker and Jason Moyer argue that Denny's theological rhetoric can best be understood as a practice of truth-telling rooted not in modern epistemological foundations but in the courage of conviction. Together the essays in this first section of the book begin to account for the work of Jesus Christ as discovered in the life and work of J. Denny Weaver.

The rest of the book explores the various historical and theological contexts in which the work of Jesus Christ is discerned in Anabaptist theology, contexts with which Denny has been engaged in his work and which remain areas of controversy and contention among Anabaptist scholars. Thus the reader will discover in these chapters lively arguments that witness to the truth of the cross, repeated instances of what Biesecker and Moyer call stewardship rhetoric, words that cultivate "God's gift of truth." I make no effort here to package for resale the fruit of this stewardship, of this cultivation, by telling a false story about how these chapters are all woven together into an orderly and integrated whole. They are not. Instead, the reader will encounter competing claims about the glorious reconciling work of Jesus Christ, claims that precisely in their difference from each other contribute to a truthful picture of what is accomplished at the cross and through the resurrection.

Indeed, the biblical studies section begins with a rather blistering critique of Denny's use of the Bible for theological purposes. One imagines that Denny will enjoy responding vigorously to Ray Person's challenge to maintain clear boundaries between historical reconstruction and theological construction. Other essays in this section take a more affirmative approach. Christopher Marshall stresses through a careful reading of Pauline texts how the nonviolence of Jesus, the first born of creation, offers the fullest revelation of God and qualifies the violent images of God found in the Old Testament accounts. Laura Brenneman suggests that a careful reading of the apostle Paul's identification with the suffering of Jesus can empower believers to resist the death-dealing powers of this world, even at the cost of security and comfort. Loren Johns argues that the images of the slain lamb found in the book of Revelation are less a reproduction of traditions of sacrificial expiation and more an exposure of the scapegoating violence that the work of Jesus Christ has overcome.

The next section of essays deals with christological themes in historic Anabaptist texts and practices. Tom Finger finds that Anabaptist writers like Balthasar Hubmaier and Peter Riedemann stress the dynamic power of the atonement to transform the lives of believers, without neglecting the political powers confronted by Jesus. Gerald Mast discovers in Menno Simons' conviction that Jesus received his flesh from heaven a powerful affirmation of the capacity for human flesh, joined together in Christ's earthly body, to become God's new creation. Ray Gingerich applies convictions about the incarnation to a definition of Anabaptism ordered by a canonical commitment to those peaceful communal practices that make the resurrection power of Jesus visible in the world.

While Gingerich's vision of incarnational community rejects the sacralization of the church's practices, the theological section of the book begins with an essay by Harry Huebner that challenges much of

Denny's work by recuperating sacramental experiences by which believers participate in the life, death, and resurrection of Jesus Christ through God's remembrance of us rather than through our own efforts. Also challenging many of the assumptions found in Gingerich's essay, and aligning well with Huebner's theological vision, Alex Sider reconsiders the theology of powers that has shaped much contemporary Anabaptist theologizing, including Denny's. Sider rejects the idea that God is engaged in a conflict with his own creation, arguing instead for a "non-competitive" doctrine of God that highlights human participation in God's powerful actions. By contrast, from a perspective shaped by contemporary womanist and feminist writers, as well as by the writings of Julian of Norwich, Malinda Berry aligns herself with Denny Weaver's critique of substitutionary atonement, emphasizing the creative potential in the experience of being satisfied by God, rather than of needing to satisfy God.

Jane Roeschley, meanwhile, argues for an inclusive vision of God's eternal salvation, one in which all creatures and persons are reconciled and restored and in which hell is forever vanquished. Such a vision of universal restoration is a profound resource for congregations who seek to be agents for God's repair of the world, Roeschley suggests, because it provides a horizon of ultimate resurrection power that can sustain the ministries of the church.

Turning to the ongoing and future life of Christ's earthly body—the church—the next section of essays considers matters of ecclesiology. Drawing on his experience as a church worker in Palestine/Israel, Alain Epp Weaver advances a nonviolent missiological perspective that recognizes the present limits of risky discipleship, while proclaiming the good news of ultimate reconciliation heralded by the imperfect and constrained witness of the present moment. Randy Keeler offers a model for youth ministry based on the story of Jesus shaped by the Christus Victor motif rather than by the propositional theology of the four spiritual laws. Keeler urges churches to invite young people into communities that "embody the story of Jesus" rather than into individualistic relationships with Jesus. Janeen Bertsche Johnson draws on biblical images from the Jewish exile and the apocalypse of John to sketch a theology of worship and praise for a church that in today's cultural captivity witnesses to Jesus' defeat of death and evil.

The final section of the book explores the blessed and fallen creation being restored through the work of Jesus Christ. Trevor Bechtel explores the relationship between the body of God found in creation and the body of Scripture said to be God's Word. Working both with contemporary theological writers and sixteenth-century Anabaptist texts, Bechtel assures us that our bodies and God's body are crucial dimensions of the hermeneutical work involved in reading God's Word together as members of Christ's body. Bringing a poet's consciousness to the details of everyday life amid the world and its creatures, Jeff Gundy revisits ancient Gnostic texts rejected as heretical and draws on numerous poets and spiritual writers to rehabilitate a delight in the surrounding gifts of the world, a delight that shapes both inner life and outer journeys. Fittingly, this book of essays concludes with a chapter by Kathleen Kern which shows how the Christus Victor atonement narrative provides a persuasive account of the work of Christian Peacemaker Teams, an organization Denny enthusiastically supports. All of this creative and challenging writing has been thoroughly and competently indexed by Anna Yoder, a Bluffton University student who serves as a research assistant in the Communication and Theatre Department.

Running through many of these essays are issues and questions familiar to readers of J. Denny Weaver's theological work: the role of language and narrative in the work of salvation, the power of the resurrection over the forces of sin and death, interconnections between Christology and ecclesiology, and the relationship between the body of Christ and the body of the world. The book will no doubt be responsible for many contentious conversations, since it embodies the conflicted and controversial theological terrain J. Denny Weaver takes great delight in exploring together with his interlocutors. May the church discover in such vigorous conversations the presence of the Holy Spirit and the peace of Jesus Christ.

Part 1

THE WORK OF JESUS IN THE LIFE AND THEOLOGY OF J. DENNY WEAVER

CHAPTER ONE

J. DENNY WEAVER: A BIASED APPRECIATION

Alain Epp Weaver

J. Denny Weaver is a biased man—biased in favor of the Anabaptist-Mennonite tradition, biased toward nonviolence, biased against the reckless militarism of U.S. foreign policy, biased against theologies (such as Anselmian substitutionary atonement theology) he fears undermine commitment to Jesus' way of peace. Denny's biases, moreover, are not subtly disguised. Be it as a friend or as an academic adversary, Denny is passionate and outspoken.

As Denny's son-in-law, I cannot pretend to write anything resembling an objective assessment of his life and times. I first met Denny shortly after I had begun dating his oldest daughter, Sonia. Denny was visiting the Bethel College campus to give a lecture in which he not only summarized the key points of *Becoming Anabaptist*, which had just appeared, but also of some of the first articles in which he began to question the extent to which Anabaptist-Mennonite concerns about nonviolence and peace could be adequately expressed in the categories of Nicene-Chalcedonian orthodoxy. Over the coming years Denny proved generous in filling me in on the Mennonite theological landscape and in taking me seriously as a conversation partner about his emerging work on the creeds, the atonement, and the theology of history, even though my own theological understandings were woefully uninformed and undeveloped.

He also gave me helpful advice as I started an academic career. I specifically value two pieces of advice about academic writing he gave me when I was still in college: always take an editor's critiques and suggestions seriously—after I was frustrated by initial editorial comments on a journal article I had submitted—and never publish a book without an index. Denny will be glad, I trust, to see that Gerald and I have heeded his admonition by including an index in this book.

What I remember most from our first meeting, however, has nothing to do with theology. Denny happened to be on the Bethel campus at the same time as the physicist Edward Teller, in North Newton for a "peace" lecture about the atomic bomb he helped to create. Denny was staying in the same campus guest house as Teller, so Sonia and I went over one evening to visit. We became involved in a vigorous game of Boggle, with lots of loud conversation. (Denny is not the shy and retiring type.) Soon the elderly hostess of the guest house came to the living room where we were playing and shushed us, saying that Dr. Teller needed to get his rest. Denny was delighted that, even if Teller's conscience did not bother him, our noise had disturbed the slumber of the eminent physicist/apologist for nuclear weaponry.

Much of Denny's academic career can be fruitfully viewed as an attempt to disturb what he viewed as the Mennonite church's slumber on questions of peace and nonviolence. Throughout his career Denny has passionately defended the Anabaptist-Mennonite commitment to peace and nonviolence. This commitment, Denny has argued, is under threat from different forms of assimilation: on the one hand, the influence exerted on many Mennonite congregations by mainstream evangelicalism, even fundamentalism, and American "civil religion"; on the other, an ecumenical drive to identify common, core beliefs (such as the creedal affirmations of Nicaea-Chalcedon), with denominational distinctives left outside of that core and thus, arguably, marginalized and rendered unessential.

Denny's critics, for their part, worry that his critique of the creeds for what they omit and his attack on substitutionary atonement lead, contrary to Denny's intention, in the direction of another type of assimilation, an assimilation to a liberal Protestant devaluation of the centrality and finality of God's revelation in Jesus. Whether or not his critics are correct about the possible effects of his theology, Denny himself certainly would resist any christological devaluation: even as he questions the adequacy of Nicaea-Chalcedon for contemporary theology, throughout his writings Denny argues (in a manner, I would suggest, that is compatible with Nicaea-Chalcedon) that God fully and definitively discloses who God is in the life, ministry, death, and resurrection of the particular human being Jesus of Nazareth. From start to finish, Denny's writings are about proclaiming the gospel of Jesus for the building-up of his church.

Denny's concern for the future of the church's witness grows out of a lifetime of having been shaped by a Mennonite family, Mennonite churches, and Mennonite institutions. Denny did not grow up in one of the traditional centers of American Mennonite life like Goshen, Indiana; North Newton, Kansas; or Lancaster County, Pennsylvania, but rather in the urban setting of Kansas City, Kansas. When Denny was born on March 20, 1941, his father, Alvin, was on his way to becoming a master craftsman whose hand-made furniture acquired a devoted following among connoisseurs of fine wood-working. As a child, Denny spent countless hours, along with his brother, Gary, and his mother, Velma, helping his father with the family business and with the work-in-progress that was their home in the forested hills of Kansas City. He attended public schools through high school while worshipping at Argentine Mennonite Church, affiliated with the (Old) Mennonite Church, where he was baptized at age eight.

An often-told Weaver family story provides a snapshot of the Argentine congregation in the 1940s. One Christmas Eve in the early 1940s, with the family struggling to make ends meet, young Denny had become so sick that his younger brother Gary had been sent to the hospital to keep him from catching the illness. A car of Argentine elders came to the house of the young family to offer comfort and support, Alvin and Velma assumed. Instead, the elders informed Alvin that they had decided that he could teach Sunday school at the church if he would agree to stop wearing a tie. Alvin continued wearing ties. Later in life, Velma and Alvin would move to the General Conference-affiliated Rainbow Mennonite Church, where they became beloved fixtures of a predominantly young, urban, professional (and unapologetically inclusive) church until their deaths in the early 1990s. If Denny learned the importance of church from his parents, which he certainly did, he also learned from them the importance of stubborn determination in persisting in the course of action one believes to be right.

Denny's post-high school studies, and later his teaching career, took him to most centers of Mennonite learning in the U.S. He spent his first two undergraduate years at Hesston College in Kansas, before completing his bachelor's degree work in mathematics at Goshen College in Indiana in 1963. Even as he completed his mathematics degree, however, Denny's interests had shifted toward theology, and after college he began seminary studies at Goshen Biblical Seminary. These studies were interrupted as Denny, like many young men of his generation, participated in Mennonite Central Committee's Teachers Abroad Program (TAP), serving in France and then at the Lycée Al-Salam in Al-Asnam, Algeria, together with his wife, Mary, from 1965 to 1968.

After a year of study at the Theologische Hochschule in Bethel bei Bielefeld, Germany, Denny returned to Elkhart, where he completed his Master of Divinity degree in 1970. Denny's generation was perhaps the last in which the default assumption was that training as a Mennonite theologian meant immersion in and a primary focus on Anabaptist history and theology. As a doctoral student at Duke University, Denny concentrated in historical theology. Under the direction of David Steinmetz, he produced a dissertation on the doctrine of God held by different Anabaptists and received his PhD in 1975.

After teaching the 1974-75 year at Goshen College, Denny took a teaching position at Bluffton College (now Bluffton University), where he stayed for the rest of his academic career, apart from a sabbatical in 1990-1991 spent at Canadian Mennonite Bible College. Denny served as a devoted faculty member at Bluffton for over three decades, working tirelessly to help make Bluffton a center of Mennonite scholarship. From his arrival at Bluffton in 1975 onwards, Denny time and again insisted that Bluffton, instead of sliding willingly or inadvertently into becoming a mainstream evangelical institution of higher learning, needed to embrace its Anabaptist-Mennonite heritage and to highlight the church's teachings regarding peace and nonviolence. Particularly during his last fifteen years or so at Bluffton, Denny thrived, excited by what he perceived as the institution's recovery and embrace of its Mennonite past, and by the arrival of a new generation of scholars committed to making Bluffton a leading center of Mennonite learning.

Denny's involvement at Bluffton extended well beyond the classroom. He acted as faculty advisor for the peace club during much of the 1970s and 1980s; Kathy Kern of Christian Peacemaker Teams recalls Denny defending the peace club's decision to sponsor a vote at Bluffton to make the campus a nuclear-free zone, a vote that some at Bluffton feared would bring unwelcome attention to the college.

Denny's commitment to nonviolent peacemaking has included involvement with Christian Peacemaker Teams (CPT): He participated in one of CPT's first delegations to Haiti and has provided theological input to CPT's training sessions for its activists. For much of the 1990s until his retirement, Denny chaired the religion department. He played an instrumental role in founding the increasingly influential C. Henry Smith Series, an interdisciplinary set of studies engaging culture from out of the Anabaptist-Mennonite tradition, and has served as editor of the series since its inception in 2000.

An avid amateur athlete, Denny relished his role as Bluffton's NCAA faculty representative, a position he held for twenty-two years. In 2006 the Heartland Collegiate Athletic Conference honored this service, noting that, "Like Paul," Denny had "recognized that athletics teach competitors valuable life lessons which are also very applicable to their Christian growth." He also put his own athletic talents at the university's disposal, one time wrestling a bear as part of a Bluffton fundraiser. For many years Denny regularly contributed commentary, often in a humorous vein, to the campus newspaper, *The Witmarsum*. Some of the titles of these commentaries give a sense of their often tongue-in-cheek quality: "The Split Infinitive and Other Threats to Civilization as We Know It," "The Pros and Cons of Junior Orals: Con," and, under the pseudonym Good E. Trachschuhs, "An Opinion: Plodding for Jesus."

While he became a major part of Bluffton's identity over three decades, Denny's influence extended well beyond Bluffton, both within Mennonite academia and within Mennonite churches. He has preached widely in Ohio Mennonite churches and beyond. Denny had the rare honor of being invited to present the prestigious C. Henry Smith lectures hosted by Goshen and Bluffton not once, but twice. Denny's work has been pivotal in debates from the 1980s until the present about the nature and possibility of a distinctly Mennonite theology. Mennonites, Denny is convinced, do not simply have a distinctive set of ethical commitments; rather, they have something distinctive to say about God.

From a purely quantitative perspective, Denny's output has been impressive: he has written four books and edited another; served as the series editor for five more books; written fifteen articles for collections of scholarly essays; published over thirty academic articles in Mennonite and non-Mennonite journals; contributed fifteen entries for academic handbooks and encyclopedias; written over forty-five reflections for church periodicals; penned scores of book reviews;

presented more than 110 papers at academic and church conferences; and preached and made Sunday school presentations more than one hundred times.

Considered from a qualitative perspective, the impact and influence of Denny's work matches the quantitative weight of his writing. In works like *Becoming Anabaptist* and *Keeping Salvation Ethical*, Denny turned to the Anabaptist and Mennonite past with the aim of recovering a viable theology for Mennonites today. *Becoming Anabaptist* has enjoyed wide use as an introductory text for high school, college, seminary, and Sunday school classes and, thanks to ongoing demand, appeared in an updated second edition in 2005. In his more recent works, like *Anabaptist Theology in Face of Postmodernity* and *The Nonviolent Atonement*, Denny's constructive agenda moves to the fore, as he argues for a "narrative Christus Victor" understanding of the atonement.

As he has worked on his constructive agenda, Denny has forged alliances with other theologians, including feminist and womanist theologians, who share some of his theological concerns. His work, in collaboration with Gerald Mast and many other members of the Bluffton faculty, on nonviolence in the liberal arts disciplines culminated in the ground-breaking volume, *Teaching Peace*, a study that will for years to come spur Mennonite and other colleges to think about how Christian commitment to nonviolent peacemaking should shape and suffuse the entire curriculum. While Denny's theology has certainly had influence within Mennonite academic circles, with his articles regularly appearing in leading Mennonite journals like *The Mennonite Quarterly Review* and *The Conrad Grebel Review*, his influence has, arguably, been even greater among pastors and lay leaders, with frequent articles in *Gospel Herald* and *The Mennonite* presenting his theological views in accessible form to a wide readership.

If many Mennonites and other Christians have come to know Denny through his academic and popular writing as a provocative theologian, a proper appreciation of Denny as an individual must account for the non-academic sides of his life. Denny is a dedicated husband, father, and grandfather. While at Goshen, Denny met Mary Wenger, daughter of Ruth and J. C. Wenger, the prominent Mennonite theologian and church leader. Mary and Denny married in 1965, and shortly thereafter, under the auspices of Mennonite Central Committee, moved to Belgium and then to Algeria, at a time when Algeria was being rocked by anti-colonialist unrest. Together, with Denny teaching at Bluffton and Mary for much of the time working as a nurse, they spent over three decades in Bluffton, raising a family and tending a home, before moving to Madison, Wisconsin, to be closer to children and grandchildren. As a father, Denny takes great pride in the accomplishments of his three daughters Sonia, Lisa, and Michelle, all of whom have inherited their father's stubborn determination and passionate concern for justice and peace. As a father-in-law, Denny is welcoming and generous, and as a grandfather to six he is doting, eager to introduce a new generation to the thrills of bird-watching, baseball, and stamp-collecting; and he is game for playing catch, building wooden-block towers, and having tea parties with dolls.

While some might call him an idiosyncratic packrat, Denny would undoubtedly prefer the more dignified label of "collector." He loves to troll through flea markets and antique stores looking for additions to his many collections: charms, mechanical pencils, stamps, key-chains, and coffee mugs. An avid bird-watcher, Denny faithfully updates his "life-list" of birds spotted. One of his collections is thoroughly ironic: memorabilia sent by televangelists like Oral Roberts to fictitious persons named after Denny's dogs—Mimi Thedogg and Penelope Derhund—that he placed on the televangelists' mailing lists. Denny's dedication to collecting and recording has undoubtedly also helped him in his regular discipline of journaling—Mennonite archivists and historians of the future will be deeply appreciative of the care Denny has taken to maintain this daily record of events and reflections. Denny's love of compiling lists extends to his bibliography, which records letters to the editor published in *Sports Illustrated* and the *Toledo Blade* alongside academic articles in distinguished journals like *Archiv für Reformationsgeschichte*.

Throughout his life Denny has been a passionate athlete and a devoted fan. From early childhood on, he has loyally cheered on the Chicago Cubs, perhaps appropriate for a man who had dedicated his theological career to the Sisyphean task of convincing other Christians that Jesus' way of nonviolence should be normative for Christians. As a college and later as a seminary student, Denny played catcher in baseball leagues in the Hesston and Goshen areas. Denny's love of athletic competition brings out an aggressive side that some might find incongruous with his being an ardent proponent of pacifism. Some of his Bluffton colleagues have been surprised by his vociferous cheering of decisive checking at minor-league hockey games in Toledo.

Denny is aware that some might find his delight in vigorous physical competition odd and has addressed it in print in a defense of why Christian pacifists can properly enjoy watching and playing football. While as a spectator Denny seems able to become interested in almost any sport—he claims to have become enamored with curling during a sabbatical year in Canada in the early 1990s—as an athlete he was for years dedicated to handball, an intense sport popular among Marines which he first learned to play while a graduate student at Duke. Denny has eagerly proselytized on behalf of handball, extolling its primal virtues, the way it pits one alone in an enclosed room against one's opponent without equipment save the ball and one's hands. He successfully convinced other Bluffton faculty members to take up the sport; beating Denny in a game of handball was considered a major achievement.

Denny has brought the intensity of a handball player to his theological engagements and interventions, and for that the church can be grateful. Denny has worn his theological biases on his sleeve and has been unapologetic in arguing vigorously for the centrality of God's nonviolent defeat of the powers of sin and death through Jesus. For the contributors to this book, both those who affirm and extend Denny's theological legacy and those who question and contend with parts of his work, Denny has been a dedicated teacher and colleague, mentor and friend. We offer these essays in appreciation for the way in which Denny has goaded us, the Mennonite church, and Christians in general, to take the Anabaptist-Mennonite tradition seriously as a theological tradition, to renew reflection on how commitment to nonviolent discipleship shapes and is shaped by our doctrinal affirmations, and to commit ourselves to the task (and joyful mission) of strengthening the church's witness to her nonviolent Lord.

CHAPTER TWO

A FRESH RIFF ON J. DENNY WEAVER'S A-THEOLOGY OR PROLEGOMENON TO A STEWARDSHIP RHETORIC

Susan L. Biesecker and Jason R. Moyer

Many people tell [him that his] style is [horrific]; it is kind of different, but let's get specific.[1]
—KRS One

INTRODUCTION

J. Denny Weaver's "theology" is irritating. Its style is impolite, its substance improper. Weaver writes, albeit in postmodern fashion, as one who speaks the truth. Although he recognizes that his truth is particular to an Anabaptist perspective, he also notes that every other truth-claim is similarly particular. However, while refusing to adopt common responses to this condition—polite tolerance, on the one hand, or self-righteous fundamentalism, on the other—Weaver nevertheless confesses that his truth has universal aspirations.[2]

Further, Weaver does not present his truth in an objective manner. Rather, his style is that of the advocate of a truth that carries definite implications not only for our collective politics but also for our individual salvation. Weaver's style is impolite also in the sense that it is not deferential to theological authority, whether that authority derives from tradition and takes the form of orthodoxy or grows out of privileged institutional positions and follows methodological protocol. He does not assume that well-recognized and respected theological approaches have any special claim on truth. On the contrary, he views such approaches with skepticism, assuming that their respectability has more to do with privilege than insight. Weaver also does not seek our approval; instead, he demands our assent. Rather than rationalize our present beliefs or practices, he challenges us with the truth, demands that we agree, and calls us to be transformed.

Finally, Weaver's style is relentlessly argumentative. He welcomes others' rebuttals as opportunities to sharpen his case, confident that ultimately he can win any argument. Moreover, he never tires of making his case and will make it anytime, anywhere, to anyone. In all these ways Weaver's theological style is presumptuous, irreverent, and contentious—in short, impolite.

The substance of Weaver's theology is improper when measured against the standards of traditional theology. Weaver's theology does not take up in systematic fashion the traditional categories of theology like Christology, soteriology, ecclesiology, pneumatology, etc., to theorize them in relation to each other for a comprehensive understanding. Instead, his theology speaks to traditional theological categories as a response to perceived crises within the church. For instance, Weaver takes up the atonement not to develop some larger theological system but to respond to a problem that he sees—namely, that the church's understanding of the atonement authorizes violence. In this sense Weaver's theology is deeply historical rather than primarily philosophical.

Additionally, to resolve the problems he identifies, Weaver does not turn to classical theological systems from which he might construct an alternative. Instead, he turns to Anabaptist sources, not as "heroes to emulate or principles to adopt," but as historical examples whose "struggle for faithfulness" yields a truthful interpretive lens for understanding Jesus and his relationship to the world.[3] Through this interpretive lens we can read the true story of Jesus which, if we will choose to enter it, provides a genuine Christian posture from which we may engage the world.

Not only are the sources for Weaver's theology atypical in the sense that they are historical rather than philosophical, they are also sources once (and by some still) considered heretical: Anabaptists who did not produce their own "proper" theology; who had no unified theological, sociological, or political origin; who had no reputable spokesperson (like a Luther, Calvin, or Zwingli); who were itinerants jotting down apocalyptic musings while on the run from the authorities; and who even today resist easy categorization—neither Catholic nor Protestant, neither evangelical nor fundamentalist. Non-systematic, deeply historical, and based in "heretical" sources, we could say that more than a theology, Weaver's is an a-theology.[4]

Weaver's a-theology not only breaks with the conventions and protocols of traditional theology, it also upends the purpose and disrupts the substance of proper theology. Weaver challenges the primary purpose of traditional theology, to reveal the true nature of God, by insisting that theology is always political. For Weaver theology is never purely theoretical; it is also always a practice. That is, Weaver is always interested in what theology does by way of what it says.

In *Keeping Salvation Ethical,* for instance, Weaver shows that the politics of theology, in this case nineteenth-century Mennonite atonement theology, justified violence. Thus, he argues that *"nineteenth-century Mennonite atonement theology contained a latent threat to the peace theology and to the peace practice of succeeding Mennonite generations* (italics in original)."[5] In his later study, *The Nonviolent Atonement,* Weaver continues to develop a corrective to those nineteenth-century theologies that authorized violence. His answer is what he calls narrative Christus Victor atonement theology, a theology which, he argues, is inherently nonviolent and, therefore, incapable of authorizing violence:

> Above all, in narrative Christus Victor salvation and justice are no longer based on the violence of justice equated with punishment. Salvation does not depend on balancing sin by retributive violence. Making right no longer means the violence of punishment. Justice and salvation are accomplished in narrative Christus Victor by doing justice and participating in God's saving work.[6]

So important are the politics of theology for Weaver that his starting point for producing theology is by definition political. Specifically, rather than begin with the nature of God as would a traditional theology, Weaver's theology begins with Jesus and, moreover, not just any Jesus. Weaver's theology finds its logical origin in the nonviolent Jesus of John Howard Yoder's *The Politics of Jesus.* Thus, for instance, Weaver's theology of atonement takes as its foundational premise the nonviolent politics of Jesus:

> The working assumption in development of this model [of narrative Christus Victor] is that the rejection of violence, whether the direct violence of the sword or the systemic violence of racism or sexism, should be visible in expressions of Christology and atonement.[7]

With a nonviolent political Jesus at its center, Weaver's "theology" disrupts the substance of proper theology by disturbing the normative status of the so-called ecumenical creeds. Traditionally the creeds are understood as a collection of uncontestable truths that serve as the foundation of Christendom. For Weaver the creeds are true yet problematic because they do nothing to shape the church in the direction of Jesus' teachings on the rejection of violence. Because they are silent on the teachings of Jesus, he argues, they do not do the political work that is needed—namely, to help the church witness to the nonviolent reign of God. So troubling is this argument for proper theology that it is worth quoting at length:

> Recall that Nicea's central claim is that Jesus is "one substance" or "one being" with the Father. Recall that the formula of Chalcedon proclaimed Jesus as "fully God and fully man." With awareness of the nonviolent character of the reign of God made visible in the narrative of Jesus and expressed in narrative Christus Victor, I simply ask, "What is there about the formulas of Nicea and Chalcedon that express the character of the reign of God, in particular its nonviolent character?" "What is there about these formulas that can shape the church that would follow Jesus in witnessing to the reign of God in the world?" Answer: virtually nothing. If all we know of Jesus is that he is "one substance with the Father," and that he is "fully God and fully man," there is nothing there that expresses the ethical dimension of being Christ-related, nothing there that would shape the church so that it can be a witness to the world. When these formulas serve as the summary touchstone of Christian faith, there is nothing of the particularity of Jesus to enable the Christ-related person to shape the church as an extension of Jesus' presence in the world.[8]

As texts that, according to Weaver, fail to recognize the centrality of the rejection of violence not only to Jesus but to the reign of God, the creeds should not be taken as they have been for so long as defining statements about what it means to be a Christian, even if the content of their specific propositions is accurate.

Challenging the creeds in this way renders them inadequate for current ecumenical efforts which presume that a condition of possibility for catholicity is an affirmation of the creeds as the universal and common core for all Christian theology, belief, and practice. Mark Noll observes that one of the great rifts within the Christian faith—that is, between Catholics and evangelicals—has largely been sutured by the growing recognition among these two groups that they share in common core beliefs articulated by the creeds. Thus Noll writes:

> Among evangelicals and Catholics who are open to cooperation there now exists a broad and deep foundation of agreement on the central teachings of Christianity. Such evangelicals and Catholics affirm together the Trinity, the sinfulness of humanity, the saving love of God extended to sinners in the person and work of Jesus Christ, the redeeming power of the Holy Spirit to change men and women into servants of God, and the wholesome integrity of God's law.... Differences on basic Christian convictions between Catholics and evangelicals fade away as if to nothing when compared to secular affirmations about the nature of humanity and the world.[9]

If the church's catholicity depends on core documents like the apostles' Creed or the evangelical "four spiritual laws" that omit the central truth of Jesus—the rejection of the sword—then the project of ecumenism excludes the most important feature of Christian faith. Thus, Weaver's theology disturbs the ecumenical project by suggesting that the unity it buys comes at the price of marginalizing the essential truth of Christianity—God's rejection of violence.

From the perspective of style, Weaver's theology is impolite. From the perspective of form, it is improper. From the perspective of substance, it is political. From the perspective of ecumenical efforts, it is troublemaking. Indeed, in all these ways it is irritating.

TRUTH TELLING

I came to you in weakness with great fear and trembling. My message and my preaching were not with wise and persuasive words, but with a demonstration of the Spirit's power, so that your faith might not rest on human wisdom, but on God's power.
—Paul of Tarsus (1 Cor. 2:3-5, NIV)

To better contextualize the character of Weaver's irritating, improper theology, we turn to the work of the French philosopher, Michel Foucault. Throughout his writings, Foucault seeks to describe the ways the particular discourses of psychiatry, punishment, sexuality, and even grammar discipline our subjectivity by enabling us to speak, but only according to the modes authorized by these discourses. In his study, *Fearless Speech,* Foucault takes up a question raised in the third volume of his *History of Sexuality*: How is it that, even as individual subjectivities are constituted and spoken by particular discourses, we might (and in fact do) nevertheless say something else, speaking in ways that are disruptive of available modes of making sense. To pursue this question, Foucault, as is his wont, turns to the ancient Greeks, seeking in them an idea or a practice foreign to us. What he finds is the practice of *parrhesia,* or truth telling, a practice that disturbs our still-modern understanding of truth by making it possible for us to imagine speaking truth to power even without secure epistemological foundations.

According to Foucault, the ancient Greek practice of parrhesia or truth telling speaks truth not by way of a correspondence between, say, word and reality but, instead, through a set of relationships among self, power, and morality that constitute the parrhesiastes, or truth teller. For Foucault, what this ancient Greek practice gives us is a way to tell truth that transgresses our problems with a modern understanding of truth by constituting a certain ethos or position within language and culture that enables truth telling.[10] As we will see below, this demanding ethos requires that the truth teller occupy a particular position within language and culture characterized by *frankness, truth, danger, criticism,* and *duty.*

By *frankness* Foucault means a correspondence between thought and word. The truth-teller is someone "who says everything that [she] has in mind: [she] does not hide anything, but opens [her] heart and mind completely to other people through [her] discourse."[11] The parrhesiastes practices frankness because she understands herself to speak the truth. By *truth* Foucault means a correspondence between what is believed and what is true. For Foucault, the truth-teller is someone who "says what is true because [she] *knows* it *is* true; and [she] *knows* that it is true because it really is true."[12] However, the guarantor of the truth-teller's access to truth is not a modern epistemology but, instead, her moral quality. Moreover, the sign of the truth-teller's high moral quality is her courage: "If there is a kind of 'proof' of the sincerity of the *parrhesiastes,* it is [her] *courage.*

The fact that a speaker says something dangerous—different from what the majority believes—is a strong indication that [she] is a *parrhesiastes*."

By *danger*, Foucault signals that parrhesia always involves taking a risk. For Foucault, a parrhesiastes is one who in speaking the truth takes a risk because she speaks that truth to power. That risk may or may not be life-threatening. It might involve anything from the loss of popularity, to the loss of a friendship, to the loss of life. In any case, the parrhesiastes is one who makes herself vulnerable by telling someone in power a truth they do not want to hear. Moreover, she does so because she would rather suffer on behalf of truth than gain security through falsehood. As Foucault puts it, the truth-teller takes this risk because "When you accept the *parrhesiastic* game in which your own life is exposed, you are taking up a specific relationship to yourself: you risk death to tell the truth instead of reposing in the security of a life where the truth goes unspoken."[13]

What makes the truth that the parrhesiastes tells potentially objectionable to the other in power and, therefore, risky is its critical character. When the parrhesiastes confesses a truth critical of herself, she risks punishment from the other in power. When the parrhesiastes tells a truth critical of the other in power, she risks the wrath of the other. Such risk is an integral part of truth telling for Foucault since the truth-teller is always in a subordinate relationship to the other: "[p]arrhesia is a form of criticism, either toward another or toward oneself, but always in a situation where the speaker or confessor is in a position of inferiority with respect to the interlocutor. The *parrhesiastes* is always less powerful than the one with whom [she] speaks. The *parrhesia* comes from 'below,' as it were, and is directed toward 'above.'"[14]

The parrhesiastes takes the risk of speaking a critical truth to power because she knows it to be her duty to correct an error that she or the other has made. However, in order for her to exercise her duty, she must choose it. For Foucault, parrhesia can never be coerced by another even as it is it undertaken out of an intense feeling of obligation: "To criticize a friend or a sovereign is an act of parrhesia insofar as it is a duty to help a friend who does not recognize his wrongdoing, or insofar as it is a duty toward the city to help the king to better himself as a sovereign. *Parrhesia* is thus related to freedom and to duty."[15] Parrhesia, in summary, is:

> a kind of verbal activity where the speaker has a specific relation to truth through frankness, a certain relationship to his own life

through danger, a certain type of relation to himself or other people through criticism (self-criticism or criticism of other people), and a specific relation to moral law through freedom and duty. More precisely, *parrhesia* is a verbal activity in which a speaker expresses his personal relationship to truth, and risks his life because he recognizes truth telling as a duty to improve or help other people (as well as [herself]).[16]

Initially we might be surprised to find Foucault, a postmodern philosopher of great renown, advancing a characterization of truth telling. As conventionally understood, postmodern philosophy poses a profound challenge to truth or at least to modern conceptions of a stable, coherent, and universal truth. Yet this text describes an ethos conducive to truth telling. However, truth telling for Foucault does not involve establishing an epistemological link between language and reality, but rather cultivating a mode of being within discourse that makes possible a move beyond conventional wisdom toward the articulation of something else, something new, something true. The conditions of possibility for that ethos are frankness, truth, danger, criticism, and duty.

WEAVER'S A-THEOLOGY AS TRUTH TELLING

If Anabaptists, Catholics, and Protestants shared as much in common as [Arnold] Snyder's approach, it would then follow that neither side understood the issue at stake (pun intended!).[17]
—J. Denny Weaver

With Foucault's retrieval of the ancient Greek practice of parrhesia in mind, we may read Weaver's a-theology as parrhesia and Weaver as a parrhesiastes. Indeed, the features of parrhesia make for an apt characterization of the style and substance of Weaver's a-theology.

Earlier when we were arguing that Weaver's style is impolite, we defended that claim by pointing out that it is relentlessly argumentative. Also in that connection we noted that he actively seeks out opportunities to argue his a-theological positions. Now we may say that Weaver's style or, better put, his a-theological ethos, exhibits frankness. Like the parrhesiastes, Weaver displays a correspondence between his thought and speech. It is as if he is incapable of holding back his arguments. Weaver exhibits the quality of frankness because he knows that he speaks the truth. There is nothing in Weaver's style to indicate that he hesitates about the truth he espouses. The only question for him is how to present that truth in the most logically compelling way possible.

When we earlier argued that the substance of Weaver's a-theology is improper, we said that it did not meet traditional standards of theology because it is neither systematic nor ahistorical, neither apolitical nor creedal. Instead, we said that Weaver's a-theology is always shaped by contemporary exigencies within the church. Weaver does not focus on developing a coherent theological system that will stand the test of time but, instead, on faithfully continuing that historical struggle to make the church into the visible instantiation of God's reign within the contingencies of the present. Given Weaver's Anabaptist understanding that the church makes the reign of God visible when it presents itself as an alternative community faithful to the nonviolent politics of Jesus, Weaver's a-theology is thoroughly political. Finally, we noted that Weaver's a-theology disrupts the status of the creeds by simultaneously drawing our attention to the fact that the creeds say nothing on behalf of nonviolence and insisting that nonviolence be at the center of all things theological. For all these reasons, then, we called Weaver's an a-theology—that is to say, an improper theology.

As such, Weaver's a-theology is dangerous. It is dangerous for Weaver as a theologian because it breaks the rules of the theological guild. In advancing his a-theology, then, Weaver risks marginalization or worse among proper theologians. Further, Weaver's a-theology is dangerous in the sense that it speaks truth to power. He tells theologians something that they do not want to hear—namely, that all theology is political and, further, that theirs does not have the right politics. In addition, as someone who bases his improper theology on the thinking of heretics and, in addition, locates himself in a contemporary religious tradition often taken to be sectarian, Weaver finds himself in an inferior position with respect to other theologians. As someone who challenges the theological guild from what that guild derides as a 'sectarian' position, it can be said that Weaver adopts an inferior position through his a-theology and, thus, may rightly be called critical in the sense Foucault means in his discussion of parrhesiastes.

At the crux of Weaver's a-theology is the necessary choice that all Christians must make at the foot of the cross and in the light of the resurrection between living according to the reign of God or accepting the rule of *the not-yet-reign-of-God*. For Weaver the atonement is not a matter of the sacrifice of divine flesh for human sin which, according to Anselmian substitutionary atonement, grants us God's grace. In Weaver's a-theology the Christ event represents the inbreaking of the reign of God which creates an *aporia* or impasse that all Christians must resolve by way of their own choice. Salvation obliges a choice about faith in Jesus' victory over the powers. While necessary for salvation, however, this choice is insufficient. Having made this choice the Christian must then live accordingly. She must witness to the truth in which she has faith—that the reign of God is victorious—by living according to its logic rather than according to the logics of sin and death. Thus, all that she thinks, says, and does should correspond to that reign-of-God logic.

If Weaver takes his own a-theology seriously, which he surely does, then he is obliged to tell others the truth that he knows, to tell them that their salvation depends not only on recognizing the ultimate supremacy of the reign of God but also, having done so, to witness to that choice in all that they do. He is obliged to tell this truth since he has himself made this choice. Thus, everything he thinks, says, or does, including his a-theology, must serve as his witness. Truth telling is a matter of his own salvation. It is also a matter of his duty to the other. Knowing as he does that the fate of the other's soul is at stake, Weaver is obliged to tell the other what she does not want to hear—namely, that discipleship and the conduct of life is a matter of salvation. Or, put another way, faith, although necessary, is insufficient.

Recalling what Foucault says about the relationship between freedom and obligation, we may say both that Weaver's a-theology of atonement is parrhesiastic and that Weaver is a parrhesiastes. It is parrhesiastic, first, because it depends upon the Christian's freedom to choose whether to tell the other the truth. The Christian has the option to witness to the reign of God or not. It is parrhesiastic, second, because this truth telling involves confronting the other with something she does not want to hear. Finally, Weaver is a parrhesiastes since he freely chooses to tell this discomforting truth to the other for her benefit. It is on behalf of her salvation that he freely engages in this a-theological witness to the reign of God.

We opened this paper with the claim that J. Denny Weaver's a-theology is irritating because its style is impolite and its substance improper. We supported our claim by showing how Weaver's style and substance may easily be read in that way. With a turn to Foucault's reading of parrhesia, however, we have attempted to write a "fresh riff," or a new take on that easy read. Thus, we have argued that

Weaver's a-theology should not be read as simply irritating but, instead, should be understood as parrhesiastic because it frankly criticizes power out of a sense of duty even in the face of danger. Having said this much we also want to say that neither Weaver's parrhesiastic a-theology nor his ethos as a parrhesiastes are unique to him. On the contrary, the characteristics we have identified in Weaver's a-theology may also be read amid many sixteenth-century Anabaptist texts.

SIXTEENTH-CENTURY ANABAPTISM AS TRUTH TELLING

Two Dominican friars also came to her, the one as a confessor, and the other as an instructor. The latter showed her the crucifix, saying: "See, here is your Lord and your God.' She answered: 'This is not my God; the cross by which I have been redeemed, is a different one. This is a wooden god; throw him into the fire, and warm yourselves with him."[18]
—Martyrs Mirror

Ques. "What do you hold concerning the holy oil?"
Ans. "Oil is good for salad, or to oil your shoes with."[19]
—Martyrs Mirror

The origins of Anabaptist truth telling may be found among the stories recounted in *Martyrs Mirror*. In those stories we hear of Anabaptists who willingly and frequently defied church-state authorities by instructing those authorities in what they knew to be the truth of the Christian faith. For this truth telling, thousands were executed by the authorities and many more were severely tortured or exiled. One such story goes like this:

> About the year 1553 . . . a shopkeeper, named Simon, . . . stood in the marketplace, to sell his wares. When the priests passed him with their idol, this Simon did not dare give divine honor to this idol made by human hands, but, according to the testimony of God presented in the holy Scriptures, would worship and serve only the Lord his God. He was therefore apprehended by the maintainers of the Roman antichrist, and examined in the faith, which he freely confessed, rejecting their self-invented infant baptism together with all human commandments, and holding fast only to the testimony of the Word of God; hence he was sentenced to death by the enemies of the truth, and was thus led without the city, and burnt for the testimony of Jesus.[20]

In his defiant stance on the street that day, Simon frankly spoke the truth about idols by refusing to perform an act of subservience to them. He further instructed the authorities in that truth, thereby criticizing them, by not bowing down to them. His was an especially visible critique that, according to the account and the engraving that accompanies it, was known to him, to the authorities, and to all assembled on the street that day and could not go unanswered. Answered it was, of course, by his prompt execution.

Speaking of the hundreds of Anabaptist martyr stories he had compiled for *The Martyrs Mirror,* Thieleman van Braght writes the following about the freedom and even boldness with which these truth tellers went forth to their executions for their frankness and truth:

> Yet to look upon all this [death and torture] will not cause real sadness, for though the aspect is dismal according to the body, the soul will nevertheless rejoice in it, seeing that not one of all those who were slain preferred life to death, since life often was proffered them on condition that they depart from the constancy of their faith. But this they did not desire; on the contrary, many of them went boldly onward to meet death; some even hastened to outstrip others, that they might be the first, who did not shrink from suffering anything the tyrants could devise, nay more than could be thought possible for a mortal man to endure.[21]

Simon's story was not unique, Braght tells us. Despite differences in the details among the stories recounted in *Martyrs Mirror,* Simon's story is paradigmatic of the rest, at least in terms of truth telling. As we said above, then, Weaver's particular parrhesia and his ethos as a parrhesiastes can be understood as a reiteration of the thousands of sixteenth-century Anabaptist parrhesiastes who preceded him.

Reading Weaver through Foucault allows us to recognize that it is not the case that Weaver has a theology that just happens to be argued in an irritating way. Weaver's theology is irritating precisely because it is a truth telling. And truth telling is always irritating because it is always antagonistic, which in this case is to say that it is contrary to the interests of the powers. Finally, this reading via Foucault has enabled us to say that it is antagonistic in this way for reasons of faith.

THE GIFT OF TRUTH

What God-word brings, may we embrace; success and suff'ring greet us; confronting evil face to face, as scorn and anger meet us. For freedom's

sake we bend we break, a sign to ev'ry nation that we have found a solid ground; God's Word our sure foundation.[22]
—Ausbund Hymn

In *Fearless Speech* Foucault draws attention to the fact that for ancient Greeks, unlike moderns, the acquisition of truth was not a problem. For moderns who, since Descartes, are modern insofar as they are suspicious of truth, the method by which truth is obtained is the central problem. In modern epistemology truth is secured through the proper and orderly application of reason, logic, and evidence. By contrast, for ancient Greeks who were not suspicious of truth, their concern was not with method but with the moral character of the one speaking truth. As Foucault puts it:

> [s]ince Descartes, the coincidence between belief and truth is obtained in a certain (mental) evidential experience. For the Greeks, however, the coincidence between belief and truth does not take place in a (mental) experience, but in a *verbal activity*, namely, *parrhesia*.[23]

As we noted in our earlier discussion of truth as a dimension of parrhesia, the activity of truth telling depends on the moral character of the truth teller rather than on proper method. To quote Foucault again: "In the Greek conception of *parrhesia* . . . there does not seem to be a problem about the acquisition of the truth since such truth-having is guaranteed by the possession of certain *moral* qualities: when someone has certain moral qualities, then that is the proof that he has access to truth—and vice versa."[24] Thus, the condition of possibility for parrhesia is an ethos understood not in the generic sense of credibility but in the more particular sense of moral character.[25]

Earlier we noted that in recovering the activity of parrhesia (as it includes frankness, truth, danger, criticism, and duty), Foucault makes it possible for us to imagine a subject position from within which contemporary modes of making sense may be disrupted. In addition we indicated that imagining such a subject position is enabled by the fact that parrhesia circumvents the modern problematic of truth.

Now we see how this is so. By recuperating a decidedly premodern practice of truth, Foucault shifts the question from one of truth to truth telling, from one of knowledge to ethos, from one of method to ethics. In so doing he makes it possible for us postmoderns, who are no more capable of confidence in the modern regime of truth than we are able simply to give up its methods for securing truth, to imagine a way to speak truth to power.

For sixteenth-century Anabaptists, the acquisition of truth was also not the problem. Like the ancient Greeks, the Anabaptists did not doubt the truth that they knew. Further, as we argued above, they told that truth as parrhesiastes—that is as truth tellers who frankly criticized the powers in the face of danger and out of a sense of duty. Although they shared the practice of parrhesia with the ancient Greeks and in this sense occupied a similar ethos, their ethos was shaped by its relationship to a peculiar truth that was not derived but awaited, not fixed but messianic, not discovered but given.

Unlike modern truth, derived from the rigors of logical deduction, empirical verification, and objective scrutiny, Anabaptist truth is collectively awaited. Following the Rule of Paul, sixteenth-century Anabaptists sought truth in the congregation gathered around Scripture and awaiting the Holy Spirit. According to John Howard Yoder, "[i]t is a basic novelty in the discussion of hermeneutics to say that a text is best understood in a congregation. This means that the tools of literary analysis do not suffice; that the Spirit is an interpreter of what a text is about only when Christians are gathered in readiness to hear it speak to their current needs and concerns."[26] Further, Yoder argues, this mode of truth-seeking implies that every member of the congregation has the potential to speak truth.[27] In other words, every member of the congregation has the potential to speak as a parrhiastes. Furthermore, the congregation is not bound either by creedal statements or tradition as it seeks the truth. In such a context for seeking truth, there is no historical *a priori* ground by which truth may be secured.[28] The Holy Spirit is in charge of those gathered and leads the congregation toward what may likely be an altogether new understanding of the text and thus of truth.

An additional implication of this mode of seeking truth is that truth is not fixed or static but arrives by way of the Holy Spirit and is on the move. It does not keep repeating itself but often makes unexpected claims. This seems to be the point that sixteenth-century Anabaptist Pilgram Marpeck makes when he writes about the nature of the truth of the cross: "The living cross and hand of Christ shows the way, does not stand immovable in one place, never has and never will, for it is itself the way from which the truth comes and is the truth from which life comes. This life comes from faith and faith gives birth to all virtue and the knowledge of Christ."[29] Like the cross, all Christian truth within this view is understood as messianic, as ongoing revelation that, in not being ahistorical, is subject to change. As such, this sort of truth may at any time throw interpretive tradition, conventional wisdom and, inevitably, social relations into crisis.

Further, this truth comes not by way of ruthless examination, but as a patiently awaited gift from God.[30] Sixteenth-century Anabaptists focused their attention not on the question of right belief or orthodoxy, but rather on right relationship or obedience to messianic truth. To quote Marpeck again: "The spiritual in Christ are committed to obedience to the Father in patience and love through the Word even as Christ, the Righteous one, became obedient unto death."[31] Again, the problem is not truth, its status, or its acquisition, but instead one's relationship to God's gift of messianic truth. For the Anabaptist parrhesiastes the practice of truth telling involves not only a certain relationship to the powers to which one speaks truth out of duty, but also a certain relationship to an unruly truth received as a gift from the One who gives all.

So far we have argued that we should read Weaver's a-theology as parrhesia. Further, we have argued that doing so is important because it enables us to see that his arguments are not merely irritating. Rather, the manner in which they are made, their rhetoric, similar as it is to the practice of parrhesia among ancient Greeks, is a form of not-modern truth telling. Weaver's practice of truth telling is important for us in these postmodern days because, as we argued earlier, it shows a way to get around the modern problem of truth through ethics. The truth teller tells the truth not by way of a certain methodologism but via a certain moral ethos. Thus, noticing how Weaver and other Anabaptists tell the truth in this way can put us on the track of how we might also speak truth to power in our postmodern context.

Along the way we noted two distinctives of Anabaptist truth telling: first, that the truth Anabaptists tell is always received as an unruly truth in the sense that it is a truth on the move; and second, that it comes as a gift from God.[32] Thus, Anabaptist truth telling is not the same as the truth telling that Foucault describes. Because we are interested in enabling truth telling in our postmodern times in a distinctly Anabaptist manner, we want to advocate an Anabaptist ethos of truth telling that presumes that the truth told is received as an unruly gift of God. In preparation for that argument we want first to say something about our relationship to God's gifts and about rhetoric.

STEWARDSHIP

Like good stewards of the manifold grace of God, serve one another with whatever gift each of you has received. Whoever speaks must do so as one speaking the very words of God; whoever serves must do so with the strength that God supplies, so that God may be glorified in all things through Jesus Christ. To him belong the glory and the power forever and ever. Amen.[33]
—Peter of Jerusalem (1 Pet. 4:10-11)

Thinking about God's gifts and our relationship to them is an ancient preoccupation at least as old as the Judeo-Christian story of the origins of creation. In the first account of creation, for instance, we read the following: "God said, 'See, I have given you every plant yielding seed that is upon the face of all the earth, and every tree with seed in its fruit; you shall have them for food. And to every beast of the earth and to every bird of the air, and to everything that creeps on the earth, everything that has the breath of life, I have given every green plant for food'" (Gen. 1:29-30). Thus God creates all and gives all to human beings. But even as the whole creation is a gift of God, God retains ownership of all. The Psalmist writes: "The earth is the Lord's, and the fullness thereof; the world, and they that dwell therein" (Ps. 24:1). In the context of God's creation, gift, and ownership of all, human beings are positioned as stewards of the creation.[34]

We learn something of what it means to be a steward in Genesis when man is placed within the context of that gift: "The Lord God took the man and put him in the garden of Eden to fill it and keep it" (Gen. 2:15). The responsibility of human beings as stewards is not to create things, but instead, like gardeners, to cultivate God's gifts from within a posture of submission. Genesis' message is

> that the responsibility of every man is like the gardener's, to know that though he creates nothing he is responsible to cultivate what God has given; that growth cannot be forced by any human haste and that the silent process of the divine unfolding must be trusted; and that those who have grown most in grace, like men who must have their gardens grow in sun and rain and changing seasons, will be most humble in themselves and most reverent before the unfolding mysteries of God.[35]

The steward of God's gift who submits and cultivates displays an ethos called for by her relationship to the one who creates, gives, and owns the creation. Since Anabaptists understand truth to be a gift of God, we suggest a particular practice of truth telling that presumes a posture of stewardship in relationship to truth.

RHETORIC

For Jews demand signs and Greeks desire wisdom, but we proclaim Christ crucified, a stumbling block to Jews and foolishness to Gentiles, but to those who are the called, both Jews and Greeks, Christ the power of God and the wisdom of God. For God's foolishness is wiser than human wisdom, and God's weakness is stronger than human strength.
—Paul of Tarsus (I Cor. 1: 22-25)

As Foucault acknowledges throughout *Fearless Speech*, truth telling is rhetorical. "*Parrhesia*," according to Foucault, "is thus a sort of 'figure' among rhetorical figures, but with this characteristic: that it is without any figure since it is completely natural. *Parrhesia* is the zero degree of those rhetorical figures which intensify the emotions of the audience."[36] As a mode of speaking that disavows its rhetoricity, parrhesia is especially rhetorical.[37] But to say that parrhesia is rhetorical is only a start because, as Foucault points out, there are multiple rhetorics or multiple ways of thinking about the relationship between truth telling and rhetoric.

Considering the two predominant views on rhetoric and truth from the ancient Greek context, for instance, we see that truth telling, following Plato, may be understood as the opposite of rhetoric—that is as speech that is transparent to truth rather than veiled in eloquence. Or truth telling, following Aristotle, may be understood as made possible by rhetoric when two opposing viewpoints are set against one another in debate so that the audience, given its propensity to appreciate when a position has been demonstrated, can recognize the position that is true. But rather than adopt either of these philosophical perspectives on rhetoric that understands truth to be, by definition, static, we take up a sophistic view of rhetoric since, as we shall see, its view of rhetoric in relationship to an unruly truth is well suited to Anabaptist parrhesia.

For the Sophists, who were itinerant teachers of rhetoric throughout the Greek city-states in the fifth-century BCE, truth understood in absolute terms is at best elusive. According to Protagoras, a leading Sophist, knowledge about ultimate things like the gods is unavailable to human beings: "Concerning the gods," Protagoras argues, "I cannot know either that they exist or that they do not exist, or what form they might have, for there is much to prevent one's knowing: the obscurity of the subject and the shortness of man's life."[38] Similarly, Gorgias, another prominent Sophist of the time, is said to have argued that nothing exists but that even if anything exists it is incomprehensible and, further, that even if anything is comprehensible, it is incommunicable.[39] What human beings do have access to are the human truths (or *doxa*) that emerge relative to their own experience and which, therefore, vary from place to place and time to time. Thus, Protagoras writes that "Of all things the measure is man, of things that are that they are, and of things that are not that they are not."[40]

For the Sophists, then, truth is elusive on two registers: first, at the level of an absolute, Truth is elusive since, even if it exists, human beings have no access to it; and second, at the level of human experience, truth is elusive since it changes over time and space. Insofar as Sophistic truth is not static like philosophical truth but, instead, inaccessible and ever changing, we may say that it is also unruly.[41]

Not only did the Sophists understand truth to be unruly. More importantly for our purposes they thought that it was the job of rhetoric to encourage its unruliness. In a fragment attributed to Protagoras, for instance, he articulates the sophistic principle that rhetoric's aim is to "mak[e] the weaker argument the stronger."[42] Since Protagoras does not believe that human beings have access to truth, we should not take him to mean by "the stronger argument" the one that is truer when measured against some external truth standard. Instead, we must take him to mean the argument that most closely reiterates accepted human truth. To say that the aim of rhetoric is to make the weaker argument the stronger, then, is to say that rhetoric's task is not only to challenge but to transform the dominant truths of a culture by articulating an alternative one.[43]

To transform truth requires, according to the Sophists, attentiveness to time and occasion. Since truth is bound by time and context, any effort to transform it must be likewise constrained. Thus, John Poulakos, scholar of sophistic rhetoric, argues that "The Sophists stressed that speech must show respect to the temporal dimension of the situation it addresses, that is, it must be timely. In other words, speech must take into account and be guided by the temporality of the situation in which it occurs."[44] As kairotic discourse, rhetoric is obliged to speak into the particularities of the moment and, especially, the urgencies at hand. Indeed, as Poulakos argues, "what compels a rhetor to speak is a sense of urgency" and further, "to intervene and, with the power of the word, to attempt to end a crisis, redistribute justice, or restore order."[45]

Crucial here, however, is that any attempt to transform truth can only be successful if it is spoken in the moment that calls it into being: "ideas have their place in time and unless they are given existence, unless they are voiced at the precise moment they are called upon, they miss their chance to satisfy situationally shared voids within a particular audience."[46]

By implication, then, when the particularities of the moment do not call forth a rhetorical response, silence should be the order of the day.[47] An important implication of the kairotic dimension of rhetoric is that anyone who dares to speak into the moment does so at some risk since "his timing might not coincide with the temporal needs of the situation."[48] The rhetorician may mistake the moment and, in so doing, speak a discourse at the wrong time and, therefore, fail to move the audience to an alternative truth.

In a similar manner, the Sophists recognized that rhetoricians must be attentive to the formal demands of the occasion in which they speak. Audiences have expectations about the kind of rhetoric that suits, say, a funeral versus a wedding versus a typical Sunday morning worship service. According to the Sophists, for any rhetoric to be successful in transforming accepted truth, it has to respond appropriately to the character of the occasion and the expectations of the audience.[49] As with *kairos*, *prepon* (or appropriateness to occasion) also involves risk: "If what is spoken is the result of a misreading on the part of the rhetor, it subsequently becomes obvious to us, even to him, that 'this was not the right thing to say.'"[50] Likewise, "If silence is called for and the response is speech, we have a rhetor misspeaking to an audience not ready to listen, or not ready to listen to what he has to say, or ready to listen but not to the things he is saying."[51] Taken together, then, kairos and prepon characterize rhetoric as discourse that says the right thing at the right time to transform accepted truth into alternative truth.

With all of this emphasis on the moment and the occasion, we might think that sophistic rhetoric is all about the present and what already exists. But this is not so. As we have already said, a key characteristic of sophistic rhetoric is its aim to make the weaker argument the stronger, to displace dominant truths with alternative ones, to transform the actual into the possible. Beginning in the here and now and attentive to kairos and prepon, the rhetorician nevertheless "tries to lift [the audience] from the vicissitudes of custom and habit and take them into a new place where new discoveries and new consequences can be made."⁵²

In this way, sophistic rhetoric, whose only foundation can be found in the exigencies of the moment and the expectations of the audience, seeks to transport its audience to the realm of the possible wherein the limits of current time and space are transgressed by aspiration and hope.

In this sophistic theory of rhetoric we hear deep resonances with Anabaptism. Like Anabaptism, sophistic rhetoric understands truth to be unruly and disruptive of the status quo. Moreover, like Anabaptism sophistic rhetoric takes as its aim the encouragement of such disruption through public discourse. Given these resonances, we bring a sophistic (rather than philosophical) view of rhetoric to this prolegomenon for a stewardship rhetoric. Thus, in what follows we apply the sophistic ideas of *kairos* and *prepon* to the question of what should characterize Anabaptist parrhesia.

A RHETORIC OF STEWARDSHIP

*He became angry, and said that what I advanced was only sophistry. . . . Thereupon I said that Paul writes that we should not be shaken in mind, neither by spirit nor by word, nor by letter, as sent from them; or even though an angel from heaven should come, and teach us anything different from what is written in the holy Gospel, he should be accursed.*⁵³
—Martyrs Mirror

If one sought to identify the ethos of Anabaptism with a single concept, that concept would surely be *Gelassenheit*. From sixteenth-century Anabaptist martyrs to present-day Old Order Amish, Gelassenheit characterizes a genuine Anabaptist posture in relationship to God.⁵⁴ Robert Friedmann argued that Gelassenheit became central to Anabaptist identity because it defined so well Anabaptist faith in the context of persecution: "their own teaching of obedience and discipleship almost required this attitude as the precondition of a reborn soul to walk the narrow path. The idea of martyrdom becomes bearable only on such a basis of self-surrender and joyous acceptance of God's will. Only through Gelassenheit may suffering become the royal road to God."⁵⁵ Almost 1,500 years later, in a context largely devoid of persecution, Old Order Amish identity features Gelassenheit as well. Donald Kraybill argues that Gelassenheit provides the key to unlocking all the riddles of Amish culture:

The solution to the riddle of Amish culture is embedded in the German word Gelassenheit. Roughly translated, Gelassenheit means 'submitting, yielding to a higher authority.' Rarely used in speech, it is an abstract concept that carries a variety of specific meanings—self-surrender, resignation to God's will, yielding to God and to others, self-denial, contentment, a calm spirit."[56]

Yielding as Submission

At the heart of the various translations given for Gelassenheit is the notion of yielding to God, to other, to community. Yielding is often paired with submission to get more fully at the meaning of Gelassenheit. Yieldedness as submission is a deeply biblical idea and one that is closely tied to how we are to receive God's gifts—or, put another way, how we are to be stewards of God's gifts. Indeed, throughout the Old and New Testaments we learn that people who receive God's gifts are called to submission. This is so whether the gift received is the whole creation (Adam and Eve), great expanses of land and many descendants (Abraham), the deliverance of his people (Moses), the infant Messiah (Mary), or revelation (Paul).

In each case God calls the receiver of the gift to submit her life to God's will in ways that are profoundly disruptive to her, her community, and even the social order. In the case of Mary, for instance, at the Annunciation she willingly submits all of her life to God upon hearing that she has found favor with God and will give birth to the Messiah: "Here am I, the servant of the Lord; let it be with me according to your word" (Luke 1:38). In her response to God's gift, Mary gives herself entirely to God's purpose setting no limits or qualifications on her submission to God's word. Of course, since she was a virgin and engaged to Joseph, her submission to God's plan compromised her social position and, indeed, her whole life.

In the same way, Paul responds to the gift of God's truth by submitting his whole life so that he loses all his possessions and the value system within which he treasured them. More importantly, he submits to a whole new understanding of salvation according to which he is required to abandon his once ardently held conviction that righteousness comes from obedience to the law and, instead, to develop faith in the claim that salvation comes through following Jesus all the way to the cross. Thus, Paul writes in Ephesians, "[f]or his sake I have suffered the loss of all things, and I regard them as rubbish, in order that I may gain Christ and be found in him, not having a righteousness of my own that comes from the law, but one that comes through faith in Christ, the righteousness from God based on faith" (3:8-9).

Paul's submission is important for stewardship rhetoric since in his example we see how we are to respond to God's gift of truth and, in particular, to the truth of the cross. For Anabaptists, as we have noted more than once, the truth of the cross is the most important truth. But that truth is not simply the conventional one—that by Jesus' blood we are saved. Rather, as John Howard Yoder has taught us, the cross (and with it always the resurrection) represents the breaking of the sovereignty of the Powers who enslave us to their truths and by their claim to be all powerful.[57]

At the cross we are invited to see that the power claimed by the Powers is a ruse and, thus, that the Powers are false gods. Once we see that this is so and willingly submit (as Jesus did) to the truth that God is sovereign even over the Powers, that the whole creation has already been reconciled to God (in actuality, even if not apparently), then we are not only freed from the enslavement of the Powers but free to join in the reconciling work of the new creation that is the church.[58] With this truth as our gift, then, the submission to which we are called is obedience to a radically unruly truth that always promises to relativize all that we know, believe, and value.

As receivers of a gift such as this, a gift of truth that is radical and unruly, what should be our posture as its stewards? If we take Paul as our example, then we may say first of all that we are called to submit all that we have and are to it. Like Paul we must be willing to give over to this truth not only all of our possessions and the values by which we treasure them but also, and more importantly, our deepest convictions. If we are to take as our task the dissemination of this truth as its rhetoricians, then we must be willing to subject all that we know to its relativizing power. The ethos of a stewardship rhetorician must be as one who is always available to God's new truth, truth we cannot yet imagine but that is on the way. Indeed, we must be relentlessly attentive to God's inbreaking revelation in our contemporary context no matter how disruptive it may be of what has become obviously true for us. If this is so, then our stewardship rhetoric must likewise be available to the radically transformative force of God's next revelation. It cannot become too fixed or static. It must remain contingent on what new word God is trying to give us.

But even as we submit to God's ongoing and unruly revelation we are also called to submit to the truth we already know, the truth of the cross—namely, that victory over death and the Powers has already been won, the reign of God is among us, and, therefore, our task is not to force history to come out right.[59] Rather, our task is to follow Jesus by freely giving away the good news of that victory all the way to the cross. If we submit to this truth as we submit to God's ongoing revelation, then even as we energetically disseminate God's truth, we cannot as stewardship rhetoricians force it on the other. In the end, we are called as stewards of the truth that is Jesus Christ to yield to the other's unbelief, even to the other's rebellion against God's truth.

Yielding as Cultivation

The constellation of terms used to capture the meaning of *Gelassenheit* includes yielding as well as resignation, self-surrender, obedience, contentment, and calm spirit. Taken together these terms may suggest a posture that is passive not only in relationship to God but to the whole world as well. Interestingly, however, the notion of yielding entails not only submission but also cultivation in the sense that a field yields a crop or a well placed financial investment yields a profit. Cultivation denotes careful tending toward the production of a yield. Yielding as cultivation is most surely not passive as it often involves both planning and ongoing care.

Perhaps the biblical text that most strongly speaks of a yield cultivated out of God's truth is the great commission, wherein Jesus' followers are commanded by him to cultivate disciples into the body of Christ: "Go therefore and make disciples of all nations, baptizing them in the name of the Father and of the Son and of the Holy Spirit, and teaching them to obey everything that I have commanded you. And remember, I am with you always, to the end of the age" (Matt. 28:19-20). Thus we are called not only to receive God's truth and to submit our whole lives to it but, having done so, to help it grow by making, baptizing, and teaching disciples with this truth. Rather than enter into the complexities of missiological debate here about how best to answer that commandment, we do well to remember Yoder's argument that before perfecting our missiology, we are first called to announce and to celebrate the reign of God.[60]

To cultivate God's gift of truth, a stewardship rhetoric must first take into account the fact that, though victorious, that truth is not widely recognized. Indeed, the Powers do not believe in the truth of the cross and largely live and work in rebellion against it. In addressing those who do not yet acknowledge the reign of God, stewardship rhetoric must be mindful that its task is, as it was for the Sophists, to make the weaker argument the stronger. This posture of speaking from the underside of conventional wisdom should be familiar from Jesus' teachings and, of course, his work on the cross. As stewardship rhetoricians, then, our aim is to disrupt the stronger argument with the weaker argument of the truth of the cross.

To succeed in making the weaker argument of the cross appear stronger, the stewardship rhetorician must begin as the Sophists did in a certain moment and place with a particular audience in mind. We must begin amid all of the pre-existing beliefs and values of our audience as well as the various constraints and realities of the present moment. But although our stewardship rhetoric must begin there, it cannot remain there, since to do so would be merely to reproduce the status quo. Instead, in recognition of the timely (*kairos*) and the fitting (*prepon*), but with attention focused on the gap between those who acknowledge the reign of God and those who yet do not, the stewardship rhetorician is called to craft appeals capable of articulating the audience into the reign of God.

To craft a stewardship rhetoric able to move an audience from obedience to the stronger argument, which will always be the argument of the Powers, to obedience to the weaker argument, which is the reign of God, takes the utmost in rhetorical sensitivity and skill. The stewardship rhetorician will, like the Sophist, need to be someone who is keenly perceptive of the present that she and her audience occupy and who can fashion out of a common language new arguments and appeals on behalf of radical transformation.

These days we hear important calls for a certain kind of exchange with the other in which we may make our arguments to the best of our ability so long as we also make ourselves available to the transforming power of the other's argument.[61] This is mutually transformative dialogue, we are told, and it is ethical insofar as both interlocutors are ultimately willing to submit to the otherness of the other's argument. To take up this posture is tempting because it seems to solve the ethical problem of advocacy. I can freely advocate my position without having to worry that I am somehow oppressing the other so long as I make myself available to the arguments of the other. But is it possible or even desirable for me to assume that posture of availability to the other's argument?

First, as to its possibility, how would I go about choosing to make myself available in that way? By what psychological mechanism could I excise or bracket from my mind my deeply held convictions such that I could hear the arguments of the other? Indeed, is my availability to the other a question of choice? Is it possible for me to decide that I will make myself available to radical transformation or, instead, is radical transformation something that happens despite my own volition? Second, as to its desirability, if my deeply held convictions are faithful to the truth that is the cross, do I even want to make them available to such radical transformation? We believe that it is neither probable that faithful Christians can nor desirable that they should bracket the truth of the cross.

Rather than try to make ourselves available to the arguments of the other to solve the ethical problem of persuasion, the stewardship rhetorician is obliged by the call to cultivation of God's gift of truth to make her arguments as persuasively as she can in the context of the moment and the situation. As she does so, she necessarily takes the risks that she may have misunderstood the moment or the occasion and, thus, misspeaks. She must risk the possibility that she may speak when she should not, or that she may say the wrong thing. In addition to taking these risks, we propose that she take another—that is, that she risk the possibility that she will speak wrongly to the other, perhaps even to the point of oppressing the other. The stewardship rhetorician must recognize that this is a possibility—that her speech may coerce and that she may engage in moral error. Further, if she does, then she must own that ethical failure.

To reduce the chances that she will make such an error, the stewardship rhetorician must consider carefully to whom, when, and where she speaks. Having a true word to say is not sufficient for speaking it. The stewardship rhetorician will have to weigh whether a certain audience is in a moment and place in which it can hear that word. If not, then the stewardship rhetorician should choose to remain silent and make the case another day. Importantly, then, the choice of the stewardship rhetorician is not about adapting the truth to her audience to make it easier to take. Neither, however, is her choice about making certain that in speaking the truth, she guarantees that the audience knows she is willing to subject that truth to radical revision by the audience. Instead, it is about discerning the moment and knowing when to speak and when to remain silent.

Of course, the stewardship rhetorician must receive and take seriously the arguments of the other. Again, however, the point in receiving them is not to make the truth of the cross available to radical transformation by the other's argument. Instead the point is to listen to the argument of the other through the truth of the cross. If upon listening carefully to it, the stewardship rhetorician decides that the argument of the other is in rebellion against the truth of the cross, then she is called to dissuade the other from it. In addition, the stewardship rhetorician should listen for the ways in which the truth of the cross may be troubling the other's argument. By listening for the gaps or fissures within an argument and between one and another argument, the stewardship rhetorician seeks to yield a new truth of the cross.

With these last two points made about the cultivation of God's gift of truth on the part of the stewardship rhetorician, we need to recall three crucial points previously made. This is so since these two points about cultivation may seem to say that the stewardship rhetorician is the lone advocate for a truth about which she is certain. This is not the case. First, if we remember that the stewardship rhetorician only gains access to truth in the context of the body of Christ gathered around Scripture in the presence of the Holy Spirit, then we know that she is not alone. On the contrary, she is accountable to that community for the truth she tells. Second, if we remember that she (in the context of that community) always avails the truth she knows to radical revision by God, then we know that she holds the truth of the cross humbly in relationship to the one who gives it. Third, if we remember that she speaks truth always as the weaker argument to the stronger, which is to say from below in a relationship of power in society and history, then her unwillingness to make the truth of the cross available to the radical transformation of the other can be seen as not an instance of domination by persuasion but, instead, as a practice of witness.

CONCLUSION

Christ's servants follow him to death and give their body, life, and breath on cross and rack and pyre. As gold is tried and purified they stand the test of fire.[62]
—Ausbund Hymn

Robert Friedman lamented that as Mennonites have become acculturated to a society that puts a premium on individualism and achievement they have largely abandoned Gelassenheit.[63] Seeing Gelassenheit as too passive for engagement with the world, Mennonites who have left behind what are often understood as the backward and sectarian ways of the Old Orders reject yielding. But if we take into account the two senses of yielding we have been developing here—that is, both submission to God and others and cultivation of the reign of God through persuasive speech—then even we Mennonites who want most to engage the world may imagine a posture or ethos that embodies our sixteenth-century ancestors' identity in Gelassenheit, but in a way that is neither passive nor sectarian.

That posture, of course, is the ethos of the stewardship rhetorician, characterized by submission to God and an unwillingness to coerce the other. Adopting this posture is an act of faith and discipleship because it only makes sense to one who knows that the sovereignty of the Powers has been broken. But the ethos of the stewardship rhetorician is also, like Weaver's and the sixteenth-century Anabaptists, that of the parrhesiastes who speaks truth to power out of duty and in the context of risk to cultivate the reign of God within the church and beyond.

As we bring this essay to a close, we are reminded of the words of a seventeenth-century stewardship rhetorician, Thieleman van Braght, who endeavored to remind the acculturated Mennonites of his time of the need for a reinvigorated faith based in submission and cultivation. In the opening paragraph of the preface to *The Bloody Theater or Martyrs Mirror*, he warns his brothers and sisters in the faith that the story he has to tell is not pleasant, perhaps even irritating. He writes:

> But most beloved, do not expect that we shall bring you into Grecian theatres, to gaze on merry comedies or gay performances. Here shall not be opened unto you the pleasant arbors and pleasure gardens of Atlas, Adonis or Semiramis.... True enough, we shall lead you into dark valleys, even into the valleys of death, where nothing will be seen but dry bones, skulls, and frightful skeletons of those who have been slain; these beheaded, those drowned, others strangled at the stake, some burnt, others broken on the wheel, many torn by wild beasts, half devoured, and put to death in manifold cruel ways; besides, a great multitude who having escaped death bear the marks of Jesus, their Savior, on their bodies, wandering about over mountains and valleys, through forests and wilderness, forsake of friends and kindred, robbed and stripped of all their temporal possessions, and living in extreme poverty.[64]

To be sure, stewardship rhetoric is not for the faint of heart. It is no easier to speak than it is to hear and least of all to embody as an ongoing practice. But a cloud of witnesses has gone before us, whether Jesus, the martyrs, or J. Denny Weaver, to show us not only the way, but that this way is the only way. As sisters and brothers in the body of Christ, we are called both to submission and to cultivation because, as the third-century church father Tertullian put it so concisely, "the blood of the martyrs is the seed of the church."

NOTES

1. We have adapted this line from the song "South Bronx" on the album *A Retrospective* by KRS-One and Scott LaRock. KRS-One, *A Retrospective* (Jive Records, 2000).

2. Weaver characterizes the truth he offers and his relationship to it in the following manner: "Conversely, it is clearly a postmodern stance to point out the particularity of classic theology and to confess a truth with universal intent from the particular perspective of the Anabaptist peace church tradition that can critique Christendom's violence-accommodating theology." See J. Denny Weaver, *Anabaptist Theology in Face of Postmodernity: A Proposal for the Third Millennium* (Telford, Pa.: Pandora Press U.S., 2000), 27. It is worth pointing out here that Weaver's claim that the truth he espouses is particular is not contradictory to the claim that it is nevertheless true. Notice, that Weaver "confesses" rather than merely asserts this truth with universal intent. Thus, Weaver is not trying to have it both ways—that is, as both postmodern and modern. Rather, he is recognizing that all truths are particular while holding that some truths are actually true.

3. J. Denny Weaver, *Becoming Anabaptist: The Origin and Significance of Sixteenth-Century Anabaptism* (Scottdale, Pa.: Herald Press, 1987), 202.

4. Our purpose in using this term is to underscore the degree to which Weaver's theology does not follow the rules or meet the expectations of traditional theology. In this sense, our use of the term resonates with Mark Taylor's use. We differ in our use of the term insofar as we do not mean to say that Weaver's is a negative theology. Clearly, Weaver's is not. See Mark C. Taylor, *Erring: A Postmodern a/Theology* (Chicago: University of Chicago Press, 1984).

5. J. Denny Weaver, *Keeping Salvation Ethical: Mennonite and Amish Atonement Theology in the Late Nineteenth Century*, ed. Theron F. Schlabach, vol. 35, Studies in Anabaptist and Mennonite History (Scottsdale, Pa.: Herald Press, 1997), 27.

6. J. Denny Weaver, *The Nonviolent Atonement* (Grand Rapids, Mich.: Wm. B. Eerdmans, 2001), 212.

7. Weaver, *The Nonviolent Atonement*, 7.

8. Ibid., 93. For more argumentation along these lines, see Weaver, *Anabaptist Theology in Face of Postmodernity*, 124-27.

9. Mark A. Noll and Carolyn Nystrom, *Is the Reformation Over? An Evangelical Assessment of Contemporary Roman Catholicism* (Grand Rapids, Mich.: Baker Academic, 2005), 230.

10. Foucault's theorization here of the truth-teller resonates with his work on subject position. To put it all too briefly, a subject position or what Foucault also calls an I-slot is a space made available within a discourse that enables an

individual to speak but for the most part only in accordance with the rules of that space. Importantly, here Foucault is theorizing a subject position for resistance to the ruling truths. For his theorization of subject position, see Michel Foucault, *The Archaeology of Knowledge: And the Discourse on Language* (New York: Pantheon Books, 1972), 88-105.

11. In a footnote to this portion of text, editor Joseph Pearson notes that Foucault uses the masculine pronoun because he is referring there to *parrhesia* as it was understood and practiced in ancient Greek society which deprived women of the use of *parrhesia*. Since the context about which we are speaking is the twenty-first-century, we have decided to use a feminine pronoun in recognition of the fact that among us these days are female truth tellers. Michel Foucault, *Fearless Speech* (Los Angeles: Semiotext(e), 2001), 12.

12. Ibid., 14.
13. Ibid., 17.
14. Ibid., 17-18.
15. Ibid., 19.
16. Ibid.
17. Weaver, *Anabaptist Theology in Face of Postmodernity*, 229.
18. Thieleman J. van Braght, *The Bloody Theater Or Martyrs Mirror of the Defenseless Christians Who Baptized Only Upon Confession of Faith, and Who Suffered and Died for the Testimony of Jesus, Their Saviour, from the Time of Christ to the Year A. D. 1660*, 14th. ed. (Scottdale, Pa.: Herald Press, 1985), 423.
19. Ibid.
20. van Braght, *The Bloody Theater or Martyrs Mirror of the Defenseless Christians*, 540.
21. Ibid., 6.
22. Anonymous, "The Word of God Is Solid Ground," in *Hymnal: A Worship Book*, ed. Rebecca Slough (Scottdale, Pa.: Mennonite Publishing House, 1992), #314.
23. Foucault, *Fearless Speech*, 14.
24. Ibid., 15.
25. With this sense of ethos we reclaim the etymological connection between *ethos* (habit, custom, disposition, character, and especially moral character) and *ethics*.
26. John Howard Yoder, "The Hermeneutics of the Anabaptists," in *Essays on Biblical Interpretation: Anabaptist-Mennonite Perspectives*, ed. Willard Swartley (Elkhart, Ind.: Institute of Mennonite Studies, 1984), 21.
27. Ibid.
28. Ibid.
29. Walter Klaassen, Werner Packull, and John Rempel, eds., *Later Writings by Pilgram Marpeck and His Circle* (Kitchener, Ont.: Pandora Press, 1999), 29.
30. For a theological discussion of a radical epistemology of patience and vulnerability that rejects methodologism, see Chris Huebner, "Globalization, Theory and Dialogical Vulnerability: John Howard Yoder and the Possibility of a Pacifist Epistemology," *Mennonite Quarterly Review* 76/1 (2002): 49-62.
31. Klaassen, et al., *Later Writings by Pilgram Marpeck and His Circle*, 31.
32. In *Fearless Speech* Foucault writes about a variety of ancient Greek *par-*

rhesiastes from fifth-century BCE dramatists (Euripedes) to fourth century BCE philosophers (Socrates and Plato) to fourth-century BCE rhetoricians (Isocrates). The parrhesiastes he describes tend not to speak a truth that is on the move. While fifth century BCE Sophists are well known for speaking truths on the move (indeed, this was Plato's primary accusation against them), Foucault does not include them in his argument. Thus, we identify this aspect of Anabaptist truth telling as distinctive.

33. For this citation and the remainder of the essay, all biblical references are to the NRSV.

34. According to Milo Kauffman's reading of biblical stewardship, "To recognize and acknowledge the ownership of God is a fundamental principle of Christian stewardship." Milo Kauffman, *Stewards of God* (Scottdale, Pa.: Herald Press, 1975), 37.

35. George Arthur Buttrick, *The Interpreter's Bible: The Holy Scriptures in the King James and Revised Standard Versions with General Articles and Introduction, Exegesis, Exposition, Exposition for Each Book of the Bible*, vol. 1 (New York: Abingdon Press, 1952), 496.

36. Foucault, *Fearless Speech*, 21.

37. Surely one of the most famous disavowals of rhetoric appears in Plato's dialogues on rhetoric. For a discussion of this and other puzzles in Plato's works, see Jean Niemkamp, *Plato on Rhetoric and Language* (Mahwah, N.J.: Hermagoras Press, 1999), 1.

38. Hermann Diels and Rosamond Kent Sprague, *The Older Sophists: A Complete Translation by Several Hands of the Fragments in Die Fragmente Der Vorsokratiker, Ed. Diels-Kranz and Published by Weidmann Verlag (Vaduz, Liechtenstein) (by Whose Permission the Translations Have Been Made): With a New Edition of Antiphon and of Euthydemus* (Columbia, S.C.: University of South Carolina Press, 1990), 20.

39. This summary of Gorgias' position on being and not being is paraphrased from a fragment titled "On the Nonexistent or On Nature." Ibid., 42-46.

40. Ibid., 18.

41. As John Poulakos puts it in his essay, "Toward a Sophistic Definition of Rhetoric: "In distinction to *episteme*, rhetoric does not strive for cognitive certitude, the affirmation of logic and, satisfied with probability, lends itself to the flexibility of the contingent." John Poulakos, "Toward a Sophistic Definition of Rhetoric," *Philosophy and Rhetoric* 16/1 (1983): 37.

42. Diels and Sprague, *The Older Sophists: A Complete Translation by Several Hands of the Fragments*, 21.

43. This practice of making the weaker argument the stronger is readily seen in the extant speeches of the Sophists. For instance, in his speech, *The Choice of Heracles,* Prodicus (a fifth-century Sophist) challenges conventional wisdom about morality by articulating through a new rhetorical form a democratic subject of deliberation and decision-making in a context accustomed to patriarchal forms of decision-making based in the moral lessons of epic texts like *The Illiad*. Similarly, in his *Encomium of Helen,* fifth-century BCE Sophist, Gorgias, challenges the conventional view of Helen of Troy as a

woman who caused the Trojan War by her betrayal of her husband and, thereby, the Greeks. Gorgias makes the weaker argument offering four reasons why Helen cannot be blamed for the war. In so doing, Gorgias makes a case for the power of rhetoric in a context accustomed to relying on poetry for life's lessons. For readings of the weaker/stronger argument in these texts and their political implications, see Susan Biesecker-Mast, "Rhetorical Discourse and the Constitution of the Subject: Prodicus' *The Choice of Heracles*," *Argumentation* 5 (1991): 159-169 and John Poulakos, "Gorgias' *Encomium to Helen* and the Defense of Rhetoric," *Rhetorica* 1 (1983): 1-16.

44. Poulakos, "Toward a Sophistic Definition of Rhetoric," 39.

45. Ibid.

46. Ibid.

47. Poulakos writes, "Moreover, the two examples [of sophistic rhetoric] seem to restrict speaking to only those times calling for it, and to suggest that silence be the alternative at all other times." Ibid.

48. Ibid., 40.

49. Poulakos writes about this dimension of rhetoric in the following way: "A complement to the notion of *kairos*, *to prepon* points out that situations have formal characteristics, and demands that speaking as a response to a situation be suitable to those very characteristics." Ibid., 41.

50. Ibid., 42.

51. Ibid.

52. Ibid., 43-44.

53. van Braght, *The Bloody Theater or Martyrs Mirror of the Defenseless Christians*, 621.

54. Sandra Cronk, "*Gelassenheit*: The Rites of the Redemptive Process in Old Order Amish and Old Order Mennonite Communities," *Mennonite Quarterly Review* 55/1 (1981): 5-44.

55. Robert Friedmann, "Gelassenheit," in *The Mennonite Encyclopedia*, ed. Cornelius Krahn (Scottdale, Pa.: Mennonite Publishing House, 1982).

56. Donald B. Kraybill, *The Riddle of Amish Culture*, revised ed. (Baltimore: Johns Hopkins University Press, 2001), 25.

57. For Yoder's argument on this point, see "Christ and Power," in *The Politics of Jesus*. John Howard Yoder, *The Politics of Jesus: Vicit Agnus Noster*, revised ed. (Grand Rapids, Mich.: Wm. B. Eerdmans, 1994), 134-161.

58. As John Howard Yoder makes this point: "the powers have been defeated not by some kind of cosmic hocus-pocus but by the concreteness of the cross; the impact of the cross upon [the powers] is not the working of magical words nor the fulfillment of a legal contract calling for the shedding of innocent blood, but the sovereign presence, within the structures of creaturely orderliness, of Jesus the kingly claimant and of the church which is itself a power and a structure in society. Thus the historicity of Jesus retains, in the working of the church as it encounters the other power and value structures of its history, the same kind of relevance that the man Jesus had for those whom he served until they killed him." Ibid., 158.

59. We are borrowing this notion of resisting the temptation to force history to come out right from John Howard Yoder, who made this point in a va-

riety of places including the following in which he offers a reading of Revelation 13:10: "The key to obedience of God's people is not their effectiveness but their patience (13:10). The triumph of the right is assured not by the might that comes to the aid of the right, which is of course the justification of the use of violence and other kinds of power in every human conflict. The triumph of the right, although it is assured, is sure because of the power of the resurrection and not because of any calculation of causes and effects, nor because of the inherently greater strength of the good guys. The relationship between the obedience of God's people and the triumph of God's cause is not a relationship of cause and effect but one of cross and resurrection." Ibid., 232.

60. For a postmodern Anabaptist take on missiology, see Susan Biesecker-Mast, "The Aporetic Witness," in *Practicing Truth: Confident Witness in Our Pluralistic World*, ed. David W. Shenk and Linford Stutzman (Scottdale, Pa.: Herald Press, 1999), 130-147.

61. In his *Mennonite Quarterly Review* essay on pacifist epistemology, Chris Huebner makes a similar call when he argues that "radical reformation consists of a dedicated willingness to subject one's own standpoint to criticism and a corresponding attitude of vulnerable openness to new and potentially hostile voices." Huebner, "Globalization, Theory and Dialogical Vulnerability," 60.

62. Anonymous, "Who Now Would Follow Christ," in *Hymnal: A Worship Book*, ed. Rebecca Slough (Scottdale, Pa.: Mennonite Publishing House, 1992), #535.

63. Friedmann puts it this way: "Present-day Mennonitism has lost the idea of Gelassenheit nearly completely." Friedman, "Gelassenheit."

64. van Braght, *The Bloody Theater or Martyrs Mirror*, 6.

Part 2

THE WORK OF JESUS IN THE SCRIPTURES

CHAPTER THREE

HISTORICAL RECONSTRUCTION AND THEOLOGICAL CONSTRUCTION IN TENSION IN THE WORK OF J. DENNY WEAVER

Raymond F. Person Jr.

*H*istorical reconstruction represents a necessary and vital task for any constructive theologian. Like our Christian sisters and brothers of the past, we must engage in some level of historical reconstruction to take seriously the beliefs and practices of historical figures in the Church Universal, be they Jesus, Paul, Menno Simons, or John Howard Yoder. Historical reconstruction, we could even say, is a necessary precursor to any theological construction. We must take inherited theologies seriously within their historical contexts as we construct our own theological discourses within our historical contexts. However, the theologies of the past do not necessarily determine the exact details of our own contemporary theologies. To keep our theologies relevant, we must continually reevaluate and reconstruct our theologies, holding on to those elements that we understand to be essential and releasing those elements that appear to be no longer (if they ever were) pertinent.

J. Denny Weaver has passionately engaged in both historical reconstruction and constructive theology. Although there is much to commend in Weaver's contributions, in this essay I want to contribute to the conversation engendered by his work by arguing that his use of historical reconstruction is often flawed because the reconstruction appears too often to be influenced negatively by his own theological agenda. Below I will first summarize how historical reconstruction and constructive theology relate in Weaver's discussion of selected biblical texts in his development of a "nonviolent atonement." I will then further explore Weaver's appropriation of Pauline theology before closing with a discussion of how my critique of Weaver's historical reconstruction affects my appraisal of Weaver's constructive theological program.

THE BIBLE AND HISTORICAL RECONSTRUCTION

Early in his study, *The Nonviolent Atonement*, Weaver presents interpretations of biblical passages to provide a biblical basis for his understanding of what he calls the narrative Christus Victor understanding of the atonement.[1] Weaver discusses Revelation, the Gospels, Paul, Leviticus, and the epistle to the Hebrews. Although he notes that his "survey of biblical material has not been exhaustive" (69), he nevertheless operates under an apparent assumption that much of the Bible must have the same theological message. Weaver concludes that his narrative Christus Victor model is consistent with the Gospels, Paul's letters, Hebrews, and Revelation—that is, the vast majority of the New Testament—and has significant connections with the Old Testament, including the sacrificial system described primarily in Leviticus (69).

This drive to find theological consistency throughout the New Testament and into the Old Testament is, I argue, extremely problematic, especially from an historical perspective on the Bible. In fact, there are hints that Weaver is aware of this difficulty, where he notes that "a minimalist conclusion is that the survey has demonstrated that satisfaction atonement is neither the only reading nor the required reading of the Bible" (69). Such a minimalist conclusion, in my opinion, is uncontroversial in biblical studies, because most biblical scholars have given up the idea that there is one consistent theology in the Bible. In other words, most biblical scholars would automatically suspect any argument that a specific theology is the "only reading" or "required reading" of the multi-vocal biblical text. However, despite his occasional awareness of this difficulty, Weaver still concludes the following: "And more importantly, it [this book] proposes narrative Christus Victor as a reading of the entire Bible story, making explicit an understanding that had fallen out of view" (228). Even if what he intended to communicate by this conclusion is a theologically motivated reading of the entire Christian Bible, it appears that he understands that this theology has some consistent historical basis throughout the biblical text. That is, he strives to accomplish more than demonstrating that satisfaction atonement is not the only biblical understanding of atonement. He strives to supplant the biblical basis for satisfaction atonement theory completely with a comprehensive argument for the biblical basis of narrative Christus Victor. Here Weaver runs into problems of historical reconstruction that then undermine his own theological construction.

Below I will briefly evaluate Weaver's interpretation of Revelation, Jesus in the Gospels, Leviticus, and Hebrews. In the following section I will then discuss more fully his interpretation of Paul. In both of these sections we will see that his interpretation of biblical passages tends to be theologically motivated to a degree that adversely affects his historical reconstruction. In many cases Weaver's conclusions are not generally accepted by biblical scholars but are based on his limited reading of secondary sources and, in one case, what I believe is a misreading of a scholar's work.

The Book of Revelation provides the strongest evidence for Weaver's argument in that "the slaughtered lamb" of Revelation "signifies the (nonviolent) manner of the victory" of good over evil (20). Weaver's discussion of the nonviolent message of Revelation draws not only from his own interpretation of the text but also from the work of various biblical scholars of Revelation, demonstrating some breadth of knowledge of the secondary literature. Here it seems that he has a sound basis for arguing that his narrative Christus Victor theology has biblical roots.

In his brief discussion of the historical Jesus and the Gospels, Weaver clearly draws heavily from the work of John Howard Yoder and Walter Wink. He acknowledges that his discussion focuses mostly on Luke; in fact, it focuses mostly on the Q material in Luke. On the basis of Q alone I think he may have an argument for a nonviolent Jesus. However, the gospel tradition is much broader than Q, and few biblical scholars are willing to limit authentic material to Q.

Those gospel passages that are problematic to arguments for a nonviolent Jesus are generally ignored. Although Weaver mentions the cleansing of the temple as an act of the historical Jesus to demonstrate that Jesus was not passive (39), he does not acknowledge that this same act can be interpreted in violent terms.

Another passage that creates real difficulty with the historical reconstruction of a nonviolent Jesus is Jesus' encounter with the Syrophoenician woman, where his ethnocentrism assumes a just social division between Jews ("children") and Gentiles ("dogs") (Mark 7:24-30). When attempting a historical reconstruction, it is not difficult to reconstruct an historical Jesus with such an ethnocentric view, since he was a first-century Jew. In fact, the real difficulty would be to explain why later tradition would develop a portrayal of Jesus with such an ethnocentric view that clearly went against the early accommodation of Gentiles into the church.

Such historical reconstruction has led New Testament scholar Hisako Kinukawa to conclude that there were various encounters in which the historical Jesus was pushed to become who he was intended to be, because of his interactions with women. For example, Jesus' first response to the Syrophoenician woman reflected his own cultural background, but the woman's response led him to break down that barrier and exorcise the demon from her daughter, thereby becoming more fully who he was destined to be.[2] Therefore, when attempting to construct a biblical basis for a nonviolent theology, such passages present theological challenges, because of probable historical reconstructions. In Weaver's discussion of Jesus in the Gospels there is no recognition of this problem. Rather, he begins with the following inadequately supported assumption: "That Jesus lived and taught nonviolence seems generally, if not universally, accepted" (12).

Weaver correctly notes that the sacrificial system of ancient Israel is generally assumed to supply the model for satisfaction atonement. Since he seems to have the goal of excluding interpretations of any New Testament text supportive of satisfaction theory, Weaver strives to undermine the Old Testament basis for these interpretations and concludes that the sacrificial system "cannot or should not be appropriated as an image of satisfaction atonement in which the blood or death is thought to satisfy a legal penalty imposed as the price of sin" (59). However, in this section there is no indication that Weaver is even aware of the secondary literature that supports the very arguments he strives to reject, in that there are no references to biblical scholars whose area of specialization concerns Leviticus, the Priestly writer, or ancient Israelite ritual.³ The current scholarly consensus understands the sacrificial system as including blood satisfaction, as evidenced by the following comment on Leviticus 17:11 by Jacob Milgrom: "Thus v. 11 ... explains why the Israelite, but not the alien, must first offer up all his meat as sacrifice (i.e., a well-being offering)—to ransom the Israelite's life for spilling the life-blood of the animal to enjoy its meat."⁴

Weaver's reading of the book of Hebrews is based on one essay by Michael Hardin.⁵ Following Hardin, he concludes that the sacrificial language in Hebrews is used for the purpose of repudiating the sacrificial hermeneutic, thereby denying the use of Hebrews to support satisfaction atonement. Again, Weaver gives no references to the work of the vast majority of biblical scholars whose interpretations are contrary to his own.⁶

In summary, with the notable exception of Revelation, Weaver's reading of secondary literature is highly selective and generally ignores the scholarly consensus concerning the interpretation of the historical Jesus, Old Testament sacrifice, and the Book of Hebrews. Biblical scholars reading Weaver's work are left with the impression that he simply looked for any interpretation of these texts that might support his understanding of narrative Christus Victor without fully struggling with the rationales behind the scholarly consensus. In the following section, we will see further evidence of such theologically motivated reading of the secondary literature, this time concerning the Pauline corpus, to provide a historical reconstruction for a basis of his narrative Christus Victor theology.

PAUL AND HISTORICAL RECONSTRUCTION

In Weaver's own words, Paul is "the New Testament's most important theologian" (10), so it should be of no surprise that Weaver desires to find support in the writings of Paul for his narrative Christus Victor theology. Furthermore, Paul's writings and the Book of Hebrews are often the biblical texts that are indicated as the basis of satisfaction atonement. Therefore, if he can demonstrate that these texts do not support satisfaction atonement but rather undergird narrative Christus Victor, then he has not only provided support for his own theological interpretation but has undermined the theological position that he identifies as most problematic for Christian pacifists. Weaver begins his discussion of Paul with some recognition of this dynamic, when he observes that "it is frequently assumed that the apostle Paul's language about the cross, sacrifice, and fulfillment of the law are the foundation of satisfaction atonement" (49). Weaver's language here suggests that he understands this "assumption" to be ill-founded and most likely based simply on a theological imposition of satisfaction atonement theology on the work of Paul due to the Constantinian church's effort to justify the use of violence.

I certainly agree with Weaver's conclusions that Paul's theology was not identical to the satisfaction atonement of Anselm (54) and that those who strive to demonstrate such equivalency are probably theologically motivated in their historical reconstruction of such a theology. However, agreement with this conclusion does not rule out that Paul's theology nevertheless is closer to satisfaction atonement theology than to Weaver's narrative Christus Victor. Therefore, Weaver should have engaged in a careful analysis of interpretations of those passages that are often interpreted as supporting some form of satisfaction atonement, rather than simply dismissing them as assumptions.[7]

Weaver only refers to one biblical scholar to support his interpretation of Paul, J. Christiaan Beker, and, as we will see below, Weaver's interpretation of Beker's work is arguably a misreading and, therefore, in my view does not support Weaver's interpretation.[8] Weaver is well aware of Beker's language including sacrifice when talking about Paul's understanding of Christ's death. Weaver, for example, cites Beker's contention that "Christ's death is a sacrificial death that acknowledges our just condemnation by the law, and yet the dominion of the law ceases with the sacrifice of Christ"[9] (52). He also quotes Beker on the matter of blood sacrifice: "Paul reinterprets the traditional Christian concept of the righteousness of God as covenant renewal, of Christ as expiation or as the Paschal Lamb (Rom. 3:24-26; 1 Cor. 5:7), of the sacrificial blood of Christ (Rom. 3:24-25; 5:9), in terms of his understanding of the death of Christ as the judgment of the powers of this age"[10] (53).

Weaver then proceeds to cite Beker's contention that "Paul's reinterpretation of the death of Christ is remarkably apocalyptic"[11] (52). Weaver apparently believes that Beker's apocalyptic reading of Paul's thought places Beker at odds with those who would appropriate Paul's work to justify satisfaction atonement. This assumption, that an apocalyptic interpretation of Christ's sacrificial death must somehow be divorced from or reject any type of satisfaction atonement, does not appear to be consistent with Beker's larger argument. Weaver's misreading of Beker occurs, I believe, because Weaver misunderstands what Beker meant when he wrote about Paul's reinterpretation of earlier Christian theologies.

Beker's interpretation of Paul's theology certainly takes seriously how Paul's apocalyptic worldview requires a reinterpretation of certain earlier Christian beliefs. Consider, for example, Beker's discussion of Paul's discussion of the atonement in Galatians:

> Galatians 3:13a, then, does not permit a Marcionite interpretation, as if the phrase "Christ redeemed us from the curse of the law" simply means an abolition of an outdated law that moreover never conformed to God's intention. To the contrary, Paul takes over from the Antioch church the confession of the death of Christ "on our behalf" (Gal. 3:13b. = "for our sins," 1 Cor. 15:3). The Antioch church interprets Jesus' death as a sacrificial death, that is, as the forgiveness of the sins that judgment of the law imposes on a disobedient people. However, Paul radicalizes this confession, because the death of Christ "for us" (that is, "for our sins") does not simply mean forgiveness under the law.[12]

Or again, Beker's examination of Paul's analysis of Jesus' death in Romans:

> the death of Christ does not refer *primarily* to the death of an innocent suffering martyr, which evokes remorse and moral cleansing; its does not mean a new moral beginning for the "old" person or *primarily* the forgiveness of sin so that one can begin again with a clean slate. To the contrary, the death of Christ addresses itself to sin as a cosmic power, that is, to the human condition "under the power of sin" (Rom. 3:9).[13]

In both of these instances it is clear that, according to Beker, Paul is building upon an earlier traditional understanding that characterized Christ's death as a sacrifice that in someway satisfied the Jewish law. Paul "takes over" this theology and "radicalizes" it so that his understanding of Christ's sacrificial death is not "primarily" about "the forgiveness of sin." Nothing in what Beker writes requires that Paul reject the satisfaction atonement dimension of the traditional understandings. Beker rather notes that the requirements of the law are not simply satisfied, because the power of sin itself is abolished. When Beker discusses the rabbinic background of the satisfaction theory, he makes a similar distinction, arguing that "according to the rabbinic understanding forgiveness means acquittal of punishment, but not the destruction of the power of sin or the 'new creation' that comes through participation in the resurrection life of Christ."[14]

Again, this does not require that Paul completely reject the rabbinic understanding. Instead, Paul understands that the rabbinic understanding is true to a point, but incomplete—that is, the death and resurrection of Christ brings not only "acquittal of punishment" according to the law but also "the destruction of the power of sin," which the law was incapable of doing. This reading of Beker clarifies why he can continue to use traditional language of "sacrificial death" for Paul's understanding, while at the same time interpreting Paul as meaning something more than the Jewish understanding of "sacrificial death."

If my reading of Beker is correct, then Beker was not out of the scholarly consensus that understands Paul's theology to include some basis for satisfaction atonement theology. In fact, to my knowledge, no one other than Weaver has interpreted Beker as diverging from this consensus.[15]

HISTORICAL RECONSTRUCTION AND THEOLOGICAL CONSTRUCTION

Theological construction cannot occur in an historical vacuum; theologians must therefore engage in historical reconstruction to better understand the theological issues facing the contemporary church. However, historical reconstruction cannot determine the exact outcome of contemporary theological construction. It can provide some limits to theological construction, but what these limits are is always itself a matter of theological debate. From my perspective as a Christian who, like Weaver, strives to identify with the theological voices of various liberation theologians (feminist, womanist, African-American, Third World), the fact that historical reconstruction cannot determine contemporary theology is itself liberating. For example, any accurate historical reconstruction of Paul must take seriously aspects of his thought that many contemporary Christians find particularly problematic, especially including his views on slavery.

Although I wish I could honestly reconstruct a historical Paul whose views on violence, gender, sexual orientation, and slavery were the same as mine, any honest historical reconstruction of Paul must result in someone who was a first-century Jewish Christian living and working primarily in Asia Minor. Another way to state this point is that, although I am aware that my own social location limits my own worldview and theology, I am nevertheless also conscious of the fact that when engaging in historical reconstruction I must allow the significant differences of time and space to be present in my historical reconstruction. Any historical Paul (or historical Jesus, or historical Beker) that easily conforms to my own thought is suspect.

If historical reconstruction of biblical theologies can only lead to theologies that fit in the first-century, then theological constructions must necessarily be free of these historical limitations or they must by implication be archaic and irrelevant to our times. Because I understand theological construction to be free of such one-to-one historical limitations, my above criticisms of Weaver's historical reconstructions do not lead me to reject his theological construction. In fact, I find his theological contribution of narrative Christus Victor intriguing. I too have theological problems with any theological construction that requires violence and applaud his efforts to combat such theologies.

My above critique of Weaver's historical reconstruction should in no way be considered a theological defense of satisfaction atonement, a position I have long found problematic. I find his theological construction of narrative Christus Victor to have a biblical basis in the Book of Revelation (although again it is certainly not a one-to-one relationship). In this way I can certainly agree with his "minimalist conclusion . . . that satisfaction atonement is neither the only reading nor the required reading of the Bible" (69).

However, I find puzzling his effort to reconstruct a consistent theology throughout the Christian Bible that supports his own theological construction. His effort not only runs counter to the consensus of biblical scholarship but is also inconsistent with the other theologies he identifies with (feminist, womanist, African-American, pacifist), all of which understand that there are biblical theologies which require suspicion and, in many cases, resistance. Therefore, I can agree theologically with Weaver that satisfaction atonement should be resisted, even though I disagree with his historical reconstruction that minimizes how much of a biblical basis there is for satisfaction atonement. I hope that readers of this essay understand that my critique of Weaver's historical work is an effort to strengthen his theological agenda to provide a nonviolent theology for the church rather than an attempt to weaken it.

NOTES

1. J. Denny Weaver, *The Nonviolent Atonement* (Grand Rapids, Mich.: Wm. B. Eerdmans, 2001). All further citations from this work will be noted paren-

thetically in the text.

2. Hisako Kinukawa, *Women and Jesus in Mark: A Japanese Feminist View* (Maryknoll, N.Y.: Orbis Books, 1994).

3. See the following articles and the bibliographical entries in these articles for the consensus understanding of the sacrificial system of ancient Israel: S. David Sperling, "Blood," in *Anchor Bible Dictionary* (hereafter *ABD*), ed. David Noel Freedman (New York: Anchor, 1992), I:761-63; Baruch A. Levine, "Leviticus, Book of," in *ABD* IV:311-21; Gary A. Anderson, "Sacrifice and Sacrifical Offerings (OT)," in *ABD* V:870-86.

4. Jacob Milgrom, *Leviticus: A Book of Ritual and Ethics* (Minneapolis: Fortress Press, 2004), 191.

5. Michael Hardin, "Sacrificial Language in Hebrews: Reappraising René Girard," in *Violence Renounced: René Girard, Biblical Studies, and Peacemaking*, ed. Willard M. Swartley (Telford, Pa.: Pandora Press U.S., 2000), 103-12.

6. See the following articles and the corresponding bibliographical entries for the consensus understanding of how sacrifice relates to Christology and soteriology in the book of Hebrews: Harold W. Attridge, "Hebrews, Epistle to the," in *ABD* III:97-105; Hans-Josef Klauck, "Sacrifice and Sacrificial Offerings (NT)," in *ABD* V:886-91.

7. See the following articles and the corresponding bibliographical entries for the consensus understanding of Paul's Christology and soteriology: Hans-Dieter Betz, "Paul," in *ABD* V:186-201, esp. 195-96; and Hans-Josef Klauck, "Sacrifice and Sacrificial Offerings (NT)." For an extended discussion of satisfaction atonement theory in the New Testament, see Martin Hengel, *The Atonement: The Origins of the Doctrine in the New Testament* (Philadelphia: Fortress Press, 1981). Hengel demonstrates that satisfaction atonement was not only developed under the influence of the Jewish understanding of sacrifice, but also from Greco-Roman understandings of sacrifice. Hengel also provides a fairly standard discussion of Paul (34-39).

8. Weaver does also refer to the work of two other theologians who apparently have similar interpretations of Paul—Raymund Schwager and Timothy Gorringe—but his analysis most closely follows his interpretation of Beker's work.

9. Weaver is quoting from J. Christiaan Beker, *Paul the Apostle: The Triumph of God in Life and Thought* (Philadelphia: Fortress Press, 1980), 187.

10. Weaver is citing Beker, *Paul the Apostle*, 191.

11. Quoting Beker, *Paul the Apostle*, 189.

12. Beker, *Paul the Apostle*, 186.

13. Beker, *Triumph of God: The Essence of Paul's Thought* (Philadelphia: Augsburg Fortress, 1990), 82. Emphasis mine.

14. Ibid., 85.

15. See, for example, three New Testament essays in *Biblical Theology, Problems and Perspectives: In Honor of J. Christiaan Beker*, ed. Steven J. Kraftchick, Charles D. Myers Jr., and Ben C. Ollenburger (Nashville: Abingdon, 1995), Hendrikus Boers, "Paul and the Canon of the New Testament," 196-208; Charles D. Myers Jr., "The Persistence of Apocalyptic Thought in New Testament Theology," 209-221; and James H. Charlesworth, "Ancient Apocalyptic

Thought in New Testament Theology," 222-32. All three essays note Beker's important contribution to the emphasis on apocalyptic thought in New Testament theology, but none suggest that Beker's interpretation of Pauline Christology and soteriology rejects satisfaction atonement theory.

CHAPTER FOUR

THE VIOLENCE OF GOD AND THE HERMENEUTICS OF PAUL

Christopher D. Marshall

*T*he jarring dissonance between the God of vengeance and violence in certain parts of the Old Testament and the God of indiscriminate love and mercy proclaimed by Jesus in the Gospels has long perplexed Christian interpreters. Echoing the verdict of many, Paul Anderson maintains that reconciling these contrasting portraits of God constitutes "the greatest theological and hermeneutical problem in the Bible."[1] It is a theological problem because it challenges the notion of a unitary and self-consistent divine will. It is a hermeneutical problem because it forces the question of how apparently contradictory views of God can exercise authority as equally part of sacred Scripture. It is also a moral problem, for the way believers resolve this tension will have implications for how they live their lives as servants of God, even if the common assertion today that violent religious texts lead directly to violent behavior must be dismissed as simplistic.[2]

These difficulties are not unique to Christians, of course. Jewish interpreters, too, have long wrestled with how the compassionate God of, say, Ezekiel 33 is to be reconciled with the punitive God of, for example, Numbers 16.[3] But these problems of interpretation confront Christian readers in a particularly acute way in light of the theological, moral, and hermeneutical privilege which Christianity accords, at least in theory, to the Jesus tradition.

One early solution to the dilemma, proposed by Marcion and the Gnostics, was to unhook Jesus entirely from the God of the Jewish Scriptures, who was deemed to be a lesser deity. This option was roundly rejected by the early church. The heresy of ditheism not only leads to theological oblivion, it actually inscribes competitive violence in the nature of ultimate reality, something which biblical monotheism avoids. Christian orthodoxy has therefore always insisted that the God and Father of our Lord Jesus Christ must be none other than the one true God of Israel, the Creator of all that exists.

But what does this identification tell us about God? Has God changed? Did God give up his violent ways with the advent of Christ in favor of nonviolent love? Is God's fearsome career as a warrior over? Or does God remain fundamentally unchanged? Is God, by definition, unchangeable: the same yesterday, today, and forever? If so, what does that tell us about God's involvement in violence? Is lethal coercion still an important part of God's repertoire of methods for achieving saving and judging purposes in human affairs as it was in biblical times?

If the testimony of Christian history and doctrine are indicative, the latter appears to be the most common conclusion Christians have reached, since God's use of violence has continued to be as notable a feature of the Christian story of God as it was in the earlier Israelite story of God. Much atonement theology, for instance, as Denny Weaver spells out so clearly, envisages a patriarchal God who visits punitive violence on his only son to defend his personal dignity or uphold his superior justice.[4] Similarly the post-Constantinian church's majority endorsement of Christian participation in war has disclosed a willingness, if not an eagerness, to equate the violent shedding of human blood with the work and will of God.

Then there is the projected violence of final judgment. Even those who feel squeamish about the idea of God using human agents to visit wrath on his enemies in present history still often espouse a concept of eschatological judgment where God, patience finally exhausted, violently destroys the wicked—or, worse, callously consigns them to the everlasting violence of eternal torment. It is not uncommon even for Christian pacifists, who conscientiously renounce lethal violence themselves, keenly to anticipate God's retribution on the ungodly at the end of time. Some even argue that Christian renunciation of violence is materially dependent on the reality of God's ultimate retributive justice on evildoers, for only an absolute confidence in God's perfect judgment can free believers from the need to take matters into their own hands in the interim.[5] Put crudely, from this perspective Christian nonviolence is sustainable only if there is a violent God giving ultimate backup.

So Christian belief and practice have not, by and large, done away with the concept of divine violence. Even peace theology has not felt the need to posit a nonviolent God. Of course, retention of a militant deity eases the hermeneutical dilemma mentioned earlier, in that the violent God of early Israel does not cease to be violent in the Christian era but merely becomes less blatantly so. Instead of regularly deputizing human agents to slay the wicked, God now largely reserves that task for God's self at the end of time (although exceptions may apply in the event of justifiable war).

Yet arguably a theology that substitutes a conspicuously violent God with a cautiously violent God remains mired in what Walter Wink famously calls the myth of redemptive violence—the belief that violence saves, that war brings peace, that might makes right.[6] As long as God is understood to rely on lethal force to achieve redemptive goals, whether in present history through appointed human instruments or at the end of time by God's own clenched fist, disturbing implications follow, and especially for Anabaptist peace theology.

One such implication is the absolutizing or deifying of violence. To reserve to God the right to use overwhelming violence is to pay violence the ultimate compliment. Violence is dignified by its association with God, and God is diminished by dependence on violence. Indeed, the more violence is reserved as God's prerogative alone, the more uniquely and terrifyingly violent God appears. "It is a fearful thing to fall into the hands of the living God."[7] But if frail humans are expected to feel angry without resorting to violence, why should not the same be expected of God? Is God unable to withstand the temptation to hit back? Is crushing the opposition God's only solution?

Again, a willingness to exempt God from the normative requirement of nonviolence sustains the kind of exceptionalism that always leaves the door open for human beings to perpetrate violence on God's behalf or approve of it when done in God's name. As long as killing is sanctioned by God—whether now in times of war or during some future apocalyptic maelstrom—no moral condemnation can apply to those who carry out the killing.

Note, however, that whenever exceptions are permitted, there is a human propensity to expand the loophole endlessly. Each and every act of violence can be defended as a legitimate exception to the rule. Not surprisingly, it is always the perpetrators of violence, not its victims, who appeal to exceptional circumstances to legitimate their actions. Something similar happens with respect to those who cherish the expectation of God's final destruction of sinners. They exempt themselves and their loved ones from the awaited firestorm while insisting that God's justice requires others to be consumed by it.[8]

The grounding of Christian non-retaliation on trust in God's eschatological vengeance also has troubling corollaries. The more one waits for God's violent intervention to rectify the world, the less incentive there is to work for peaceful change now. Indeed, it could be argued (and often has been historically) that since God is clearly not yet riled enough by sin and injustice to intervene to overturn it, the unjust status quo ought to be accepted as something God permits to exist. Christians should not then actively oppose it, for that would be to usurp God's work. Pacifism then slides into a passivism that leaves it over to God to sort out the mess while keeping one's own hands clean. Although John Howard Yoder rejects such quietism, this could be one way of construing (or misconstruing) his contention that Christian nonviolence bears witness to Christians relinquishing control of history. Their call is to be faithful to the slain lamb, not to be "effective" in directing historical processes, a goal which is frequently taken to justify violence and is an illusory ambition at the best of times.[9]

Does this then mean that assuming responsibility for the direction of human history necessarily requires violence, even for God? Is violence an inescapable corollary of exercising supreme authority? Perhaps a better grounding for Christian pacifism would be the recognition that, in a real sense, humans *are* in charge of this world, and that it is only by emulating the nonviolent rule of God that we have any real chance of undoing the yokes of oppression and recovering the true purpose of our existence. After noting the vast literature written on theodicy and on whether God can ever be forgiven for the atrocities permitted on his watch, such as the incineration of a five year old girl called Esther before the eyes of her parents, or the random assassination carried out by a Palestinian gunman called Omar, J. Harold Ellens comments:

> I have figured out that the question is erroneous. It is not a question of justifying God or of bringing God to justice. It is not a question of forgiving God or holding God accountable. It is a matter of recognizing the limitations of God. God is not in

charge of this world. We are. We should have gotten that clue at a more profound level of awareness than we seem to have done, from Genesis 1:28, where the ancient Israelite narrative informs us that God assigned us the task of dominion in this world, to bring it to its potential fruitfulness. If we do not take care of beautiful blond and blue-eyed Esther, God cannot. If we do not find reconciliation with Omar, God cannot stop the mass murders. If we do not reach beyond the alienations and transcend the terror of the terrorists, God cannot save us.[10]

But perhaps the biggest problem with continuing to imagine a God who employs violence to advance his cause in the world is that it leads to an incoherent Christian monotheism. On the one hand, Jesus Christ is held to be the perfect revelation of the one true God. On the other hand, the God whom Jesus is said to reveal bears little resemblance to Jesus.

JESUS AS THE NONVIOLENT ICON OF GOD

The Christian story rests on two fundamental truth claims which set it apart from all other religious and ideological systems. First, it claims that the Creator God is made most fully known in the human person of Jesus Christ. If we want to know what God is really like, the New Testament authors submit, we must look at Jesus. He is the supreme benchmark for our understanding of Deity. "He is the image of the invisible God," the apostle Paul writes, the one in whom "all the fullness of God was pleased to dwell."[11] "He is the reflection of God's glory and the exact imprint of God's very being," Hebrews declares. He is also the one "through whom God created the worlds."[12] "All things came into being through him," John's Gospel begins, "and without him not one thing came into being. What has come into being in him was life, and the life was the light of all people."[13] "For in him all things in heaven and on earth were created, things visible and invisible, whether thrones or dominions or rulers or powers—all things have been created through him and for him."[14] Jesus, then, is both the human embodiment of God's very being and the one through whom and for whom God created the universe.

This conviction invests the words and deeds of Jesus of Nazareth with unparalleled revelatory significance. When Jesus teaches and practices nonviolence, therefore, it is not enough to see it as a tactical expedient he employs because revolutionary violence against the Roman superpower was not a viable option at that time.[15] It must be understood more profoundly as an articulation of what God is like and of how God exercises divine rule. That is why Jesus explicitly grounds his summons to enemy love and non-retaliation in the imitation of the heavenly Father, who "makes his sun to rise on the evil and on the good, and sends rain on the righteous and the unrighteous."[16] Jesus instructs his followers to conduct themselves as "children of the Most High, for he is kind to the ungrateful and the wicked." They are to be merciful "just as your Father is merciful."[17] Jesus' ethic of nonviolence, in other words, is predicated on the premise of a nonviolent God, a God who, as Raymund Schwager puts it, is "exactly the opposite of violence," a God whose "limitless forgiveness and boundless love are distinct in every respect from the mechanism of violence and the vicious cycle of mutual destructiveness."[18] Those who claim to follow this God must therefore be nonviolent too.[19]

The second truth claim Christianity makes is that God has acted uniquely in the life, death, and resurrection of Jesus to restore the world to its originally intended state of freedom. In Jesus, God has entered fully into the human condition, shackled as it is to the power of sin and subject to the scourge of suffering and death, and has acted through him to defeat the power of evil and reconcile its victims to himself. "He has rescued us from the power of darkness," Paul rejoices, "and transferred us into the kingdom of his beloved Son, in whom we have redemption, the forgiveness of sins. . . . For through him God was pleased to reconcile to himself all things, whether on earth or in heaven, by making peace through the blood of his cross."[20]

Not only is "the blood of his cross," by which Paul means his violent death on a Roman gallows, the decisive event that defeats evil and brings about peace, it is also the definitive revelation of what God is really like. Christian faith asserts that God is never more truly God than he is in the dying of Jesus. In the cross, as the gospel writers put it, the veil of the temple is torn in two and God stands revealed. God's justice also stands revealed.[21] The cross shows that God's justice is a peacemaking justice,[22] a reconciling, restoring, and healing justice. The God who is made climactically known in the cross of Christ is a God who secures justice not by violent imposition of his will on his enemies but by freely subjecting himself in suffering love to the violent impulses of humanity to liberate creation from its bondage to violence and to restore people to relationship with God and with each other.

These, then, are the two mind-boggling assertions the New Testament authors make. They dare to propose that Jesus of Nazareth is the human face of God, "the flesh and blood embodiment of the perfections of God,"[23] and that the true character and the justice of this God are nowhere more evident than in his death and resurrection. But this is not all. From these two claims they arrive at a critically important deduction—that what we learn of God in the story of Jesus is the key to understanding the meaning, inter-connectedness, and destiny of all created reality. As Ephesians states, "All things have been created through him and for him. He himself is before all things, and in him all things hold together."[24] In him God has made known his "plan for the fullness of time, to gather up all things in him, things in heaven and things on earth."[25]

What an astonishing assertion this is! All things have been created for, they are sustained by, and they find their ultimate meaning in Jesus Christ. All things are eternally imprinted with the moral character and career of the crucified and risen Lord. From this it follows that the central principle of creation is not naked power, or control, or order, or balance, but vulnerable, passionate, reconciling, self-giving love, a love which subverts evil, not by an overwhelming display of coercive force, but by acting in amazing grace to redeem offenders and to heal sin's victims, and at great cost to itself. In short, the Jesus story reveals that God's nonviolent love is the ground of the universe.

This is not a wholly new revelation, however. It is already evident in the creation narratives of Genesis. It is hugely significant that, notwithstanding the violence ascribed to God in the pages of the Bible, the canonical record opens and closes with surprisingly peaceful scenes—the two accounts of creation (Gen. 1-2) and the presentation of the New Jerusalem (Rev. 21-22). Peace is both ontologically anterior to violence and eschatologically posterior to it. Violence has no role in God's work of creation; it only enters into the picture later as a result of human sin and will eventually come to an end.[26] This is quite different from other ancient Near Eastern creation myths, such as the Babylonian Emuna Elish, where creation is the result of a violent act of deicide and humans are created from the blood of the murdered god. There evil precedes good, chaos is conquered by violence, and the king serves as Marduk's representative on earth, ruling by means of holy war. By contrast, as Walter Wink observes:

> The Bible portrays a good God who creates a good creation. Chaos does not resist order. Good is before evil. Neither evil nor violence is a part of the creation, but enter later, as a result of the first couple's sin and the connivance of the serpent (Gen. 3). A

basically good reality is thus corrupted by free decisions reached by creatures. In this far more complex and subtle explanation of the origins of things, violence emerges for the first time as a problem requiring a solution.[27]

The creation narratives, in other words, presuppose a divine ontology of peace. They portray a nonviolent God who speaks the world into existence and who makes human beings in the divine image and likeness to cultivate creation as devoted gardeners, not to pillage it as rapacious warriors. Things go badly wrong, however, and violence invades this peaceable reality.[28] This is no minor problem that can be easily fixed. It not only escalates out of all control in the human community,[29] it even provokes God to an act of massive counterviolence, something God apparently later regrets.[30] Thus begins the long canonical story of divinely induced violence, a story which stands in stark contrast to what we have seen of God in the story of Jesus and cries out for some theological explanation.

It is important that this explanation is *theological* in character, not just traditio-historical or psycho-cultural or phenomenological, because the canonical text is principally intended to exercise a theological role in the community that created and preserves it. The biblical traditions, for all their diversity, once gathered together as canonical Scripture, combine to tell a single overarching story about Israel, God, and the world. The texts constitute a narrative world into which readers enter, with its own plot, its own cast of characters (including God), and its own universe of meanings, a story which serves authoritatively to interpret God to Israel and Israel to itself.[31] In this connection it matters little whether the biblical accounts are historically reliable in all their details; of primary importance is the theological claim they make to narrate the story of God. This means that the problem of divine violence cannot be dealt with adequately simply by deeming this or that episode to be legendary or fictitious.[32] Whether or not God actually killed the children of Egypt, the biblical story *says* God did. This is how the biblical writers understand the involvement of God, and it is their interpretation of God that has normatively shaped and conditioned how the subsequent community of faith (including Jesus) has apprehended God.

What is needed, then, is some explanation for God's violence that both accords with the inner logic of the plotted narrative and that accounts for *why* it is that God is characterized in this way, especially when there are strong indications at the outset of the story that the Creator God works by peaceable means. Given the many incidents of divine violence that follow, it is also worth pondering how Jesus could possibly have conceived of God as being unfailingly kind to the ungrateful and wicked when he knew full well that within the biblical drama God discriminates in favor of friends, bears grudges against opponents for generations, and visits retribution on sinners.

THE VIOLENCE OF GOD IN SCRIPTURE

The Hebrew Bible has a reputation for being one of the bloodiest works in existence. Firmly fixed in the popular mind is the image of the "Old Testament God" as a God of war and destruction, a brutal, reactive, and ruthless deity who brooks no rivals and leaves no infraction unpunished. Whether this menacing reputation is fully deserved is debatable. Patricia M. McDonald argues that there is far less violence in the Hebrew Scriptures than is generally supposed and that the deepest concern of the biblical authors is to encourage ways of living that overcome violence and foster compassion. The problem with any textual portrayal of violence, she suggests, is that it tends to have a disproportionate impact on readers. Violent language and imagery take over our imagination and absorb our interest, so that we "find" more violence than is actually there.

This rhetorical impact of the violence also diverts attention away from other themes in the text that are often of more fundamental importance to the author. The peripheral thus becomes central and the central peripheral. Nor, McDonald adds, does all the violent imagery used in the Bible function to endorse actual violence. The specifically military imagery for God, for example, is plainly metaphorical. God's defeat of Egypt may be spoken of as a triumph of war,[33] but in practice it was achieved by non-military terms. Although Yahweh uses "weapons" to overthrow his enemies, his weapons are the forces of the natural order. The language is analogical, not literal, although, as McDonald concedes, this choice of military analogies did encourage dangerous perceptions about God to emerge.

As helpful as these considerations are, the fact remains that the biblical narrative attests to a deep and pervasive association between God and deadly violence. The connection between them is varied and complex. Sometimes God resolutely opposes the use of violence and identifies wholly with the victim. At other times God is portrayed as the perpetrator of violence, either by direct fiat or by organizing and sanctioning others to visit judgment on a disobedient people. Often it is precisely God's capacity for superior violence that serves to establish Yahweh's credentials as the only true God. Violence thus emerges as the most frequently mentioned activity in the Hebrew Bible. Schwager has counted some 600 passages in which violence is recorded and at least 1,000 verses in which God's violence is described. In some 100 passages God expressly commands people to kill others, and in some stories God tries to kill people for no apparent reason.[34] God's violence is particularly evident in the wilderness stories. It has been calculated that in the forty year period between Israel's exodus from Egypt and their entry to Canaan, the Lord executes at least 30,000 of his own people.[35] Three times Yahweh threatens to annihilate them entirely,[36] and on a number of occasions strikes them with plagues as he did the Egyptians.[37] Even greater in number than such narrative acts of violence are the potential acts of violence commanded in the enforcement of the laws of the Sinai covenant.[38]

The blood of Israel's enemies runs even more freely. Yahweh smites innocent Egyptian children in Exodus 12, drowns the Egyptian army in the sea in Exodus 14-15, opens up the ground to swallow the Korahites in Numbers 16, orders the impaling of Baal worshippers in Numbers 25, calls for reprisal on the Midianites in Numbers 31, and orders the conquest of Canaan in Joshua 1. The most chilling of all biblical texts to do with war and violence are those that refer to the *herem* or "ban," under which all human beings among the defeated are "devoted to destruction," sometimes at God's explicit command.[39] Emotions of pity are expressly forbidden in such cases.[40] Susan Niditch identifies two main ideologies undergirding and justifying this practice of genocide. In one, the ban is understood as a sacrificial offering to God, which presupposes a God who appreciates human sacrifice. In the other, the ban is viewed as an act of divine justice upon idolatry, which was thought to threaten Israel's own purity and survival. In both cases mass slaughter is a means of gaining God's favor.[41]

It is possible to identify certain ameliorating features in the institution of *herem*. McDonald mentions, for example, its role in discouraging the use of war purely for plunder, since all captured possessions were to be destroyed.[42] Niditch detects a paradoxically high view of human dignity implicit in the ban. The "terrifying completeness and fairness" of the ban's indiscriminate massacre "may be viewed as admitting more respect for the value of human life than other war ideologies that allow for arbitrary killing of soldiers and civilians."[43] This sounds like special pleading. But even if it were true, God is still cast in the role as author or condoner of immense brutality, the instigator of repeated episodes of ethnic cleansing, the perpetrator of what today would be termed crimes against humanity. According to one critic, the God of Exodus, Deuteronomy, and Joshua is little better than a violent, murderous, genocidal land thief. "Troubling images of God cascade from biblical texts like waterfalls after a violent storm. God's repugnant words and pathological behavior are so widespread as to be considered normative behavior for God!"[44] This judgment may be one-sided. But the fact that it can seriously be made at all is testimony to the extent to which God is deeply embroiled in gut-wrenching brutality in many parts of the biblical narrative.

The most graphic accounts of divinely approved violence are set in the context of Israel's early history, even if they were composed at a later stage. With the establishment of the monarchy, the pure ideal of holy war comes to an end and Israel learns to rely on conventional military might. War still carries a sacral element to some extent, but, as Mark McEntire explains "God is removed from the battlefield and eventually closed off in the temple along with the ark . . . the presence of God is no longer an essential element of a battle."[45] In later prophetic and apocalyptic literature, emphasis shifts from the mediation of divine violence through historical agents to the expectation of God's eschatological victory, which is portrayed in language no less violent than is found in Deuteronomy and Joshua. The Psalms also celebrate and anticipate the coming of the "God of salvation" who will "shatter the heads of his enemies" and will enable his own people to "bathe their feet in blood" and to feed their enemies to their dogs.[46]

Not that God ever deserts the cut and thrust of present history. McEntire points out that the Hebrew canon (unlike the Greek canon and Christian Old Testament canon) closes with 2 Chronicles 36, which tells of the destruction of Jerusalem by the Babylonians. Although the term *herem* is not used, the many parallels between 2 Chronicles 36 and Joshua 6 give the unmistakable impression that the city has fallen because God has instituted a ban on Israel. The classical prophets toyed with the possibility of Yahweh turning against Israel for breaking covenant;[47] now it has happened. Yahweh disowns his people and brings devastation upon the holy city. No mercy is shown to its inhabitants; the chosen people are either killed or carried off into exile. "Yahweh begins the story as the compassionate, patient God of a disobedient people. As the story progresses, Yahweh becomes a wrathful avenger whose actions are confused with and indistinguishable from those of an earthly tyrant."[48]

To be sure, bringing such episodes of divine violence into the limelight in this way is potentially misleading, for there is quite another side to God's character in the biblical accounts as well. Hosea 11, for example, depicts Yahweh in emotional turmoil, torn apart by conflicting feelings of outrage at his people's sin and tender compassion for their plight, contemplating terrible punishment but recoiling in horror from the prospect of executing fierce anger against them and promising never again to destroy Ephraim. Elsewhere too God is revealed as a God of mercy, forgiveness, and love, a God who displays a special concern for the most vulnerable members of the covenant community, a God who liberates the poor from oppression and who heals and restores the victims of violence.[49] Indeed, this biblical notion of a God who sides with the weak and the downtrodden is radically different from that which prevailed in the ancient Near East, where the gods inaugurated and upheld the hierarchical structures of wealth and power.[50]

Even so, God's concrete actions at times belie God's words. Yahweh appears not only as the God of victims but also as the God who devours victims. How the head-smashing God of the historical narratives, the psalms, and the prophets can be reconciled with the nonviolent God disclosed by Jesus still needs to be answered.

HERMENEUTICAL STRATEGIES

Many different interpretive strategies have been employed to try to resolve this problem. One common tactic is to refuse to question anything God does, as a matter of principle, for God's ways are higher than our ways and God's thoughts higher than ours (Isa. 55:9). God is sovereign and holy; it is simply wrong for human beings as mere creatures to subject God's actions to moral scrutiny.

But this pious concern to save God from criticism ducks the problem. Even Abraham was prepared to challenge God's projected violence against the inhabitants of Sodom on the ground that the judge of all the earth has a moral obligation to abide by the principle of justice.[51] If God's deeds are beyond all moral valuation, so that nothing God ever does can be called bad, then it is equally true that nothing God does can ever be called good, and no way finally exists to differentiate between God and the Devil. There is also no ground for challenging religious zealots today who cast themselves in the role of human agents of divine wrath on the basis that whatever God is said to have done in sacred Scripture must be inherently good.

Another common strategy is to offer pleas of mitigation on God's behalf, to find in each episode of bloodletting a justifiable reason for divine judgment. The dispossession and extermination of the Canaanites, for example, is seen as fitting punishment for their idolatry and wickedness. It is also often observed that given Israel's precarious predicament in a hostile world, God simply had to employ lethal violence to safeguard the chosen instrument of salvation for the benefit of us all. God's violence is an example of "good violence" rather than "bad violence" because it is a redemptive or salvific violence.[52]

Such appeals to mitigating circumstances, however, come perilously close to an ends-justifies-the-means style of moral reasoning. It is true that the conquest of Canaan is sometimes defended in the biblical text as deserved retribution for the idolatry of the inhabitants.[53] But the justice of the penalty is by no means self-evident. As McEntire points out, "The inhabitants of Jericho, and Canaan in general, are never accused of anything other than two dubious transgressions. They happen to live in the land Yahweh promised to Abraham and they do not exclusively worship a god, Yahweh, who has never been revealed to them." McEntire notes that "As punishment for these transgressions, they become victims of destructive violence." The net result is "people minding their own business becoming dead so that nomads can become farmers."[54]

It is also true that the continued existence of Israel as a holy people is of overriding importance to the story of salvation and that God favored their interests for the ultimate good of all humanity. But it is extremely doubtful that every episode of divinely sanctioned bloodshed was critical to the maintenance of Israel's national and religious integrity. Sometimes relatively minor infractions attract massive retribution while at other times mercy is extended to serious breaches of covenantal boundaries. It also needs saying that the ease with which some interpreters defend the necessity and morality of the "redemptive violence" employed in biblical history attests to an imaginative failure on their part to recognize the hideous suffering endured by its victims. Christian readers recoil in horror at the Christmas story of Herod's slaughter of the infant boys in Bethlehem,[55] yet often barely flinch when reading of God ordering the massacre of the Amalekite infants, and some two centuries after the offense for which the people were allegedly being punished.[56] Readers may delight in the sparing of Rahab and her family when Joshua "fit de battle of Jericho" but spare no thought for all the other inhabitants of the city who were "devoted to destruction by the edge of the sword, both men and women, young and old, oxen, sheep, and donkeys" (Josh. 6:21).

A third interpretive strategy is to sanitize the real-life violence of the biblical text by allegorizing or spiritualizing it. There is a long and venerable approach to biblical interpretation that is so convinced of the text's divine origins that where the literal sense of the words produces impossible results, one must look for a deeper allegorical meaning, a meaning, as Origen put it, that is "worthy of God." By this method stories of war and mayhem are transposed into uplifting moral and spiritual truths. But despite its impressive pedigree, allegorization is hardly a viable method in the modern world for dealing with offensive texts. Moreover, even if the allegorical meaning may be counted as worthy of God, the literal historical meaning remains deeply problematic.[57] Allegorists and Sunday school teachers may find comforting spiritual messages disclosed by violent texts, but the texts themselves were initially intended to portray and validate actual bodily suffering and death.

Yet another hermeneutical strategy is to dismiss the violent portrayals of God in the biblical text as historically and theologically false. They are the product of the biblical authors projecting onto God their own violent fantasies and vengeful impulses, seeking to justify human atrocities by claiming God decreed them. God thus gets the blame for what in reality were acts of human malice. This means that rather than blithely accepting the truthfulness of everything the text says about God as guaranteed by divine revelation, it is important to separate the wheat from the chaff, to distinguish the voice of divine truth from the voice of human self-deception.[58] Nelson-Pallmeyer makes this point with uncompromising clarity:

> The Bible tells us more about human beings than it does about God, and it does so even when it claims to be talking about God. Revelation within the biblical story, in my view, is rare, and often overwhelmed by distorted human projections. The Bible is both sacred and dangerous. It is sacred because God is revealed partly within the experiences of those responsible for its pages. That is why many of us return to it day after day and year after year in search of meaning and guidance. It is also a dangerous book because we often ascribe divine will to the many human distortions it contains. We undermine the sacredness of the Bible and fuel its dangers whenever we fail to discern the difference between distortion and revelation. . . . Stated simply, the Bible can inform our religious experience, but it is often wrong about God.[59]

For Nelson-Pallmeyer it is not enough just to recognize the metaphorical character of the violent images used for God. Violent metaphors must be utterly repudiated as false and abusive. They distort the truth of God and should be expunged from the language of theology and worship. Other scholars, however, warn against discarding such morally offensive material, for, as John Collins suggests, violent texts still possesses revelatory power insofar as they give "an unvarnished picture of human nature and of the dynamics of history, and also of religion and the things that people do in its name."[60]

This fourth hermeneutical strategy is helpful in alerting us to the complexity of the interface between divine revelation and human reception. Comprehending God's self-disclosure in the biblical narrative is like following a fine silver thread woven into a dense and colourful tapestry, a tapestry embroidered from a wide range of human reflections and actions that are always culturally conditioned and ideologically slanted. Accordingly, just because God's permission is frequently evoked by biblical figures does not necessarily mean that God has spoken in every one of those instances. Yet how do we make allowance for this possibility without remaking God in our own image? How do we avoid simply favoring those parts of Scripture that suit our own prejudices and biases and discarding the rest as false projections, thus reducing the text to an echo-chamber of modern liberal values and preconceptions? And how is the canonical status of the text sustained if we accept only the nice bits?

The violence of God material is not easily separable from other more peaceful conceptions of divine activity. In one form or another, divine violence is woven into warp and woof of almost the entire biblical tradition. The self-same texts that extol God's graciousness and mercy and forgiveness and slowness to anger, also warn of God visiting the iniquity of the parents on their children for three or four generations.[61] No wonder Nelson-Pallmeyer is forced to conclude that revelation is rare in the Bible.

This brings us to a final, and more promising, hermeneutical strategy, one that allows for a substantial change in God's relationship to violence in the course of the biblical story. In this approach the violent texts are not to be rejected as a simple distortion of divine reality. They are a reliable reflection of how God was experienced at this time. Amid the violence that pervaded human life and society, people encountered God as someone directly involved in the messiness of human life and conflict. They knew that God abhorred the squandering of human life, for it was invested it with sacred significance. Yet they also wanted a God who would employ coercive power in great measure to punish, protect, and correct. Elijah, for instance, invited God to cast fire down from heaven to consume his opponents, for this was how any self-respecting deity should prove his superiority when challenged by competitors.[62]

With the coming of Jesus, a fresh experience of God is afforded. When Jesus' disciples wanted to emulate Elijah by calling down fire on a Samaritan village, Jesus "turned and rebuked them."[63] He did so not simply because such an extreme reprisal would be unfair in this particular circumstance, but because he considered violent vengeance to be wrong in principle and because he knew that God should no longer be understood to work in this way.[64] God has disarmed! God's perceived involvement in the infliction of violence is over. God no longer fights fire with fire. God has changed—or, perhaps more accurately, the human experience of God's association with violence has changed. God will no longer permit his identity to be defined by violence; God actively repudiates the violent behavior which has hitherto clouded his character so that the duplicity of violence itself may be exposed and defeated.

GOD'S CHANGED RELATIONSHIP TO VIOLENCE

I noted earlier that the creation narratives presuppose a divine ontology of peace. Violence is neither part of God's creative activity nor of God's internal being. Violence appears only after the human community has fallen into sin. Interestingly the subsequent account depicts an initial reluctance on God's part to employ violence, then a decision to do so, followed by a recoiling from its drastic consequences. This imaginative portrayal of divine ambivalence toward violence in the early scenes of the human story is, I suggest, an important key for understanding what follows. It dramatizes a profound insight into the perversity of violence, namely, that once violence is entrenched in human society, even the sacred is captured by its allure. Once "the earth is filled with violence" (Gen. 6:11,13), humanity's apprehension of the divine is inescapably framed by its desire to have a deity whose power is greater than that of human violence and whose greatness is shown precisely in a heightened capacity for violence. The violence-of-God material that pervades the biblical narratives is thus symptomatic of this capture while also disclosive of it.

God's reply to Adam and Eve's disobedience is not, at first, a violent one. Along with other consequences they are banished from the

Garden to prevent their fallen condition from becoming everlasting (Gen. 3:22-24). When in the second generation the problem of sibling rivalry arises, God tries to warn Cain off from succumbing to his feelings of jealousy and resentment, but without success. Sin is personified as a hungry animal lying at the door ready to spring (4:6-7). It is so powerful that it overcomes the will of God and overtakes the passions of Cain, and he turns to violence. After Cain murders his brother, God still does not respond violently; instead the Lord acts to protect the life of the killer, though now *threatening* sevenfold vengeance against any who disregards the protective mark on Cain (4:15). God's next response to human sinfulness is to impose a 120-year limit on the human life span (6:3) and to express regret over the decision to create human beings in the first place (6:6). But as violence spins out of control and fills the land, God plans, for the first time, an act of violent retribution in which "everything that is on the earth shall die" (6:17). In due course God carries out the plan, blotting out all but a tiny handful of creatures (7:21-24).

Afterward, however, God is deeply disturbed by the indiscriminate nature of the punishment employed. Non-human creation has been made to bear the brunt of humanity's sin. At the same time, God recognizes that wiping out sinful people still has not actually removed the problem of sin, "for the inclination of the human heart is evil from youth" (8:21, cf. 6:5). God therefore promises never again to curse the ground and destroy all living creatures because of human evil (8:21-22; 9:11, 15). As McDonald observes, "God tried violence once and now knows better."[65] God then makes two telling concessions to the descendants of Noah: humans may now kill animals for food (9:3-4), and those who take human life will face the death sentence (9:5-6), an attempt to use judicially circumscribed violence to break the spirit of vendetta displayed earlier by Lamech (4:23-24). In a sense, God makes a compromise with violence. Lethal violence in the human community is forbidden, but those who resort to it can expect God to respond in like manner.

The patriarchal narratives that follow are remarkably peaceful. There is very little violence described at all, although God is often involved in what does occur, such as the destruction of Sodom and Gomorrah,[66] and God's long-term plan to dispossess the Canaanites of their land is frequently alluded to.[67] Violence only becomes more pronounced during and after the deliverance from Egypt, and especially during the conquest of Canaan where, as we have seen, genocide is commanded. Thereafter in the waxing and waning of Israel's fortunes, God is frequently depicted as the author and instrument of violence, ranging from incidents of individual retribution to episodes of large-scale war-making.

God's actual responsibility for authorizing this violence is, of course, doubtful, if not impossible. It is a standard feature of biblical idiom to ascribe a causative role to God for almost everything that happens, both good and bad, as well for narrators to assume a God's eye perspective in interpreting events. It is crucial to recognize this interpretive technique. Raymund Schwager divides the texts that speak of God's violence in the Old Testament into four categories: those where Yahweh strikes out irrationally for no apparent reason (which are extremely rare),[68] those where God personally takes revenge on human wrongdoing,[69] those where God uses other human beings to punish evildoers,[70] and those where the wicked are punished by their deeds rebounding back on them under God's supervision.[71]

But the distinction between these categories is more rhetorical than real, for the narrative texts show that even where God's direct retribution is talked of, it is almost always mediated through human instruments.[72] Both direct and indirect divine violence amount to the same thing; "it is always a question of human power interpreted as God's action."[73] Direct heavenly intervention is rare, though it does happen (and presumably here natural calamities are being attributed to God).[74] Much the same applies to those texts which speak of self-punishment. The penalty may be conceptualized as the inherent consequence of a wrongful deed boomeranging back on the doer, but in practice the penalty might still be inflicted by another person or be initiated by God.[75] While violence, then, is explicitly ascribed to God in the biblical text, it is almost always committed by human beings. Texts on Yahweh's violence normally refer to human deeds that are thought in some way to be related to God's will, so that we may safely assume that "human violence is meant when there is talk of divine anger and retribution."[76]

But why is it that human violence is so naturally identified with the action of God? Why is God conceived as the author of so much carnage? Why are harmful human experiences viewed as the punishments of God? Part of the answer lies in the desire to affirm God's transcendent immanence in all of historical experience, and part of it lies in the corrupting impact of violence itself. Such is the intrinsic nature of violence that once unleashed it changes everything, including humanity's experience of God. In the Genesis story God is initially portrayed as one who resists and opposes violence, albeit without success. But as violence grows and spreads God is driven to counter-violence. Once this step is taken however, God is enmeshed in the very problem that needs addressing.[77]

Redemptive violence takes on an irresistible logic of its own, so that even the knowledge of God falls victim to it. It is almost as if once it is imagined that God compromises with violence, God ends up being compromised. Consistently in the Bible the experience of violence changes people's identity, the way individuals are perceived and known and relate to one another.[78] The same happens to God's identity, as the peaceable God of creation is inexorably defined in militant and aggressive ways. Counter-themes of love and mercy and forgiveness and restraint are always present, but the larger conceptual framework fundamentally remains one of redemptive violence.

Once conceived as violent, God's only option is to tarry with humanity in its misconceptions to win redemption by other means. God is forced to accommodate revelation to the limitations of human perception, not least so that the ultimate futility of redemptive violence—already intimated in Genesis 8:21—might become apparent.[79] In the process horrendous acts of violence are attributed, or misattributed, to God. But God's apparent capture by the categories of sacred violence becomes the precondition for exposing violence for what it is—an enslaving and self-perpetuating deception that contaminates all that it touches, including knowledge of God.[80] With the coming of Jesus however, God finally casts off the illusions surrounding righteous violence to disclose "the plan of the mystery hidden for ages in God who created all things" (Eph. 3:9)—to reconcile all things by an act of self-giving, nonviolent, victorious love. Significantly this requires God-in-Christ personally to fall victim to divinely sanctioned lethal violence,[81] making it plain once and for all that God-authored violence is a falsity, that "whenever sacred violence is mentioned, it is always human beings attacking one another."[82]

It is God's definitive renunciation of redemptive violence in the life, death, and resurrection of Christ that requires us to re-read the earlier biblical narratives of divine violence in such a way that God can no longer be seen as the ultimate author of the cruelty and killing they record. Certainly these bloody narratives attest to God's providential presence amid human degradation. But insofar as they ascribe to God responsibility for acts of barbarism, they attest only to the veil of violence through which the experience of God has been filtered since the days of Cain. In Christ, however, the veil is taken away and God stands fully revealed.

I am suggesting then that the biblical accounts of divine violence are both true to how God was experienced following the entry of sin, yet ultimately untrue to God's real character. In this respect they are hermeneutically complex. It could be objected that allowing for such misrepresentation of God's initiative in violence by the biblical authors undermines the authority and trustworthiness of the scriptural text.[83] But this is not necessarily so. The text remains trustworthy in that it reliably discloses how God has been apprehended in history and how God perseveres with human fallibility. Those passages that ascribe violence to God should not be censored or sanitized or discarded; instead they should be read with a "critical charity" that embraces them, for all their gruesomeness, as a gift of God to aid in our instruction and formation.[84] But neither should such passages be absolutized as an unassailable revelation of God's true being; that role belongs to Christ alone.

Objections might also be raised to the notion of God being "captured" by the mythology of violence, of God allowing the divine identity to be clouded by images of vengeance and viciousness. But this phenomenon can be seen as testimony to the seriousness of the cognitive and moral distortions created by the entry of sin and the irruption of violence (cf. Rom. 1:18-23). Also there are precedents within Scripture itself for questioning whether established understandings of God's behavior are truly consonant with the character of God. Jeremiah, for example, despite repeated affirmations in sacred tradition that God employs the practice of collective punishment, extending down through many generations,[85] looks forward to the day when this will no longer be so,[86] and Ezekiel is rebuked by God for failing to see that the principle no longer applies.[87]

An even more instructive analogy is the way in which the apostle Paul rethinks the role of the law in salvation. Paul faces a hermeneutical dilemma similar to the one explored above. He discovered that when God played his trump card in Jesus Christ, it looked disconcertingly different from what God's hand had hitherto looked like. Until that point, God had insisted that obedience to the Torah was the indispensable source of righteousness for the chosen people and the ground of hope for Israel's redemption. The law was central to God's saving purposes. But then something unexpected happened. When God finally intervened to secure salvation for Israel, it took place "apart from the law,"[88] in some respects even contrary to the law.

Paul was therefore forced to think his way through how and why God's familiar ways in the past had altered so dramatically. The zealous young Pharisee, who himself had been prepared to use righteous violence to defend and uphold the law,[89] was compelled to read the Scriptures afresh, to interpret them from a new perspective, to discern in them a new understanding of God hitherto hidden from sight but now revealed through his son. In doing so Paul suggests a relationship between God, sin, death, and the law that parallels, in broad outline, the relationship between God and violence I have sketched above.

PAUL'S TREATMENT OF THE LAW AS A HERMENEUTICAL PRECEDENT

The meaning and self-consistency of Paul's extensive reflections on the place of the Mosaic law in the Christian era is a storm center in current Pauline scholarship. Over the last twenty-five years, the so-called "New Perspective on Paul" has thrown up a series of objections to the traditional or "Lutheran" understanding that has dominated the interpretation of Paul since the time of the Reformation. Yet the New Perspective is itself coming under sustained criticism, with some scholars claiming that it lacks the theological depth and exegetical precision of the traditional model. No consensus has yet emerged, although there is a growing feeling that some mediating position is required that combines the insights of both older and the newer perspectives. There is no room here to explore this further. Suffice it to say that any satisfactory explanation of Paul's critique of the law must, in my opinion, do justice to three main realities: the diversity of views on the Torah in first-century Judaism, Paul's radical commitment to Gentile inclusion in the messianic community, and the apostle's darkly pessimistic view of the human condition. All three inform and shape his reconsideration of the role of the law in God's purposes, now that the Messiah has appeared.

It is noteworthy that Paul approaches the issue within a narrative framework. That is to say, he reads Scripture primarily as a story, with an overarching plot, a set of characters, and a forward-reaching momentum that climaxes in the life, death, and resurrection of Christ. Paul recognizes that there are different ways of interpreting this story. As a Pharisee, he read the biblical story through the lens of the Torah, with Moses being the key actor in the drama and Israel's holiness being its central concern. Now as a Christian, Paul has learned to read the story through the lens of Jesus Christ, with Abraham being the key figure and the eschatological uniting of Jew and Gentile in a new covenant community being its true message. Of course, for Paul, these two readings of the biblical narrative are not equally valid. The former is the product of viewing Scripture through a "veil" of ignorance, of lacking true enlightenment about the real import of God's saving righteousness. Only in Christ is this veil removed; only in him do the lights come on.[90] Only then does the true meaning of God's activity in preceding history come clearly into view.

From this hermeneutical vantage point, Paul is able to see the Torah in a completely new light. Once he viewed the law as God's answer to Adam's sin, the gracious means by which Israel could recover humanity's true role in the world and secure admission to the world to come. Now, however, Paul considers the law to be part of the problem, not part of the solution. Paul faults the law on three main counts. First, the law has proven powerless to free God's people from the grip of sin. Far from controlling sin, as God intended, the law actually makes the situation worse, because it simultaneously highlights Israel's accountability to God's requirements (Rom. 2:12; 3:19) and her impotence to achieve genuine righteousness no matter how sincerely she strives for it (9:31, cf. 2:17-29). Consequently the law cannot deliver the hoped for vindication; on the contrary it brings "the knowledge of sin" (3:20; 5:13; 7:7), the weight of God's wrath (4:15), and the inevitability of God's curse (Gal. 3:10). More than that, it actually exacerbates human sinfulness. The law functions to stir up the very passions it condemns (Rom. 7:5), so that the coming of the law resulted in trespasses being multiplied rather than being reduced (5:20).

The reason for this sorry state of affairs is that the law, for all its divine qualities, is unable to overcome the indwelling and all-pervasive power of sin (3:9-18; 7:14-25; Gal. 3:22). The law is fatally "weakened by the flesh" (Rom. 8:3; 7:14, 25); it is stymied by that fallen human condition that "does not submit to God's law, indeed it cannot" (8:7). The law has even become a weapon in the hands of sin (7:7-13), so much so that Paul can boldly declare that "the power of sin is the law" (1 Cor. 15:56, cf. Rom. 7:22-23). What God intended for life has become a vehicle of death.[91] The source of the problem is not the law itself, which Paul considers to be "holy, just and good" (Rom. 7:12, 14, 16). The problem is the deep-rootedness of sin, which lies beyond the reach of any external legal code, even one given by God.

The second problem Paul finds with the law is that it is limited to one ethnic community. Notwithstanding the ironical tone of his comments, Paul accepts the premise that the law was given uniquely to Israel to enable her to be "a guide to the blind, a light to those who are in darkness, a corrector of the foolish, a teacher of children, having in the law the embodiment of knowledge and truth" (Rom 2:19-20). But this mission has been subverted by Israel's failure to practice what she preaches, so much so that Paul can even charge the covenant people with causing God's name to be blasphemed among the Gentiles (2:24). What Israel's track record proves, Paul argues, is that sin is no respecter of ethnic boundaries. Nor, conversely, is the capacity to perceive and obey God's will. Paul believes that it is quite possible for uncircumcised Gentiles, who do not possess the Torah, "instinctively to do what the law requires" since "what the law requires is written on their hearts, to which their own conscience bears witness" (2:14-15, 27).

So law and righteousness are not co-extensive realities; there is no necessary overlap. If there were, justification could legitimately come through the law and Gentiles would need to become observant Jews to appropriate it. But Israel's own servitude to sin proves that this is not the case. In any event, even if it were the case, an additional problem would arise, for God would then be reduced to the status of a tribal deity rather than universal lord, and God's promise to bless all the nations of the world through Abraham would be null and void (4:9-16; Gal. 3:15-22). If the unity, sovereignty, and justice of God—to which the law itself bears witness—are to be vouchsafed, justification must come by some means other than the law. It must potentially be open to every member of the human family.

> For we hold that a person is justified by faith apart from works prescribed by the law. Or is God the God of Jews only? Is he not the God of Gentiles also? Yes, of Gentiles also, since God is one; and he will justify the circumcised on the ground of faith and the uncircumcised through that same faith. Do we then overthrow the law by this faith? By no means! On the contrary, we uphold the law. (Rom. 3:28-31, cf. 10:11-13)

The third problem Paul has with the law is that an overriding emphasis on law-keeping shifts the spotlight from God's empowering grace to autonomous human achievement. Paul is adamant that justification cannot come from reliance on "the works of the law."[92] Now it is true that by this phrase Paul most likely has in mind ceremonial practices such as circumcision, food laws, purity regulations, and Sabbath observance which served visibly to demarcate the boundary between the law-keeping covenant community and the Gentile world. He is not thinking of legalism in a moral sense but of proud reliance on badges of ethnic distinction. He is not accusing Judaism of advocating an individualistic works-righteousness whereby people can earn their own salvation by merit. He is more likely targeting some conception of national-righteousness, whereby adoption of certain Jewish distinctives was thought essential to securing final vindication. Even so, Paul still recognizes the potential for a law-centered spirituality to over-emphasize human capability and to underestimate the insidiousness of sin and the necessity of grace.

Viewed from the perspective of law-keeping, sin tends to get equated with a set of external behaviors that can be avoided with sufficient vigilance, rather than being recognized for what it really is—a deadly poison that permeates the entire life-system of humanity, a cosmic power that enslaves all humanity by habituating everyone to self-centeredness and idolatry.[93] A certain kind of complacency can therefore emerge that is so assured of its own sincerity that it underrates the unmerited nature of grace (cf. Phil. 3:4-16). This is partly why Paul sets law and grace in such stark opposition.[94]

The only solution to this predicament, Paul argues, is the rupturing of sin's lordship and the radical renewal of human nature from the inside out so that God's law is written on the human heart by means of the indwelling of the Spirit. This is exactly what Christ achieves through his death and resurrection on behalf of all humanity, as a kind of second Adam.[95] Those who participate through baptism in Christ's victory (Rom. 6:1-14) are empowered by the eschatological Spirit to fulfil the true intention of God's law (8:1-4). That intention is a life of freedom wholly devoted to the love of God and the love of neighbor,[96] including even the love of enemies (12:9-21). Paul saw his own life experience as proof of this. Once supremely zealous for God's law, he perpetrated violence on God's behalf.[97] Now graciously freed from the grip of sin through faith in Christ, he proclaims the peace of God, even taking up the cause of his former opponents in the interests of universal reconciliation.

In light of this analysis, Paul concludes that the regime of law was only ever intended by God as a temporary holding measure, until Christ should come (Gal. 3:19-26). It served negatively to imprison all under sin (Gal. 3:22; Rom. 10:32) in preparation for the great liberation which Christ would win through his vicarious death and resurrection. Those united with Christ in this way are no longer "under law but under grace" (6:15). They have "died to the law" (7:4; Gal. 2:19), they are "discharged from the law" (7:6), they are "freed" and "redeemed" from the law (Gal. 3:13; 4:5; 5:1), they are "no longer subject" to the law's rule (Gal. 3:25) or its condemnation (Rom. 8:1). "For Christ is the end-goal [*telos*] of the law" (10:5). Things have changed!

In none of this, of course, is Paul wrestling with the problem of divine violence (he is actually struggling to make sense of the prodigiousness of God's mercy!)[98] But there are several features of Paul's approach to the law that constitute a kind of hermeneutical template for the type of approach to divine violence I have advocated above. To begin with, in both cases, the presenting problem is a substantial shift in God's *modus operandi* from what was apparent in previous tradition. Paul openly acknowledges that God's methods have changed. This is implicit in the ringing adversative declaration "But now, apart from law . . ." that commences his account of the revelation of saving justice in Christ in Romans 3:21-26. It is also evident in the way he divides Israel's story into sequential phases (Adam to Abraham, Abraham to Moses, Moses to Christ), with the law entering 430 years after the promise to Abraham and serving as a disciplinarian "until Christ came," after which time "we are no longer subject to a disciplinarian" (Gal. 3:15-26). Paul thus allows for real change in God's ways.

The sheer radicalism of this change ought not to be underestimated. It required for Paul a thoroughgoing revision of understanding of what had hitherto been the most fundamental ingredients of covenantal faithfulness—circumcision, Sabbath observance, food laws, and separation from all sources of impurity, including Gentiles. That the apostle can boldly declare that "I know and am persuaded in the Lord Jesus that nothing is unclean in itself" (Rom. 14:14) and that "neither circumcision nor uncircumcision is anything but a new creation is everything" (Gal. 6:15), is a measure of the extent to which he reckoned on a major revolution having occurred in God's way of working.

Second, in problematizing the law Paul seeks an explanation that both accords with the plot of the canonical story and explains why God appears to act differently than previously thought, which is exactly what I have said is needed to deal with the issue of divine violence. Paul accepts that radical changes have taken place in God's priorities, but he is equally emphatic that there is a profound consistency between the realities of the present and the revelation of the past. The "new creation" afforded in Christ is not arbitrary or capricious; it accords with the deepest themes of the previous story. It is both "attested by the law and the prophets" (Rom. 3:21, 31) and compatible with God's own being (3:29). That authentic righteousness can come "apart from the law," Paul argues, is already evident in the story of

Abraham as a foreshadowing of what was to come (4:1-25), and it is only by transcending the limitations of Mosaic law that the promise of universal blessing to Abraham can possibly be realized (Gal. 3:6-17).

The negative role of the law is thus balanced by its positive role in anticipating and illuminating eschatological events.[99] Even Moses can now be heard to speak of "the word of faith that we proclaim" (Rom 10:8)! It is the fulfilment of eschatological hope in Christ and the Spirit that accounts for why God's activity now seems so different. It is also what impels Paul to read the canonical story afresh to discern in it a meaning and dynamic once hidden from view. A similar strategy is needed, I have suggested, with respect to the narratives of divine violence.

Finally, and most tellingly, Paul does not shrink from depicting God's law as having been captured by the power of sin and becoming a source of enslavement and death. The law itself, Paul is clear, is imbued with the very attributes of God; it is "holy, just, and good," it is even "spiritual" (Rom. 7:12, 14, 16). But regardless of its divine credentials the law has been bamboozled by sin. Seizing the opportunity created by the revelation of God's will, sin commandeered the law to deceive and kill its adherents (7:11). Consequently, despite its intrinsic goodness, and despite its promise of life to those who observe its commandments, the law has in effect functioned to lock in, as it were, Israel's servitude to sin and death.

This is an incredibly daring claim for Paul to make! He asserts that not only has Gentile humanity's knowledge of God been corrupted by the tyranny of sin (1:18-23, cf. 1 Cor 1:20-25), even Israel's apprehension of God's intentions in the law has fallen victim to sin's death-dealing deception. It is only by taking this insight with full seriousness that we can begin to make sense of the attribution of violence to God in the biblical record. Arguably part of sin's deception is the identification of human violence with the will of God. Jesus Christ explodes this deception, and in him a new humanity emerges that is now in the process of "being renewed in knowledge according to the image of its Creator" (Col. 3:10).

In these ways, then, Paul's grappling with the ambiguities of the law in salvation history furnishes something of a hermeneutical analogy for the approach to divine violence sketched out in this chapter. To be absolutely clear: I am not suggesting that Paul's ruminations on the law in themselves relate to the issue of God's recorded violence, only that he models a style of hermeneutical engagement with Scripture that can be usefully reapplied to this question. Whether the biblical stories of violence caused any discomfort for the apostle is hard to say. Certainly he never explicitly disavows a violent God. If anything, the real scandal for Paul was not the violent exclusivity of God's past actions but the gratuitous inclusiveness of God's saving activity in the present. When Paul takes refuge in the inscrutability of God's ways it is not to justify divine violence but to underscore the mystery of God's indefatigable mercy, a mercy displayed equally toward disobedient Israel and toward wider Gentile humanity (Rom. 11:28-36).

Paul may never have consciously reflected on how best to reconcile this present experience of God's mercy with past episodes of grotesque violence. But it was his apprehension of the crucified and risen Christ as the "image of the invisible God" (Col. 1:15) that transformed Paul from a violent religious zealot into a peacemaker extraordinaire. It was this that led him to speak distinctively of God as "the God of peace,"[100] the God who has reconciled the entire world to God's self not by violent conquest but by self-giving sacrifice. This crucified God is the same God who made the world and everything in it, the same God who called Abraham and chose Israel, the same God that Jesus called Father, and the same God to whom Jesus pointed his followers as the supreme paradigm for the way of nonviolent discipleship.

NOTES

1. Paul N. Anderson, "Genocide or Jesus: A God of Conquest or Pacifism," in *The Destructive Power of Religion: Violence in Judaism, Christianity, and Islam*, ed. J. H. Ellens (Westport, Connecticut & London, Praeger 2004), 4:31-52 (at 31).

2. See D. Andrew Kille, "'The Bible Made Me Do It': Text, Interpretation, and Violence," in *Destructive Power of Religion*, ed. Ellens, I:55-73. See also Charles Mabee, "Reflections on Monotheism and Violence," in *Destructive Power of Religion*, ed. Ellens, 4:111-18. Cf. also Karen Armstrong, "Unholy Strictures," *Guardian Weekly* (Aug. 19-25, 2005): 13.

3. As Dale C. Allison Jr. notes, ". . . the problem of conflicting theologies was not born with Christianity. The problem was already internal to Judaism . . . . If, after Marcion, the issue for Christians became which God to acknowledge, this was only a later variant of the earlier question, Which texts should we sanction?" "Rejecting Violent Judgment: Luke 9:52-56 and its Relatives," *Journal of Biblical Literature* 121/3 (2002): 459-78 (at 478).

4. See J. Denny Weaver, *The Nonviolent Atonement* (Grand Rapids, Mich.: Wm B. Eerdmans, 2001). I am in general sympathy with the direction of Weaver's argument, though I depart substantially from him on his reading of the New Testament evidence. See my "Atonement, Violence and the Will of

God," *Mennonite Quarterly Review* 76/1 (2003): 67-90.

5. See. for instance. Miroslav Volf, *Exclusion and Embrace: A Theological Exploration of Identity, Otherness, and Reconciliation* (Nashville: Abingdon Press, 1996), esp. 275-306. Cf. also Kenneth R. Chase, "Christian Discourse and the Humility of Peace," in *Must Christianity Be Violent? Reflections on History, Practice and Theology*, ed. Kenneth R. Chase and Alan Jacobs (Grand Rapids, Mich.: Brazos Press, 2003), 119-34 (esp. 128-31); Dan McKanan, "Is God Violent? Theological Options in the Antislavery Movement," in *Must Christianity Be Violent?*, 50-68.

6. Walter Wink, *Engaging the Powers: Discernment and Resistance in a World of Domination* (Minneapolis: Fortress Press, 1992), 1-31; idem, *The Powers That Be: Theology for a New Millennium* (New York: Doubleday, 1998), 63-81.

7. Heb 10:31

8. I attempt to construct a non-retributive view of final judgment in my *Beyond Retribution: A New Testament Vision for Justice, Crime and Punishment* (Grand Rapids, Mich.: Wm B. Eerdmans, 2001).

9. John H. Yoder, *The Politics of Jesus: Vicit Agnus Noster* (Grand Rapids, Mich.: Wm B. Eerdmans, 1994), 228-47.

10. J. Harold Ellens, "Revenge, Justice and Hope: Laura Blumenfeld's Journey," in idem, *Destructive Power of Religion* 4:227-235 (at 235).

11. Col. 1:15, 19, cf. 2 Cor. 4:4

12. Heb. 1:2-3

13. John 1:3-4

14. Col. 1:16

15. N. T. Wright offers a powerful presentation of Jesus' nonviolent opposition to Rome in *Jesus and the Victory of God* (London: SPCK, 1996). But he stops short of grounding it in any distinctive apprehension of God's character by Jesus.

16. Matt. 5:44-48

17. Luke 6:35-36

18. Raymund Schwager, *Must There Be Scapegoats? Violence and Redemption in the Bible* (New York: Harper & Row, Gracewing & Crossroad Publishing Company, 1987), 207. So too Wink, *Powers that Be*, 89. Jack Nelson-Pallmeyer observes that "Jesus was not the first Jew to promote or use nonviolence when resisting injustice.... Jesus may have been the first, however, to specifically reject the violence of God as the foundation for nonviolent resistance. Rather than rooting nonviolence in the assurance of God's ultimate and redeeming violence, Jesus saw nonviolent action as a faithful embodiment of a nonviolent God, that is, as reflective of the very Spirit that is God." —*Jesus against Christianity: Reclaiming the Missing Jesus* (Harrisburg, Penn.: Trinity Press International, 2001), 320.

19. Cf. Ulrich Mauser, *The Gospel of Peace: A Scriptural Message for Today's World* (Louisville: Westminster John Knox, 1992), 183-84.

20. Col. 1:15, 20

21. Rom. 1:16-17; 3:20

22. Rom. 5:1

23. John C. Haughey, "Jesus as the Justice of God," in *The Faith that Does*

Justice: Examining the Christian Sources for Social Change, ed. J.C. Haughey (New York: Paulist Press, 1922), 279. See also Marshall, *Beyond Retribution*, 259-63.

24. Col. 1:16-17
25. Eph. 1:10
26. Gen. 4: 8; Rev. 21:3-4,24; 22:2
27. Wink, *The Powers That Be*, 44-48, at 46. Also Patricia M. McDonald, *God and Violence: Biblical Resources for Living in a Small World* (Scottdale, Pa. and Waterloo, Ont.: Herald Press, 2004), 35-49.
28. Gen. 4:1-16
29. Gen. 4:23-24; 6:5-7, 11-13
30. Gen. 7:1-24; 8:21-22; 9:11-17
31. This is not to deny that the canonical tradition is full of tensions, disagreements, contradictions, and revisions. Later biblical authors and tradents felt free to disagree with the perspective of their predecessors on certain theological positions even while accepting the authority of the tradition they bequeathed. Indeed, the authority of the tradition is shown precisely in the commitment of later recipients to engage in radical rethinking of its meaning and implications. See further Ellen F. Davis, "Critical Traditioning: Seeking an Inner Biblical Hermeneutic," *Anglican Theological Review* 82/4 (2000): 733-51.
32. Of course, legendary elements may well exist in the tradition. As Simon De Vries notes, "Battle and war passages in the Old Testament range from the legendary to the mythical, to the realistic and immediate, from the schematic and ideological, to the bizarre and apocalyptic." —"Human Sacrifice in the Old Testament: in Ritual and Warfare," in *Destructive Power of Religion*, ed. Ellens, I: 99-121 (at 120).
33. Exod. 15:1-3
34. Schwager, *Must There be Scapegoats?*, 47-71.
35. Jack Miles, "The Disarmament of God," in *Destructive Power of Religion*, ed Elkins, 1:123-167 (at 147).
36. Num. 11:1-6; 14:10-12; Deut. 1:34-40
37. Num. 12:1-16; 14:10-12; 16:41-50; 25:6-9, cf. Exod. 11:4-5; 12:12,13, 23, 37
38. Mark McEntire, *The Blood of Abel: The Violent Plot of the Hebrew Bible* (Macon, Georgia: Mercer University Press, 1999), 61-62.
39. Relevant texts include Exod. 17:8-13; Num. 21:1-3, 23-24; Deut. 2:30-35; 7:2-6; Josh. 6: 1-16, 7:1, 24-26a; Judg. 3:16-25; 4:6-7, 9-10, 13-15, 17, 21-22; 15:4-8; 1 Sam. 17:12-18:2; 31:1-13; 2 Sam. 18:6-9, 14-15; 1 Kings 22:31-38; 2 Kings 9:30-35; Isa. 2:4; Mic. 4:3; Ezek. 38:14-23; Joel 3:9-10; 2 Chron. 14:9-15
40. For example, Deut. 7:2; Josh. 11:20.
41. Susan Niditch, *War in the Hebrew Bible: A Study in the Ethics of Violence* (New York & Oxford: Oxford University Press, 1993), 28-89. See also John J. Collins, "The Zeal of Phineas, the Bible and the Legitimation of Violence," in *Destructive Power of Religion* I: 12-33, ed. Ellens (at 13-17).
42. McDonald, *God and Violence*,123, 126, cf. 127, 128, 131.
43. Niditch, *War in the Hebrew Bible*, 50. Collins is unconvinced. "Rather than respect for human life, the practice bespeaks a totalistic attitude, which

is common to armies and warfare, where the individual is completely subordinated to the interests of the group."—"Zeal of Phineas," 14.

44. Nelson-Pallmeyer, *Jesus Against Christianity*, 37, cf. 40.

45. McEntire, *Blood of Abel*, 90.

46. Ps. 68:20-23, cf. Habakkuk 3:13-16.

47. Amos 2:4-16; 5:127; Isa. 43:28. See Niditch, *War in the Hebrew Bible*, 78.

48. McEntire, *Blood of Abel*, 114.

49. See my *Crowned with Glory and Honor: Human Rights in the Biblical Tradition* (Telford/Scottdale, Pa.: Pandora Press U.S./Herald Press, 2001).

50. McEntire, *Blood of Abel*, 44.

51. Gen. 18:16-33

52. In *Violence, Hospitality, and the Cross: Reappropriating the Atonement Tradition* (Grand Rapids Mich.: Baker Academic, 2004), Hans Boersma argues that in a sinful world violence is necessary to defend the boundaries which enable hospitality to function. In such a world, God employs "redemptive" violence, which is a "good violence" because it serves to uphold monotheism, to punish immorality, and to protect the poor and underprivileged. But Boersma makes little attempt to measure this sweeping defense of divine violence against the concrete suffering endured by its victims. See my critical review in *Stimulus* 13/3 (2005), 51-52, which includes my own attempt to spell out the semantic parameters of the term *violence*.

53. For example, Gen. 13:13; 15:16; Deut. 9:5; 20:17-18. The general perfidy of the Canaanites is pervasive in the biblical tradition, although the purported wickedness of the Canaanites is never actually substantiated within the conquest accounts.

54. McEntire, *Blood of Abel*, 118.

55. Matt. 2:16-18

56. 1 Sam. 15:2-3, cf. Exod. 17:14,16; Num. 24:20; Deut. 25:17-19

57. So Collins, "Zeal of Phineas," 24-25.

58. So Anderson, "Genocide or Jesus," 51.

59. Nelson-Pallmeyer, *Jesus Against Christianity*, 16.

60. Collins, "Zeal of Phineas," 25.

61. Exod. 34:6-7; Num. 14:18-19; Deut. 5:9-10

62. 2 Kings 1:11-12, cf. Gen. 19:24; Lev. 10:1-2; Job 1:16; Ps. 97:3

63. Luke 9:54-55

64. So rightly Allison, "Rejecting Violent Judgment," 476.

65. McDonald, *God and Violence*, 54, cf. 57.

66. Gen. 12:3, 17; 14:20; 15:14-16; 18:20; 19:15-29; 22:1-19; 38:10

67. Gen. 12:7; 13:14-17; 15:16; 17:8; 22:17; 28:3-4, 13-15; 35:12; 48:4; 50:24

68. For example, Exod. 4:24-26; 2 Sam. 6:6-7.

69. See Lev. 26: 14-39; Exod. 12:29; Ezek. 21:3-4, 9-15; Jer. 25:32-33.

70. For example, Deut. 20:16-17; 1 Sam. 15:2-3; Isa. 19:2; Jer. 51:20-24; Ezek. 21:31; Ps. 44:11-12; Zech. 8:10.

71. For example, Isa. 50:11; Jer. 44:8; Ps. 7:13-17; Prov. 8:36; 26:27

72. See, for example, Ezek. 21:31; Jer. 22:25-26; Isa. 19:2; 13:17

73. Schwager, *Must There Be Scapegoats?*, 63.

74. For example, Gen. 19:24; Num. 16:29-32.

75. See, for example, Isa. 64:6-7; Ps. 81:11-12.
76. Schwager, *Must There Be Scapegoats?*, 63 (emphasis mine).
77. Whether some actual primeval act of violence by God is the reason for God's subsequent identification with violence, or whether the flood story itself is the product of prior projection of violence onto heaven, is open to discussion.
78. This is one of the major findings in McEntire's study *Blood of Abel*.
79. Cf. Wink, *Engaging the Powers*, 146-47.
80. God's sovereign self-disclosure is the necessary presupposition for all and any knowledge of God. But divine revelation is also necessarily filtered through fallible human language and categories, which can distort as well as report God's truth, and often both at the same time. For a helpful discussion of the relationship between revelation and Scripture, see William C. Placher, *The Domestication of Transcendence* (Louisville, Ky.: Westminster John Knox, 1996), 181-200.
81. Jesus is condemned to death on the charge of blasphemy (Mark 14:55-64), a capital crime in Mosaic law (Lev. 24:15-16).
82. Schwager, *Must There Be Scapegoats?*, 67.
83. Collins is clear that what makes violent religious texts dangerous is not their violent content but the certitude with which they are received by readers as divine revelation, "Zeal of Phineas," 23-26. So too Nelson-Pallmeyer, *Jesus Against Christianity*, 277.
84. I borrow this term from Ellen Davis, "Critical Traditioning."
85. Exod. 34:6-7; Num. 14:18-19; Deut. 5:9-10
86. Jer. 31:29-30
87. Ezek. 18:1-4
88. Rom. 3:21; 8:1-4
89. Gal. 1:13; Phil. 3:6; 1 Cor. 15:9; cf. Acts 9:1-2; 22:4; 26:9-11. On the violent implications of "zeal," see Terence L. Donaldson, "Zealot and Convert: The Origins of Paul's Christ-Torah Antithesis," *Catholic Biblical Quarterly* 51/4 (1989): 655-82; Vincent M. Smiles, "The Concept of 'Zeal' in Second-Temple Judaism and Paul's Critique of It in Romans 10:2," *Catholic Biblical Quarterly* 64/2 (2002): 282-99; Mark R. Fairchild, "Paul's Pre-Christian Zealot Associations: A Re-Examination of Gal 1:14 and Acts 22:3," *New Testament Studies* 45/4 (1999): 514-32. For a thematizing of the place of zeal in the biblical tradition and American self-understanding, see Robert Jewett and John Shelton Lawrence, *Captain America and the Crusade Against Evil: The Dilemma of Zealous Nationalism* (Grand Rapids, Mich.: Wm B. Eerdmans, 2003).
90. See 2 Cor. 3:12-18; Rom. 10:2-4.
91. Rom. 7:5, 9-10; 10:5; Gal. 2:19, cf. 3:12, 21; 1 Cor. 15:56; 2 Cor. 3:6-7
92. Rom. 3:20, 27-28; Gal. 2:16; 3:2,5,10, 12, cf. Rom. 3:27; 4:2,6; 9:12, 32; 11:6; Eph. 2:9
93. Rom. 1:18-32; 3:9-20; 5:12-21; 612-14, 20-21; 7:7-25; etc.
94. Rom. 4:16; 5:20-21; 6:1,14; 11:5; 1 Cor. 15:10; Gal. 1:6; 2:21; 5:4; cf. Eph. 2:5-6.
95. Rom. 5:6-21; 1 Cor. 15:42-49; Col. 1:10; 3:10
96. Rom. 5:5; 13:8-10; 14:15; Gal. 5:6, 13-14, 22-23; Phil. 1:9; 1 Cor. 8:1; 13:1-8;

16;14; Col. 3:14, cf. Eph. 4:32-35.
    97. Gal. 1:13; Phil. 3:5-6; 1 Cor. 15:9; cf. Acts 9:1-2; 22:4; 26:5, 9-11.
    98. See Rom. 11:28-36.
    99. Cf. Rom. 4:23-24; 15:4; 1 Cor. 10:11; 9:10.
    100. The phrase *God of peace* is a favorite of Paul's (Rom. 15:33; 16:20; 2 Cor. 13:11; Phil. 4:9; 1 Thess. 5:23; 2 Thess. 3:16, cf. Eph. 2:14), though he did not invent it (Heb. 13:20). In early Jewish literature the phrase occurs only once (*Test. Daniel* 5:2).

CHAPTER FIVE

IMITATION AS PARTICIPATION: DISCIPLESHIP IN PAUL'S LETTERS

Laura L. Brenneman

*T*hroughout his writing and in his personal encounters, J. Denny Weaver shows himself to be an earnest child of God. Weaver's passion for theological reflection comes through in how he talks and how he acts. The stated objective in his study, *The Nonviolent Atonement*, is also confessional: "it is my fervent hope," he writes, "that this essay about the past for the present will make *Christ*ian faith more Christlike in future years."[1]

In this essay I consider another Christ-focused earnest child of God, the apostle Paul. I seek to complement Weaver's own work on Paul in *The Nonviolent Atonement*[2] by examining the atonement texture of three Pauline texts: Romans 6:2-14; 2 Corinthians 4:7-18; Phillipians 3:2-4.1. It is not possible to explore all of the Pauline passages about Christ's death and resurrection within one essay. Thus I have chosen to limit myself to the study of how Paul describes the Christ event in various passages where he exhorts believers to live as participants in the story of Jesus. In his call to followers of Jesus to be participants Paul talks about suffering—that is, Christ's suffering, his own suffering, and believers' suffering. The close relationship he suggests between suffering and faithfulness may strike the modern reader as odd, or even repulsive. However, I will argue that there is a poignant relationship in these texts between the author's beliefs and his actions. Furthermore, Paul expects that followers of Christ will similarly link faith and praxis. Thus we will find considerable connection between Paul's outlook and that of Weaver.

PAUL'S APOCALYPTIC OUTLOOK

Weaver aims in his section on Paul's writings to disrupt the well-established view that his "language about cross, sacrifice, and fulfillment of the law are the foundation of satisfaction atonement."[3] In issuing his challenge, Weaver concentrates on Paul's language about Christ's resurrection, which gives readers a glimpse of Paul's apocalyptic outlook.[4] Weaver argues that God's action in raising Christ from the dead signals the dawn of a new era, in which the fallen creation is being transformed. In fact, the resurrection marks that "the end (or goal) of history, namely the reign of God, is breaking into the present and beginning the process of transforming all of creation."[5] Few Pauline scholars now seriously debate this point,[6] and Paul's own language bears out this observation (e.g., Rom. 8:18-25; 2 Cor. 5:16-21).[7] Paul acknowledges that Christ's resurrection is a decisive action, the first fruits of God's inbreaking reign (1 Cor. 15:20, 23). It marks the beginning of the end of the present age (Gal. 1:4; 1 Cor. 10:11).

Weaver focuses on Paul's resurrection language because to him it demonstrates God's sovereignty and the "proleptic presence of the reign of God."[8] Following Beker, Weaver reads Paul as declaring Jesus' crucifixion to be God's confrontation with the powers of the old age (the law, sin, and death) in which Jesus' death confirms "our just condemnation by the law."[9] God's resurrection of Jesus, then, signals the new potential for the wholeness of humanity and all creation. But if it is God's will to bring about the fullness of creation, why was Jesus' death necessary? To answer this question Weaver draws on the work of Raymund Schwager.

Schwager primarily looks at Romans 8:3, Galatians 3:13, and 2 Corinthians 5:21 to demonstrate that God was not responsible for Jesus' crucifixion, which is in concert with Weaver's own critique of classical atonement theories. Schwager affirms that Jesus' crucifixion was a condemnation of sin. He finds in Romans clear statements that humans are victims of sin and that only "through pure grace and through faith in redemption in Christ can they become just before God."[10] Under the influence of sin, humans are enemies of God (Rom. 5:10); through Jesus' death on the cross comes reconciliation. The crucifixion reconciled enemies whereas the law, provided by God but weakened by the flesh, could not (8:3).

Schwager relies on Galatians 3:13 to show just how thoroughly sin pervades the created world, even tainting the God-given law. The passage states that Jesus was cursed by the law because he was hung on a tree. Those who see this curse as God's direct act of condemnation of the Son do not appreciate how much the law and humans trying to fulfill the law were weakened by the flesh and co-opted by sin. Schwager's interpretation is that "the power of sin is so cunning that it can get completely within its grasp the good and holy law and so can distort it that it works against God and his envoy."[11] Thus the world is in a state of rebellion against God, and it was human rebellion that led to Jesus' death. Schwager considers 2 Corinthians 5:21 to show that others "projected the evil in their hearts onto [Christ], and thus made him the bearer of sins."[12]

This is where Weaver sees Beker's and Schwager's work dovetailing. Beker's Paul, with a thorough-going apocalyptic outlook, demonstrates that God is acting in history to set things right in creation. Thus Jesus, as a sinless man, was in conflict with the world in which he lived. On this point Schwager contends that the powers of the sinful creation rebelled against God's plan and crucified Jesus. However, not their violent action, but God's resurrection of Christ, had the last word. Moreover, Christ is the "first fruits" of all redeemed creation. Weaver concludes that Paul saw "the death of Jesus ... as the confrontation between the reign of God and evil powers. Resurrection then becomes the victory of the reign of God over the power of sin."[13] So, Weaver interprets Paul's writings as supporting narrative Christus Victor atonement theology and as standing against classical satisfaction atonement theories.

THE NARRATIVE OF SUFFERING

Having reviewed Weaver's interpretation of Paul's atonement language, I now turn to several Pauline passages that underscore the ethical dimension of his theology (Rom. 6:2-14; 2 Cor. 4:7-18; Phil. 3.2-4.1). In each of these passages Christ's crucifixion and resurrection serve as the bases for Paul's message of the inseparable nature of belief and conduct. The texts evoke participatory language: believers do or experience particular things because they are a certain kind of people. In addition, although the passages differ in form, their function is the same: in each Paul reminds believers that they participate in the Christ event.

The passage from Romans displays Paul's theological reasoning behind his understanding of the believers' participation in the Christ event. As such, I will examine it first, even though, chronologically, Romans was probably the last of Paul's letters. Next, I will turn to 2 Corinthians. From Paul's extant writings to the Corinthians we see that their relationship was stormy: Paul often understood "pastoral care" to mean exercising his apostolic authority as disciplinarian.[14] In 2 Corinthians 4:7-18, Paul appeals to his role as their leader to demonstrate that other believers should see him as the model of how life "in Christ" is experienced. The final passage, Philippians 3:2-21, represents what scholars assume to be Paul's "mature" thought, probably a retrospective reflection over his career. If this is so, we see that believers' imitation of him (Phil. 3:17) and his imitation of Christ continue, as in his earlier letters (1 Thess. 1:6; 1 Cor. 4:16; 11:1; Gal. 4:12), to be important components of Paul's message to believers.

These passages display how Paul writes, more generally, about the meaning of Jesus' death and resurrection. For Paul, this narrative is the gospel that he proclaimed to his churches (see 1 Cor. 2:2). Although one cannot know the full content of his message (for example, whether Paul's *kerygma* was the same as the Gospels' narrations of Jesus' crucifixion), one can determine from passages such as Romans 1-8, 1 Corinthians 1-4, and 1 Thessalonians 1 that Paul thought that the gospel should be transformative. In fact for Paul, all of history and God's actions before that time find their focal point in the Christ event. All that Paul writes is theologically charged; his exhortations are shaped by how he saw God acting in the world through Christ. Paul presents sweeping overviews of the Christ event and its relationship to history; theologians and biblical scholars alike spend lifetimes trying to unravel the knotty theological questions Paul raises.[15] I will approach Paul's complex writings by considering him as a pastor calling on the congregations to whom he ministers to participate in Christ's story.

Paul's apocalyptic view of history, sketched so well by Beker, is invitational. Paul invites his readers to acknowledge that we live in a world in which God has acted, is acting, and will act to return every created thing to goodness. Romans 6:2-14, with its discussion of power and dominion, shows that Paul understood the Christ event as the best way to grasp God's intent in the world. Individual moral agency does not concern Paul; rather, Paul perceives that we exist in relation to the rulers of the age, God and death.[16] One belongs either to God through Christ or to death through sin (see also 1 Cor. 6:19-20). Paul speaks of enslavement (v. 6, *douleuō*) and lordship (v. 9, *kurieuō*), as well as of participation. One is not simply an unwilling slave or prisoner of a particular master; one participates in that enslavement or subjugation. People either exist "in sin" (vv. 1-2 [*tē harmartia*], also vv. 12, 14) or "in Christ" (vv. 3-6 [*eis Christos Iēsoun*], also v. 8). Although everyone exists as a servant of either Christ or sin/death, the default position, according to Paul, is death. Death through sin holds sway over everyone; unless a person chooses differently, death chooses her or him (Rom. 5:12-21; 6:12-14).

Romans 6:2-14 reveals that God has given humans a choice of masters. Here Paul calls on his readers to live within the story of God's redeeming activity. The believer can "walk in newness of life" (6:4), but to do so means a transfer from one master to the other. This change of masters is physical and occurs through baptism.[17] Believers are baptized "into Christ," a baptism into Christ's death (6:3-5, 7-8): they are "buried with him" (v. 4, *synthaptō*), and "crucified with him" (v. 6, *systaurō*).[18] Baptism involves a dying to sin (6:2, 6-7, 11), a dying which releases the person from death. Choosing union with Christ means that believers will also experience a resurrection like his (vv. 5, 8, 11, 13); they are "dead to sin and alive to God in Christ Jesus" (v. 11).

Paul extends his invitation to participate in Christ's death and resurrection to those who would hear the gospel message. Paul's language is metaphorical and pushes scholars to ask what being buried, crucified, and dying with Christ signifies. We can begin to answer by examining Paul's description of his own life. Paul commonly calls attention to his status of being "in Christ," stressing his participation in the story of Christ.[19] Take, for example, 2 Corinthians 4:7-18,[20] one of Paul's so-called "hardship catalogues" (see also 1 Cor. 4:9-13; 2 Cor. 11:23-28; Phil. 4:10-13). On the one hand, Paul is clearly doing more than providing a dry enumeration of his hardships: he constructs his argument carefully to elicit *pathos*, a goal of any effective communicator. In 2 Corinthians 4, Paul exhorts the congregation to have confidence in his authority, despite his physical weaknesses (e.g., 2 Cor. 12:7-10) about which the Corinthians likely were scornful of him (2 Cor. 10:11). On the other hand, the "hardship catalogues" also convey Paul's understanding of what Christian identity should be.

The theological crux of Paul's argument is that his own body manifests the death of Jesus (2 Cor. 4:10), granting him apostolic authority and making him an exemplar for believers. As Charles Cousar contends, Paul's hardship lists do not only present biographical information concerning one unusual person; "instead, the experiences are reported and function as a paradigm, to illustrate how the preaching of the crucified Christ is to work itself out in the life and service of every 'ordinary' Christian."[21] Even though Paul serves as the Corinthians' apostle, he declares himself to be their servant (v. 5, *doulos*),[22] a posture he also exhorted Christ's followers to espouse in relation to God (Rom. 12:11; 14.18; 1 Thess. 1.9) and to one another (Gal. 5:13).[23] Moreover, being a servant, according to Paul's "Christ hymn," is the very identity adopted by Jesus himself (Phil. 2:7).

Paul's claim of his body manifesting Christ's death in 2 Corinthians 4:10 is thus multivalent. Paul and his co-workers are "always carrying in the body the death of Jesus, so that the life of Jesus may also be made visible in our bodies." Paul's suffering demonstrates that he is "in Christ." Intriguingly, however, Paul here and in the following verse uses the name *Jesus* by itself, an unusual rhetorical move for Paul who typically speaks of "Jesus Christ," "our Lord Jesus Christ," or "Lord Jesus."[24] Paul's emphasis in this verse falls on the earthly man Jesus, on his earthly life and death. The life that Paul says is manifested in "our" (signifying Paul, his co-workers, and the Corinthians) bodies is patterned after Jesus' life. This, however, does not exhaust Paul's meaning, for what the lives of believers (their "earthen vessels") demonstrate is the power of God (v. 7). God's power renews the "inner nature" of believers (v. 16), giving them hope for the "eternal weight of glory beyond all comparison" (v. 17). Participation in Christ's suffering is paired with participation in the cosmic event of Christ's resurrection: The invitation to participate in Christ is thus an invitation to live in the narrative of suffering and hope incarnated by Jesus and written on Paul's body.[25]

Paul's description of his hardships is marked by an eschatological confidence. "We are afflicted in every way, but not crushed," he proclaims: "perplexed, but not driven to despair; persecuted, but not forsaken; struck down, but not destroyed" (2 Cor. 4:8-9). By the time he wrote the last chapters of 2 Corinthians, Paul had experienced considerable trials: he had received thirty-nine lashes five times; three times he was beaten with rods; once he was stoned; another three times shipwrecked; and he had been subjected to countless other difficulties (11:24-29). Paul's testimony about his confidence in the power of God is thus profound. He was afflicted but not crushed, struck down but not destroyed. Grappling with his own weaknesses, Paul was even able to boast about his infirmities (12:5).

He refers to a weakness as a "thorn in the flesh" placed by a messenger of Satan (2. Cor. 12:7). On three occasions Paul asked the Lord to remove this particular weakness from him. However, rather than being granted this request, Paul came to understand his weakness as the way in which God's power was made known. If Paul's message did not come in an improbable package, then what would keep converts from praising human wisdom rather than the power of God (see 1 Cor. 2:1-5; also Phil. 3:8-9)? "My grace is sufficient for you, for power is made perfect in weakness" (2 Cor. 12:9), God assures Paul concerning his thorn in the flesh; Paul's response was to be "content with weaknesses, insults, hardships, persecutions, and calamities for the sake of Christ; for when I am weak, then I am strong" (v. 10).

Thus Paul's interprets his own suffering theologically. He opens and closes 2 Corinthians 4:7-15 with references to God's power and glory. God has triumphed; Christ is raised; the dominion of death and sin is broken in believers; but followers of Christ still live in a world enslaved to sin and death. The suffering the earthly Jesus experienced should therefore also be expected by his earthly followers.[26] Paul identifies with this narrative so strongly that he calls his marks of suffering on his body the *stigmata* of Jesus (Gal. 6:17).[27] Indeed, in another letter to the Corinthians, Paul calls the believers to imitate him, even as he imitates Christ (1. Cor 11:1). Such exhortation also characterizes our final focal passage, Philippians 3:2-4.1.

In v. 17 of this section we see Paul's call to the Philippians to imitate him (*symmimētai*[28] *mou ginesthe*, literally "become co-imitators of me"[29]) and others who live like him (*tous houtō peripatountas*[30]). The passage follows Paul's rejection of the ministry of some "evil-workers" (3:2, *tous kakous ergatas*) and a recommendation of his own ministry (vv. 7-14). His tone here is urgent. He wishes to warn the Philippians to guard themselves against what Paul believes to be false doctrine. Paul begins with an imperative statement, "watch out" (*blepete*), and refers to his opponents as dogs (3:2). The final statement of the passage reveals his intent, that the Philippians stand firm "in the Lord" (4:1). Paul has equipped them by offering his own life as an example (v. 17, *typos*).

Paul puts forward his weakness as a model to the Philippians, contrasting his lack of status with the position of his opponents. Paul's antagonists propose that the Philippians be circumcised to become full participants in God's covenant (3:2-3),[31] a position already strenuously opposed by Paul in another place, his letter to the Galatians. Paul not only considers circumcision unnecessary for Gentile followers of Jesus, given that they are "adopted" into the covenant as they are (Gal. 4:4-7); he also believes circumcision for Gentiles entails rebellion against God's act of grace through Christ (Gal. 5:2-4).

Instead of following the same theological arguments he deployed in Galatians, in Philippians Paul chooses to question his opponents' motives by inferring that they have a misplaced confidence "in the flesh" (Phil. 3:3-4). Rather than launching a critique of his opponents, Paul seeks to prove why, if success by human standards is important, he would have a more legitimate claim for confidence in the flesh. Paul notes his status as a Jew of good lineage, legal training, religious zeal, and perfect adherence to the law (3:4-6). However, from the standpoint of his faith "in Christ" (v. 9) all of Paul's human success completely missed the mark. He writes,

> whatever gain I had, these I have come to regard as loss because of Christ. More than that, I regard everything as loss because of the surpassing value of knowing Christ Jesus my Lord. For his sake I have suffered the loss of all things, and I regard them as rubbish, in order that I may gain Christ and be found in him, not having a righteousness of my own that comes from the law, but one that comes through faith in Christ. (3:7-9)

Paul's message here is similar to his claim in 1 Corinthians 1:18–3:23, where he maintains that seeking human badges of honor is at odds with living in faithful accordance to God's plan. In fact, Paul asserts that God intentionally chooses those who are weak to shame the strong (1 Cor. 1:27), for "God's weakness is stronger than human strength" (1:25). In Philippians 3, meanwhile, Paul writes about those who live as "enemies of the cross of Christ" (v. 18), who focus solely on their desire: those whose god is in their belly,[32] who glory in their shame, and whose minds are set on earthly things (v. 19). For these people, according to Paul, "their end is destruction" (v. 19), precisely what Paul wants the Philippians to avoid. The Philippians are, Paul exhorts, to stand firm (4:1), because in return for living a life in Christ, God will change their lowly bodies into glorious ones, like Christ's (3:21). Followers of Christ are to live with resurrection hope, not with trust in human achievements.

Hope is the operative word here, for Paul does not think believers can fully participate in Christ's glorified existence while on earth. He emphasizes that he still "presses on," recognizing that he has not yet reached perfection (3:12, *ēdē teteleiōmai*). He has not yet reached the goal, and so he strains forward, as if in a foot race, for the prize "of the heavenly call of God in Christ Jesus" (3:13-14). He urges the Philippians to do the same. In v. 15, Paul says that those who are mature (*teleioi*)[33] will be "thus-minded" (*touto phronōmen*), a claim reminiscent of his exhortation in Phil 2:5: "Let the same mind be in you, that was yours in Christ Jesus (*Touto phroneite en humin ho kai en Christō Iēsou*)."

Paul has asked the Philippians to look to the interests of others and to do nothing in selfishness or conceit (2:3-4). Following immediately upon v. 5 comes what is commonly called the "Christ hymn" (2:6-11), here employed to elaborate upon what a common mind "in Christ" means. In this poem, Christ's qualities of humility ("emptied himself," v. 7; also v. 8), willingness to serve (v. 7), and obedience, even to the point of death on a cross (v. 8), are emphasized. Paul's ample use of these terms in reference to himself and his call that believers emulate him demonstrate that Christ's followers should expect the sort of suffering that Jesus experienced.

But the Christ hymn also reveals that hope is justified, for, as Paul writes, God has exalted Christ and made his name above every name (v. 9), "that at the name of Jesus every knee should bend, in heaven and on earth and under the earth" (v. 10). God has already won the victory, even if believers cannot yet fully participate in this perfection (3:12-14). Therefore, the tension in Paul's language between what has already been achieved and what is still to come should not be collapsed. In his examination of Rom 6:1-11, Dunn remarks that "it is this tension which is at the basis of Christian ethics and conduct."[34] What we know about God's action through Christ is the story that Paul invites his readers to live in, a narrative in which the dominant rebellious powers that rule this world, sin and death, are broken. This narrative disturbs the way the world works; thus those who reorient themselves to live in that story will walk out of step with the rebellious "god of this world" (2 Cor. 4:4; see also Rom. 12:2). Paul experienced this and he expected those in his churches to feel this conflict with the world—a conflict that will result in the believer's suffering. To have a different experience would mean that a person was not living faithfully (see Rom. 8:17).

These passages display Paul's commitment to a distinctive kind of life based upon his theological understanding. His faith determines his actions. In Romans 6, when Paul writes about the believers' relationship to their Lord, he uses participatory language. They live "in Christ," having been buried with him so that they might also be raised with him. In 2 Corinthians 4, Paul writes about what participating in Christ's death has been like for him. He has endured many hardships, hardships he interprets as how God demonstrates power in weakness. Despite human frailty, God triumphs. Rather than seeing vulnerability and suffering negatively, Paul takes heart that God is working in him. Moreover, Philippians 3 contains one of Paul's exhortations to believers to imitate him. He holds up his rejection of earthly honors as an example of having his priorities straight. Once again he mentions sharing in Christ's sufferings and his death; once again he holds up his hope of participating in Christ's resurrection. In this way, we see how Paul integrated his faith with life and that he expected all believers to live similarly. Paul asks followers of Christ to live within the narrative of what has already happened, Jesus' crucifixion and resurrection, and what will happen, their own resurrection.

LIVING WITHIN THE TENSION

How should Christians today read Paul's message? Is his gospel of life "in Christ," including the certainty of suffering, a message that still speaks to believers? These questions go right to the concern of every person who takes the Bible seriously for faith and conduct. Exegesis and interpretation go hand in hand for a believer. These questions also lead us to consider the voices of those who have challenged traditional church teachings about the value of suffering.

Denny Weaver has a special concern for how atonement theology has affected some of society's most mistreated members. In *The Nonviolent Atonement* Weaver dedicates considerable attention to the ways in which black, feminist, and womanist theologians have critiqued the classical Anselmian satisfaction view of atonement.[35] One of the main difficulties various theologians from these traditions, as well as Weaver himself, have with satisfaction atonement is that it explains Jesus' suffering and violent death as redemptive. To many people who have been systematically subjected to violence, a glorified narrative of suffering does not convey a message of hope. In fact, it only serves to legitimate the claims of those who benefit from systems of violence and, as a result, actually perpetuates the suffering of vulnerable people.

Weaver engages feminist theologians who are cautious about the language of suffering, suspicious that some Christian teachings have contributed to abuse of women and children. Feminist theologians, Weaver explains, have shown how "the image of Christ on the cross teaches that suffering is redemptive, and that for women to be of value, they should likewise sacrifice themselves."[36] For those in vulnerable positions, that "divine model of submission to victimization . . . can have dangerous consequences."[37]

Paul's words about Jesus' crucifixion and suffering have undeniably been used in support of theologies that justify the victimization of women. My question, however, would be whether or not Paul's discussion of the crucifixion and of suffering must be appropriated in this fashion, or if more possibilities exist. To nuance Joanne Carlson Brown and Rebecca Parker's critique of traditional atonement models, Weaver examines the interpretations of Jesus' suffering offered by another feminist, Julie Hopkins, and by womanist theologians Delores Williams, Karen Baker-Fletcher, JoAnne Marie Terrell, Katie Cannon, and Clarice Martin. Instead of viewing the crucifixion as God's endorsement of violence and victimization, "the suffering and death of Jesus show that God clearly identifies with and understands the plight of oppressed and suffering people."[38] In particular, for Williams, the image of Jesus on the cross is not that of an abused son or a powerless victim; it is the face of the collective human sin that rose up against Jesus and continues to rise up against his followers.[39]

Williams' theological analysis of Jesus' death, I would suggest, meshes well with Paul's interpretation of the crucifixion. Paul tells believers that when they accepted the lordship of the Christ, they were buried with Jesus. This burial was a death to sin, death to the destructive power that still holds sway over most people's hearts.[40] Since believers have been set free from sin, they are empowered to resist it as Jesus did. In Paul's mission to proclaim this good news of freedom (e.g., Gal. 5:13) obstacles presented themselves, including hardships and suffering. These, however, he counted as joy because he knew that they were the death throes of an age subject to the sovereignty of God. Paul's confidence in God's authority allowed him to resist and endure. Furthermore, his appeal to other believers to imitate him was also based on the hope that, as God had glorified Christ, his followers would also experience a resurrection like his. Paul's call to believers to imitate Jesus is, I believe, in concert with Weaver's atonement theology. "Identifying with or following the Jesus of narrative Christus Victor may indeed be costly," Weaver stresses: "it may indeed entail suffering and even death. But that suffering," he continues, "is no longer suffering that is salvific in and of itself.... This is suffering that is the result of opposing evil, as Jesus' suffering and death were the result of opposing evil. This suffering is an ethic of risk."[41]

Although Paul does not use the word *discipleship* in his writings, his call to believers to imitate him arguably constitutes a call to discipleship.[42] Paul himself, certainly, is a model of radical discipleship. Much as Jesus counseled disciples to "render unto Caesar the things which be Caesar's" (Luke 20:25, KJV), Paul advised the Roman believers not to usurp the authority of rulers (Rom. 13:1-7). However, just as Jesus experienced trouble throughout his whole career from various religious and political rulers, so did Paul. Both ultimately died at the hands of human rulers because of the message they preached. Stereotypes of an apolitical Paul cannot, therefore, be sustained: He was too much of a troublemaker to be adequately characterized as apolitical.[43]

Like Paul, Martin Luther King Jr. faced accusations of stirring up trouble. When Alabama clergymen accused King of acting unwisely and in an untimely way, he responded that "There comes a time when the cup of endurance runs over, and men are no longer willing to be plunged into an abyss of injustice where they experience the blackness of corroding despair. I hope, sirs, you can understand our legitimate and unavoidable impatience."[44] Twice in this letter King appeals to Paul's example: once in describing their common task of carrying the "gospel of freedom" beyond their home towns[45] and once in likening Paul's suffering and extremism with King's own.[46] Paul's message and character are compelling to those who resist the powers of sin and death. Although Paul preaches the triumph of God, he does not engage in triumphalism. Better than most people, he knew that living a life in Christ meant suffering. He did not glorify but did accept suffering. Put another way, Paul did not collapse the tension in the story of Jesus' crucifixion and resurrection. One cannot glibly claim to partake of the fruits of the resurrection while still existing in the overlapping ages. Those fruits are the believers' hope in the future.[47]

Thus, with Cousar, I am troubled by some contemporary Christian messages proclaiming a relationship between God's blessings and material prosperity. After relating a story about a pastor who likened Jesus' cross to the hardships that all successful people must endure and overcome, Cousar provocatively argues that

> A theology that rings loudly the joyful note of Easter without the sobering, dissonant sounds of Good Friday inevitably tends to-

ward triumphalism.... As with the television preacher, negative experiences are often viewed as no more than obstacles to be overcome in the journey to something more—to success and positive living.⁴⁸

I am compelled by Paul's message that belonging to Christ entails suffering in this world. Paul offers a denunciation of all that is enslaved by sin and death, not a glorification of suffering: Because believers belong to a different master, they will encounter hardship in a world in the grips of a sinful power. Paul's words provide encouragement and hope amid sorrow, freedom in places of bondage, courage in the face of oppression.

Denny Weaver is certainly right that much of the Pauline corpus buttresses his narrative Christus Victor understanding of the atonement. What one misses from Weaver's work, however, is close attention to Paul's language about Jesus' crucifixion and the believers' participation in it. Without following Paul's understanding of the disciples' participation in Jesus' suffering, one could easily get lost in a false sense of a "realized resurrection," precisely Paul's critique in 1 Corinthians of the believers.⁴⁹ We must cling to the tension in Paul's narrative. As Cousar poignantly observes, "the church does not interpret the cross, but the message of the cross interprets the church."⁵⁰ Obedience to God's will asks that believers be servants of God as Jesus and Paul were. Obedience calls for the ethic of risk. At odds with the world, such obedience will not prove to be a popular way; one living within the narrative of Christ will therefore willingly risk temporal defeat rather than comply with the powers of sin and death.

NOTES

1. J. Denny Weaver, *The Nonviolent Atonement* (Grand Rapids, Mich.: Wm. B. Eerdmans, 2001), xiii, emphasis original.
2. Ibid., 49-58.
3. Ibid., 49.
4. On these points, Weaver refers extensively to J. Christiaan Beker, *Paul the Apostle: The Triumph of God in Life and Thought* (Philadelphia: Fortress, 1980), chapters 8 and 9.
5. Weaver, *The Nonviolent Atonement*, 50.
6. Among others, Beker was instrumental for prompting scholars to take Paul's apocalyptic thinking seriously. For an overview of trends up to that point in theological and biblical studies regarding apocalypticism in Christianity, see Beker, *Paul*, 135-49.

7. For an examination of Paul's apocalyptic statements see J. Paul Sampley, *Walking between the Times: Paul's Moral Reasoning* (Minneapolis: Fortress, 1991), especially 7-24.

8. Weaver, *The Nonviolent Atonement*, 54.

9. Ibid., 52.

10. Raymund Schwager, *Jesus in the Drama of Salvation: Toward a Biblical Doctrine of Redemption* (New York: Herder & Herder, 1999), 160.

11. Ibid., 168.

12. Ibid., 169.

13. Weaver, *Nonviolent Atonement*, 58.

14. Paul also characterizes his apostolic authority as being parental (both father [see 1 Cor 4:14-15; 1 Thess 2:11; Phm 10] and mother [1 Thess 2:7-8]).

15. See James D. G. Dunn, *The Theology of Paul the Apostle* (Grand Rapids, Mich.: Wm. B. Eerdmans, 1998), 19-23, for an outline of representative scholars' attempts to capture the organizing center of Paul's theology.

16. This is also Dunn's evaluation. See his analysis of Rom 6:2 in James D. G. Dunn, *Romans 1-8*, vol. 38A of *Word Bible Commentary* (Dallas: Word, 1988), 307. In this section of Romans Paul builds on his earlier claim in Rom 5:21 that "just as sin exercised dominion in death, so grace might also exercise dominion through justification leading to eternal life through Jesus Christ our Lord." All Bible citations are from the NRSV unless otherwise noted.

17. Leander Keck also talks about baptism "'into Christ' as an 'objective' transference into a domain of power. To be baptized into Christ is to be included in the domain of Christ, his field of force."—Leander E. Keck, *Paul and His Letters* (Philadelphia: Fortress, 1979), 57-58.

18. The verbs occur with a form of the preposition *syn*, "with," emphasizing the participatory nature of these actions. David Stanley characterizes these verbs, apparently created by Paul, as neologisms. Functionally they "express what he meant by declaring himself to be an imitator of Christ by being united with him in the twofold event proclaimed by the gospel, death and resurrection."—David Stanley, S.J., "Imitation in Paul's Letters: Its Significance for His Relationship to Jesus and to His Own Christian Foundations," in *From Jesus to Paul: Studies in Honour of Francis Wright Beare*, ed. Peter Richardson and John C. Hurd (Waterloo, Ont.: Wilfrid Laurier, 1984), 132.

19. The phrase "in Christ" is characteristically Pauline, representative of what some scholars call "Paul's Christ mysticism." Dunn explains that "in some sense [Paul] experienced Christ as the context of all his being and doing. . . . Here we focus . . . on the evident sense of Christ's presence as more or less a constant factor, from within which Paul consciously and subconsciously drew resource and strength for all his activities"—Dunn, *Theology of Paul*, 400. Keck, meanwhile, connects Paul's "in Christ" language with Paul's apocalyptic outlook and his understanding of proper conduct: "The ethical meaning of the already/not yet is the dialectic of the indicative and the imperative: You are in Christ, live in Christ."—Keck, *Paul*, 89.

20. Although Paul does not use the word *mimetai* ("imitate") here, he nevertheless portrays himself as embodying Christ's qualities, essentially his definition of *mimēsis* elsewhere. Jo-Ann Brant laments the English translation

"imitation" for this word, arguing that this translation fails to capture the depth of the Greek. Paul, she notes, considers the act of *mimēsis* to be "a process by which the imitator brings to expression an immutable principle," one that seeks to express "the essential characteristics of the object that one imitates."—Jo-Ann A. Brant, "The Place of *Mimēsis* in Paul's Thought," *Studies in Religion* 22/3 (1993): 286-87.

21. Charles B. Cousar, *A Theology of the Cross: The Death of Jesus in the Pauline Letters* (Minneapolis: Fortress, 1990), 136.

22. Paul Barnett concurs that this passage is about more than Paul's apostolic vocation. "Rather," he asserts, "it is [about] the essential nature of his ministry as the slave of Christ, which is applicable to all believers and which Paul models before the people to that very end, that they might understand it and do it."—Paul Barnett, *The Second Epistle to the Corinthians* (Grand Rapids, Mich.: Wm. B. Eerdmans, 1997), 238.

23. Stanley remarks that even though a slave was able to achieve fairly prominent positions in ancient society, "he was never his own man: his entire existence was ordered necessarily to his master."—Stanley, "Imitation in Paul's Letters," 131.

24. Paul uses "Jesus Christ" or "Christ Jesus" sixty-five times in the undisputed letters, some combination of "Lord Jesus Christ" forty-one times, and "Lord Jesus" twenty-one times. He refers to the name Jesus alone fourteen times in eleven passages. Five of those occur in 2 Cor. 4:10, 11, 14; for the others, see Rom. 3:26; 8.11; 1 Cor. 12:3; 2 Cor. 11:4; Phil. 2.10; 1 Thess. 1:10; 4.14.

25. Suffering is not the only characteristic of living "in Christ." Brant also highlights how Paul's *mimēsis* language invokes an "ethic of self-renunciation."—Brant, "*Mimēsis* in Paul's Thought," 286.

26. On this point, we appreciate how Rom 6:2-12 provides Paul's theological underpinning of participation "in Christ." "We should note," observes Dunn, "how quickly Paul jumps from a deep theological concept (union with Christ in his death) to talk of daily conduct. For Paul, evidently, *the character of daily conduct is actually determined by these deeper realities*, the hidden self-understandings and sources of strength which come to expression in day-to-day living."—Dunn, *Romans 1-8*, 330, emphasis original.

27. Reflecting on this passage Ernst Käsemann, a main proponent of *theologia crucis* as the center of Paul's thought, writes, "It is not only according to Gal. 6:17 that Paul views the stigmata of the one who was crucified (stigmata which even assumed physical form) as the sign of his belonging to Christ and as the mark of the true apostle and follower of Jesus. He was unable to separate faith from these stigmata."—Ernst Käsemann, "The Saving Significance of the Death of Jesus in Paul," in *Perspectives on Paul*, trans. Margaret Kohl (Philadelphia: Fortress, 1971), 38.

28. *Symmimētai* is another word compounded by the preposition "with," emphasizing its corporate nature. This is one of the relatively few places where Paul overtly calls for believers to imitate him; however, he consistently invokes this concept throughout his career (early [1 Thess. 1:6], middle [1 Cor. 4:16; 11.1], and late [Phil. 3:17]; see also Gal. 4:12), which suggests that he found himself to be a fine model for all of his *paranæsis*.

29. The word "co-imitators" is a call to unity, also indicated by Paul's use of the vocative *adelphoi*, "brothers and sisters," in this verse. This plea underscores Paul's wish for the Philippians to "stand firm" (4:1; also 1:27) and to be of the same mind (2:2; 3:15). See Adele Reinhartz, "On the Meaning of the Pauline Exhortation: '*Mimētai Mou Ginesthe*—Become Imitators of Me,'" *Studies in Religion* 16/4 (1987): 400.

30. Paul uses *peripateō*, the word for "walking," to refer to how one conducts life. People can either walk according to human standards (1 Cor. 3:3) or they can walk according to the Spirit (Gal. 5:25), "in newness of life" (Rom. 6:4). Paul's use of *peripateō* is influenced by the Hebrew *halak*, from which is derived *halakah*, the Jewish reflection about proper behavior as derived from the law.

31. From the context of the passage it is not certain if these opponents are already spreading this message to the Philippian believers, or if Paul is preemptively warning about them. See also Gordon Fee, who contends "that Paul does not mention them again would seem to indicate that they are *not* present."—Gordon D. Fee, *Paul's Letter to the Philippians* (Grand Rapids, Mich.: Wm. B. Eerdmans, 1995), 294, emphasis original.

32. See also Rom 16:18. Paul's discussion in Phil 3:19 relates closely to his analysis of how those who exchange the creature for the creator live (Rom 1:25).

33. "Perfection" in v. 12 and "mature" in v. 15 have the same underlying Greek root. Paul's close association between maturity and the conformity of one's mind to Christ demonstrates the radical nature of the believer's reorientation towards God; that is, the goal is nothing less than perfection.

34. Dunn, *Romans 1-8*, 330.

35. Weaver, *Nonviolent Atonement*, 99-178.

36. Ibid., 126. Weaver is referring to the work of Joanne Carlson Brown and Rebecca Parker, "For God So Loved the World?" in *Christianity, Patriarchy and Abuse: A Feminist Critique*, ed. Joanne Carlson Brown and Carole R. Bohn (New York: Pilgrim Press, 1989), 1-30.

37. Weaver, *Nonviolent Atonement*, 127-28.

38. Ibid., 135. Here Weaver is specifically looking at Julie M. Hopkins, *Towards a Feminist Christology* (Grand Rapids, Mich.: Wm. B. Eerdmans, 1995); see also Delores S. Williams, *Sisters in the Wilderness: The Challenge of Womanist God-Talk* (Maryknoll, N.Y.: Orbis, 1993); Karen Baker-Fletcher and Garth Kasimu Baker-Fletcher, *My Sister, My Brother: Womanist and Xodus God-Talk*, The Bishop Henry McNeal Turner/Sojourner Truth Series in Black Religion (Maryknoll, N.Y.: Orbis, 1997); JoAnne Marie Terrell, *Power in the Blood?*, The Bishop Henry McNeal Turner/Sojourner Truth Series in Black Religion (Maryknoll, N.Y.: Orbis, 1998); Katie Geneva Cannon, "'The Wounds of Jesus,'" in *A Troubling in My Soul*, ed. Emilie M. Townes, The Bishop Henry McNeal studies in North American Black Religion (Maryknoll, N.Y.: Orbis, 1993), 219-31; Clarice J. Martin, "Biblical Theodicy and Black Women's Spiritual Autobiography," in *A Troubling in My Soul*, 13-36.

39. See Williams, *Sisters in the Wilderness*, 161-67; also Weaver, *Nonviolent Atonement*, 164-66.

40. Although Paul states that God has triumphed over sin and death, he also is clear that they are allowed to continue their dominion in the time before Christ's return *(parousia)*. Along with Rom 5:21-6.23, see 1 Cor 15:20-28.

41. Weaver, *Nonviolent Atonement*, 174-75. Weaver borrows the phrase, "ethic of risk," from Karen Baker-Fletcher. See Baker-Fletcher and Baker-Fletcher, *My Sister, My Brother*, 79.

42. In his essay about Paul's exhortation to imitation in Philippians, Hawthorne observes that it is "perhaps the best New Testament writing to correct erroneous views of discipleship by clearly showing, not in words, but in life, what it truly means to be a disciple of Jesus today."—Gerald F. Hawthorne, "The Imitation of Christ: Discipleship in Philippians," in *Patterns of Discipleship in the New Testament*, ed. Richard N. Longenecker (Grand Rapids, Mich.: Wm. B. Eerdmans, 1996), 164.

43. Even Luke, who earnestly argues for Paul's good name (see, for example, the speech of King Agrippa at Paul's trial in Acts 26:31-32), reports his imprisonments (Acts 16:20-40; 22:22-26:32; 28.16), the attempts to kill him and run him out of cities (Acts 9:23-24; 14:5, 19-20; 17:5-10, 13; 18:6, 12-17; 19:23-41; 20:3; 21:27-36; 23:12-16; 25:1-3), and, ultimately, Paul being delivered in chains to Rome (Acts 25:10-12; 27:1-28:16).

44. Martin Luther King Jr., "Letter From a Birmingham Jail," in *A Testament of Hope*, ed. James Melvin Washington (San Francisco: Harper San Francisco, 1986), 293.

45. Ibid., 290.

46. Ibid., 297.

47. On this point, I find support from John Howard Yoder: "The cross is not a recipe for resurrection. Suffering is not a tool to make people come around, nor a good in itself. But the kind of faithfulness that is willing to accept evident defeat rather than complicity with evil is, by virtue of its conformity with what happens to God when he works with us, aligned with the ultimate triumph of the Lamb."—John Howard Yoder, *The Politics of Jesus: Vicit Agnus Noster* (Grand Rapids, Mich.: Wm. B. Eerdmans, 1972), 238. Käsemann also espouses this view. He writes, "'Through the Cross to the Crown' is the slogan which in the name of devotion vulgarizes such a view and pushes the death of Jesus into the shadow of his exaltation, either with the aid of a theory of redemptive history or by means of a moralizing model of the Christian life which enables us still to believe that we can (not of course without divine impulse and divine help) transcend both our earthly existence and nature."— Ernst Käsemann, "The Pauline Theology of the Cross," *Interpretation* 24 (1970): 174.

48. Cousar, *Theology of the Cross*, 90-91.

49. The Corinthians seem to assume that they have already reached the goal of salvation (e.g., 4:8), which has led to a relaxed attitude about conduct, particularly concerning sexual and dietary matters. From 2 Corinthians one observes that the Corinthian believers may be picking up this perspective from Paul's opponents who followed him to Corinth to "correct" his teaching. Calvin Roetzel notes that "Paul's rivals in Corinth promised what everyone desires—an immediate rescue from the one great absolute—death. By

contrast, Paul's gospel spoke only of a future resurrection, coupled with a call to suffer with Christ in the present."—Calvin J. Roetzel, "'As Dying, and Behold We Live': Death and Resurrection in Paul's Theology," *Interpretation* 46 (1992): 18.

50. Cousar, *Theology of the Cross*, 184.

CHAPTER SIX

ATONEMENT AND SACRIFICE IN THE BOOK OF REVELATION

Loren L. Johns

*T*he book of Revelation has played an important role in the theological work of J. Denny Weaver, both in his teaching and writing.[1] In developing a "narrative Christus victor" model of the atonement, Weaver has turned to Revelation's narrative as a resource for modifying the classic "Christus victor" model as articulated by Gustaf Aulén.[2]

After a few preliminary remarks outlining the historical and conceptual context for his book, Weaver begins his most substantial theological treatise, *The Nonviolent Atonement*, with an exposition of the book of Revelation. He does this in part because he (rightly, in my view) considers Revelation "virtually an extended, multifaceted statement of the Christus Victor image."[3]

In this essay I will examine the themes of atonement and sacrifice in Revelation with the intent of uncovering the primary theological significance of Christ's death in this book. I will argue that both *atonement* and *sacrifice* (or *sacrificial*) are slippery words that require careful definition and qualification. In Revelation, as I will explain, Christ's death is the key to God's victory over evil; the unfolding of God's reign on earth, however, requires believers to emulate the faithful witness that led to Christ's death, even though John expects that such faithfulness will mean their own martyrdom. Thus, while Christ's death is uniquely salvific, it is also exemplary—a model for believers to follow. Insofar as Revelation supports a theory of the atonement, it clearly supports a narrative Christus victor model over Anselm's satisfaction theory.

THE DEATH AND RESURRECTION OF CHRIST IN REVELATION

The death of Christ plays a pivotal role in Revelation. However, determining whether the author's primary concern is with "the atonement" requires some provisional understanding about what *atonement* signifies. If *atonement* signifies primarily a sacrificial death that expiates sin and puts humanity right with God, we would naturally investigate the book to evaluate the centrality of and the relationship among the concepts of sin, sacrifice, expiation, alienation from God, and restored relationship with God. If *atonement* refers to the larger cosmological significance of Christ's death as it relates to the overcoming of evil and the working out of God's purposes on earth, then we would naturally investigate whether the book says much about the broader cosmological significance of Christ's death and how evil is overcome.

At one level the difference lies between different theories of the atonement—especially between Anselm's satisfaction theory and the Christus Victor theory. At another level the difference lies between the personal or individual appropriation of the power of the cross on the one hand, and the broader cosmological or social significance of the power of the cross on the other. At yet a third level, the difference is between a unique, once-for-all event and an exemplary event that is to be emulated by those who follow the Lamb wherever he goes.

Right relationship with God figures prominently in Revelation. However, right relationship is tied directly to hearing and responding to God's call in life, not with "believing" apart from works. The first of the seven blessings in Revelation falls on the one who reads aloud the words of the prophecy and on those who hear *and who keep* what is written in it (1:3). Keeping the commandments—or the words of this prophecy (i.e., Revelation)—is quite important in this book.[4] Doing "works" (*erga* in Greek) is also important. The word *ergon* (a "work" or "deed") occurs twenty times in Revelation, second in the New Testament only to the gospel of John, where the word usually refers to the "works" that *Jesus* does—works that bear witness to who he is.

Seventeen of the twenty occurrences are in the letters to the seven churches (Rev. 2–3), where the word is always used in the positive sense as something that Christ expects of the churches. The criterion for judgment in Revelation is works, not faith. Revelation 2:23 says, "I will give to each of you as your works deserve." Revelation 2:26, "To everyone who conquers and continues to do my works to the end, I will give authority over the nations." Revelation 20:12, "And the dead were judged according to their works, as recorded in the books." And 22:12, "See, I am coming soon; my reward is with me, to repay according to everyone's work." The verb *believe* (*pisteuō*) does not appear at all in Revelation, while the noun *faith* (*pistis*) appears four times (Rev. 2:13, 19; 13:10; 14:12) with the sense of "faithfulness."[5]

This is not to suggest that there is a basic disagreement between John and Paul regarding Jesus' death as a means of justification. We simply do not have enough evidence to render such a verdict, since the occasion for Paul's letters was quite different from the occasion for the book of Revelation. Despite an emphasis on God's just *judgments* in Revelation,[6] *justification* in the Pauline sense is not of much concern to John. Revelation 1:5[7] and 5:9-10[8] suggest that John is aware of and accepts the idea that Christ's death was unique and efficacious—and perhaps even vicarious in some way. However, a closer look at how John deals with Christ's death in Revelation shows that his primary interest lies in Christ's death as the key turning point in divine warfare—a warfare in which the army of believers follow the Lamb wherever he goes (i.e., in his faithful witness all the way to martyrdom).

The treatment in Revelation of Jesus' death should not be opposed to or separated from its understanding of his resurrection. The first entrance of the Lamb in the key visions of Revelation 4 and 5 portray the Lamb as "*standing* as if it had been slaughtered.*"* The idea here is not only that Jesus had been killed, but also that he had risen from the dead and was now victorious. Jesus' victory came not only in his death, nor only in his resurrection, but in his death *and* resurrection.[9]

Bauckham is right to treat the book of Revelation as an extended "Christian war scroll."[10] David Barr similarly entitles the second half of Revelation (i.e., Rev. 11:19–22:21), "The War Scroll."[11] In keeping with the idea that Jesus' death is *exemplary* in Revelation, John calls Jesus the "firstborn" from the dead (1:5), since more deaths and resurrections are on their way.

However, Christ's uniquely efficacious death is by no means minimized in Revelation. Indeed, it is the key to the working out of God's plan for creation, the means by which evil is conquered. In the crucial scene in heaven in chapter 5, the connection between Christ's slaughter and his worthiness to open the scroll is made explicit: "You are worthy to take the scroll and to open its seals, for you were slaughtered and by your blood you ransomed for God saints from every tribe and language and people and nation; you have made them to be a kingdom and priests serving our God, and they will reign on earth" (5:9-10).

The ransoming of the saints here is not primarily *from* something (e.g., sin or death), but *to* or *for* something: to be a kingdom and priests serving God and reigning. Christ's death is the key to God's victory over evil, but the establishment of God's reign on earth requires the believers to emulate the faithful witness that led to Christ's death, even though John expects that it will mean their own martyr deaths as well. Although Stanislas Lyonett and others have attempted to find behind the concept of "purchase" in 5:9-10 evidence of the Old Testament sacrificial system, Dale Martin and Stephen Finlan claim that it is much more natural to see behind this term "the ordinary sale of a slave by one owner to another."[12] At this level (*how* believers participate in Christ's death), there does appear to be a difference of perspective between John and Paul.

THE WASHING OF ROBES

The final blessing in Revelation comes on those who "wash their robes" (22:14).[13] The author of Revelation refers or alludes several times to the concept of washing one's robes. As R. H. Charles has noted, "those who wash their robes" is functionally equivalent to "the one who conquers" in 2:7, since in both passages the reward to those who have conquered is access to the tree of life.[14]

Aune considers the washing of robes to be "clearly a metaphor for moral and spiritual cleansing or reformation,"[15] and such an association seems natural on the surface. Bauckham's discussion of this metaphor in the context of warfare, however, is more convincing.[16] The question is whether Revelation is more interested in moral or spiritual *cleansing*, or in *holy warfare*. The latter is clearly the case. In the religion of Israel, before warriors could worship, they were required to wash their garments as part of a purification ritual following a battle in which blood was shed (Num. 31:19-20, 24; cf. also 1QM 14.2-3; 1 Enoch 90:31). The purification of which John is speaking here draws from that holy war motif. It is the purification that comes through maintaining a faithful witness to the point of death. Martyrdom effectively sealed that witness and resulted in the paradoxical image of washing one's robes white in the blood of the Lamb (7:14; cf. 3:4; 22:14).

SIN IN REVELATION

The word *sin* does not appear often in Revelation. In the New Testament, *sin* is most prominent in Romans (NRSV, 57 times; NIV, 74; KJV, 57). Second is Hebrews (29, 34, and 27 times respectively), then 1 John (27, 28, 24), then the Gospel of John (23, 21, 23). With only three instances of the word (*hamartia* in each case; 4 in NIV,[17] 3 in KJV), Revelation is near the bottom of the list, especially when its length is taken into consideration.[18]

The first appearance of *sin* is in the opening doxology in 1:5-6: "To him who loves us and freed us from our sins by his blood, and made us to be a kingdom, priests serving his God and Father, to him be glory and dominion forever and ever. Amen." The second and third occurrences refer to the sins of Babylon and come in the context of judgment upon Rome and warning the believers not to participate in her sins. Thus, only once in Revelation (1:5) is there a reference to believers' sins being atoned by the blood of Christ.

Sin is rarely if ever seen as a "problem" that separates humanity from God. The problem is the presence of evil and the ongoing battle for the establishment of God's reign on earth. Although Jesus' death and resurrection were decisive in that battle, the believers' participation in it continues. As Richard Bauckham puts it, John "takes largely for granted that Christ's sacrificial death has liberated Christians from sin (1:5) and made them the eschatological people of God (1:5; 5:9-10). What is important, in the context of Revelation . . . is the role it [the church] has to play in the universal coming of the kingdom." Because the imagery of Christ's death is not concerned primarily with the once-for-all sacrifice that puts humanity right with God, but with the victory won by Christ in which believers *continue to participate* in overcoming evil, the references to "the blood of the Lamb" in Rev. 7:14 and 12:11 should not be understood as referring exclusively "to Christ's death, but to the deaths of the Christian martyrs."[19] Christians participate "in the death of Christ through faithful witness to the point of martyrdom,"[20] as 12:11 implies.

CHRIST'S DEATH AS SACRIFICE

As we have already seen, the relationship between sacrifice and atonement in the book of Revelation is fraught with terminological challenges. It would be possible to foreclose the entire question about theories of the atonement by treating the word *atonement* itself as a virtual synonym for Anselm's satisfaction theory of the atonement. The word itself derives from the idea of being reconciled, or put "at one," with another (at-one-ment), and might thus be considered roughly equivalent to expiation and reconciliation. But that would be to beg the question of Revelation's own understanding of Christ's death.

Similarly, simply to call the theology of the cross in Revelation "sacrificial" is inadequate and misleading.[21] As Christopher M. Tuckett warns, "One must . . . be wary of making sacrificial language too monochrome. The sacrificial cult within Judaism and elsewhere was very varied and included provision for many different kinds of sacrifice."[22] Just as the practice of religion today is varied and reflects many different theologies, so the practice of sacrifice in the Greco-Roman world was varied and reflected many different theologies.

Revelation is shot through with scenes of worship that incorporate temple and sacrificial cult imagery—along with images of royalty.[23] For instance, the decisive scene in heaven (Rev. 4–5) includes a central throne surrounded by thrones, and golden crowns. But it also has a temple, an altar, and a censer with incense (5:8; 6:9; 8:3-5; 9:13; 11:1; 14:17-18; 16:7), though there is no temple in the New Jerusalem (21:22). Even the seven bowls of God's wrath probably derive from the utensils used in temple worship. The fullness of God's reign is characterized as turning the community of faith into a kingdom of priests (1:6; 5:10; 20:6). As Robert Daly says, "The entire work is a series of visions about, or occasioned by, the liturgy of the heavenly sanctuary or (after 21:1) of the New Jerusalem."[24] The question is not how important such worship and temple imagery are in Revelation, but rather how those elements function. That is, with what kind of rhetorical force is it employed?

Elisabeth Schüssler Fiorenza has contrasted the *political nature* of the book's rhetoric with its *liturgical form*. Although she notes that the book's rhetoric is "replete with cultic language and imagery," she maintains that its social location and theological goal are "not liturgical but political."[25] Such a sharp dichotomy between the liturgical and political may not be warranted. As Jean-Pierre Ruiz has established in several publications,[26] the worship scenes in Revelation are essentially political in their rhetorical force.[27] Specifically, "the mediation of meaning through ritual worked to shape a strategy of resistance."[28] Revelation implies that the function of worship is political. But one might also maintain that all of the political language in Revelation ultimately serves John's interest in proper worship of God and of the Lamb. Thus, while Fiorenza is probably right to see in the cultic imagery of Revelation a political-ethical intent, it may not be legitimate or warranted to posit such a hard line between liturgical and political agendas.

In most Greco-Roman religions, sacrifice was synonymous with worship, without any necessary connection with expiation or forgiveness, though it often was connected with a community's or individual's obligation to appease the gods. Ritual sacrifice was widespread in the ancient world. In Greece it was as common in the ancient period as it was in the Hellenistic and Roman eras. In the Archaic and Classical periods it was not considered proper to consult or petition a deity without bringing a sacrifice. Sacrifice was "one of the three principal acts of worship"[29] in the ancient world and was perhaps even the most important form of action in Greek religion.[30]

Even within Second Temple Judaism, understandings of the religious significance of sacrifice varied, and within the sacrificial cult itself, sacrifices were quite different from each other and were carried out with different purposes. The problem is not just that "diverse images associated with the word 'sacrifice' have become widespread in Christian tradition," as Jonathan K. Smith has noted, but that the theology and practice of sacrifice were exceedingly diverse already in ancient times.[31]

In biblical thought, sacrifice was much broader theologically than expiation. This was even more obviously the case in the Greco-Roman religions. In the Old Testament, only *some* sacrifices were considered expiatory. Sacrifice was the central feature of worship in Israelite religion. The burnt offering was prominent in Israel's theology and practice of sacrifice, but expiation was not the focus of burnt offering, and the lamb was not the primary offering of expiation. In other words, *lamb* was not an obvious symbol for expiation in the sacrificial cult.[32] There were other sacrifices for which sin was not at issue. For instance, the peace offerings included the thank offering, the free will offering, and the votive offering, none of which had anything to do with atonement.

Even the so-called "sin" offering, which Jacob Milgrom, Gary Anderson, David Aune, and others prefer to call the "purification offering," was not *primarily* about the expiation of sin. Indeed, this offering sometimes purified when sin was not even in view. Anderson offers for consideration "the cases of the parturient (Lev. 12), the person suffering from a discharge (Lev. 15), the Nazirite who completes a vow of abstinence (Num. 6), or the installation of a new altar (Lev. 8). In each of these cases," Anderson argues, "the act of sacrifice serves to purge or purify something rather than to remove sin."[33] After the destruction of the second temple, sacrifice continued to play a theoretical role in the theology of Rabbinic Judaism. In the twelfth century, Maimonides famously systematized the sacrificial system as no one before or since. Nevertheless, he was capable of being quite critical of the whole system.[34] In any case, "burnt-offerings and sacrifice . . . are of secondary importance."[35]

Even if one grants that *some* understanding of Old Testament sacrifice must lie behind the Lamb symbolism of Revelation, it is not at all clear how that helps us understand the theology of Revelation, given the wide range of associations related to sacrifice. As David Aune puts it,

> While it is likely that the figure of the Lamb in Revelation must be understood at least in part on the basis of O[ld] T[estament] sacrificial ritual, it is not at all clear *which* type of sacrifice is primarily in view, for sheep or lambs were used as sacrificial victims in several different types of sacrifice in the OT and early Judaism.[36]

For instance, two lambs were sacrificed every day as a burnt offering in the Tamid (the daily offering). However, this daily burnt offering never carried with it any atoning significance.[37] The Passover lamb was a type of peace offering (*šelâmîm*), which had nothing to do with atonement.[38] In general agreement with Gary Anderson, David Aune concludes that

> it seems apparent that the historical *realia* of the Israelite sacrificial cult . . . do not provide anything more than a general context in which the metaphor of the slaughtered Lamb whose blood somehow effects redemption can be understood. The sacrificial features of the Lamb of Revelation are primarily a *textual phenomenon* with only very loose associations with actual cultic practice.[39]

REVELATION AS ANTI-SACRIFICIAL

There is, in fact, some linguistic evidence that the author of Revelation took care to *avoid* a sacrificial interpretation of the death of Christ. As Sophie Laws and others have pointed out, the Seer consistently uses the Greek word *sphazō* to speak of the Lamb as having been slaughtered, or murdered, rather than *thyō*, the word that would normally have been used when speaking of ritually "sacrificing" an animal. The verb *thyô* does not appear in Revelation. *Sphazô* is slaughterhouse language, not Temple language. Though all animal sacrifice involved slaughter, not all slaughter involved sacrifice. *Sphazō* means to kill or to slaughter. Its use in Revelation to speak of deaths *other than* the Lamb's indicates how the author likely understood its meaning with regard to the Lamb: Once in Revelation it refers to the killing or murder of people (6:4). Twice it refers to the slaughter of God's people in martyrdom (6:9; 18:24).

In none of these cases is the slaughter considered expiatory, reducing the possibility that the rhetorical force of the slaughter of the Lamb in Revelation is primarily expiatory.[40] However, unlike *apothnēskō* ("murder"), *sphazō* may have some ritual overtones. If so, this would lend some credence to the argument of Marc Bredin that John understands the death of Jesus to challenge the mimetic desire at work in the sacrificial system.[41] At the very least, John's use of the word *slaughter* for both the death Jesus and the death of the saints implies some kind of *participation* of the latter in the shed blood of Jesus.[42]

The word used for Lamb in Revelation is *arnion*, not *amnos*, which is the word used in the Septuagint as well as in other parts of the New Testament to refer to Jesus as Lamb with regard to his atoning death. *Arnion* is diminutive in form and although one should probably not translate it as a diminutive ("little lamb" or "lambkin"), it probably does serve to underline its vulnerability. In the Septuagint, *arnion* is used only of lambs that symbolize vulnerability, whereas *amnos* is used almost exclusively of sacrificial lambs.[43]

To maintain that Christ's death is not understood primarily in sacrificial terms in Revelation does not mean that the death of Christ has no salvific import. On the contrary! The death of Christ is central to the theology of Revelation and to the Revelation's conception of how God will establish God's kingdom on earth. Richard Bauckham maintains that Christ's death and resurrection are "fundamental to Revelation's whole understanding of the way in which Christ establishes God's kingdom on earth."[44]

We have already considered signs of a more traditional atonement theology in the opening doxology, which says, "To him who loves us and freed us from our sins by his blood, and made us to be a kingdom, priests serving his God and Father, to him be glory and dominion forever and ever. Amen" (Rev. 1:5-6). Here Christ's death is explicitly connected with being freed from sins, a feature of Anselm's satisfaction theory of the atonement. However, four considerations temper this connection.

First, in an analysis of the hymns of Revelation, David Carnegie concludes that the hymn in Rev. 1:5-6 is likely the only one that comes from the Christian tradition—i.e., that was not created by John in the writing of the book.[45] This could suggest that although John knows and accepts this traditional theology, it is not his primary concern in the book.[46] Second, the verb *lyō* ("freed") here[47] is more apocalyptic than forensic in its force. It is an active verb associated with redemption rather than forgiveness.[48] Third, as we saw above, Revelation has little interest in the problem of sin as such. Fourth, the doxology in this verse is "to the one who loves us," suggesting that Jesus' death is in part an expression of God's love for humanity. This was the key contribution of Abelard in response to Anselm's atonement theory.

There are, to be sure, alternative ways of understanding Revelation's theology of Christ's death.[49] For instance, Sir Isaac Newton (1642–1727) saw the temple as the place where *all* of the action in Revelation took place. Thus, "every aspect of the temple—its physical layout, vessels and ceremonies . . . becomes critical to the unraveling of the secrets held in the Apocalypse."[50] In the 1930s, Johannes Pedersen argued that the concepts of expiation and atonement were becoming more and more important within the sacrificial cult in Judaism.[51] Pedersen wrote in an era that was apt to use later rabbinic sources as reliable guides to the variegated Judaism of the Second Temple Period and to psychologize religious traditions.[52] Austin Farrer's *Rebirth of Images* also emphasized the connections with the temple cult.[53]

More recently, John and Gloria Ben-Daniel developed an interest in cultic life and thought and wrote a book that pushes the Old Testament sacrificial cult for all its worth as a key to understanding the book of Revelation.[54] For the Ben-Daniels, the blood of the Lamb in Revelation "has a profound expiatory effect."[55] The book of Revelation is for them an elaborate liturgy of atonement in which Satan is the scapegoat Azazel, yet the martyrdom of the saints is part of the heavenly liturgy that eventuates in atonement for the world.

In addition, some conservative evangelicals see Anselm's satisfaction theory of the atonement behind every mention of Christ's death in the New Testament. For instance, Roy Zuck claims that "the Johannine Epistles and the book of Revelation . . . emphasize the sacrificial nature of Jesus' death as part of God's plan of salvation."[56]

Similarly, *Nelson's New Illustrated Bible Dictionary* suggests that

> John's reference to Jesus as the Lamb of God calls to mind the Old Testament sacrificial system. In the sacrifice God accepted the blood of animals as the means of atonement for sin. It is likely that John had many themes from the Old Testament in mind when he called Jesus the Lamb of God. These themes probably included the sin offering (Lev. 4), the trespass offering (Lev. 5), the sacrifice on the Day of atonement (Lev. 16), and the Passover sacrifice (Exod. 12).[57]

And Gregory Beale concludes that

> the Lamb's death is best understood as a removal of the divine wrath barring entrance to God's presence by means of the Lamb bearing that wrath himself as a penal substitute for his people. This notion is based on the OT sacrificial background, especially the Day of atonement, where the sacrificial animal is a representative penal substitute for Israel.[58]

In each of these cases, the controlling context for understanding the meaning of Christ's death in Revelation seems to be orthodox theology, rather than the book of Revelation itself.

A key conviction in Revelation is the call for believers to conquer, just as Christ conquered. Christ clearly conquered *through his death as a faithful witness* (cf. Rev. 3:21; 5:5). The blessing to each of the seven churches is upon the one "who conquers," and the messages climax with the final blessing: "To the one who conquers I will give a place with me on my throne, just as I myself conquered and sat down with my Father on his throne."

Thus, the washing of robes in 7:14 refers not simply to their reception of cleansing or forgiveness, but to the idea that "the moral probity of their lives as faithful witnesses is sealed in their martyrdom and is their active participation in the redemption won for them by Christ."[59] Those who wash their robes are those who have come out of the great "ordeal," or "suffering" (*thlipsis* in Greek).

THE WORD *ATONEMENT*

As I noted above, one of the problems with using atonement terminology is its lack of precision. Does Revelation even *have* a theology of the atonement? It depends on what one means by *atonement*. Although the death of Christ in Revelation is central to its theology and clearly salvific, the book's primary focus is on how evil is conquered and how God's reign is established on earth, *not* on how sin is dealt with forensically in putting humanity into right relationship with God.

It is impossible to speak of atonement and sacrifice without some underlying understanding of how God saves—and from what. The word *sacrifice* is often associated with Anselm's satisfaction theory of the atonement—and for good reason. Anselm saw humanity as owing a debt that it could not pay. Humanity was atoned when Jesus' death "expiated" humanity's sin. The analogy in the immediate background was the sacrificial system, with which nearly everyone in the Greco-Roman world, whether Jew or Gentile, would have been familiar, though less so in Anselm's day. So the relationship between sacrifice and Anselm's satisfaction theory is a natural one.

But if one uses the word *atonement* to refer to John's understanding of Christ's death in Revelation, then one must take care not to import unwarranted expiatory or sacrificial inferences if, as I have maintained, those inferences do not derive authentically from the text itself. As Charles E. Hill notes in his essay on atonement in Revelation, the book is remarkable in part because of its emphasis on the *ethical* implications of Jesus' death and resurrection.[60]

RENÉ GIRARD AND MIMETIC DESIRE

According to René Girard, the word *sacrifice* in its primary sense "stems from originary victimization or scapegoating."[61] As a result, in Girard's earlier work, *sacrifice* itself was a synonym for the whole scapegoating system, since the practice of animal sacrifice likely derived from the earlier practice of human sacrifice. As a system of ritually controlled vengeance, sacrifice lies near the heart of what is wrong with all human religious systems, in Girard's view.

In his later years, however, Girard began to accept an alternative, more positive understanding of sacrifice as giving oneself to others and to God out of love and faithfulness to the other.[62] Any understanding of the atonement through Christ that claims or implies that God the Father arranged for his Son's murder to satisfy God's wrath would be an example of scapegoating and unworthy of the gospel. However, the New Testament Gospels do not portray Jesus' death as a sacrifice. Instead, "by focusing on the innocence of the victim, the Bible exposes the sacred justification of violence against the victim."[63]

Unfortunately, little attention has been given to the book of Revelation in Girardian studies.[64] Some exceptions have been Mark R. Bredin,[65] Raymund Schwager,[66] Ted Grimsrud,[67] Judith Kovacs and Christopher Rowland,[68] and more recently, Stephen Finamore.[69] To be sure, students of Girard have said quite a bit about "apocalypse," (small a) but they tend to treat "apocalypse" as a broad philosophical category roughly equivalent to the "myth of violence" or "sacralized violence,"[70] rather than read John's Revelation carefully on its own terms. Girard maintains that the apocalyptic violence that we see in the Gospels "is always laid at the door of humanity . . . and never blamed on God."[71] In fact, the book of Revelation is sometimes treated as the epitome of sacral violence in Girardian circles.[72]

Mark Bredin argues that the Greek word *pharmakos* in Revelation 21:8 and 22:15 refers to the scapegoating mechanism, which the Seer rejects, rather than to sorcery, as it is normally translated. The word *pharmakos* did indeed refer to the scapegoat from at least Hipponax in the sixth century BCE in classical Greek literature.[73] In the Septuagint the word usually refers to sorcery, although in Wisdom of Solomon 1:14, it appears to refer to the scapegoating mechanism as a virtual synonym for evil.[74] The NRSV and most other versions (probably following Jerome's *"medicamentum exterminii"*) translate the word "destructive poison," even though *scapegoat* or *scapegoating* fit the context much better. Wisdom 1:12-15 reads,

> [12]Do not invite death by the error of your life,
> or bring on destruction by the works of your hands;
> [13]because God did not make death,
> and he does not delight in the death of the living.
> [14]For he created all things so that they might exist;
> the generative forces of the world are wholesome,
> and there is no destructive poison [*or scapegoat*] in them,
> and the dominion of Hades is not on earth.
> [15]For righteousness is immortal.

The following chapter in Wisdom goes on to describe and condemn the scapegoating mechanism.

In this sense, *pharmakos* is a synonym for *peripsēma, katharma,* and *perikatharma*.[75] Liddell, Scott, Jones, and McKenzie translate pharmakos as "*one sacrificed* or *executed as an atonement* or *purification* for others, *scapegoat*."[76] Sadly, Wisdom 1:12-15 has largely been ignored by Girardian scholars.

Thus, while sacrificial images and language pervade the book of Revelation, they are used in such a way to support a message that is primary ethical. Rather than reify the sacrificial cult, these images are molded and reshaped for a different intent—one that rejects the internal logic of a scapegoating sacrificial system. As Bredin puts it, "Satan deceives the world into blaming others for the violence that is in society resulting in the violence of scapegoat sacrifice." But, he continues, "Jesus conquers Satan by uncovering this deception; he shows that the way of God is that of nonviolent faithful witness."[77]

THE CHALLENGE OF IDEOLOGICAL CRITICISM

In a growing body of scholarship focusing on ideological criticism of Revelation—especially in the United States—a new challenge to such a Girardian reading has been levied.[78] This ideology has drawn significantly on recent work in feminist scholarship and rhetorical criticism but is maturing into a recognizable school of interpretation in its own right with significant implications for Revelation studies. A number of scholars, including Robert Royalty Jr.,[79] Paul Duff,[80] Tina Pippin,[81] and Greg Carey[82] have focused their study of Revelation on the struggle for power and ascendancy among the prophetic leaders *within* the Christian communities in Asia.

These scholars agree that even if there is some unmasking of mimetic desire with regard to Jesus' death on the surface of the text, we can see a re-victimization going on at the rhetorical level. That is, at the rhetorical level, John is engaging in unethical argumentation.[83] For instance, "John tries to discredit his rival [unnamed in the text, but derisively dubbed 'Jezebel' by John] by indirectly tying her by means of homology and irony—to the satanic realm."[84] The primary "crisis" facing the seven churches of Revelation is an internal one that involved not only theological differences but also conflicts over social position and economic mobility; it was *not* primarily an external crisis, such as persecution from outside.[85] Even the way that John uses the Old Testament is an expression of this power struggle.[86]

This struggle for power among the leaders of the seven churches is clearly visible within the text of Revelation itself. Especially in the letters to the seven churches, we see many negative sobriquets (e.g., Nicolaitans [2:6,15], Jezebel [2:20], Balaamites [2:14]) and references to people who "call themselves" one thing (2:2, 9, 20) but "are not" (2:2, 9), to the blasphemy of those who consider themselves part of the believing community (2:9), to the synagogue of Satan (2:9; 3:9), to liars (2:2), and to evildoers among the people of God (2:2). Besides suggesting that the author does not share his readers' assessment of the current situation, these references bear witness to a power struggle among the leaders of the community—a power struggle that the author is waging with questionable ethical integrity at the rhetorical level.

Greg Carey maintains that "however one negotiates Revelation's violence, liberationist interpretations are left with a difficult moral ethos, which is inclusive in that it takes the side of the marginalized but is also exclusivist in identifying persons, groups, and structures with oppression."[87] If Carey is right, and I think he is, the ethos of Revelation is unstable in that it is torn between egalitarian and authoritarian impulses. A similar observation has been made by Tina Pippin.

This look at the school of ideological criticism within Revelation studies indicates that, even if a Christus Victor reading of Revelation is legitimate and warranted by the text, this does not necessarily save the book from some of the ethical problems that have dogged Anselm's theory of the atonement.

In conclusion, we see no victimization or re-victimization in the Revelation of John with regard to the death of Jesus. Jesus is portrayed as Lamb precisely because the image underscores Jesus' vulnerability—a vulnerability manifested and sealed in his murder. But ironically, his is a vulnerability without victimization, since it is precisely through his death that Jesus overcame, or conquered. Jesus' death in the Apocalypse is not portrayed as an expression of mimetic desire, or of sacral violence, but rather as a repudiation of it.

"Atonement" in its classic, Anselmian sense was not important to the author of Revelation. While John seems to know and accept the tradition that Jesus died for humanity's sins, his primary understanding of Jesus' death is that it was the ultimate victory over evil.

The sacral or cultic imagery we find in Revelation is designed primarily not to correct the believers' mode of worship or understanding of sacrifice, but rather to redirect that worship from the emperor and/or the emperor's gods to the one true God and to the Lamb. The irony is that this book, which is perhaps second only to Hebrews in the pervasiveness of cultic language and imagery, is not concerned with the proper observance of cult, except that it is the God of Israel who is to be worshiped, not the emperor. Instead, its burden is to elicit the kind of allegiance to God that allows no compromise with Greco-Roman religion or with emperor worship. It calls for a kind of nonviolent resistance to those forces that may well lead to the reader's death—a death that will seal the believer's salvation. In short, there is a kind of spiritualization of sacrifice and of cultic terms in this book.[88]

There is a war going on in Revelation at several levels. The war in heaven symbolizes and gives new perspective for the war taking place on the earth.[89] But there is a rhetorical war going on as well among the leaders of the seven churches, to which we have only one remaining witness: the book of Revelation itself.

What does this mean for the believing Christian today? What difference does it make if Revelation reflects a Christus Victor understanding of the significance of Jesus' saving death and resurrection?

Revelation's view regarding what Jesus did privileges the ethical and political. Whatever else Jesus' death is in this book, it is not exclusively, or even primarily, vicarious: it is unique and salvific, but it is also exemplary. In Revelation, Christ's death and resurrection are the keys to God's victory over evil in a battle whose outcome has already been settled, but the *working out in history* of which requires that believers maintain the same kind of faithful witness that eventuated in Jesus' own death. Revelation thus exhibits an understanding of Jesus' death and resurrection that directly supports a vision for discipleship. For those who wish to follow the Lamb wherever he goes must follow him in faithful witness . . . and perhaps even in death.

NOTES

1. In his teaching, Weaver often began his theology courses with a session on Revelation, focusing on how it has been and should be read. His first substantial foray into the Christus Victor view of the atonement appeared in his article, "Atonement for the Non-Constantinian Church," *Modern Theology* 6/4 (July 1990): 307-23. Subsequent work in this area includes J. Denny Weaver, "Violence in Christian Theology," *Cross Currents* 51/2 (Summer 2001): 150-76, esp. 164-67; J. Denny Weaver, "Christus Victor, Ecclesiology, and Christology," *Mennonite Quarterly Review* 68/3 (July 1994): 277-90; J. Denny Weaver, "Some Theological Implications of Christus Victor," *Mennonite Quarterly Review* 68/4 (October 1994): 483-99; J. Denny Weaver, *Keeping Salvation Ethical: Mennonite and Amish Atonement Theology in the Late Nineteenth Century* (Scottdale, Pa.: Herald Press, 1997), 39-43; J. Denny Weaver, "Reading the Past, Present, and Future in Revelation," in *Apocalypticism and Millennialism: Shaping a Believers Church Eschatology for the Twenty-First Century*, ed. Loren L. Johns (Kitchener: Pandora Press, 2000), 104-18. Weaver re-

vised and expanded much of his work on Revelation in his book-length study, *The Nonviolent Atonement* (Grand Rapids: Eerdmans, 2001), esp. 20-33.

2. See Gustaf Aulén, *Christus Victor: An Historical Study of the Three Main Types of the Idea of Atonement*, (New York: Macmillan, 1969). For a succinct introduction to theories of the Atonement, see Timothy J. Geddert, *Mark* (Scottdale, Pa.: Herald Press, 2001), 387-9.

3. Weaver, *The Nonviolent Atonement*, 20. Oddly enough, Aulén himself almost completely ignored the book of Revelation in his survey of the New Testament theology of atonement.

4. For other instances of the word *tēreō* ("keep"), see 2:26; 3:3, 8, 10; 12:17; 14:12; 16:15; 22:7, 9.

5. Note that the parallel expressions in these verses may help to explain the author's understanding of faith (*pistis*) in these verses. In 2:13 the parallel expression is holding fast to Christ's name; in 2:19 they are love, service, works, and endurance (*hypomonē*), which Elisabeth Schüssler Fiorenza translates as "consistent resistance." See Elisabeth Schüssler Fiorenza, *The Book of Revelation: Justice and Judgment* (Philadelphia: Fortress, 1985), 4, 182; in 13:10 it is endurance (*hypomonē*); and in 14:12 they are endurance (*hypomonē*) and keeping the commandments.

6. See 6:10; 15:4; 16:5, 7; 18:20; 19:2, 11, 20:4.

7. "To him who loves us and freed us from our sins by his blood, and made us to be a kingdom, priests serving his God and Father, to him be glory and dominion forever and ever. Amen."

8. "You are worthy to take the scroll and to open its seals, for you were slaughtered and by your blood you ransomed for God saints from every tribe and language and people and nation; you have made them to be a kingdom and priests serving our God, and they will reign on earth."

9. See David E. Aune, *Revelation 1–5* (Dallas: Word Books, 1997), 352, on the significance of the lamb *standing*.

10. Richard Bauckham, "The Book of Revelation as a Christian War Scroll," *Neotestamentica* 22 (1988): 17-40, reprinted in Richard Bauckham, *The Climax of Prophecy: Studies on the Book of Revelation* (Edinburgh: T&T Clark, 1993), 210-237. Summarizing his research, Bauckham says that "John carefully takes up Jewish expectations of a messianic war in which God's people are to fight and to win a military victory over their enemies, and reinterprets them, substituting faithful witness to the point of martyrdom for armed violence as the means of victory. Though military means are repudiated, the imagery of holy war is employed in the interests of active participation by Christians in the divine conflict with evil, following up the decisive victory which their Messiah, the Lamb, has already won" (Bauckham, *Climax of Prophecy*, xv). Elsewhere he notes, "The messianic army is an army of martyrs who triumph through their martyrdom, because they are followers of the Lamb who participate in his victory by following his path to death" (Bauckham, *Climax of Prophecy*, 229).

11. David L. Barr, "Tales of the End," in *Tales of the End: A Narrative Commentary on the Book of Revelation* (Santa Rosa, Calif.: Polebridge Press, 1998), 101.

12. See Stanislas Lyonnet, "The Terminology of Redemption," in *Sin, Redemption and Sacrifice: A Biblical and Patristic Study* (Rome: Biblical Institute, 1970), 61-184; Dale Martin, *Slavery as Salvation: The Metaphor of Slavery in Pauline Christianity* (New Haven: Yale University Press, 1990), 63; and Stephen Finlan, *The Background and Content of Paul's Cultic Atonement Metaphors* (Atlanta: Society of Biblical Literature, 2004), 166.

13. Some manuscripts have "do his commandments" here (followed by the KJV) instead of "wash their robes," but the latter reading is to be preferred. For a discussion of the issues here, see Bruce M. Metzger, *A Textual Commentary on the Greek New Testament: A Companion Volume to the United Bible Societies' Greek New Testament*, 3rd. ed. (London and New York: United Bible Societies, 1971), 690; and David E. Aune, *Revelation 17-22* (Nashville: Thomas Nelson Publishers, 1998), 1197-8.

14. R. H. Charles, *A Critical and Exegetical Commentary on the Revelation of St. John* (Edinburgh: T&T Clark, 1920), 177. Cf. also Aune, *Revelation*, 1219.

15. Aune, *Revelation*, 1219.

16. For Bauckham's handling of this metaphor, see Bauckham, *Climax of Prophecy*, 226-9.

17. The NIV supplies the word *sin* in 2:14, where it reads, "You have people there who hold to the teaching of Balaam, who taught Balak to entice the Israelites to sin by eating food sacrificed to idols." The Greek has simply "taught Balak to put a stumbling block before the Israelites."

18. The word *sin* does not appear in Philippians, 2 Thessalonians, Philemon, or 2 or 3 John.

19. Richard Bauckham, *The Theology of the Book of Revelation* (Cambridge and New York: Cambridge University Press, 1993), 75. Similarly, David Aune notes that "though the idea of martyrdom is very much present" in 12:11, "the notion of atonement is absent." See David E. Aune, *Revelation 6–16* (Nashville: Thomas Nelson Publishers, 1998), 474.

20. Bauckham, *Climax of Prophecy*, 228.

21. Much as I appreciate Mark Bredin's work in *Jesus, Revolutionary of Peace*, I find his question "sacrificial lamb or military figure?" misleading. See Mark Bredin, *Jesus, Revolutionary of Peace: A Nonviolent Christology in the Book of Revelation* (Carlisle, Cumbria, U.K.: Paternoster Press, 2003), 182-5. Not only must "sacrificial lamb" be defined and nuanced; so also must "military leader." I have demonstrated that although Friedrich Spitta in the nineteenth century attracted many twentieth-century followers in his positing of the existence of a militaristic lamb redeemer tradition in Early Judaism, this tradition never existed—at least not prior to the writing of Revelation. See Loren L. Johns, *The Lamb Christology of the Apocalypse of John: An Investigation Into Its Origins and Rhetorical Force* (Tübingen: Mohr Siebeck, 2003), 76-107. Thus, if Jesus is a military leader in Revelation—and I would argue that he is—then he is a military leader of a much different sort—a nonviolent one. And if the Lamb is a sacrificial character—and he is, in a way—then he is a very different sort of sacrificial character.

22. C. M. Tuckett, "Atonement in the N[ew] T[estament]," in *Anchor Bible Dictionary*, ed. David Noel Freedman (New York: Doubleday, 1992), 1.519.

23. For considerations of the pervasiveness of Revelation's language of the Hebrew sacrificial system of worship—and its implications for understanding the message of Revelation—see Richard Bauckham, "Prayer in the Book of Revelation," in *Into God's Presence: Prayer in the New Testament*, ed. Richard N. Longenecker (Grand Rapids, Mich.: Wm. B. Eerdmans, 2001): 252–71; and Jon Paulien, "The Role of the Hebrew Cultus, Sanctuary, and Temple in the Plot and Structure of the Book of Revelation," *Andrews University Seminary Studies* 33/2 (Autumn 1992): 245-64. The role of the temple and of Temple worship also plays largely in the monographs by Farrer and Niles: Austin M. Farrer, *A Rebirth of Images: The Making of St. John's Apocalypse* (Albany, NY: State University of New York, 1986); and Daniel Thambyrajah Niles, *As Seeing the Invisible* (New York: Harper, 1961). Cf. also Michael D. Goulder, "The Apocalypse as an Annual Cycle of Prophecies," *New Testament Studies* 27 (April 1981): 243-67; and Robert J. Daly, *Christian Sacrifice: The Judaeo-Christian Background before Origen* (Washington, DC: Catholic University of America Press, 1978), 295–307.

24. Daly, *Christian Sacrifice*, 296.

25. Elisabeth Schüssler Fiorenza, *Revelation: Vision of a Just World* (Minneapolis: Fortress, 1991), 103.

26. See Jean-Pierre Ruiz, "Betwixt and Between on the Lord's Day: Liturgy and the Apocalypse," in *Society of Biblical Literature 1992 Seminar Papers* (Atlanta: Scholars Press, 1992), 654-72; and Jean-Pierre Ruiz, "The Politics of Praise: A Reading of Revelation 19:1-10," in *Society of Biblical Literature 1997 Seminar Papers* (Atlanta: Scholars Press, 1997), 374-93, reprinted in Jean-Pierre Ruiz, "Praise and Politics in Revelation 19:1-10," in *Studies in the Book of Revelation*, ed. Steve Moyise (Edinburgh and New York: T&T Clark, 2001), 69-84.

27. Nowhere, for instance, does Revelation ever mention or describe the worship of the Christian church. Cf. Daly, *Christian Sacrifice*, 297, 304, 307.

28. Ruiz, "Praise and Politics in Revelation 19:1-10," 84.

29. Everett Ferguson, *Backgrounds of Early Christianity* (Grand Rapids, Mich.: Wm. B. Eerdmans, 1987), 144.

30. See "Sacrifice Traditions" in Johns, *The Lamb Christology of the Apocalypse of John*, 62-5.

31. See the discussion in Raymond Schwager, "Christ's Death and the Prophetic Critique of Sacrifice," trans. P. Riordan, *Semeia* 33 (1985): 120.

32. "The connection between the shedding of the Lamb's blood and redemption from sin . . . [is] somewhat problematic." See Charles E. Hill, "Atonement in the Apocalypse of John," in *The Glory of the Atonement: Biblical, Historical and Practical Perspectives, Essays in Honor of Roger Nicole*, ed. Charles E. Hill and Frank A. James, III (Downers Grove, Ill.: InterVarsity Press, 2004), 200. See my discussion of these matters in Johns, *The Lamb Christology of the Apocalypse of John*, esp. p. 30.

33. Gary A. Anderson, "Sacrifice and Sacrificial Offerings (Old Testament)," in *Anchor Bible Dictionary*, ed. David Noel Freedman (New York: Doubleday, 1992), 5.879.

34. See Moses Maimonides, *The Guide for the Perplexed: Translated from the Original Arabic Text* (New York: Dover Publications), 325. See also Anderson,

"Sacrifice," 5.871; and Jacob Neusner, et al., *The Encyclopedia of Judaism* (New York: Continuum, 1999), 2.532. For a more thorough and appreciative consideration of Maimonides' theology of sacrifice, see Josef Stern, *Problems and Parables of Law: Maimonides and Nahmanides on Reasons for the Commandments* (Ta`Amei Ha-Mitzvot) (Albany, N.Y.: State University of New York, 1989).

35. Maimonides, *The Guide for the Perplexed*, 326.
36. David E. Aune, *Revelation 1–5* (Dallas: Word Books, 1997), 372.
37. Aune, *Revelation 1–5*, 372; cf. also C. H. Dodd, "Messiah," chap. 9 in *The Interpretation of the Fourth Gospel* (London: Cambridge University Press, 1960), 230-8.
38. Aune, *Revelation 1–5*, 372.
39. Aune, *Revelation 1–5*, 373.
40. Cf. Johns, *The Lamb Christology of the Apocalypse of John*, 129.
41. See "René Girard and Mimetic Desire" below.
42. See Bauckham, "Prayer in the Book of Revelation," 260-61.
43. Cf. Johns, *The Lamb Christology of the Apocalypse of John*, 31-2, 38-9.
44. Bauckham, *The Theology of the Book of Revelation*, 73.
45. D. R. Carnegie, "Worthy is the Lamb: The Hymns in Revelation," in *Christ the Lord: Studies in Christology Presented to Donald Guthrie*, ed. Harold H. Rowdon (Downers Grove, Il.: InterVarsity Press, 1982), 246–7.
46. Cf. Johns, *The Lamb Christology of the Apocalypse of John*, 130.
47. Although some manuscripts have *louō* ("washed") instead of *lyō*, Metzger strongly prefers the originality of the latter "because it has superior manuscript support ... because it is in accord with Old Testament imagery (e. g. is 40.2 LXX); and because it suits better the idea expressed in ver. 6a. The reading *lousanti*, which may have been pronounced like *lysanti*, seems to have arisen 'due to failure to understand the Hebraic use of *en* to denote a price and a natural misapplication of 7.14' (Hort, 'Notes on Select Readings,' ad loc.)." See Metzger, *A Textual Commentary on the Greek New Testament: A Companion Volume to the United Bible Societies' Greek New Testament (3d ed.)*, 662.
48. Hill, "Atonement in the Apocalypse of John," 192.
49. In addition to what follows here, see fn. 23 above.
50. Matt Goldish, *Judaism in the Theology of Sir Isaac Newton* (Dordrecht, The Netherlands: Kluwer Academic Publishers, 1998), 96.
51. Johannes Pedersen, *Israel: Its Life and Culture* (reprint, 1926-40; Atlanta: Scholars Press, 1991) In contrast, Stephen Finlan has more recently argued that although "it will not do to be dogmatic and to insist that there were no penal ideas in Hebrew sacrifice, ... it is true that the clear expressions of this idea are all late (rabbinic)." See Finlan, *Background and Content*, 163.
52. Ronald Ernest Clements, *A Century of Old Testament Study* (Guildford, England: Lutterworth, 1976), 150-1.
53. Austin M[arsden] Farrer, *A Rebirth of Images: The Making of St. John's Apocalypse* (Albany, NY: State University of New York Press, 1986).
54. John Ben-Daniel and Gloria Ben-Daniel, *The Apocalypse in the Light of the Temple: A New Approach to the Book of Revelation* (Jerusalem: Beit Yochanan, 2003).
55. Ben-Daniel and Ben-Daniel, *The Apocalypse in the Light of the Temple*, 30.

56. Roy B. Zuck, *A Biblical Theology of the New Testament: From Members of Dallas Theological Faculty* (Chicago: Moody Press, 1994), 212; cf. also 215.

57. Ronald F. Youngblood, ed., *Nelson's New Illustrated Bible Dictionary* (Nashville: Thomas Nelson, 1995), s.v. "Lamb of God".

58. G[regory] K. Beale, *The Book of Revelation: A Commentary on the Greek Text*, in *The New International Greek Testament Commentary*, ed. I. Howard Marshall and Donald A. Hagner (Grand Rapids, Mich.: Eerdmans, 1999), 660.

59. Bauckham, *Climax of Prophecy*, 229.

60. Hill, "Atonement in the Apocalypse of John."

61. James G. Williams, ed., *The Girard Reader* (New York: Crossroad, 1996), 292.

62. Williams, *The Girard Reader*, 292.

63. Weaver, *The Nonviolent Atonement*, 48.

64. As one example, the Book of Revelation is not even mentioned once in the issue of *Semeia* devoted to the work of René Girard: A. McKenna, ed., *René Girard and Biblical Studies* (Atlanta: Scholars Press, 1985).

65. See Mark R. Bredin, "Hate Never Dispelled Hate: No Place for the *Pharmakos*," *Biblical Theology Bulletin* (Fall 2004), 105-13. See also Mark Bredin, *Jesus, Revolutionary of Peace*, esp. 16-19.

66. Raymund Schwager, *Must There be Scapegoats? Violence and Redemption in the Bible* (San Francisco: Harper & Row, 1987), esp. 218-9.

67. Ted Grimsrud, "Scapegoating No More: Christian Pacifism and New Testament Understandings of the Death of Jesus," in *Violence Renounced: René Girard, Biblical Studies, and Peacemaking*, ed. Willard M. Swartley (Telford, Pa.: Pandora Press, 1994), 49-69; see esp. 61-64.

68. Judith Kovacs and Christopher Rowland, *Revelation: The Apocalypse of Jesus Christ* (Malden, Mass.: Blackwell Publishing Ltd., 2004), 79-80.

69. Finamore's book is a revision of his 1997 doctoral dissertation at Oxford. See Stephen Finamore, *God, Order and Chaos: René Girard and the Apocalypse* (Paternoster Press, 2006). In addition, see Paul S. Fiddes, *The Promised End: Eschatology in Theology and Literature* (Oxford: Blackwell, 2000), 19, and n. 57.

70. Cf. René Girard, *Things Hidden Since the Foundation of the World* (Stanford: Stanford University Press, 1987), 185, 253-62.

71. Girard, *Things Hidden Since the Foundation of the World*, 186.

72. Cf., e.g., Robert Hamerton-Kelly, ed., *Violent Origins: Walter Burkert, René Girard, and Jonathan K. Smith on Ritual Killing and Cultural Formation* (Stanford: Stanford University Press, 1987), 142-3.

73. Henry George Liddell, comp., "*Pharmakos*," in *A Greek-English Lexicon: With a Supplement*. ed., rev. and augm. throughout by Henry Stuart Jones, et. al., (Oxford: Clarendon Press, 1968). For an explanation of how Greek religions ignorant of Israel's religions expressed their own understandings of the scapegoat mechanism, see Gerhard Friedrich, ed., Geoffrey W. Bromiley, trans., *Theological Dictionary of the New Testament*, vol. 5 (Grand Rapids, Mich.: Wm. B. Eerdmans, 1967), s.v. *peripsēma*, 6.84-93.

74. Cf. also James Moffatt, *A Critical and Exegetical Commentary on the Epistle to the Hebrews* (Edinburgh: T&T Clark, 1924), 34.

75. See also 1 Cor. 4:13, where Paul may be claiming that he has been a scapegoat of the world, and the terms *katharos* and *peripsēma* in *Theological Dictionary of the New Testament*, ed. Gerhard Kittel, trans. Geoffrey W. Bromiley (Grand Rapids, Mich.: Wm. B. Eerdmans, 1964–76), 3:413-31 and 6:84-93. For "scapegoat" in translation of 1 Cor. 4:13, see Walter Bauer, *A Greek-English Lexicon of the New Testament and Other Early Christian Literature*, 3rd. ed.; ed. Frederick W. Danker (Chicago: University of Chicago, 1999), s.v. *perikatharma*.

76. Liddell, *"Pharmakos."*

77. Bredin, "Hate Never Dispelled Hate," 112.

78. Michael Harris apparently issued such a critique already in 1988 in Michael A. Harris, "Deceit, Desire, and Violence: A Critique of Girard's Reading of the Apocalypse," unpublished paper (Society of Biblical Literature, 1988). For an introduction to ideology criticism of the Bible, see David Jobling and Tina Pippin, eds., *Ideological Criticism of Biblical Texts* (Atlanta: Society of Biblical Literature, 1993).

79. See Robert M. Royalty Jr., "The Rhetoric of Revelation," in *Society of Biblical Literature 1997 Seminar Papers* (Atlanta: Scholars Press, 1997), 596-617; Robert M. Royalty Jr., *The Streets of Heaven: The Ideology of Wealth in the Apocalypse of John* (Macon, Ga.: Mercer University Press, 1998); esp. 125-133; and especially Robert M. Royalty Jr., "Don't Touch This Book!: Revelation 22:18-19 and the Rhetoric of Reading (in) the Apocalypse of John," *Biblical Interpretation* 12/3 (2004): 282-99.

80. Paul Brooks Duff, *Who Rides the Beast? Prophetic Rivalry and the Rhetoric of Crisis in the Churches of the Apocalypse* (Oxford; New York: Oxford University Press, 2001).

81. Tina Pippin, *Death and Desire: The Rhetoric of Gender in the Apocalypse of John* (Louisville: Westminster/John Knox Press, 1992). See also Tina Pippin, "The Heroine and the Whore: Fantasy and the Female in the Apocalypse of John," *Semeia*, no. 60 (1992): 67-82; Tina Pippin, "Eros and the End: Reading for Gender in the Apocalypse of John," *Semeia* 59 (1992): 193-217; and Tina Pippin, "Jezebel Re-Vamped," *Semeia 69/70: Intertextuality and the Bible* (1995): 221-34.

82. Greg Carey, *Elusive Apocalypse: Reading Authority in the Revelation to John* (Macon: Mercer University Press, 1999); and L. Gregory Bloomquist and Greg Carey, eds., *Vision and Persuasion: Rhetorical Dimensions of Apocalyptic Discourse* (St. Louis, Mo.: Chalice Press, 1999).

83. Although Elisabeth Schüssler Fiorenza's reading of the Apocalypse is fundamentally rhetorical, her readings emphasize the constructive ethical message of the text, rather than the problematic ethos created by the author's argument. Although she considers the feminine images in Revelation to be problematic, even misogynistic, she believes that they can and should be "translated" into appropriate symbols and images for our own day. See Fiorenza, *The Book of Revelation: Justice and Judgment*, esp. 199; and Fiorenza, *Revelation: Vision of a Just World*. Similarly, although Leonard Thompson's rhetorical criticism led him to deny the existence of any outside threat or crisis at all behind Revelation, his reading does not lean in the direction of ideology criticism. See Leonard L. Thompson, *The Book of Revelation: Apocalypse and*

Empire (New York, Oxford: Oxford University Press, 1990).

84. Duff, *Who Rides the Beast?* 82.

85. See Duff, *Who Rides the Beast?* 14.

86. Cf. Royalty Jr., "Don't Touch This Book!"

87. See Carey, *Elusive Apocalypse* and Steve Moyise, "The Apocalypse and Its Ambiguous Ethos," in *Studies in the Book of Revelation*, in *Studies in the Book of Revelation*, ed. Steve Moyise (Edinburgh and New York: T&T Clark, 2001), 163-80.

88. I use the word *spiritualization* here with some caution: not in the sense of radical dematerialization, but rather in the sense of pursuing the inner, spiritual, or ethical significance of the Hebrew Temple workshop. See the comments of Robert J. Daly regarding the limits and usefulness of the word *spiritualization*. Daly, *Christian Sacrifice*, 4-5.

89. "The 'battle' depicted between forces of God and forces of Satan [in Rev. 12] was really the confrontation *in history* between the church, the earthly institution that represented the rule of God, and the Roman empire, the earthly structure used to symbolize the rule of Satan. The so-called cosmic battle was really imagery that gave . . . cosmic significance [to] the confrontation between the Roman empire and Jesus and his church." See Weaver, "Violence in Christian Theology," 165.

Part 3

THE WORK OF JESUS IN ANABAPTISM

CHAPTER SEVEN

RETRIEVING HISTORIC ANABAPTIST CHRISTOLOGY FOR CONTEMPORARY ANABAPTIST THEOLOGY

Thomas N. Finger

*A*mong J. Denny Weaver's contributions to contemporary Anabaptist theology is his notion of *two lists*. When Anabaptists theologize, Weaver shows, they often take doctrines from a *standard mainline theology*, or one *list*; and ethics from another, *distinctively Anabaptist*, list. But surely, Weaver observes, our ethical efforts to obey God will be influenced by our theological understanding of God's character.

Weaver is most concerned about the tension between the ethics of nonviolence and the doctrine of satisfaction, or substitutionary, atonement. Weaver insists that divine violence is "intrinsic to any and all forms of satisfaction. . . ."[1] Consequently, people who unreflectively accept both teachings can fall into inconsistencies—like practicing forgiveness in personal relationships but supporting their governments in wars.

Weaver connects satisfaction (formulated by Anselm in 1098), at least indirectly, with the classical Christology exemplified by the

Nicene Creed (381) and the Chalcedonian Definition (451). He calls all three products of "Constantinianism," or of an imperial Christianity that suppressed Jesus' ethics and legitimated state violence. In contrast to satisfaction, Weaver champions a "narrative Christus Victor" approach to atonement. His association of substitution with classical Christology implies that Christus Victor is at least somewhat discordant with classical Christology.

Although Weaver does not base his theology on Anabaptist historiography, he has worked in this field and values its discoveries. Yet despite his efforts to link doctrine with ethics, this discipline has often conveyed the impression that what I will call *historic Anabaptism* (from roughly 1525-1575) was not concerned with theology, but only with practical matters—or *one list*. At present, though, some historians like Arnold Snyder are arguing that historic Anabaptist practice was deeply informed by theology. Nonetheless, Snyder claims that "In matters of doctrine . . . Anabaptism was not very unique. Anabaptists tended to repeat what the early radical reformers had already said."[2] Boiled down to the popular level, this means not only that "Anabaptists doctrines were not . . . very distinctive," but that today's Anabaptists should contribute their "'practical spirituality'" to ecumenical discussions and learn about "theological reflection" from others.[3] While Snyder hopes that such an exchange will encourage Anabaptists to theologize, his distinction, reflecting a common outlook in his field, could legitimate the two lists approach today. For if historic Anabaptists borrowed their doctrines from others, why should their heirs not do the same? This distinction, moreover, leads one to expect that historical Anabaptism will yield rich ethical insights, but little doctrinal creativity or variety.

In Christology this *two lists* approach often seems to operate as follows. Some historians assume that Christology means classical Christology. In asking whether historic Anabaptists had a Christology, they search for classical concepts and titles (or for their refutation). Robert Friedmann, for instance, noticed that Anabaptist writers occasionally used such terms, and that ordinary Anabaptists affirmed the creeds when put on trial for denying them. These comparatively rare references to classical Christology (a first list item) meant that it was "not the center, the decisive element in this faith . . ." Decisive instead was a second list theme: "the model of the life of Christ and . . . His death on the cross."[4]

In this essay, I want to challenge the two lists approach to historic Anabaptist Christology. I can only begin that task, since space considerations limit me to two writers: Balthasar Hubmaier and Peter Riedemann.[5] In the process, I will draw implications for current Anabaptist Christology, including those atonement issues crucial for Weaver.

To help our approach to the material, I will begin by asking how well it falls into Christology's traditional distinctions between Jesus' *person* and his *work*, and among three models of the Jesus' work (atonement): *substitution* (or satisfaction), *moral influence* and *Christus Victor*. I will employ these categories provisionally, however, to spot not only data which fits them but also that which does not. Our two historic Anabaptists Christologies (those of Hubmaier and Riedemann) will be seen eventually to overflow these traditional distinctions. Weaver, in contrast, insists that the three atonement models are "separate and distinct approaches" and strongly opposes attempts to integrate them.[6]

BALTHASAR HUBMAIER

The Person of Jesus Christ

Hubmaier was the most educated early Anabaptist leader by far. If we are to find classical christological terms anywhere, it should be in his writings. Indeed, we read that Jesus Christ was "God and Lord" (397), "God and Savior" (237), "true God" (538, 539), and also "true God and man" (236, 539). He existed "from eternity" (105). Presently, his risen, bodily humanity is in heaven, but his deity is omnipresent (415, cf. 336).[7] Yet such classical terms are relatively few, scattered through Hubmaier's corpus.

Hubmaier's last writing, however, urged Christians not simply to recite but to thoroughly understand these expressions, since many "bad Christians" were claiming "that Christ is not God" (539). Hubmaier penned this from prison to the Austrian King Ferdinand. Yet he was not simply agreeing as much as possible with Catholic orthodoxy in hopes of saving his neck. More specifically, Hubmaier was being charged with teaching that "Christ is not God, but a prophet, to whom the speech or word of God was commanded"; and that "Christ has not atoned for the sin of the whole world."

These were two of the "Nikolsburg Articles," whose origins are much debated.[8] However, most scholars now think that they do not express Hubmaier's own views but rather are his representation of the views of his radical apocalyptic antagonist, Hans Hut, when they debated in May 1527. Charged with these teachings in January 1528, Hubmaier repudiated them strongly, as did Hut (542-543, 556). Yet as Weaver rightly concludes, these Articles did not accurately express Hut's theology but rather Hubmaier's understanding of what it implied.[9] This indicates that Hubmaier strongly opposed challenges to classical Christology, real and imagined, throughout his career, even though he seldom explicated it in his writings.

But if so, why did not Hubmaier employ traditional conceptuality more often? Most likely, because he was strongly influenced by late medieval nominalism, which resisted speculation about divine nature and intra-divine relationships, and focused instead on God's revealed will.[10] Hubmaier was far less interested in titles for, and general claims about, Jesus than in his dynamic, salvific activity.

Might we, then, discover a genuine Christology in Hubmaier—a significant understanding of who Jesus is and was and what he did and does—not mainly by searching for classical conceptions of Christ's nature, but by focusing on his action and power? At first glance, this route seems unpromising. Hubmaier claimed that Jesus' bodily humanity was in heaven, which meant it could not be present in the Lord's Supper, and that churches must be responsible for discipline and virtually all other affairs since Jesus no longer affected these directly.[11] Even though Christ's deity was somehow omnipresent, was not his risen reality too remote to exercise any action or power? Yes—with one striking exception. To examine this exception, we must cross the traditional division between Christ's *person* and *work*.

The risen Jesus, according to Hubmaier, called, rebuked, comforted, and bestowed salvation through the preached Word. Hubmaier could represent this preached message as Jesus' own personal address, saying, "Believe the gospel that clearly shows that I am . . . the only giver of mercy, reconciler, intercessor, mediator and peacemaker toward God." This speaker was "the Samaritan . . . Christ Jesus" who "brings along medicine, namely wine and oil, which he pours into the wounds of the sinner. Wine: he leads the person to repentance. . . . He brings oil, by which he softens his pain and drives it away."[12]

"The Word," then, on one level, was the preached message of salvation, sent by the risen Christ and pointing to him. However, this Word exercised judgment and bestowed pardon and new life directly enough to function, quite often, less like a message about Jesus than as Jesus himself.[13] Hubmaier, indeed, could render this identification explicit, referring to "the preached Word of God, which is God himself and which has become human," citing John 1:14.[14]

However, since nominalist Hubmaier focused on the divine will and resisted speculation about divine nature, might this Word have been not the risen Jesus, but one mode, or expression, of a single divine will? Further examination of salvation's dynamics, or of atonement's continuing operation, indicates that people are called and regenerated in "two forms, outwardly and inwardly" (362). Outwardly, they are awakened, convicted, pardoned, and granted new life by the Word, while the Spirit draws, convinces, and enlivens them from within.[15] In Hubmaier's portrayals of so intimate a transformation, activities of Word and Spirit sometimes overlapped. Yet the overall process involved direct interaction and cooperation between two distinct agents—not differing phases or modes of a single force.

In many writings, then, Hubmaier indicated that both the risen Son[16] and the Spirit were involved in atonement's present operation. A similar distinction between the Son and the Father emerged in Hubmaier's sophisticated discussion of the freedom of the will. Many theologians who denied human freedom championed predestination, which stemmed from God's eternal omniscience and will. Hubmaier critiqued predestination in nominalist fashion, for peering into secrets beyond the range of revelation and human comprehension. He acknowledged that God's omnipotent, hidden will could damn people before they were born.[17]

However, theology cannot be based on God's hidden will but only on "the revealed and preached will of God . . ." For this will is "God himself . . . which has become human . . . as the only begotten Son of the Father" (473-474). "We should listen to the incarnated God . . . and not concern ourselves with . . . investigating further God's omnipotence, omniscience, and eternal foreknowledge. . ."(467). Here, for Hubmaier, Christ himself functions as God's will revealed in his historical life, much like he does as God's Word, revealed in preaching.

Hubmaier also conceptualized the distinction between God's revealed and hidden wills as one between God's facing or conversive, and God's withdrawing or aversive, wills (475). Yet he acknowledged that talk of two wills is a concession to human finitude and ignorance. Only one will really exists in God (473, 475). Did this possibly mean that the distinction between two wills, which Hubmaier associated with the Father and the Son, really designated modes of a single will? To answer fully, we must consider Jesus' historical *work*, especially the roles of Father and Son.

To prepare for this, let us, before formally leaving Christ's *person*, ask this: What was Jesus' *human nature* like? Hubmaier held that all other people are "conceived and born in sin" (361, 434, 518). Jesus, though, was not, and this entailed significant socio-political consequences. While Hubmaier often seemed optimistic about salvific transformation, it was limited by this difference between Jesus and us. For this kept us from participating in his "nature,"[18] through which he alone belonged to that kingdom which is "not of this world."[19] The rest of us are stuck in the sinful kingdom of this world "right up to our ears" until we die (434, 497, cf. 242). For this reason, Hubmaier argued, even Christians must be governed by "the sword" and can be rulers who wield the sword when necessary.

What has this investigation yielded so far? Had we limited it to Hubmaier's use of classical expressions and titles, we might have concluded that, yes, he affirmed these—but seldom enough that Christology was "not the center, the decisive element" for him. But recognizing Hubmaier's nominalist distaste for talk of "natures" and intra-divine relations, we shifted to atonement's continuing dynamics and thereby the divine will. We found that the divine Word and the revealed divine Will were central there. We have, in fact, already crossed the line between Jesus' person and work. Let us now turn to the latter's earthly phases.

The Atoning Work of Jesus Christ

As we might expect, Hubmaier cited Jesus' teachings often. He affirmed, generally, that the way to union with God's will is to hold "Jesus before our eyes and follow his life and teaching. . ." (468). Yet Hubmaier almost never brought Jesus' behavior into view.[20] Before his passion, Jesus' only significant function, apparently, was giving commands. The most important of these were not ethical principles but directives for Anabaptist church practices of believers' baptism, discipline, and the Lord's Supper. Hubmaier also emphasized Jesus' teachings on biblical authority, on keeping his commands, and on himself, as Christ and Son of God, as the church's foundation.[21]

Hubmaier frequently cited the Sermon on the Mount—but often to counter interpretations which forbade wielding the sword.[22] These arguments undergirded his broadest affirmation about Jesus' work during his life: Jesus came not to pass judgment on civil matters but "to save people by the Word" (500). But if Hubmaier linked Jesus' life loosely to his atoning work, it was quite otherwise with Jesus' death and resurrection.

Hubmaier's understanding corresponded at points with each traditional atonement model. Like substitutionary theorists, Hubmaier believed that all humans, because they fail to meet God's demands, deserve "eternal damnation" (145). To elaborate this, Hubmaier used many concepts common to substitution. Jesus' death procured forgiveness by making *satisfaction* (236, 332), or paying our *debt* (236, 332, 347, 348) with his "crimson blood" (330, cf. 332). Jesus acquired *merit* which draws the Father to look favorably on us (443, 444, 468). Since we could not produce the righteousness demanded by God's *law*, Jesus' "foreign righteousness" delivered us.[23]

Many such passages, however, intermix these themes with those common to moral influence. While God the Father did demand a price, which his Son painfully paid, Jesus' death manifested, much more centrally, the Father's love in sending his Son. This "sacrifice" of his Son for "payment" of sins, the believer confesses, "has so moved, softened and penetrated my spirit and soul" that I am ready to offer myself for others (399-400, cf. 404). The cross, which revealed God's "grace and kindness" (117), draws our prayers to the "gracious," "merciful" and "tender" Father (242), who is "good, gentle, benevolent and merciful ... who carries, protects and shields us as ... his child...."[24] In fact, faith itself is "the realization of the unspeakable mercy of God, his gracious favor and goodwill ... through his most beloved Son" for he "delivered him to death for our sakes that sin might be paid for, and we might be reconciled to him..."(348, cf. 32, 85, 146). At the same time, Jesus' "distress, torture and bitter dying" revealed his own "greatest and highest love..." (236, cf. 355, 395).

If all versions of substitution portray "God as either divine avenger or punisher and/or as a child abuser"[25] and "*depend on God-induced and God-directed violence,*"[26] as Weaver claims; and if, further, the traditional atonement models are "separate and distinct approaches,"[27] how could Hubmaier employ multiple substitutionary concepts but chiefly emphasize something like moral influence?

The main clue, I think, appears in one definition of faith: confidence in God "through the favor, grace, and good will which God the Father has for his most-beloved Son...."[28] The Father, that is, is "gracious and favorable to you through the grace and favor which he has toward Christ" (145). In other words, the main relationship between Father and Son is one of favor and love. Although the Father sent his Son to pay sin's painful price, the basic relationship between Father and Son was never altered. This relationship, which Hubmaier derived not from speculation but from historical revelation, and the fact that atonement draws us into it, is a major reason why Father and Son must be distinct agents, not modes of a single will.[29]

Hubmaier's atonement theology, then, overflowed substitutionary and moral influence categories, and combined aspects of each which seem to clash. Moreover, features common to the third historic model also appeared often, sometimes intermixed with the other two.

Christus Victor imagery occasionally functioned like, and was perhaps reducible to, substitution. To call sin an unpayable debt is similar to envisioning people bound in a "debtors prison" (347), or as captives to "sin, the devil, hell, and eternal death" (242, cf. 496-497). To call atonement release from debt is similar to calling it release from jail and these jailers. Hubmaier consequently could affirm, in the same breath, that Jesus had "paid and done satisfaction" and then led prisoners "mightily out of captivity" (236); and also that "the Law is now fulfilled in Christ, who has paid the debt" and "vanquished death, devil, and hell" (347).

Nevertheless, victory involved more than removing the death penalty. Victory also brought captives to life. Hubmaier accordingly highlighted an event minimized by substitution and moral influence, yet magnified in Christus Victor: Jesus' resurrection. Jesus, Hubmaier stressed, not only forgave us through his death but also justified and made us righteous through his resurrection.[30] Resurrection and Christus Victor themes combined in Jesus' descent to hell, to free the partriarchs imprisoned there. Jesus proclaimed that he had "paid and done satisfaction" for sins. Yet this, by itself, did not release these prisoners. Jesus also needed to rise from their prison and lead "them mightily out of captivity" (226, cf. 347-348).

Resurrection and Christus Victor also joined when Hubmaier explained salvation another way, via a tripartite anthropology. In this schema, the human *spirit* had never participated in "the Fall" but always remained wholly good and oriented toward God. The *soul*, however, had been assigned the task of obeying either the *spirit* or the *body*. Originally, the *soul* turned toward the latter and its desires, and "lost the knowledge of good and evil" and all ability to do good (438). At present, then, the *spirit*, though still upright, is "a prisoner in the body" (434) which can only "cry as a captive to God without ceasing...."(438) The *soul's* and *spirit's* bondage to the *body* imprisons the whole person under sin, death, and the devil. When sin is conceptualized this way, Hubmaier insisted, salvation "must, must, must take place through a new birth..." (445, cf. 361, 431).

This new birth occurs through the process described above: the interaction of Word and Spirit. Resurrection was necessary to free Jesus to operate through (and even as) the Word, empowered by the Spirit, who had largely withdrawn from the world due to sin.[31]

This atonement process centers on the soul. The spirit needs no atonement, since it never sinned. It is, however, liberated from the negative effects of its prison, the body, and this "renders flesh, sin, death, devil and hell harmless."[32] The body, or flesh, however, "irretrievably lost its goodness" long ago, and is only capable of sin (433). It must continue to bear its penalty, to "suffer and return again to earth" (441), and anticipate transformation only in the next life.

Through this new birth the soul is made whole by God's "dear Son, and enlightened by the Holy Spirit" (439). They teach the soul to recognize good and evil again, and render its weaknesses "harmless, unless it follows evil wantonly" (446). Hubmaier could affirm that the soul "can will and choose good, as well as ... in Paradise."[33] This optimism may be inconsistent with his pessimistic arguments that Christians need discipline by the sword. In any case, as we noticed while considering Christ's *person*, this continuing victory over sin through divine, transforming energy was atonement's most important feature for Hubmaier.

PETER RIEDEMANN

Unlike Hubmaier, Peter Riedemann, co-leader of the Hutterites 1542-1556, was neither theologically trained, nor did he occasionally write on sophisticated levels. Riedemann nevertheless penned two confessions of faith, completed in 1532 and 1542, which Hutterites quickly accepted as guides to their belief and practice. The first was much briefer, and employed few technical concepts.[34] Yet Riedemann's second confession addressed some classical issues in classical ways, even though in popular vocabulary. It was structured around the Apostles' Creed at the beginning and organized in clear logical fashion throughout. This more formal approach was occasioned, in part, by external challenges: to explain Hutterite faith to the Lutheran Prince, Philip of Hesse,[35] and to address the challenge of Melchiorite Christology.[36] Yet the Hutterites' acceptance of both confessions strongly suggests that the second did not deviate much from the first, but explicated its basic convictions more fully.

The Person of Jesus Christ

Early on, Riedemann tackled a classical issue: if there is only one God, how could Christ be divine?[37] Echoing a common classical solution, he replied that God is Truth—not abstract truth, but in an active, living way. To be such, this Truth must express itself, or speak a Word which does not really separate from It, but always remains with and in its source.[38] In traditional terms, these will both share "one power and one essence (*eine Kraft . . . und ein Wesen*)," though they have two names.[39] In other words, the Word or Son is never without the Father, nor is the Father ever without the Son (64). From this traditional formulation, however, Riedemann drew an untraditional conclusion: Since neither Father nor Son has anything for himself, but shares all he has with the other, we should surrender all private property and share everything with each other (119, cf. 80, 204).[40]

Since the Son, or Word, comes from the Father in this unique way, he is by no means a creature (66). All things were created, presently exist, and will be completed in him (64). He is also "the brightness of the Father's glory and the image of his nature" (66). God, through the Word, created humans "in his own image," to be "his dwelling place" (171). The divine Truth "pours itself into believing souls, making them like, similar and conformable to itself."[41]

Already we can see that Riedemann's straightforward handling of divine nature and relations, though mostly in popular terms, differed markedly from Hubmaier's nominalism. This last quotation, moreover, suggests a poetic exuberance, quite unlike Hubmaier's more sober explications.[42] Riedemann also poured this exuberance into forty-six songs[43] and about forty-one letters, many expressing a profound pastoral sensitivity.[44]

To describe Jesus' *person* further, we must, as with Hubmaier, begin crossing the line between Jesus' person and work. When approached through traditional atonement models, Hubmaier approximated Christus Victor slightly more often than moral influence or substitution. Riedemann, however, when assessed in this way, clearly prioritized the first. Sin corrupted people and brought them under God's wrath. But more basically, sin rendered them powerless to escape sin, death, and their demonic agents. Death, however, could only be overcome by divine power.[45] Power, for Riedemann, was probably God's primary attribute (59, 86), and the Son was the "unparalleled power of God" (66). This theme not only shaped Riedemann's notion of Christ's deity but also his account of Christ's humanity.

With classical Christology, Riedemann spoke of Jesus' human and divine *natures*[46] and affirmed that he was "a genuine and real person, who was tempted and tested in all things, yet without sin" (69, cf. 181). Nevertheless, since the rest of us are conceived through "the seed of man and woman . . . in the weakness of the flesh," it was necessary that Christ, to do away with sin, be "conceived in the power of God" (68). This, however, made him "a different human being" who "completed his life in the power of God. . . ." Despite Riedemann's acknowledgment that Jesus was tempted, he lacked "any inclination to sin" (69).

Further, even though Jesus, through being tempted, "knows our weakness" (72), Riedemann seemed to consider weakness, which renders us unable to escape death and the powers, nearly equivalent to sin. Although the Word "stripped himself of radiant glory" (72) and became "a poor and lowly servant" (71), he retained the fullness of his divine nature and lived through its power (65, 69). Consequently, when he took "human nature upon himself" and joined it to his divine nature, the weakness of this human nature died.[47] On the cross, it perished completely. The divine nature even withdrew from Jesus and "forsook the human nature" (69-70). Did this mean that the risen Jesus is no longer human and has no body? This seems unlikely, for Riedemann insisted, like Hubmaier, that Jesus' risen body is in heaven, thus located in some sort of place, and cannot be in the Eucharist.[48] Riedemann's main point was that Jesus' resurrection filled him with divine power. When the risen Jesus dwells in people, this power enables them to escape their powerless captivity (74).

The Atoning Work of Jesus Christ

This discussion of Jesus' human *nature*, an essential component of his *person*, has already drawn us into his atoning work, as happened with Hubmaier. If we approach this theme, initially, by looking for simililarities to the three historic models, we find Riedemann, like Hubmaier, using expressions resembling substitution, though less often. Riedemann could say that Jesus "bought us with his own blood" (67), and provided atonement for our sins (72), so that they are not held against us (74). He even mentioned the Father laying our sins upon his Son, though he immediately averred that "our sins"—evidently not the Father directly—"have crucified him" (70).

But while God "has discounted, remitted, forgiven" sins in Christ, Riedemann quickly added, like Hubmaier, that he also "offered himself to me in Christ as Father," indeed, "as my utterly beloved Father, who will always seek . . . the very best for me" (196). Riedemann sometimes blended "substitutionary" expressions with "moral influence" expressions. However, he portrayed atonement as the revelation of God's love less often than Hubmaier.

On the other hand, Riedemann combined Jesus' teachings with his example more frequently than Hubmaier, integrating Jesus' ministry more clearly into his *work*. Jesus came preaching his Father's will and seeking the lost, as we must do. "He gathered those who already belonged to the Father and led them into the liberty of an heir . . . so that they would become like Christ [and] conform to his image in complete obedience to his Father. . ."(181-182). Christ continues to instruct us "by his nature, manner and character, so that he may become increasingly known to all people" (66). Surely, then, we should keep and teach others "to keep all the Lord's commands" (185).

Specifically, Jesus taught us not to repay evil for evil, but to love and forgive our enemies. This means that Christians can never go to war.[49] For when Christ "begins to work in people, he causes them to do nothing but what he himself did during his life on earth. . ." (134, cf. 222). This includes forgoing "acquiring things and holding property" (120). Such behavior was as essential as the others to deliverance from evil powers—or the overall Christus Victor theme. Why?

God, as mentioned above, created people to be "his dwelling place" (171); God seeks to pour himself "into believing souls, making them like, similar and conformable" to Godself.[50] Sin, conversely, involves filling ourselves with things other than God. Now God created the goods of the earth to be shared by all (63, 87, 119-120). Yet humans were not content with God's gifts, and sin, which "has its source and origin in wrong taking," arose.[51] That is, people began acquiring things for themselves and "vehement quarreling" broke out, "one wanting this, and the other that," which led to perpetual strife (92, cf. 119). Rather than being filled with God, people seek to fill themselves with created goods and comforts. They are glutted with the possessiveness, lies, and injustice necessary to attain and maintain such things (90, cf. 159). Those who were created to be God's temple "instead become a dwelling place of idols and all unclean spirits."[52]

How, precisely, do these evil forces inhabit and bind people? Chiefly through these sins themselves. These are the devil's snares.[53] By filling us with lust, envy, and aggression, they empty us of God's grace and render us too weak to resist these impulses. How, then, does Jesus release us from this bondage, and at-one us with God? Chiefly, much as Hubmaier said: when he, along with the Holy Spirit, fills us with his righteousness, power, and life, which drive out sin, weakness, and death. In this way, we again become God's dwelling.[54]

Riedemann nearly always described this atonement process in the present. He often traced its immediate origin, like Hubmaier, to the Spirit's operation through the preached Word.[55] But since Riedemann showed, more clearly than Hubmaier, how Jesus' life initiated the overall process, Riedemann helps us perceive atonement more comprehensively, as leading the human race back to God (176). We are directly planted or grafted into our true inheritance (61), into our heavenly nature (155) and into Christ's divine nature and character (135). But how did Jesus' death and resurrection conquer the Satanic forces?

Riedemann highlighted Jesus' destruction of their power.[56] This is connected with his theme of human weakness perishing in Jesus. For weakness, apparently more than anything else, subjects sinners to the powers' strength. Yet I cannot find Riedemann clearly indicating, congruently with what we call Christus Victor, how the cross overcame this. Was human weakness in some way abolished on the cross and replaced with resurrection power? If so, I cannot find Riedemann making such a process, or its operation, explicit.[57]

From another perspective, humans become subject to the powers' strength when God, in wrath against sin, hands people over to them (91, 133, 171, 223). Perhaps, then, Jesus' death triumphed in a more substitutionary way, as for Hubmaier. By satisfying that wrath, or paying its penalty, Jesus would have removed this barrier to his Father, reopening the channel to overflowing goodness and mercy[58]—not to an angry, violent parent.

But if the rationale for Jesus' death was somewhat vague, at least in light of traditional models, the function of his resurrection was not. Here God's strength over evil clearly triumphed, investing Jesus with royal status and power which enabled him, through his Spirit, to transmit divine strength to us, much as Hubmaier said.[59] It is this "power and strength" which ultimately overcomes "death, the world, sin and the devil" (64).

This continuing atonement, however, was more thorough than Hubmaier's. When the Holy Spirit grafts people into the risen Christ, they become, in Riedemann's poetic phrases, "one with him in mind, in his very character and nature . . . one plant and organism with him . . . one substance and essence. . . ."(97) This process, often depicted as organic growth, interacts with others in a colorful cosmic dynamism. Father, Son, and Spirit, who share all they have with each other, pour life, love, and goodness into all creatures (as anyone free from idolizing them as possessions can see [59-60, 62-63, 119-120]). These divine energies vitalize humans, and flow back and forth among them, and also between humans and other creatures, and back to God.

So often did Riedemann envision people participating in, or becoming partakers of, "the divine nature (*göttliche Nature*)," that this transformation by divine energies can be called *divinization*.[60] This, however, did not make people literally divine, or remove them from earthly concerns. It joined them to share physical labor, material goods, and life in Christ's earthly body.

Atonement as divinization carried quite different social implications than Hubmaier's less thorough renewal, which can be called *ontological transformation*. For Hubmaier, sin remained potent enough, even in Christians, to require their submission to civil society with its sword, and for some Christians to govern it. Riedemann's divinization called true Christians away from civil society, to construct an entirely new society directly governed by Jesus' radical teachings.

RESULTS

What significance does this investigation have for current Anabaptist theology? Obviously, sweeping conclusions cannot be drawn from two writers. Historical material, moreover, cannot be directly authoritative in theology, for its role is shaped by the theologian's norms and methods.

Christology in Historic Anabaptism

In contrast to assumptions that Anabaptists had little interest in this subject (except for Jesus' teachings and example), or borrowed most of its content, two creative, significantly different, broad Christologies have emerged. To be sure, we found few classical titles and themes in Hubmaier, which might suggest that this topic was marginal for him. But by crossing the traditional line between Christ's *person* and *work*, we discovered material normally classified under the latter that said much about who Jesus is and was. While Riedemann approached Christ's person in classical terms, his accounts of Jesus' work greatly enriched his presentation. This raises a question: Did other historic Anabaptists find it crucial to say who Jesus was and is—to make christological affirmations about his *person*—while deriving these affirmations more often from scriptural passages describing what Jesus did and does than from classical arguments and terms?

Hubmaier's main way of approaching the risen, divine Christ—through his activity in (and as) the preached Word—differed from classical presentations. Yet I find no evidence that it contradicted classical Christology, which Hubmaier affirmed. Further, Christ's work, for both Anabaptists, was largely present and continuing. They did not emphasize the Jesus of history over the Christ of faith but, if anything, the reverse.

Differences between these Christologies challenge assumptions that they were largely borrowed from the Radical Reformation, or any *one list*. Riedemann's straightforward references to eternal Father-Son relationships jarred with Hubmaier's nominalist avoidance of this stratosphere. Riedemann's devotional, poetic exuberance differed markedly from Hubmaier's tightly argued, academic style. Riedemann's cosmic vision of dynamic, interacting vital energies had no real parallel in Hubmaier.

Hubmaier's earthly Jesus all but disappeared behind his commands, while Riedemann's visibly trod the path leading through this life, and on through death and resurrection into our true inheritance (61, 181). Conceptually considered, however, Hubmaier's Jesus seems more fully human than Riedemann's. Hubmaier's loving, gracious God, manifested mainly through the cross to form faith's main object, was less visible in Riedemann. Finally, diverging estimates of the transforming scope of the atonement bred incompatible sociopolitical views.

These different, creative Christologies also overlapped at important points. Jesus' teachings were crucial to both, as Anabaptist historiography leads us to expect. For both, the major obstacle to following them was not lack of ethical teaching or maturity but the persistence of deep inward, ultimately demonic, bondage and corruption. Consequently, themes associated with Christus Victor formed Riedemann's, and probably Hubmaier's, primary atonement understanding. Since socio-political issues loom large in contemporary theology, let us briefly expand on how this affected their approaches to this sphere.

Hubmaier considered Satan to still be, in some very real sense, Prince of this world (497). Satan opposed the gospel by turning governments against true Christians, and inflicting great suffering through them (311, 495). Hubmaier warned such rulers, following Christus Victor logic, that God would hand them over to others to inflict the same cruelty on them.[61] Still, government's rule and punishment were salutary enough for Christians to submit to and to participate in them.

Riedemann, in contrast, insisted that government was instituted by God's wrath (130-132, 221). "It is a sign of turning away from God" which functions simply to punish "those who have deserted him...."(224) Governmental institutions, which preside over the realm pervaded by demonic forces, have no place among Christians (221). Riedemann conceded that governments preserved humankind until Jesus' coming and could still promote better behavior over worse. Christians, then, should obey rulers and pay taxes—but only when these are legitimate. Unlike most Anabaptists, Riedemann encouraged evaluation of government demands and refusal of unjust ones (225-227). As for Hubmaier, God ruled the socio-political realm in Christus Victor fashion, delivering evil rulers and nations over to each other, bringing their evil upon their own heads (130-131, 215). Christians, though, were to exit this social realm as far as possible, to construct another governed by Jesus' commands and energized by his risen life.

Jesus' atoning work, then, for both historic Anabaptists, surely opposed demonic forces in the socio-political sphere. Yet neither expected it to have great impact there. Atonement, for Riedemann, was to operate largely in a second sphere. Hubmaier expected its effects to operate within, but be significantly limited by, legitimate though sinful social structures.

For both writers, atonement mainly countered the deep corruption which linked people inwardly to demonic impulses, then swept them, too weak to resist, repeatedly into evil behaviors. This process, of course, was not simply individual. Inward bondage drew people together into corrupt behaviors shaped by corrupt institutions. Only the energies operating through Christ's earthly body could dissolve these bonds. This atonement process, both in and among individuals, functioned chiefly in the present. That is why Jesus' resurrection, Christus Victor's high point, which released these energies, was crucial for both theologians.

This continuing atonement, of course, took shape in Jesus-like behavior, especially for Riedemann. But only because it was a transforming spiritual process, whose agents were necessarily divine, could it provide the strength required for this. Neither Hubmaier nor Riedemann prioritized the earthly Jesus and his commands over his divine reality and spiritual power. If anything, their relative emphases were on the latter.

Hubmaier, Riedemann, and J. Denny Weaver

What implications can be drawn for J. Denny Weaver's concerns about atonement? Let us remember that no historical view, in and of itself, can carry direct authority for his theology or anyone else's. Hubmaier and Riedemann can only contribute small stones to a large and complex mosaic.

I noted that Jesus' teachings were indeed central for both of them, although Hubmaier differed on matters relevant to peace. I also noticed that while Christus Victor themes were favored by Riedemann, and perhaps slightly by Hubmaier, emphases common to substitution appeared in both. Substitution and Christus Victor, then, might not always be as opposed as Weaver maintains, and constitute "separate and distinct approaches." While these models provided useful starting-points for our inquiry, distinctions among them, and between Jesus' *person* and *work*, often blurred as we examined the historical materials.

These two historic Anabaptists also challenge Weaver's disjunction between Christus Victor and classical Christology. Riedemann clearly emphasized both, while Hubmaier found them compatible.[62] Riedemann explicitly, and Hubmaier more implicitly, recognized at least one intrinsic connection: only a fully divine power could conquer death and bestow eternal life.

In my own explications of Christus Victor, I distinguish a *conflictive* dimension (Jesus' opposition to evil forces) from a *transformative* dimension (Jesus' present bestowal of eternal life through the Spirit). Both dimensions have been intrinsic to Christus Victor since Justin Martyr until recently. Weaver's "Narrative Christus Victor" highlights the conflictive dimension. I have not found the transformative dimension until his latest writings, which insist that people cannot resist the powers on their own, only through God's enabling grace.[63] Weaver's most detailed comments on inner or "mystical" reality, so far as I know, find it dependent on one's temperament and history and more shaped by environmental factors than shaping the environment.[64] But while the *conflictive* dimension was crucial for Hubmaier and Riedemann, they placed more weight on the *transformative*.

Weaver's Narrative Christus Victor also locates the demonic in the socio-political sphere, as the inner ethos of sinful institutions. But again, Hubmaier and Riedemann highlighted the inner struggle. While this renewal process surely clashed with society's inner ethos, Hubmaier expected it to produce relatively few changes there, and Riedemann perhaps none.

This hardly prevents contemporary theologians from including, even stressing, the socio-political realm, or from arguing that Anabaptists like Riedemann, in setting out to construct a new society, implicitly pointed toward it. Decisions about including any historic Anabaptist elements depend on a variety of factors. Still, theologians who identify themselves as Anabaptists claim some connection with the original historic movement. I hope this beginning attempt to identify and retrieve its christological potential will help us all draw on it fruitfully.

NOTES

1. J. Denny Weaver, "Narrative Christus Victor: the Answer to Anselmian Atonement Violence" in *Violence and Atonement*, ed. John Sanders (Nashville: Abingdon, 2006), 7. "No amount of redefining or reinterpreting or supplementing or amending or enriching the satisfaction motif," Weaver insists, "overcomes that violence. It should be abandoned" (1-2).

2. C. Arnold Snyder, *Anabaptist History and Theology*, Revised Student Edition (Kitchener, Ont.: Pandora, 1997), 149: cf. 155, 161, 162, 194. These "early radical reformers" were Karlstadt, Müntzer, and Schwenckfeld (47-65). This claim is not as prominent in Snyder's more detailed *Anabaptist History and Theology* (Kitchener, Ont.: Pandora, 1995), 83-99.

3. Snyder, *From Anabaptist Seed to Worldwide Growth* (Kitchener, Ont.: Pandora, 1999), 10, 49-50. This 54-page booklet has been translated into several languages and widely distributed by Mennonite World Conference.

4. Robert Friedmann, *The Theology of Anabaptism* (Scottdale, Pa.: Herald, 1973), 55.

5. Earlier historians, including Robert Friedmann, proposed that Riedemann drew significantly on Hubmaier. See Werner Packull, "The Origins of Peter Riedemann's *Account of Our Faith*," *Sixteenth Century Journal* 30/1 (1999), 61-69. While this occurred in some areas, like baptism and preaching, I, with many recent scholars, accent their substantial differences.

6. Weaver, "Narrative Christus Victor," 2.

7. References are to Wayne Pipkin and John Howard Yoder, eds., *Balthasar Hubmaier: Theologian of Anabaptism* (Scottdale, Pa.: Herald, 1989). All page references for Hubmaier in the main text will be to this volume. Hubmaier also confessed Jesus as God's "only Son" according to the Apostles' Creed (349; "only begotten Son" on 235), and, quite significantly, the church as founded on the affirmation of Jesus as "the Christ, the Son of the living God" (352, 539). These uses of "Son" normally denoted Deity.

8. Karl Schornbaum, ed., *Quellen zur Geschichte der Wiedertäufer, Bayern I* (Leipzig: M. Heinius Nachfolger, 1934), 71. The Articles also claimed that "Christ was conceived in original sin," and that "The Virgin Mary is not the Mother of God, but only the Mother of Christ." In December 1526, as well as during his imprisonment in December 1528, Hubmaier insisted on the former

title (ed. Pipkin and Yoder, 341, 538).

9. Weaver, "Hubmaier versus Hut on the Work of Christ," *Archiv für Reformationsgeschichte* 82 (1991), 171-192.

10. See Walter Moore, "Catholic Teacher and Anabaptist Pupil: The Relation between John Eck and Balthasar Humbaier," *Archiv für Reformationsgeschichte* 72 (1981), 68-97; David Steinmetz, "Scholasticism and Radical Reform: Nominalist Motifs in the Theology of Balthasar Hubmaier," *Mennonite Quarterly Review* 45/2 (April 1971), 123-144; Eddie Mabry, *Balthasar Hubmaier's Understanding of Faith* (Lanham, Maryland: University Press of America, 1998) 118-128.

11. The church became not only the agent of the Lord's Supper, but even its content.—John Rempel, *The Lord's Supper in Anabaptism* (Scottdale, Pa.: Herald, 1993), 48, 64-65. Rempel also finds that the incarnation, for Hubmaier, was a temporary instance of divine presence, a presence not so much extended as replaced by the Holy Spirit (81, 89). I agree, with the exception I am about to mention.

12. Ed. Pipkin and Yoder, 84, almost verbatim on 144; cf. 105. As Hubmaier's view of atonement will show, this was not merely imaginative anthropomorphism, since it highlights major themes of Jesus' own historic work.

13. For discussion of this issue, see Mabry, op. cit., 40-44, 78, 81, 87, 104; and Christof Windhorst, *Täuferische Taufverständnis* (Leiden: E.J. Brill, 1976), 185-193.

14. Ed. Pipkin and Yoder, 248, 473; cf. 115-116, 294, 403, 409, 474. Hubmaier cited John 1:12 to this effect (ibid., 292, 457, 468, 477), and 1:13, where he called Jesus "the true and eternal light which became human" (431), as well as 1:14 (also 483-484). He also encouraged readers to receive the Word much as Mary received Jesus and "be conceived a new man and be born again in Thy living, indestructible Word" (236). To receive the Word was to receive the tender lamb, Jesus, who would live in one (85). He also identified Jesus' call in Matt. 11:28 with God's (475).

15. E.g. ed. Pipkin and Yoder, 75, 100, 145, 349, 362-363, 431-432, 439.

16. I would not *identify* Hubmaier's dynamic Word fully with the risen Son, although Hubmaier sometimes spoke this way. I would maintain, more precisely, that because this risen Christ acted so directly through that Word, Hubmaier was clearly speaking, Christologically, of an active divine-human *person*.

17. Ibid., 472, 474, 511, cf. 203. For the crucial nominalist distinction between God's *potentia absoluta* and *potentia ordinata* see Heiko Oberman, *The Harvest of Medieval Theology* (Durham, N.C.; Labyrinth, 1983) 30-38; Pipkin and Yoder's note on 469; and note 10 above.

18. Pipkin and Yoder eds., 519. Though Hubmaier's notion of salvation can be called *ontological transformation*, this was not as thorough as Riedemann's and most other South German/Austrian and Dutch Anabaptist notions, which can be called *divinization*.—See Alvin Beachy, *The Concept of Grace in the Radical Reformation* (Nieuwkoop, the Netherlands: B. De Graf, 1977). While divinization is defined in various ways, transformation of "human na-

ture" is nearly always included. Although our nature is transformed not *into* divine *nature,* but *by* divine *energies*, Anabaptists who believed in divinization expected human nature to change enough that Christians could not, in good conscience, wield the sword, and would seldom, if ever, need to be disciplined by it; cf. notes 46, 60 below.

19. Jesus' human nature also shared our tripartite structure; cf. note 31 below.

20. The most detailed account I find is Hubmaier's recommendation that in preparation for the Lord's Supper, the Scriptures be read so that communicants might "recognize Christ, who was a man, a prophet, mighty in works . . . and how the highest bishops among the priests and princes gave him over to condemnation to death and how they crucified him" that this "may kindle and make fervent and warm the hearts of those at the table, that they may arise in fervent meditation of his bitter suffering and death. . ." (ed. Pipkin and Yoder, 394-395). Hubmaier also described Jesus' wilderness temptations (ibid., 450-451) and John the Baptist's ministry (101-114, 208-210) to some extent, and, to a lesser extent, Jesus' post-resurrection appearance to the two disciples on the road (328).

21. Matt 16:15-19, in contrast to the Catholic interpretation of Peter as the rock.

22. See esp. his treatment of Matt 5:21 (Pipkin and Yoder, eds., 512-514), Matt. 5:40 (ibid., 501-503), Matt. 5:38-3 and Luke 6:27-29 (507-508), Matt. 5:43-48 (510-512) and also Matt. 26:52-54 (497-499). Hubmaier found direct support for his view in Matt. 18:15-17 (503-507), Luke 9:54-56 (499-500), Luke 12:31-32 (500-501) and John 18:36 (496-497).

23. Ibid., 106. C. Norman Kraus seeks to minimize, or eliminate, substitution from Hubmaier, e.g. by describing passages which sound that way as "Eucharistic and penitential" rather than legal.—"Interpreting the Atonement in the Anabaptist-Mennonite Tradition," *Mennonite Quarterly Review* 66/3 (July 1992), 298. I find Weaver's frank attribution of substitution to Hubmaier more convincing (Weaver 1991, op. cit.). However, apparently because atonement models must be "separate and distinct approaches" ("Narrative Christus Victor," 2), Weaver overlooks Hubmaier's Christus Victor themes, and the crucial "moral influence" meaning which Hubmaier, as I will now show, draws from substitution.

24. Pipkin and Yoder, eds., 116; although we "acquire" this grateful and merciful God, a phrase which probably intimates substitution, this nonetheless enables us to call on God by the intimate name "Father." (id., cf. 85, 147)

25. Weaver, "Narrative Christs Victor, 8.

26. Ibid., 9.

27. Ibid., 2. Further, since "divine wisdom" is "inrinsic to any and all forms of satisfaction atonement," therefore "no amount of redefining or reinterpreting or supplementing the satisfactory model overcomes that violence" (1-2).

28. Pipkin and Yoder, eds., 116; to pray "through the favor and good will which he has for his Son" is to pray "in the name of Jesus." (id.) "Faith is the realization of . . . [the Father's] gracious favor and goodwill which he bears to us through his most beloved Son. . ." (348).

29. How could Hubmaier perceive this in Jesus' suffering? I cannot imagine, unless he somehow pictured Jesus' Father deeply moved and pained—the opposite of angry and violent—by the anguish of the one he loved. Apparently, bearing this distress, rather than striking down Jesus' tormenters, required and revealed overwhelming mercy, gentleness, and goodness.

30. Ibid., 86, 100, 115, 348; cf. 103-104. Yet Hubmaier did not narrowly identify the two results with the two acts, but could speak of "forgiveness of sins through the death and resurrection of our Lord. . ." (ibid., 349, cf. 117, 197, 359). Weaver rightly recognizes the centrality of resurrection for Hubmaier (1991 op. cit.).

31. Ibid., 236. Along with Jesus' body, his soul descended into Hell, although it did not suffer there (ibid., 348). The unity of Jesus' body, soul, and spirit was fragmented in some way, which perhaps distantly paralleled their fragmentation in all other humans. In the process of rising, Jesus reunited his "spirit, soul and body" in the grave (236). Hubmaier also ascribed a salvific function to each of these parts. Through his spirit, Jesus nullified the capacity of the body ("prison") to harm the spirit. His soul acquired enlightenment by the Word for our souls, while Jesus' body earned for us resurrection bodies (446). This tripartite human structure could also be considered a feature of Christ's "Person" (cf. note 19 above).

32. Pipkin and Yoder, eds., 360. In their potential to affect us negatively, at least, "flesh, sin, death" and the devil "are already captured, bound, and overcome in Christ." Expressed otherwise: Jesus "crushed the head of the old serpent" and "made its poison no longer lethal to us" (ibid., 446).

33. Ibid., 439; also 361, 464; cf. 400, 444. Hubmaier's anthropology was generally more pessimistic in earlier writings than in his "Freedom of the Will" (ibid., 427-491). Previously, Hubmaier added more qualifications, such as that obedience "would be impossible for us in ourselves, without God's drawing which comes through his Word" (362). For discussion of Hubmaier on the will, see Thomas Finger, *A Contemporary Anabaptist Theology* (Downers Grove, Ill.: InterVarsity, 2004), 469-473.

34. Translated as *Love is Like Fire* (Farmington, Pa.: Plough, 1993).

35. See Packull, op cit. Riedemann wrote the second Confession when he was imprisoned by Philip in Hesse.

36. See Andrea Chudaska, *Peter Riedemann: Konfessionsbildenes Täufertum im 16. Jahrhundert* (Gütersloh: Gütersloher Verlaghaus, 2003), 257-265. According to this "monophysite" Christology, Jesus received his humanity not from Mary, but directly from God.

37. Yet even these first articles discuss Jesus' historical "work" as well as his "person." Riedemann sought to base every point on Scripture, hardly ever appealing explicitly to tradition.

38. See, e.g., Thomas Aquinas, *Summa Theologiae* I, Q. 27, a. 1.

39. John Friesen, ed., *Peter Riedemann's Hutterite Confession of Faith* (Scottdale, Pa.: Herald, 1999), 66 (cf. 64), translating Peter Riedemann, *Rechenschaft unserer Religion, Lehre und Glaubens* (Wiltshire, U.K.: Verlag der Hutterischen Brüder, 1938), 16. The Holy Spirit is the breath which accompanies that spoken Word, and can convey it to creatures. These three are "one

substance, one nature, one essence *(eine Substanz, Materie und Wesen)*" much as fire, heat, and light are one (Friesen, ed., 75; Riedemann 29). Wherever one of them is, all three are there; but if one is missing, so are all three. To express these realities, Riedemann often employed ordinary words like "power," but also several classical concepts, particularly "essence *(Wesen)*" and "nature *(Natur)*," although Friesen does not translate them uniformly, as in "nature" for "*Materie*" above (see note 46 below). Page references for Riedemann in the main text will be from Friesen's translation.

40. Weaver appreciates Riedemann's use of the trinity here, but concludes, with Gerald Biesecker-Mast, that Riedemann's treatment of the Apostles' Creed renders it "hardly recognizable any more."—Weaver, "Parsing Anabaptist Theology: A Review Essay of Thomas N. Finger's *A Contemporary Anabaptist Theology*," *Direction* 34/2 (Fall 2005) 256; quoting Biesecker-Mast, *Separation and the Sword in Anabaptist Persuasion* (Telford, Pa.: Cascadia, 2006), 145. According to Biesecker-Mast (now Gerald J. Mast), the Creed is "eclipsed" and "reconstitute[d]" by Riedemann's "gloss" (136, 138). Yet Biesecker-Mast treats it simply as an expression of "Orthodoxy" which, "by definition," construes belief as "verbal assent to specific formulations" (138), prioritizes "orderliness and precision about truth claims" (132), and considers "simply concurring with or rejecting the creed" to be crucial (145). Not only is this stereotyped definition of "Orthodoxy" questionable. Biesecker-Mast also overlooks the Creed's other functions, such as the catechetical and the expositional. From the early church to the present, the Creed has repeatedly provided a skeleton outline for elaborating a great variety of teachings, doctrines, and ethical imperatives. Riedemann was hardly eclipsing or rendering it unrecognizable, but employing it in a way for which it was designed. For my response to Weaver on this point, see "Response to J. Denny Weaver's 'Parsing Anabaptist Theology,'" *Direction* 35/1 (Spring 2006): 148-150.

41. See Friesen, ed., 60; cf. 79, 98, 115. Friesen omits "making them like, similar and conformable to itself," which I add in light of its inclusion in Riedemann (1938), 7.

42. Cf. Riedemann's description of God in *Love is Like Fire*: "So loving is his compassion! Like a spring that overflows, his mercy flows over all who desire it, calling them to his grace.... Who has ever shown anyone such love as the Ruler of all as shown, even to those who despised him?" (3)

43. See Ursula Lieseberg, *Die Lieder des Peter Riedemann* (Frankfurt am Main: Peter Lang, 1998).

44. See Chudaska, op. cit., 64-68.

45. Friesen, ed., 65; more positively stated, this required "a birth from God, which takes place only through the Word" (ibid., 176). In addition, "since death came through a human, so resurrection from the dead and salvation" had to come through a human being (65).

46. Riedemann used "Natur" in discussing Jesus' conception, birth and death (Friesen, ed. 68-70), though not in every other place where Friesen has "nature" (cf. note 39 above). Riedemann also described salvation often as participation in the "divine nature *(göttliche Natur;* cf. note 18 above); and also, like some other Anabaptists, in the "*göttliche Natur und Art* (divine nature and

character)," indicating that "nature" was not some static substance, but a way of being with moral features.

47. Friesen, ed., 72, cf. 74, 69, though I am not quite sure how. "Taking human nature on himself" was a hallmark of classical Alexandrian Christology.

48. Ibid., 114-115, 20. The risen saints, moreover will obtain bodies like Jesus' glorified body (82). Jesus initiated this human transition from earthly to glorified bodies (70).

49. Ibid., 135; Riedemann linked some commands of Jesus much more closely to his earthly ministry than did Hubmaier (e.g., on swearing oaths [ibid., 139-143, 206-208, 211-212] and nonviolence [217-219]).

50. Cf. Friesen 60; see note 41 above.

51. Instead of "wrong taking," Friesen, ed., has "embracing what is unrighteous." (94) "Wrong taking," however, better renders the original German "unrechten Annehmen," especially because Gen. 3:6 is cited in support. Riedemann formally defined sin as "disobedience" to God (Friesen, ed., 92), which "stirs up, rouses, and brings to pass all other sins..." (ibid., 93). Wrong taking, which leads to striving and fighting for possessions, is the main concrete form sin takes.

52. Ibid., 91, 171. An idol is anything "in which one seeks salvation, comfort, or help apart from God..." (ibid., 87). To set one's heart upon any created thing in this way is to set up another god (88).

53. Ibid., 74, 95. Yet Riedemann rejected the notion that the devil or serpent is simply a symbol for "the curiosity and desire of the flesh." For this desire arose out of a prior event, "the serpent's counsel" (ibid., 91).

54. Ibid., 64, 67, 74. This will not occur, however, unless one's heart turns towards God, "emptying itself from everything else" (ibid., 120); unless one "give up whatever was previously appropriated wrongly:" all private property (94).

55. Ibid., 79, 85, 100-102, 109-110, 166-167, 182.

56. Ibid., 65, 71, 74, 181, 185, 220.

57. I never find him referring to Jesus' weakness, or weakness of any kind, paradoxically triumphing as strength, as in 1 Cor. 1:18-31. Pilgram Marpeck, in contrast, found this central to atonement (see Finger 2004, op. cit., 343, 378).

58. Riedemann also mentioned occasionally that Jesus' death established or confirmed God's covenant with us (Friesen, ed., 98, 182) and did so with clarity (ibid., 99). Jesus' death, in addition, provided a model for our dying to sin, including through baptism (107, 116, 178, 198).

59. Ibid., 71, 185; cf. 65. Jesus also descended into hell, or "the place of captivity," to preach to deceased spirits who, in contrast to Hubmaier, had not believed the word preached previously (ibid., 70-71). This was also part of his atoning work which destroyed death and the devil's power, though Riedemann said little about it.

60. Ibid., 61, 76, 84-85, 116-117, 179, etc.; see note 18 above.

61. Pipkin and Yoder, eds., 309, 487-488, 498. In Christus Victor, God punishes not by inflicting penalties directly on evildoers, but by handing them over to the consequences of their evil acts.—See Finger, *Systematic Theology:*

An Eschatological Approach Vol. I (Scottdale, Pa.: Herald, 1985), 327-331.

62. Hubmaier's allowance for the sword in society might have been linked with his substitutionary views, though I have not yet found the connection. However, this *historical* appearance of satisfaction, classical Christology and the sword in Hubmaier's work cannot ground any general *theological* relationships among them.

63. Weaver, "Narrative Christus Victor," 22-23.

64. Weaver, *Becoming Anabaptist* (Scottdale, Pa.: Herald Press, 1987), 181; "Narrative Theology in an Anabaptist-Mennonite Context," *Conrad Grebel Review* 12/2 (1994), 175. Inner experience can be valid if it motivates ethical action, but detrimental if it diverts from this. See Weaver in *Anabaptist Currents,* ed. Carl Bowman and Stephen Longenecker, eds. (Bridgewater, Virginia: Penobscot, 1995), 27-37; and *Keeping Salvation Ethical* (Scottdale, Pa.: Herald, 1997), 226.

CHAPTER EIGHT

JESUS' FLESH AND THE FAITHFUL CHURCH IN THE THEOLOGICAL RHETORIC OF MENNO SIMONS

Gerald J. Mast

We teach and believe, and this is the thrust of the whole Scriptures, that the whole Christ is from head to foot, both inside and outside, visible and invisible, God's first-born and only begotten Son; the incomprehensible eternal Word, by whom all things were created, the first-born of every creature.
—Menno Simons[1]

WITMARSUM AND BLUFFTON

It is appropriate in an essay for a book engaging the life work of J. Denny Weaver to return to the writings of Menno Simons, that stubborn and argumentative sixteenth-century Dutch Anabaptist leader who gave the Mennonite church its name, and who has often been a source of embarrassment for those who seek to make Mennonites a respectable and proper church. While the distance between the sixteenth and the twenty-first century is great and while Menno's itinerant lifestyle has little to do with the relative comfort of an academic life in Bluffton, Ohio, there are nevertheless striking resemblances between the rhetorical and theological habits cultivated by the reformer from Witmarsum and the "Bluffton school" of theology perpetrated by J. Denny Weaver.

Like Menno, J. Denny Weaver is a controversial writer and teacher whose discussions of theology are often deemed extra-orthodox and even dangerous. Although Denny's books have not been outlawed, confiscated, and burned as was the case for Menno, the writing and teaching of J. Denny Weaver has evoked the kind of passion and even hostility that one can imagine would lead to book-burning and court-injunctions in a less liberal or modern society. Nevertheless, as for Menno, Weaver's theology is offered as a gift to the church, in the hope of encouraging greater faithfulness and deeper commitment to the reconciling love of Jesus Christ.

Perhaps especially in the areas of Christology and ecclesiology are the similarities between Menno and Weaver apparent. For both Menno and Weaver, the work of Christ is intrinsic to the character of the church. Both of them pursue biblical—rather than orthodox—accounts of Jesus' life, death, and resurrection which emphasize the empowerment of Jesus' disciples to make the reign of God visible in the company of the saints, to inhabit a contrast society that challenges the surrounding culture, and to live lives that are fundamentally altered in association with the body of Christ—the church.

Weaver himself acknowledges this parallel between his own theological convictions and the writings of Menno—especially on the subject of Christology. In *Anabaptist Theology in Face of Postmodernity* he notes Menno's celestial flesh Christology as an example of Anabaptist precedent for rethinking classical orthodox doctrinal categories in the interest of strengthening the church's social witness: "Menno wanted to defend the sinlessness of Jesus because he believed that the church founded by Jesus was a pure church and an extension of Christ's work on earth. This church would then be separate or distinct from the social order, rather than the church of Christendom that supports the social order."[2]

While Weaver clearly does not advocate celestial flesh Christology and has thus far not given further consideration to the social and ecclesiastical implications of Menno's christological convictions, I seek in this chapter to examine more closely Weaver's claim that Menno's views about Jesus' flesh profoundly shaped Menno's understanding of the church. Although the purpose of this chapter is not to advocate celestial flesh Christology, I do hope to demonstrate the worth of considering the work of Jesus Christ in relationship to the character and practices of the church. I also hope to suggest that celestial flesh Christology is a valid interpretation of the claim in the gospel of John that in Jesus Christ "the Word became flesh." In light of the ethical and social failures of Chalcedonian Christianity, I conclude that celestial flesh Christology contains valuable clues for strengthening Christian convictions about the relationship between Christ and the church today.

THE SCANDAL OF DUTCH MENNONITE CHRISTOLOGY

The argument that Jesus received his flesh—and therefore his humanity—not from his mother Mary but from heaven, has long been a source of controversy and embarrassment for Mennonite piety and historical theology. This view, with precedent in the second century Gnostic teachings of Valentinus and Marcion, and appearing again among such "heretical" sects as the Cathars and Bogomiles, was taken up in the sixteenth century by Radical Reformation leaders such as Caspar Schwenckfeld and Melchior Hoffman, both of whom no doubt contributed to the long shadow of celestial flesh Christology among Dutch Anabaptists.[3]

Not long after Menno joined the Dutch Anabaptist movement in 1536, following the violent apocalypse at Münster, he was wracked by doubt and anxiety regarding the celestial flesh teaching of the Dutch Anabaptist brotherhood, becoming convinced of the truth of this doctrine only after lengthy discussion, many days of fasting, and months of biblical study. Although it was not his preferred doctrinal topic, a large amount of his published writing ended up being devoted to defending celestial flesh Christology to Calvinist detractors like John a Lasco and Martin Micron. For such Reformed church leaders, celestial flesh Christology was a basis for rejecting the validity of Mennonite doctrine, a rejection that appeared again and again in Reformed (and Lutheran) confessions.

At the same time, celestial flesh Christology was a basis for division among Mennonite groups. Anabaptist communities in Upper Germany that had been in fellowship with Dutch Mennonite groups refused in 1559 to accept either strict shunning or the celestial flesh Christology of the conservative Dutch groups as confessional requirements for their congregations, thus leading Dirk Philips and other Dutch Mennonite leaders to ban the Upper Germans. This, in turn, caused more tolerant Dutch Anabaptist groups who rejected this decision to leave the main body of Mennonites in the Netherlands; these more tolerant congregations became known as the Waterlanders—after the place of origin for a significant number of the dissenters.

The question of the nature of Jesus' flesh was to play a significant role in contentious discussions throughout the seventeenth century among Dutch Mennonite communities who sought to achieve confessional unity amid multiple and repeated divisions. Confessions of faith written by Dutch Mennonites to achieve unity at different times and contexts featured celestial flesh Christology—at times emphasizing and at other times deemphasizing the doctrine. Compilers of Mennonite martyrologies in the seventeenth century edited their collections to either highlight or downplay the adherence of Anabaptist martyrs to the heavenly flesh of Jesus, sometimes producing vituperative exchanges between such editors.[4]

Modern editors of the writings of Menno Simons have sometimes flinched at the extended discussions and debates about the incarnation found in Menno's work. In John Funk's 1871 English edition, Menno's *Very Plain and Discreet Answer to Martin Micron* is abridged significantly because, according to the publisher, "in the translation of the writings of Menno Simons upon the 'incarnation of Christ'" there were parts that were considered "of no importance in the illustration and explanation of the subject," and "were not edifying to the reader."[5] These parts, it turns out, were almost invariably instances of Menno's discussion of Mary's menstrual flux (*menftrual bloet*), where Jesus' seed was said to have coagulated, and which Menno argued was the extent of Mary's contribution to Jesus' bodily origin.[6]

These references to Menno's mistaken understanding that women contribute nothing to the formation of the human embryo were included in the 1956 translation by Leonard Verduin, but with an introduction by J. C. Wenger in which he labeled Menno's treatment of the issue as "tedious and tiresome" and wished that Menno "would have had more good sense than to waddle through the mire."[7] Wenger urges the reader to avoid reading the majority of the *Reply to Micron*, identifying section X as "the only edifying section in the entire *Reply*."[8]

More recent retrievals of Menno's theological convictions have also expressed discomfort about his view of the incarnation. Abraham Friesen's otherwise instructive book on the role of Erasmus' interpretation of the great commission in Anabaptist baptismal polemics assumes that Menno held to celestial flesh almost entirely as a pragmatic concession to Dutch Anabaptist conventions—an assumption that seems unlikely given Menno's stubborn refusal to be conformist in practically every other issue he confronted, either inside or outside the brotherhood.[9] More recently, Tom Finger has described Menno's "tedious" advocacy of "heavenly flesh Christology" as a conviction he held "most embarrassingly for Mennonites today."[10]

A few months ago, I received an e-mail from a member of the Christian Reformed Church who was studying article 18 of the Belgic Confession, which opposes "the heresy of the Anabaptists, who deny that Christ assumed human flesh of his mother."[11] This correspondent asked me whether Mennonites still denied that Christ received his flesh from Mary. His hope was that if Mennonites no longer made such a denial, perhaps the Belgic Confession could be revised to reflect this development. I, of course, responded that this view was peculiar to the Dutch Mennonites, that it had pretty much died out by the eighteenth century, and that no Mennonite group today that I knew of denied that Christ received his flesh from Mary.

That I would need to reassure an ecumenical partner today about Mennonite christological beliefs illustrates the longstanding significance of Menno's stubborn adherence to celestial flesh Christology. Perhaps the time has come not to simply reassure ourselves and others that Mennonite Christology is orthodox but to reexamine again what Menno taught to see if there is anything we might learn from this strange conviction from a different time and place.

MENNO'S UNDERSTANDING OF JESUS' FLESH

While not advocating celestial flesh Christology, I will nevertheless investigate the possibility that Menno's solution was a valid theological effort to recover the heavenly power of the earthly Jesus to save us from our sins, from which we could learn today. My reading of Menno's views on the incarnation has been shaped significantly by William Keeney, whose extensive and, in my mind, definitive exploration of the grammar of Menno's Christology has proven Menno's thoroughgoing, if militant, Christian humanism.

According to Keeney, Menno was convinced that Jesus became flesh in Mary without receiving his flesh from her.[12] Menno argues that although Jesus was born out of (*uit*) Mary, he was not born from (*van*) Mary, but rather from (*van*) God.[13] This distinction was crucial for Menno because he assumed that had Jesus been born from Mary, he would also have received corrupted flesh from her and would thus have been unable to be the bearer of human salvation.[14] Menno supported his view of Jesus' origin by invoking the Aristotelian theory of human conception, whereby only the male seed contributes substance to the embryo, while the female body provides nourishment and birth.[15] Keeney points out that the Aristotelian view was widely held in the centuries leading up to the time of Menno, including by Thomas Aquinas and Hilary of Poiters, although Thomas did not apply this view to the incarnation as did both Hilary and Menno.[16]

While Menno did not believe that Jesus received his flesh from Mary, he did assume that Jesus' flesh was human, although the humanity of Jesus' flesh was derived from the same substance as that of Adam's nature before the Fall.[17] Menno therefore did not assume the inherently evil nature of human flesh, but rather the fallen nature of post-lapsarian human flesh. He is thus distinguished from the gnostic writers mentioned earlier who assumed that flesh, like matter itself, was intrinsically evil.[18]

Furthermore, it is not the case that Menno exhibited hostility to women by assuming that Jesus could not have been conceived by Mary. For Menno, the problem with Mary is not that she was a woman but that she was a fallen human being.[19] His appropriation of the Aristotelian view of male-originated conception was an incidental argument used to support his more basic conviction that Jesus' flesh came from God, not from fallen humanity. Moreover, Menno did not believe, like Valentinus, that Jesus passed through Mary like water through a pipe. Rather, Jesus "was fed and nourished in truly human fashion in her virgin body by ordinary food and drink."[20] Jesus received this nourishment, in the Aristotelian theory accepted by Menno, through Mary's menstrual blood or flux.[21] Menno's extensive discussion of the role of menstrual blood in the process of birth suggests that he is less squeamish than some of his descendants in considering the role of women's bodies in procreation—even if he was mistaken about the particulars.

In his debate with Martin Micron, Menno also rejected the view that the sinful nature of humanity "comes from the marital intimacy that was given in God's original creation."[22] Instead, Menno insisted that sin originated in Adam's transgression. This offers further evidence that Menno was not somehow hostile to bodies and human biology. Rather, he sought to offer access to the redemption of the body through association with Christ's body, a body that was fully free from the constraints of human sin and could therefore be the agent of human liberation—"the spiritual brazen serpent" and the "true bread from heaven, which is not made of natural grain or wheat (I mean of our sinful flesh) but comes of the dew of the eternal Word and is the only true food for our souls, by which we shall live forever, if we eat of Him through true faith."[23]

Thus, for Menno, Christ was both divine and human insofar as he was wholly of God, undivided in his nature, "a single person, God's own first-born Son and only begotten Son," consisting of "holy and saving flesh."[24] It is precisely since Christ was fully God that his willingness to become a servant had meaning, that his ability to minister to humans became visible, and that his obedience unto death was in fact an offering on our behalf.[25]

To fully grasp what was at stake here in Menno's argument it will be helpful to rehearse the rhetorical situation to which Menno was responding. Menno's texts concerning the incarnation were written in the context of debates with two Reformed church leaders—John a Lasco (the superintendent of the Reformed state church in East Friesland) and Martin Micron (an influential Reformed minister from Norden in East Friesland).[26] In both cases, Menno was engaging in public debates with the church party that had come into ascendancy in northwest Germany. Menno clearly recognized greater kinship with these Reformed leaders than with the Catholic regime that had put a price on his head in Holland. He initially addressed both John a Lasco and Martin Micron (and their people) as brothers and friends.

The first debate with John a Lasco in 1544 was an occasion when a Lasco sought to test how dangerous Menno's views were and also to convince him to accept the Reformed perspective. No doubt Menno hoped to prove the validity of Anabaptist faith, and perhaps to achieve some tolerance by the Reformed regime, without compromising his community's convictions and practices. The discussion with a Lasco ranged over such topics as baptism, original sin, justification, the calling of ministers, and the incarnation, with the latter topic prompting a Lasco to ask Menno for a written confession of his views on the incarnation.[27]

When Menno provided the written text for a Lasco, he then published it without Menno's consent and subsequently attacked it in a treatise published in 1545, the same year that Countess Anna of Oldenburg, acting under the influence of a Lasco, decreed that Menno and his people be required to leave the country, while the more threatening Anabaptists, including those associated with the terrorist cells of Jan van Batenburg and the spiritualist conventicles of David Joris, were to be executed. Menno's second book on the incarnation (1554) was published nine years later in response to a Lasco's attack. In the preface to the 1554 response to a Lasco, Menno no longer evinces much hope that his argument will win any tolerance from Reformed authorities: "I know very well that my truth will probably remain a falsehood in the eyes of the learned ones...."[28] Menno's motivations instead lie with "pure love for my Lord and Saviour and for his holy Word and out of love for my dear brethren" as well as "a kindly feeling which I entertain toward my opponent."[29]

The year before he published his response to John a Lasco, the events which led to Menno's debate with Martin Micron had begun to unfold. Zwinglian refugees from London had come to Wismar, where Menno and his followers offered them assistance. In the course of their fraternization, the Mennonites and the Zwinglians got into a doctrinal dispute that led to a formal public debate, with Martin Micron coming from Norden to help the Zwinglians. The first day of debate was an uninterrupted eleven hour discussion of the same issues Menno had earlier debated with a Lasco concluding with a common meal. The topic of the incarnation was reserved for a separate occasion, nine days later on February 15, 1554.

The discussion about the incarnation clearly exceeded the bounds of civility and led both to the public revelation of Menno's hiding place (which the Reformed party had promised to keep secret) and to Micron's publication of his account of the disputation two years later. Menno responded four months later with his *Reply to Martin Micron*, followed shortly with his *Epistle to Martin Micron*, the first of which dealt almost exclusively with the debate on the incarnation.[30]

One obvious dimension of the rhetorical situation then was a doctrinal conflict in which Menno was taking up the weaker position, first of all in the sense that it was held by a religious minority against the confessional regime that sought to enforce the more "orthodox" position on the incarnation—that Jesus was born from, and not merely out of, Mary. In the case of John a Lasco, the initial discussion had led to a decree of exile against the Mennonites. In the case of the dispute with Micron, which had begun with an offering by the Mennonites of material assistance and relief to beleaguered Zwinglians, the result was that Menno's hiding place was divulged and a leading Reformed minister had published another book against him. But a second aspect of the "weaker argument" taken up by Menno was that he was challenging the long-standing orthodox formulation dating back to the council of Chalcedon that Jesus had two natures: one derived from his earthly mother and the other from God. Micron's inflection of this Chaldcedonian understanding apparently accepted that Jesus contained within himself two persons—one the son of God and the other the son of Mary.[31] Against this division, Menno insisted, perhaps with some excessive redundancy, on an "undivided Christ."[32]

Yet this seemingly redundant insistence is understandable when we recognize the apparent link for Menno at this point, felt by him in a quite material way, between Reformed soteriology and Chalcedonian Christology. For Menno, the two natures or persons in Christ assumed by the Reformed were of a piece with the incongruence between the confession and practice he observed among the Reformed. How could those who claimed Christ as their salvation persecute other Christians with violence, or even use the sword of the magistrate to execute unbelievers? Writing to Micron as a follow-up to his refutation of Micron's account of their disputation, Menno asks: "If you had tasted the sweet Word of God and the fruits of the world to be, you would never afflict the pious as you have done by your untrue, false writing, nor would you encourage any of their bloody doings, but point them to the meek Lamb, and let the dead bury the dead."[33] Moreover, Menno writes, the sword of the magistrate cannot be used by Christians to kill anyone, even wrongdoers: "For he who is a Christian must follow the Spirit, Word, and example of Christ, no matter whether he be emperor, king, or whatever he be."[34] In this respect Menno eloquently recalls his response to Micron during their earlier debate, in a passage that is worth quoting at length:

> When you proposed your pharisaical, Herod-like question concerning the magistracy, I said nothing more to you than that it would hardly become a Christian ruler to shed blood. For this reason, If the transgressor should truly repent before his God and be reborn of Him, he would then also be a chosen saint and child of God, a fellow partaker of grace, a spiritual member of the Lord's body, sprinkled with His precious blood and anointed with His Holy Ghost, a living grain of the Bread of Christ and an heir to eternal life; and for such an one to be hanged on the gallows, put on the wheel, placed on the stake, or in any manner be hurt in body or goods by another Christian, who is of one heart, spirit, and soul with him, would look somewhat strange and unbecoming in the light of the compassionate, merciful, kind na-

ture, disposition, spirit, and example of Christ, the meek Lamb—which example He has commanded all His chosen children to follow.[35]

This passage exhibits vividly the social understanding of salvation assumed by Menno. For members of Christ, everyone is a potential brother or sister and thus to be treated as such. In his confession about the incarnation written for John a Lasco, Menno had acknowledged that the peace brought by Christ has an inward dimension. But, he insisted, "whoever has this inward, Christian peace in his heart will never more be found guilty before God and this world of turmoil, treason, mutiny, murder, theft," but rather such people "follow peace with all men. . . ."[36] This was the basis for Menno's understanding of "true evangelical faith," that it could not "lie dormant" but would "manifest itself in all righteousness and works of love."[37]

Such inward and social peace is rooted for Menno in the regenerative power of the work of Jesus Christ. Menno asks,

> For how could true brethren and sisters of Jesus Christ, the well-disposed children of God, who with Christ Jesus are born of God the Father and the powerful seed of the divine Word in Christ Jesus, who are regenerated by Christ, partake of His Spirit and nature, who have been made like unto Him, are Christian and heavenly minded—how can such people teach or stage turmoil of any kind . . . ?[38]

It seems clear that one way Menno imagined Christians could justify killing is to accept a divided Christ, a Christ in whom both sin and salvation co-exist. Egil Grislis defends Menno's critique of Chalcedonian Christology on precisely this point: "He (Menno) cannot be blamed for all-too-readily connecting the Chalcedonian two-nature Christology, with a doctrine of justification which all too readily admitted sin into Christian existence—and then went on to persecute, torture, and to kill."[39] Indeed, Grislis suggests, "for Menno in his time and circumstances, it was a monophysite Christology that insured the possession of truth and salvation."[40]

Grislis makes clear what was at stake for Menno in his commitment to an "undivided Jesus." The main issue has to do with what is meant by salvation. Is salvation merely a forensic event, an adjustment of our standing or status before God? Or does salvation involve practical empowerment toward liberation from sin? Menno was concerned that the orthodox or Reformed insistence that Jesus' flesh came from earthly humanity simply reinforced the intractability of sin and a weak forensic view of salvation—cheap grace. By way of contrast, Menno believed that Jesus' holy humanity, his divine flesh, offered leverage against the corruption of the Fall and freed Christians to share in Christ's divinity, to become themselves whole human beings once more, no longer divided within themselves or against others. As William Keeney succinctly restates this view, "The incarnation through the new creature in Christ offers the ontological basis for real obedience."[41]

Thus, from the perspective of Menno, the same incorruptible seed from which Christ was conceived, through which the Word became flesh and dwelt among us, will also produce fruit in the lives of those who have become members of Christ's incorruptible body. Our flesh, too, can become divine.

MENNO'S UNDERSTANDING OF THE CHURCH'S SEED

The process by which human beings can be regenerated by the "undivided Christ" necessarily involves the church—the body of Christ. Menno believed that the church had inherited from Jesus Christ the incorruptible seed that had birthed his body—both the historical Jesus and the historical church. "By faith," Menno wrote in his *Foundation of Christian Doctrine*, human beings "become new creatures, born of God and transplanted from Adam into Christ."[42] Menno makes this observation in the context of his discussion of the Lord's Supper, an event he considered a memorial meal on the one hand, but also an occasion where when the meal is rightly celebrated with "faith, love, attentiveness, peace, unity of heart and mind, there Jesus Christ is present with His grace, Spirit, and promise. . . ."[43] In his discussion of the Lord's Supper, Menno critiques the practice of including unrepentant sinners in the Supper because such a performance precisely contradicts the reality of Christ's incorruptible body as the basis for the church. Those who are joined to Christ are necessarily freed from sin, becoming "flesh of his flesh and bone of his bone, a true partaker of the body and the blood of Christ."[44] A Lord's Supper which does not make visible such a liberating participation with Christ is false.

In Menno's writing, the process of regeneration seems to precede chronologically the constitution of the church. At the same time, the existence of the church in his writings is not divided logically from the new creature that is born into Christ. As Sjouke Voolstra puts it, "For Menno Simons, incarnation is the residence of Christ in the hearts of believers and the transformation of individuals who were not obedient to God into a people subject to God in obedience."⁴⁵

There is quite clearly for Menno a specific existential choice by human individuals to accept the work of Christ. This is not primarily an intellectual decision, an acknowledgement of Christ, or a matter of belief, but rather a shift in orientation, an embrace of the Word of God, and being joined to Christ: "in your life you must become so converted and changed that you become new creatures in Christ, that Christ be in you and you in Christ."⁴⁶ This process of conversion and reorientation involves the reception of the incorruptible seed, according to Menno: "those who with Adam truly receive the promised Seed and are renewed and comforted in God, who are born from above by this same Seed, who are changed and converted from the disobedient nature of Adam to the obedient nature of the Word, Christ Jesus: these He calls flesh of his flesh and bone of His bone."⁴⁷

The incorruptible seed from which new believers are born is the basis for a change in orientation and identification. Being born from such seed immediately places one into relationship with others who have also been reborn in Christ and joined to one another in Christ. In Menno's book on *Christian Baptism* he makes explicit that the spiritual seed from which Christians are born is the seed of the "holy, Christian church." This is an "assembly of the righteous, and a community of saints; which church is begotten of God, of the living seed of the divine Word, and not of the teachings, institutions, and fictions of man."⁴⁸

The role of human choice in the reception of this "spiritual seed" is clear in Menno's book on baptism. Fallen children of Adam have the capacity, once they have reached an age of understanding, to respond to the divine Word in faith and obedience, to repent of their sins and to accept baptism, in which, according to Menno, they receive "remission of sins."⁴⁹ Yet, it is clear that salvation is the result of the work of Christ, not of a choice to accept this work and to embrace it. According to Menno, believers receive remission of sins, "not through baptism but in baptism" (*niet door den Doopfel maer in den Doopfel*) a distinction of prepositions that recalls Menno's claim that Jesus was born not from Mary but out of Mary.⁵⁰ Furthermore, while in baptism believers receive remission of sins, they are not "cleansed in baptism of our inherited sinful nature which is in our flesh, so that it is entirely destroyed in us, for it remains with us after baptism."⁵¹

Menno, in other words, is not arguing for Christian perfectionism. Rather, he writes that because of God's gift of faith through

God's Word, "we declare in the baptism (*in den doopfel*) we receive that we desire to die unto the inherent, sinful nature, and destroy it, so that it will no longer be master over our mortal bodies, even though such true believers are often overcome by sin."[52] For Menno, the capacity of humans to desire freedom from sin, a desire which is unleashed by the gift of God's enfleshed Word, is the condition of possibility for regeneration in baptism.

Elsewhere, in his *Reply to False Accusations*, Menno elaborates on the relationship between the remaining sinful nature and the freedom from that nature experienced by believers in baptism. He distinguishes between willful disobedience and actions resulting from "remnants of the old nature," the latter of which he describes as "human frailties, errors, and stumblings which are still found daily among saints and regenerate ones."[53] Although the willful disobedience of unbelievers and the lapses of conduct by regenerated believers both result from the same corrupt sinful nature, the difference is that believers "fight daily with their weak flesh in the Spirit and faith," whereas unbelievers "commit sin with relish and boldness."[54] Believers are acting, in other words, according to the new nature that they have received in opposition to the "remnants of the old nature" that remain. The "new nature" produces "evangelical fruit" such as "mercy, friendship, chastity, temperance, humility, confidence, truth, peace, and joy in the Holy Ghost," despite the "old nature."[55] The basic orientation is away from sin and toward the "doctrine, ceremonies, commands, prohibitions, and perfect example of Christ," rather than toward sin and away from Christ.[56]

For Menno, the capacity of believers to bear evangelical fruit, to live according to Christ, and to manifest "righteousness and works of love," is the result of the gift of the incarnation—the Word becoming flesh in Mary—a "single undivided person, Son and Christ, God's true and natural Son as to origin and essence, and Mary's supernatural Son as to His conception."[57] The same Word through which Adam and Eve were created has "by His almighty power raised them up again out of pure grace and love."[58] All who "firmly believe this wondrously high work . . . overcome the world; they are in God and God is in them." They "fear God, bury their sins, and turn from evil."[59] They are born of "the incorruptible seed of the holy divine Word" and will thus help their brothers and sisters "in an evangelical manner, risk and give their lives for them in time of need."[60] Menno clarifies here that an "evangelical manner" means not with "swords and muskets" but after the example of Christ, "who for our sakes did not spare himself, but willingly yielded His life, that we through Him might live."[61]

Sjouke Voolstra has commented that in celestial flesh Christology, Anabaptists like Menno witnessed to the fact that in Christ "something entirely new has entered the world," a thing so original that "it cannot be part of the Fallen creation nor can it be understood within human, philosophical categories."[62] This seemingly incomprehensible newness "does not make it less real," however. According to Voolstra, "It is the only reality which makes of the visible reality a sham and manifests itself provisionally in the disarmed community."[63] This new reality, revealed now in the faithful church, is the basis for a renewed perspective on the world and a new experience of self and other, for those who are joined to Christ's body in the church. The church, as we will see below, is the place where we are saved, even if it is not the instrument of our salvation.

HOW OUR SALVATION TAKES PLACE IN THE CHURCH, BUT NOT THROUGH IT

Egil Grislis writes that "since Christology and soteriology are correlatives, a presently perceived flaw in one will necessarily lead the community of the faithful to question and rewrite the other."[64] In Menno's time, the perception of his fellowship that prominent forms of Christianity did not manifest the evidences of salvation led Dutch Anabaptists to propose a rethinking of Chalcedonian Christology. That rethinking emphasized the power of God through the work of Jesus Christ to transform human beings, down to their very bodily knowledge and experience.

The question of whether Christianity really makes a difference is still with us today. In a recent book, Ron Sider has called attention to *The Scandal of the Evangelical Conscience*. Citing numerous statistics from U.S. polling firms such as Gallop and Barna, Sider concludes that evangelical Christians are living lives no different from, and in some cases worse than, their "unsaved" neighbors, particularly when it comes to how they spend their money, their fidelity in marriage, and the commitment to racial equality and reconciliation.[65] By such evidences, evangelical Christians commit "treason," according to Sider. "With their mouths they claim that Jesus is Lord, but with their actions they demonstrate allegiance to money, sex, and self-fulfillment."[66]

Sider recognizes that a significant cause of such "treason" is the "cheap grace" preached in many evangelical churches, along with an overemphasis on substitutionary atonement and justification at the expense of the lordship of Christ and sanctification.[66] He argues for recovering the social aspect of salvation along with the personal aspect.[68] What is absent from his framework is a meaningful consideration of how the personal and social aspect of salvation can be joined in a way that makes it impossible to recognize them separately. Menno's understanding of Jesus' holy flesh as accessible through the incorruptible seed in the church provides just such a holistic theology—an undivided Christ, an undivided salvation, an undivided humanity.

From this perspective, Jesus is not a portable deity who travels with Christians as a kind of good-luck charm or cheerful pal to secure their lives. The relationship between Christians and Jesus is not primarily "personal." And the presence of Jesus does not make an individual "perfect," as in the Wesleyan holiness doctrine of sanctification. Rather, Jesus is the one to whom we have become attached and through whom we have been regenerated insofar as we have been baptized into newness of life in the church. Our membership in Christ's body renews us and restores us because the same incorruptible seed from which Christ was born is the seed from which we have been reborn. Our "perfection" lies in our attachment to Jesus Christ, not in any deeds we are able to perform as individuals through our corruptible flesh. We are saved in the church, not apart from it. Being without spot or wrinkle is only possible when we are acting as faithful members of Christ's body.

Thus, an important reason why evangelical Christians in North America are living like the world is because they have become primarily of the world, which is to say that they don't spend enough of their life as part of the church. To become like Jesus will require that they participate in his life and suffering as members of his body. Such suffering solidarity is not a matter of despising the flesh, as Dennis Martin has accused Menno of teaching, but rather of divinizing the flesh—making bodies godly.[69]

Menno, in his version of celestial flesh doctrine, succeeded in linking the Christ of the atonement with the Christ of the creation, as J. A. Oosterban pointed out back in 1961.[70] Oosterban saw much to praise in Menno's vision of a church wherein believers share Jesus' body, becoming "flesh of his flesh and bone of his bone."[71] Oosterban also recognized that such a vision had dawned again in the writings of that great theologian Karl Barth, who wrote that "the Virgin birth at the opening and the empty tomb at the close of Jesus' life bear witness that this life is a fact marked off from the rest of human life" and that "the mystery at the beginning is the basis of the mystery at the end."[72] Thus, for Barth, as for Menno, the "Holy Spirit by which Jesus was conceived" is the same Spirit by which it "becomes really possible for the creature, for man, to be . . . free for God," and for "flesh, human nature" to be "assumed into unity with the Son of God."[73] This "freedom which the Holy Spirit gives" is for Barth, as for Menno, "the freedom of the Church, of the children of God."[74] We are saved, in other words, not simply by a personal appropriation of Jesus' saving death on the cross. We have been saved, rather, in our attachment to the church (the body of Christ), by the power of the Holy Spirit and through the birth, death, and resurrection of Jesus Christ, the Word who became flesh and dwelt among us, and from whose incorruptible seed our bodies have been regenerated.

NOTES

1. *The Complete Writings of Menno Simons*, trans. Leonard Verduin (Scottdale, Pa: Herald Press, 1956; reprint, 1978), 335-36.

2. J. Denny Weaver, *Anabaptist Theology in Face of Postmodernity: A Proposal for the Third Millennium* (Telford, Pa.: Pandora Press U.S., 2000), 104-05.

3. Cornelius Krahn, "Incarnation of Christ," in *Mennonite Encyclopedia 3* (Scottdale, Pa: Herald Press, 1957), 19.

4. Keith L. Sprunger, "Dutch Anabaptists and the Telling of Martyr Stories," *Mennonite Quarterly Review* 80/2 (April 2006): 170-73.

5. *The Complete Works of Menno Simons*, (Elkhart, Ind.: John F. Funk and Brother, 1871), 452.

6. *Opera omnia theologica, of alle de godtgeleerde wercken van Menno Symons*, (Amsterdam: Joannes van Veen, 1681), 546-48.

7. *The Complete Writings of Menno Simons*, 836-37.

8. Ibid., 837.

9. Abraham Friesen, *Erasmus, the Anabaptists, and the Great Commission* (Grand Rapids, Mich.: Wm. B. Eerdmans, 1998), 62-64.

10. Thomas Finger, "Confessions of Faith in the Anabaptist/Mennonite Tradition," *Mennonite Quarterly Review* 76/3 (July 2002): 283.

11. Philip Schaff, ed., *The Evangelical Protestant Creeds*, 6th. ed., 3 vols., vol. 3, *The Creeds of Christendom* (Grand Rapids, Mich.: Baker Books, 1983; reprint, 1998), 403.

12. William E. Keeney, *The Development of Dutch Anabaptist Thought and Practice from 1539-1564* (Nieuwkoop,: B. de Graaf, 1968), 89-100.

13. Ibid., 91. An example of this argument is Menno's answer to the fifth objection in his "Een korte ende klare belydinge," in *Opera omnia theologica, of alle de godtgeleerde wercken van Menno Symons*, 531.

14. Keeney, *The Development of Dutch Anabaptist Thought and Practice from 1539-1564*, 92.

15. Ibid.

16. Ibid. See also Joyce Irwin, "Embryology and Incarnation: A Sixteenth-Century Debate," *Sixteenth-Century Journal* 9/3 (1978): 94-96.
17. Keeney, *The Development of Dutch Anabaptist Thought and Practice from 1539-1564*, 97.
18. Irvin Burkhart's study of Menno's views on the incarnation concludes that Menno believed that "all flesh is inherently evil," a claim that Burkhart later retracted in a correction where he stated unequivocally that "Menno did not teach that the flesh of man is inherently evil." See I. E. Burkhart, "Note: Menno Simons on the Incarnation (a Correction)," *Mennonite Quarterly Review* 6/2 (April 1932): 122-23, Irvin E. Burkhart, "Menno Simons on the Incarnation (Continued)" *Mennonite Quarterly Review* 4/3 (July 1930): 179.
19. For a discussion of celestial flesh that places this conviction in the context of contemporary feminist understandings of the body, see Gerald Biesecker-Mast, "Spiritual Knowledge, Carnal Obedience, and Anabaptist Discipleship," *Mennonite Quarterly Review* 71/2 (April 1997): 213.
20. *The Complete Writings of Menno Simons*, 794.
21. Ibid., 850, Irwin, "Embryology and Incarnation: A Sixteenth-Century Debate," 95-96.
22. *The Complete Writings of Menno Simons*, 851.
23. Ibid., 820-21.
24. Ibid., 793, 820.
25. Ibid., 814-15.
26. Ibid., 19-25.
27. Cornelius Krahn, "Menno Simons," in *Mennonite Encyclopedia 3*, ed. Cornelius Krahn (Scottdale, Pa.: Herald Press, 1957), 580.
28. *The Complete Writings of Menno Simons*, 785.
29. Ibid.
30. Ibid., 836.
31. Ibid., 334-35.
32. Ibid., 865-84.
33. Ibid., 922.
34. Ibid.
35. Ibid., 920.
36. Ibid., 423.
37. Ibid., 307.
38. Ibid., 423.
39. Egil Grislis, "The Doctrine of the Incarnation According to Menno Simons," *Journal of Mennonite Studies* 8 (1990): 30.
40. Ibid.
41. William Keeney, "The Incarnation, a Central Theological Concept," in *A Legacy of Faith: The Heritage of Menno Simons*, ed. Cornelius J. Dyck (Newton, Kan.: Faith and Life Press, 1962), 64.
42. *The Complete Writings of Menno Simons*, 146.
43. Ibid., 148.
44. Ibid., 151.
45. Sjouke Voolstra, *Menno Simons: His Image and Message*, ed. John D. Thiessen, vol. 10, Cornelius H. Wedel Historical Series (North Newton, Kan.:

Bethel College, 1996), 66.
46. *The Complete Works of Menno Simons*, II: 172, *The Complete Writings of Menno Simons*, 96-97.
47. *The Complete Writings of Menno Simons*, 439.
48. Ibid., 234.
49. Ibid., 244.
50. Ibid. *Opera omnia theologica, of alle de godtgeleerde wercken van Menno Symons*, 406.
51. *The Complete Writings of Menno Simons*, 245.
52. Ibid. *Opera omnia theologica, of alle de godtgeleerde wercken van Menno Symons*, 406. Menno adds that "we are not cleansed by the washing of the water, but by the Word of the Lord . . . ."
53. *The Complete Writings of Menno Simons*, 564-65.
54. Ibid., 564.
55. Ibid., 342-43.
56. Ibid., 343.
57. Ibid., 307, 884.
58. Ibid., 884.
59. Ibid., 885.
60. Ibid., 347.
61. Ibid., 347-48.
62. Sjouke Voolstra, *Het Woord Is vlees geworden: De melchioritisch-menniste incarnatieleer*, vol. 8, Dissertationes Neerlandicae Series Theologica (Kampen: Uitgeversmaatschappij J. H. Kok, 1982), 213.
63. Ibid.
64. Grislis, "The Doctrine of the Incarnation According to Menno Simons," 31.
65. Ronald J. Sider, *The Scandal of the Evangelical Conscience* (Grand Rapids, Mich.: Baker Books, 2005), 17-29.
66. Ibid., 12-13.
67. Ibid., 55-69.
68. Ibid., 72-83.
69. Dennis Martin, "Menno and Augustine on the Body of Christ," *Fides et Historia* 20/3 (1988): 43-51.
70. J. A. Oosterbaan, "The Theology of Menno Simons," *Mennonite Quarterly Review* 35/3 (July 1961): 192.
71. Ibid., 195.
72. Karl Barth, *Church Dogmatics: The Doctrine of the Word of God. Vol. 1 Book 2* (Edinburgh: T&T Clark, 1956), 182-83.
73. Ibid., 199.
74. Ibid., 198.

CHAPTER NINE

The Canons of Anabaptism: Which Anabaptism? Whose Canon?

Ray Gingerich

*M*y purpose in this essay is to review the shifting foci of Anabaptist research since H. S. Bender's historic essay, "The Anabaptist Vision," first published in 1944.[1] This review is in the context of a search for a usable and "normative" Anabaptism—an "Anabaptist canon"—to serve us in the beginning of our twenty-first century. I do not seek to be objective, but I seek to be fair in exposing not merely the biases of some of my colleagues, but my own biases and commitments as well. My hope is that the result of this essay may honor our Anabaptist heritage and serve the Mennonite church of today by the guidelines it suggests and by further stimulating constructive dialogue.

I introduce this essay with two theses. Both theses are almost axiomatic in our age and presumably noncontroversial. I illustrate both theses with historical events in sixteenth-century Anabaptist research, although I presume that not everyone may agree with all of the illustrations.

Thesis one: What we look for is what we find. This is at least a halftruth. The biases we bring most certainly influence the outcome. Bender went about finding a usable history for Mennonites in the mid-twentieth century. And he found it.² At least many of us felt he did. He was so persuasive that the masses of those who resonated with his findings made Bender's the vision privileged with special authority for nearly half a century.

James Stayer, Werner Packull, and Klaus Depperman went about to find a different kind of Anabaptism from that which Bender had mapped out. And they found it. At least many of us felt they did.³ Today anyone entering the scholarly portals of sixteenth-century Anabaptism must still genuflect in acknowledgement to some form of polygenesis theory even if no longer needing to do obeisance of mind to it.

Thesis two: The tools we deploy determine the task we accomplish. What we set about to do is significantly influenced and sometimes outright determined by the tools we deploy. The sieves we use determine the minerals we pan (*and* the stuff that is allowed to slide back into the stream unnoticed and unchanged). Or, to shift metaphors, the focus of our lens determines which objects fall sharply into our purview and which ones form the blurred background. Hence, the tools we deploy determine not merely the precision with which we accomplish the task, but the nature of the outcome.

Social historian Claus-Peter Classen did a numbers game.⁴ He found that the persecuted and executed Anabaptists were far fewer in number than their empathizing posterity had declared. From the same disciplinary orientation, Paul Peachey, at an even earlier date, also did a numbers game. He found just the kinds of nuggets his sociological "panning screen" was designed to find—namely that Anabaptism was a genuine religious movement and was therefore not in any significant way associated with the political upheavals of the peasants' movements of the times.⁵ Fritz Blanke wrote his short history of Anabaptist beginnings in Zurich with an eye to documenting once again that Anabaptism was a religious renewal movement, not politically motivated—heroic deeds done, not by knaves, but by courageous people, whose time had not yet come.⁶

These two theses do not mean that history is but a fabrication, or that the tasks of the fiction writer and the historian are not to be distinguished from each other. It does mean, however, that there is no one who writes history objectively, "as it *really* was,"⁷ despite the fact that these claims are still echoed by certain contemporary historians, including Anabaptist ones. It also points to the necessity that as historians and theologians we need to be more conscious of our own predispositions (thesis number one above) and of the methods we use to legitimate our findings (thesis number two above).

In Section I below, I sketch the contours of twentieth-century Anabaptist research and scholarship. I also indicate the methodological requirements I think necessary for Anabaptist scholarship to have relevance for the church and the world of the twenty-first century.

In Section II, I indicate what analytical tools I am using by laying out my own presuppositions. Through these presuppositions I discern and analyze certain aspects of Anabaptism commonly ignored, even at times denied.[8] At the same time, these presuppositions allow me largely to pass over those aspects of Anabaptism that were everywhere present in the culture and religion of the times, and so, of course, were also present in Anabaptism, characteristics that didn't play a significant role in making Anabaptism distinct from the larger Christendom, or politically more radical, or biblically more faithful.[9]

In the final section I outline what it is that I perceive sixteenth-century Anabaptism has that is of special significance for the church and the world of today. What, I ask, ought to be the quality and characteristics of Anabaptism for the twenty-first century?

EXPLORING THE WRITINGS, DETERMINING CANONICAL BOUNDARIES: WHICH ANABAPTISM?

A. Steps and Stages in the Process: Determining Who the Real Anabaptists Are[10]

One can discern a series of movements within Anabaptist historiography of the past seventy years. These movements include:

1. A shift from depicting Anabaptists as heretics to considering Anabaptists to be true believers;[11]

2. A move from a literal, historical rendition of a single regional group of Anabaptists—e.g., early Swiss[12]—to a selective reading of a "normative" segment of a wider movement;[13]

3. A move from the selective reading of a normative regional movement to a selective reading of Anabaptists (or baptized ones) all over the Continent.[14] This resulted in a "lowest common denominator" phenomenon in which there was little that Anabaptists held in common except water baptism;

4. A move from a selective yet nondiscriminating[15] reading of those who were baptized (e.g., Stayer) to a more selectively discriminating reading of individual leaders of the movement;[16]

5. Whereas all of the above readings still made the tacit monogenesis assumption that at least implicitly motivated the researchers to link the various players under one umbrella—if not otherwise, then at least through (re)baptism—the next significant move is from monogenesis to polygenesis.[17] Exploding the so-called "myth of monogenesis" meant that no one could any longer seriously work on sixteenth-century Anabaptism without at some level factoring in the impact on Anabaptist historiography of multiple origins and multiple movements—and, if not multiple Anabaptisms, then at least numerous diverse strands of Anabaptism.

In going from Anabaptism with multiple origins and multiple movements, the larger question then is: What constitutes Anabaptism? How are we to interpret the phenomenon? What is the cohesive, uniting factor among the differing strands? Are Anabaptists prophetic or pastoral? Political or apolitical? Principled pacifists or pragmatic revolutionaries? Or, has the very term "Anabaptism" become clichéd and generalized beyond usefulness? Will the real Anabaptists please stand up?[18]

Anabaptism, for some, meant that which was present in all Anabaptists—regardless of whether that "something" everywhere present was a key factor in shaping the movement and in determining its values. Hence for Stayer all that was left was adult baptism, while for Snyder it was some form of spirituality (mysticism).[19] For others, recognition of multiple origins did not debunk the basic tenets of the Bender model—a visible, mutually accountable fellowship; discipleship, or following the way of Jesus; and pacifism, or nonresistance.[20] Nevertheless, with polygenesis began the fading of the Bender vision, a diminishing of that privileged perspective—with the emergence of polygenesis came the eventual rise of poly-visions.[21]

B. From the History of Ideas to an Analysis of Social Movements: Doctrine versus Ethics

The larger fault line in the research and interpretation of Anabaptism is not monogenesis versus polygenesis. The most important divide was and is between the *history of ideas* or *idea-ism* (usually described under the rubric of idealism), in which the essence or the essentialness (or substance)[22] of history is carried by the medium of ideas, versus *social history*. Here the socioculture of a particular society and age becomes the primary determinant of the nature of a movement, including its ideas and its impact on history.[23] The debate of monogenesis versus polygenesis focuses primarily on tracing direct historical continuity of specific ideas and individual leaders. The methodological orientation remains that of a "histories of ideas."[24]

Within theology, this distinction between scholastic idealism and socio-cultural history is most commonly manifested in an opposition between *orthodoxy* and *orthopraxis*.[25] This opposition in turn is expressed religiously in the differing modes of a group's worship. Two main options can be identified. On the one hand, one has a more *ritually and sacramentally oriented worship*, with its high point in either the sacrament of the sermon (Reformed) or, in another stream of traditions, a service culminating in the sacrament of the Eucharist (Catholic, Lutheran, Anglican). The alternative to ritually and sacramentally oriented worship is a worship service focusing on the people—their everyday struggles, both their victories and defeats, be they personal, social, political, economic, or spiritual—with the apex of the service being congregational sharing. Amid this celebration the teachings and example of Jesus are upheld—Jesus as a social transformer holding forth a prophetic understanding of justice, a redeemer of people in the process of creating a more life-giving community at-the-edge-of-the-old,[26] Jesus as one who initiates "the reign of God."[27]

C. From the Social History to the History of Incarnation: From Cultural Norms to Particularistic Ethics

This groundswell shift from the history of ideas to a socio-political history with its *epistemological fault line* introduces social dynamics and ethical values into the search for finding a normative Anabaptism. In earlier historiographical stages, social structures were merely *forms* that held the content; here, in what I am calling "particularistic incarnational ethics," these social structures are inseparable from the content. An Anabaptist communal ecclesiology needs a social ethic that applies not simply to individual people and groups of people but also to the church as an institution. Far more than in the sixteenth century, church institutions (both the congregations proper and the many para-church institutions) today constitute a significant component of who we are and what shapes our moral character and ethos. As an institution, at whatever level, we should be no less Christ-like than as individuals. Our institutions are integral to who we are. *We are they.*

From an Anabaptist perspective, if the structures that shape us (family, congregation, education) are not redeemed, then we too will not be redeemed. Less categorically stated, the more life-giving, just, and holistically empowering the structures that shape us, the more whole and healthy we become. Where God's movement of justice-with-peace is found, whether in the sixteenth-century Reformation or in contemporary twenty-first century life, there dynamic, normative[28] "Anabaptism," including its structures, is emerging.

Sixteenth-century Anabaptism was not the first and only place since the first century CE in which the phenomenon of justice-with-peace emerged as a renewal movement within the church.[29] Rather, sixteenth-century Anabaptism is normatively distinctive for us today because it was a life-generating, transformative movement with substantial *social rootage* so that it was both sustained and replicated throughout a longer historical period. It was not simply the reality of an idea or of a charismatic leader, but a much thicker reality of people profoundly enmeshed within the culture and politics of their times, embodying a new way of life.

If truth comes through people rather than merely through the ideas of people, if truth needs to be embodied socially and not merely represented through symbols, if truth is moral and not merely logical, then to understand the human race is to understand it socially, to understand it as community. *To understand history socially is not merely an option; it is an imperative*. If we accept the Christian claim that God is revealed through incarnational community, and not primarily through doctrinal creeds, nor through tables of stone, then both doctrinal and sacramental theology may be misleading—not because of "bad theology," but because of the deception such theology poses in its claim to reveal God and the way of salvation.

Anabaptism was a social movement of desacralization, not merely because the sacraments were viewed as magical and therefore idolatrous, but also because the sacraments were a method for the established church to maintain control of salvation—a church which, according to many, embodied neither salvation nor the hope of God's coming reign. The truth of creeds and sacramental theology is reductionist inasmuch as sacrament and dogma have displaced the larger reality they purportedly represent and communicate through sacred transmission.

Furthermore, it is qualitatively more difficult—should I say impossible?—to communicate human relationships and the life-generating dynamics of social movements through the medium of sacral language and sacraments rather than to communicate them through the lives of individuals in committed groups and movements. Grace is the transmission of dignity and hope in a social context defined by practices of dignity and the sharing of justice (righteousness) within a society that embodies justice. Hence, in our attempt to find an "Anabaptism" for the twenty-first century we look for those communities that took seriously the deceptions implicit in the sacramental and focus instead on the incarnation embodied in peoplehood.[30]

D. The Centrality of Nonviolence with Justice

As we continue the search to "determine the canonical boundaries" and to discern "which Anabaptisms" are "canonical," it should not strike us as an accident that the Anabaptist movements that endured were those that espoused a nonviolent way of life and became pacifist—a few of them from the beginning, most of them over a longer period of dialogue and struggle. Pacifism in Jesus' time, as in the sixteenth-century, was a costly venture. Such a movement does not normally and logically survive except where conviction runs deep and practice is consistent.[31]

There is scholarly consensus that those movements associated with Anabaptism that were spiritual (mystical)[32] but not nonviolent did not survive. Neither did those that were communal but not nonviolent. We may therefore rightly ask: What was that movement that survived through the decades and even centuries to which certain Anabaptists belonged, a movement which at the same time they were creating?[33] At its very core was nonviolence-with-justice,[34] that which they understood the teachings and example of Jesus to be. In its nascent stages it began with a refusal to participate in that which is death-dealing and insisted on that which is life-giving.

We can then move toward a more specific expression called "nonviolent peace-with-justice." We may look to the acute question of whether or not to baptize infants that led Conrad Grebel, Felix Mantz, Georg Blaurock, and their colleagues to the insight that adults who were sacramentally (in their understanding, magically) baptized as infants had not been scripturally baptized. Or we may examine Michael Sattler, who identified his possible affinity with the Anabaptists in his struggle against collecting taxes from the peasants.

It was the struggle with Wilhelm Reublin on how to deal with the powers-that-be that brought the issue of the use of the "sword" to a crisis within the group. It was Hans Hut who moved from the chiliastic Thomas Müntzer toward a more pacifist, life-giving stance as he experienced fellowship with the Swiss Brethren refugees in Nikolsburg. It was the followers of Hut who were most communal among the Anabaptists in the years following the Nikolsburg episode. And was it not Menno Simons in the wake of the Münster debacle who found a pacifist way of moving forward and saving the movement?

Nothing in the life of the Anabaptist movement (or, as some would prefer, of the various Anabaptist movements) *was more normatively radical, challenging the old systems to their roots and grafting new communities of life, than was engaged nonviolence practiced by the movement's participants.* At this point we need not argue whether this was the nonviolence of the "apolitical" dissidents, or the nonviolence of the "sheathed sword," or the non-biblical pragmatic nonviolence of political necessity, or the nonviolence that emerged out of the inter-Anabaptist struggle and dissension. What should be noted, however, is that (1) each of these enduring Anabaptist movements emerged out of a trajectory from a lesser to a greater, to a more fully orbed, socially rooted nonviolence; and that (2) the practice of nonviolence, as we are able to observe it within the bounds of history, does not, in itself, guarantee the continuity of the movement. God, or the Power of the Universe, we are left to believe, guides that. This is not something that human beings can control. What humanity is called to do is to live in love and generosity—i.e., nonviolently. What Christians, more specifically, are called to do is to follow Jesus.

Hence, a certain kind of sixteenth-century Anabaptism was normatively distinctive in the same way the Jesus movement was normatively distinctive for the early church. Had Jesus simply lived individually at the highest *spiritual* plane of a renewed individual without profoundly intersecting with the cultural powers of his time and his town, engaging its peoples nonviolently and creating a following, we would not know about him today. Likewise, had Felix Mantz or Michael Sattler and their companions, or Hans Hut, not belonged to a movement while at once also generating a nonviolent movement, they would undoubtedly have long ago dropped off of history's radar screen. Similarly, Menno in the wake of Münster's violence found a nonviolent way to save the movement and advance the cause.

Anabaptism was not a movement that can be reduced to numbers and quantities, nor to a resurgence of mysticism[35] or any other form of non-social, inner-oriented spirituality. Those who would say that nonviolence was not at the core of prophetic Anabaptism have history against them. *The burden is theirs to show how they interpret the prophetic endurance of the Anabaptist movement more authentically, more historically, more according to the data we have available to us*—a movement of ethical/moral values, significantly interlinked with the politics of the day—*without placing nonviolence at the center.*[36]

Linked with the nonviolent practice of refusing to go to war or to kill the enemy is the kind of theology the church practices. The Anabaptist witness of the sixteenth century (and the witness and way of Jesus of the first century) cannot, I believe, be carried forward in the twenty-first century via traditional theology.[37] Traditional theology represents control and domination by the established church of the Corpus Christianum.[38] Historically it has functioned (and continues to function so today) to legitimate the violence of church and Empire. Furthermore, *by its very nature traditional theology creates dualisms* when it is applied to contemporary social ethics. Because the spirituality it espouses (metaphysical and mystical) cannot readily and meaningfully be applied to social constructs and politics, it serves to eviscerate the holistic discipleship-ethics of Jesus.

The church today is moving toward moral bankruptcy with its dualisms: the dualism of power—affirming nonviolence for the church and violence for the state; the dualism of economics—affirming an ecclesiology of communalism and generosity, but operating both individually and institutionally on "free market capitalism" and profit-maximizing principles; a dualism of politics—a kind of theological socialism (neighbor love, sharing freely with the poor), but in practice a selective democracy of an economic elite[39] in which the rich are getting richer while the poor are getting poorer; a dualism between the individual and the institutions of our church—for personal and family life we affirm discipleship and self-sacrifice as taught in the Sermon on the Mount, but we are unwilling to apply such a self-giving gospel ethic to our institutions; a dualism of epistemology in which theologically we are Christians by belief in the creeds and the practice of the sacraments, but ethically and practically we are Christians on the basis of following Jesus.

The more we become a people who are materially affluent, the more conspicuous become our religious dualisms. The American ethos in which the Mennonite Church and other pacifist-oriented groups find themselves in the beginning of the twenty-first century is culturally seducing many of us to choose the wrong option presented by each one of these dualisms—i.e., the option that moves us away from Anabaptism. An Anabaptist vision and model for the current century will need to address our contemporary dualistic existence theologically if it is to be overcome practically.

So before I go further in outlining an Anabaptist vision that has historical integrity and contemporary relevance, let me lay out some of the presuppositions with which I am working. This will enable the reader more easily to grasp the way I am framing the vision. I will not defend these presuppositions at length, although some are more self-evident than others. My goal is to clarify where I am coming from, not necessarily to convince the reader. The question of agreement or disagreement can be considered later as the contours of the Anabaptism I am championing emerge.

CONTEMPORARY PRESUPPOSITIONS RELEVANT TO ANABAPTISM: WHOSE CANON?

The presuppositions that follow represent assumptions that I hold, assumptions that come before my suggestions for an "Anabaptist canon" but which undergird these statements. Obviously, not every so-called "Anabaptism" is of equal value. That is, not every contemporary set of values (which for heuristic purposes I am calling "canonical guidelines") correlates with the abiding life-giving values of sixteenth-century Anabaptism. Inversely, not everything common to sixteenth-century Anabaptism can or should be transferred into our world today. This is in part due to the shift in worldviews (i.e., our perceptions of the cosmos)—from the ancient worldview to the modern and postmodern.[40] What applies to sixteenth-century Anabaptism also applies in many ways to the biblical materials and the early church. The worldview of the sixteenth century was far more comparable to that of the first century CE than to the modern/postmodern worldview of our society today.

But there is a further very significant issue at stake here—not all Anabaptists were equally "right." Or, to say it less crassly, some Anabaptists were more helpful in promoting the way of Jesus than were others; some just plainly got some things wrong. Again, what applies to the sixteenth-century Anabaptists sometimes also applies to biblical writers. Ours, then, is the ongoing task of discernment—of finding that which most calls attention to the way of Jesus and directs people along that path.[41]

My first presupposition is that *power is of one essence and nature*—i.e., a mono-essence. Whether ecclesial or state, whether local, national, or transnational, whether personal, vocational, or institutional—power is ultimately of *one* nature and essence. Appearances deceive. Cultural conditioning seduces. Power shows itself in many forms and expressions, but it is not both violence and nonviolence. If the way of Jesus is true, and if we believe in the resurrection, then power—ultimate power—is nonviolent. What I have attempted to show biblically and theologically elsewhere,[42] Hannah Arendt has argued at length philosophically and politically. She succinctly summarizes: "To speak of nonviolent power is actually redundant. Violence can destroy power; it is utterly incapable of creating it."[43]

This understanding of power becomes particularly important in moving away from the historical dualism of sixteenth-century Schleitheim[44] to find the meaning and relevance of Schleitheim for today. To grasp what lies behind this presupposition—namely, that power is nonviolent and that violence is always a reflection of weakness—calls for a paradigm shift or what in religious language may best be described as a kind of conversion.[45]

Inasmuch as today Mennonites/Anabaptists play a major role in the current American Empire, and insofar as Mennonites operate consciously or subconsciously with dual understandings of power—both coercive and violent on the one hand and nonviolent on the other—the need to move beyond dualism becomes vital.[46]

Second, I presuppose that *Empire is the commonly shared political system*. The common external political context shared by the early church, by sixteenth-century Anabaptists, and by the North American church of today, particularly within the United States, is Empire.[47] In each of these eras the church (wherever it can be found) exists amid Empire and participates in Empire. This is one of the most direct parallels that can be drawn between Jesus' culture, the Anabaptists', and ours. Yet far too seldom is the connection made.

The church of today, even as the followers of Jesus and the early church did, finds its *identity* in the political context of *Empire*. The church and the Empire constitute two distinct yet commingling societies embodying distinctly contrasting political systems—the one is a system of domination, the other a domination-freeing society.[48] Nevertheless, as Wink reminds us, "God's reign does not represent the polar opposite of the Domination System. Otherwise it would need the latter to supply the tension of the opposites. The opposites are contained *within* God's reign."[49]

Where the church fails to struggle with Empire, whether because it is withdrawn or because it has been assimilated by the Empire, it fails to be the church of Jesus Christ. Empire becomes the negative political force which spurs the church to develop a keener prophetic identity. When the church loses its counter-identity it is not neutral; it then provides the religious reinforcement for the Empire.[50] The church as an institution then, de facto, becomes a Corpus Christianum and a religio-political muscle of Empire.[51]

My third presupposition is that *humans are instinctively[52] idol-worshipers*. Human nature has an overwhelming propensity toward idolatry. This has not changed one whit since the first century CE. The human being is an idol-building creature. As co-creators with God, we build our own environment: our organizational structures, our symbol systems, our laws, our institutions. We build our cultural structures with our own "hands," our own ingenuity. Once built, our culture and its institutions stand out away from us and above us. Our cultural structures surround us and penetrate our depths. They determine our habits and mold our thoughts. We in turn pay homage to all these cultural creations—to our nation and its institutions, its "free-market capitalism," its "freedom of religion," its "right to protect itself," even its sovereignty. This is idolatry. But as with all idolatry, the idolater of today does not recognize her idolatry.

Next to human nature itself, religion is the most central ingredient needed in the construction of idols and idolatrous systems. Religion is the transcendent glue that helps to make it all hang together. We socialize our thought (repeating it among us over a period of time), then call it divine doctrine. We sacralize our symbols and allow certain ones to stand in as shorthand for the sufferings of God in Christ. We laud a divine Jesus Christ in worship at the expense of a human Jesus. We sacralize our Scriptures, at times referring to them as infallible or as inspired from cover to cover. We sacralize our Mennonite institutions, supporting them with blood money, and allowing them to oppress individuals far beyond the bounds of love—all in the name of the "greater good." We sacralize meditation and mysticism, calling them "paths to God." We sacralize violence as power and, if it is wielded by the state, legitimate it for the cause of God.

This sacralization does not need to be absolute to be effective. That which is sacralized attracts. A thing holds power merely by being more "sacred" than what surrounds it. Our religion and our gods are determined less by what we confess than to whom our lives are committed and what we do. Let me show you the source of my values and the center of my loyalties, and you will know the God I worship. How we understand the person, the role of idolatry in the context of religion, and the nature of doctrine and sacraments, plays a major role in how we understand Anabaptism—and in how we determine which "Anabaptism" is the more authentic. Much of Anabaptism of the sixteenth century was a desacralizing movement.[53]

Why is this discussion of idolatry so important for our task of determining a usable and authentic Anabaptism? Our greatest danger today in an age of clamoring allegiances is not false belief, but false loyalties and commitments; not heresy, but idolatry. It is the community we live in rather than the intellectual acumen we acquire that provides the tools and the necessary social context to free ourselves of idolatry. It is the quality of relationships within the community rather than impersonal rituals and sacred sacraments of the tradition that protect us from the quest for false security leading to idolatry. The Anabaptists to be included in our contemporary "canon" were keenly aware of this.

Fourth, I presuppose that *the qualities of authentic Anabaptism cannot be determined by reducing them to a quantifiable phenomenon.* To restate, that which makes Anabaptism authentic (or worthy to be in the Anabaptist canon) cannot, in the end, be quantified. The value and authenticity of Anabaptism, as is the case with all religious, moral, ethical, and political movements, is a *phenomenon of quality and by nature does not allow quantification.* This does not mean numbers cease to matter. Nevertheless, what constitutes an authentic Anabaptist community or movement is determined less by its quantity than by its quality; less by objective tabulation than by the community's ability to be ethically discerning; less by the number of times a phenomenon appears than by what proceeds and follows that phenomenon—i.e., the societal impact it makes and the structures it challenges.

It should be clear by now that a simple "Anabaptist act"—even if that act is one of adult believer's water baptism, and even if this marks the derivation of the term *ana-baptist*, and even if this was one of the few things (perhaps the *only* thing) that all Anabaptists held in common—*it in itself does not constitute the hallmark of Anabaptism.*

The historian who attempts to do quantifiable Anabaptist research and ends up reducing the movement to its lowest common denominator does both the sixteenth-century Anabaptists and his or her contemporary readers a grave disservice. To depict sixteenth-century Anabaptist movements as having had few common distinctives except for several quantifiable religious acts (e.g., water baptism, the mark of the cross), and therefore, instead, to concentrate on what Anabaptists held in common with mainline religion (Catholic or Protestant), is likewise a disservice. Such approaches fail to capture the dynamic Anabaptist spirit of renewal for both the church and the larger society.

No historian in our postmodern era should be allowed to say, "I'm just doing history," if by that is implied that history is value-neutral, that all acts or events occurring in history are of essentially equal "weight," and that what we perceive in our reading of the documents is not affected by the values we hold.

My fifth and final presupposition is that *what "gets in the way when doing good" is the starting point for a prophetic social analysis.*[54] Social opposition when walking the way of Jesus may be an indicator that our witness is prophetically relevant for the times. When opposition, whether from Caiphas or Herod, appears, I must take note! The practices of Jesus inevitably get in the way both of established religion and of Empire. Justice,[55] dignity, and peace—such practices call for societal change and evoke mainstream opposition. The creativity and the validity of any particular social movement must, of course, be measured within its cultural context. However, when people are captured and executed, not for commonly recognized crimes, but because of the way they live (or because of the oaths they refuse to swear), I must ask: To whom were they committed? What was their cause? Who was being threatened? And what would the equivalent be in our day?

What we perceive as the task at hand determines the tools we deploy. To determine the quality and characteristics of a movement within any given culture and society—particularly when the mainstream society in which the movement is situated constitutes a system of domination and oppression—we examine not that which the sub-group shares with all of society, but that which distinctively calls for a just, more fair, more loving society. Furthermore, we identify that which raises resistance and creates opposition not as good in its own right simply because of opposition, but on the basis of whether it creates just-peace and is other-oriented, i.e., not for the enhancement of personal status or power, but for the benefit of others. We look not simply for whatever might be different, but for those distinctive things that "name the powers" and "unmask the domination system"—to use Wink's terminology. To "name" and to "unmask" the evils of a society is to alert others and to invite them to participate in renewal. It also alerts "the powers that be" and places them before a necessary choice. It is this that "gets in the way when doing good." It is this that must be taken most seriously when determining one's canon of Anabaptism.

To illustrate the contrary of what "gets in the way," we need only to look at the emphasis on spirituality. Spirituality was literally *everywhere* in the sixteenth century; it was the *modus vivendi* of the society as a whole.[56] To emphasize the spirituality of Anabaptism is to observe that Anabaptists were like all the rest of society. While in itself neither good nor bad, spirituality does not distinguish Anabaptism from the worst citizens of the Empire. Therefore, it cannot possibly be what Anabaptism was really about. To present it as such, whether in our historical studies of Anabaptism or in our contemporary teachings called "Anabaptist," we do the movement a great disservice.

Contrast this again with the refusal to use violence when the Turks (the Muslims) were pounding at the gates of Vienna; the refusal to carry weapons when ordered by the duke, the prince, or the emperor; the refusal to use violence amid a political context that makes "violence the only sensible response"—such refusal makes pacifism treasonous. Such refusal gets in the way! Such refusal makes Anabaptists distinctive for the cause of Jesus. Understandably, it places them into our canon of authentic witnesses.

CANONICAL GUIDELINES: KEY CHARACTERISTICS OF THE ANABAPTIST CHURCH OF THE TWENTY-FIRST CENTURY[57]

All this background allows us finally to ask more directly: What then are the distinctive features of Anabaptism in the sixteenth-century that have ongoing significance for the twenty-first century? *The authority of Anabaptism—and hence its normativeness—is determined not by the total corpus of sixteenth-century Anabaptist writings but by its life-giving function in society then and now.* That which is life-giving is of God and worthy to be emulated. That which is death-dealing is not of God. What are the marks of an authentic, life-giving Anabaptist vision for today?

So, within the context of the five presuppositions that I have laid out, I now set forth five distinctives that shape an Anabaptist vision for the twenty-first century and for the new millennium.[58]

a. To be Anabaptist is to be a people of community

No single feature in Anabaptism is structurally more important than the viability of its caring and prophetic community. Furthermore, no single feature in the ongoing Anabaptist vision for today is more difficult to maintain than its social structures reaching everyone at the grassroots. In saying this I am not suggesting that social structures are ends in themselves; quite the contrary. But precisely because the structures of a society both reflect and determine the quality of the society I am underscoring this point.

As human beings we cannot live without social structures. But structures also repeatedly become oppressive. Mennonites in the twentieth century became experts at building social structures—institutions. We do well at building hierarchies, but we have not learned to structure our peoplehood and our institutions horizontally. For both church and business we have taken our models from General Electric and General Motors, not from Anabaptism. Sixteenth-century Anabaptist theology is helpful in providing us with general principles for institution building. It is not very helpful in showing us how actually to do it. Not because they did it wrong: sixteenth-century Anabaptists didn't have the opportunity to do institution building.

The American Mennonite churches have moved from charismatic leadership to institutional leadership, some would say to institutional domination. We have gone from the bishop to the boardroom. We borrowed our institutional models from the world using the wisdom of the world to construct them—often using the best that was available. All of our major church institutions—but particularly our institutions of higher education and our financial and insurance agencies—look amazingly similar to their secular counterparts. We have yet to construct an "Anabaptist theology of institutions."[59]

Where the church is established in the culture of competitive capitalism and individualism, particularly in North America and Europe, the church must go beyond the nascent beginnings of the New Testament and Anabaptism. Not merely its individual members but its institutions as well must be of incarnational quality.[60]

b. To be Anabaptist is to be a community in whose midst is Jesus

Anabaptism is a movement that embodies the life-giving nature of God as revealed through Jesus of Nazareth. This second characteristic of Anabaptism for the twenty-first century focuses on Christology or "jesuology"—the *human* nature of Jesus. This, it strikes me, would be a good place to begin a "theology of institutions."

Central for the Anabaptists (from a variety of origins) was following Jesus.[61] Whatever else Jesus was, he was human; and however else Jesus is defined, it dare not distract from his humanity. John Howard Yoder continued to see the issue of Jesus' humanity as increasingly important. Toward the end of his life was making bolder statements on this subject. In what turned out to be Yoder's last major publication before his untimely death he writes, "Modern doctrinal debate has often been about the deity of Christ. For this author [referring to himself] the humanity is what counts."[62]

The sixteenth-century Anabaptists never doctrinally resolved Luther's jeering scoffs of works' righteousness at the Anabaptists, scoffs that assumed that Anabaptists thought of themselves as divine. Today, when our predominant worldview has shifted from Luther's fundamentally medieval perspective[63] to our postmodern one, this acknowledgement of the humanity of Jesus by those who claim to be his disciples no longer takes any profound insight—only honesty and courage in the face of traditionalists.

This is why those who would be Anabaptist today need to distinguish themselves from orthodoxy, from evangelicalism[64], and from all those other forms of Christianity, including Catholicism, that have orthodoxy as one of their central claims. A clear and consistent claim of the humanity of Jesus is also a forthright rejection of substitutionary atonement (traditionally understood) in today's Anabaptist vision.[65] Orthodoxy distracts from the humanity of Jesus. Orthodoxy is reductionist inasmuch as it tends to reduce discipleship to a verbal claim. Orthodoxy makes discipleship a sham—unless all Christians, individually and collectively, also belong to the Trinity, even as orthodoxy perceives Jesus as belonging to the Trinity.

A seminal contribution of sixteenth-century Anabaptists was their understanding of the church—the visible community as the body of Christ. The fully human becomes divine. We may call this an incarnational church, an incarnational ecclesiology. Anabaptists believe the church, the gathered community of believers, to be the embodiment of the person and work of Jesus. It is a community of both mutual support and accountability; a community that participates in God's grace by relying on God for sustenance, while embodying (incarnating) the divine amid a society for whom grace was in the control of the established church. An Anabaptist anthropology maintains that human beings are created in "the image and likeness of God," and therefore refuses to accept Luther's, and even more Calvin's, understanding of depravity.

But as followers of Jesus, we as individuals are not little "Jesuses." What Jesus was in his day, that the church, "the body of Christ," is to be in our day. Water baptism is the symbol celebrating the individual's entrance into the body of Christ. Alone, the task of following Jesus is too great, the forces of evil too overwhelming. What Jesus began in his day, so the Anabaptists understood, the church as a corporate body of divine presence was to continue in its day, in its era. From an Anabaptist perspective, the church has many forms, all serving one body and one Lord. Church also includes the "church scattered" throughout the week at a thousand work places. This embodiment, this collective presence, includes the institutions of the church—even those institutions operated by the church that are often said *not* to be the church. These too belong to the phenomenon called "church." But we have no theology of institutions to reflect this reality, and until we do, we will likely continue to assume that our institutions do not really belong under the lordship of Jesus.

c. To be Anabaptist is to live life with the confident assurance that power, Ultimate Power, is nonviolent

That reality which lies beyond Jesus and beyond our grasp, the reality that we call God, *is* nonviolent. Or, we can state this in a more traditional, ethical form without all of its ontological implications: Anabaptists commit themselves to the nonviolent God and to the nonviolent politics of God as practiced by Jesus.[66]

Central to the Anabaptism of the Swiss Brethren and of Hans Hut and his adherents[67] was following Jesus—to be and to do in our society what Jesus did in his. As with the followers of Jesus in the first century and as with the Anabaptists, this "modeling after" Jesus was at one point and at one point only, but then universally and consistently—at his cross.[68] This was not primarily a "doctrinal stance" in which to repeatedly recite the belief in the nonviolent way of Jesus was the equivalent of being nonviolent. Rather, it was a long struggle in a revolutionary practice.[69] The cross for the Anabaptists was not the symbol of death but the way of life through the nonviolent struggle for justice. Only when the means are of the same quality as the end envisioned do the means participate in that end. Only when the means are life-giving does the present imperfect struggle already participate in the resurrection which is yet to be realized.

Going beyond the theology of the sixteenth-century Anabaptists, but consistent with their witness, we may state: If Jesus is the fullest revelation of God given to us, then God, like Jesus, is nonviolent. If God, however else defined, is the ultimate nature of being, if this God and parent of Jesus Christ is nonviolent, then to be nonviolent goes far beyond a "discipleship of obedience." To be nonviolent is to participate in the nature of God as Jesus participated in the being of God.

d. To be Anabaptist is be God's mission of justice in a world of injustice[70]

Anabaptists believed that *to know God is to do justice*, to be the embodiment of "revealing God's way of righting wrong"—of being God's righteousness (Rom. 1:17). What a (nonviolent) theology of the marginalized is in today's "third-world" settings, that is what Anabaptism was in the sixteenth century.[71] We might also refer to this as *an epistemology of engagement with the marginalized*. To know is to "be whole," to be healed, to be saved. But the other side of the same coin is "to be in solidarity with," to participate in God's presence, to be God's ambassador—even as Jesus was.[72]

Mission was not something external to what Anabaptists *were* and *did*. Anabaptists did not view *mission* as a special *call* to a select special set of persons (missionaries) for a special task (mission work) in a special place (the mission field, usually overseas) to a special people (pagans or heathen). This is only a slight caricature of nineteenth-century Protestant missions from which Mennonites, for the large part, took their model. It is the model that still shadows major segments of Mennonite missions today. For Anabaptists, to be Christian was to be mission, to be sent for a purpose. Anabaptists were not *in* mission; they were mission, simply the *"sent ones"* of God.

The good news of mission was *healing* where there was *hurt*. Where there was injustice, justice was sought, not through coercion but through persuasion and demonstration. Where there was violence in the search for justice, and where violence had failed, an alternative was offered. That alternative was a community of sharing.[73]

Anabaptist mission was not a matter of first creating a "metaphysical hurt" and then offering a metaphysical, other-worldly healing. This does not mean, of course, that there was no call for repentance with an offer of God's forgiveness—indeed, the world of heaven and the reality of earth were viewed as an integrated whole.[74]

Mission for the early Anabaptists included what I have earlier called "desacralization"—being freed from the bonds of established religion. Desacralization included not only freedom from the sacraments but also from the Scriptures as interpreted by the established church, whether Catholic or Protestant.[75] The Bible became an open book for the common people. Those who could not read could nevertheless participate in the worship service where the Bible amid the gathered people formed the focal point of conversation and discernment.

"Canonical Anabaptism" for our day will include mission, but it will hardly be what I have sketched above as "Protestant missions." It will not be a special activity, *but a way of life that is shared with the world.* It was the Anabaptists' dynamic quality of life filled with the Spirit of God and shared with the generosity of Jesus in anticipation of a new world that attracted hundreds and constituted the backdrop for the phenomenal spread of the movement. The *medium* of a regenerate way of living was the *message* in a world of domination.

e. To be Anabaptist is to live in the resurrection

Resurrection is God's vindication of the kind of life Jesus lived (Phil. 2:11). Whatever else resurrection means, it means that violence shall not have the last word. What God did for Jesus, God will do for you and me if we live like Jesus. Resurrection, then as now, is the test of whether we have grasped who God is (number three above) and what the God of Jesus was all about (number two above).

To "live in the resurrection" is to "know," to have faith that the resurrection of Jesus as recorded in the scriptural canon is the historical epiphany of nonviolence.[76] To see the resurrection as miracle in our modern day sense, as a defiance of nature, is to fail to see the resurrection as the triumph of nonviolence; it is to fail to believe in the resurrection of Jesus. To see the resurrection primarily as a miracle, as a break in the laws of nature, is to turn the keystone of the Christian faith into just one more magical phenomenon of doctrinal belief.

Resurrection is freedom from the power of the fear of death. Being freed from the fear of death is to be *free to live one's life for others and for Jesus*. This is the ultimate social expression of *living in the resurrection*. The resurrection of Jesus is an episodic epiphany of Ultimate Reality. For the ultimate power of Empire is death: therefore, to be freed from the fear of the power of death means that Empire no longer has power. In no other way am I able to explain the steadfastness, what even appears as joy, of the Anabaptists as they faced the pyre. Only as we are free from the power of the fear of death are we free to live our lives for the other, for Jesus, and for God, in the presence of Empire.

The resurrection was a political event of revolutionary magnitude—revolutionary not in the popular sense of defeating the "bad guys" by forcing them to the bottom of the power pyramid, and letting the "good guys" at the top act like the bad guys used to act. It is revolutionary because what was thought to be weakness was power, power of a life-giving order. What was claimed to be "power" was demonstrated to be weakness manipulated by fear.[77]

The message and the ministry of Jesus' healing and wholeness is one of just-peace and is inseparable from nonviolence.[78] The paradigm of power as violence which we have inherited is dysfunctional and keeps us from seeing the greater truth proclaimed by Jesus and demonstrated in the resurrection. This Jesus is Lord because he refused, when tempted, "to make history come out right"[79] by taking up violence, or by asking others to do so, or by relying on others who did so without his asking them.[80]

Jesus is Lord and savior—by direct implication Caesar is not. Unlike Caesar, Jesus neither used violence to defend his personal status, nor an Empire to leverage that status. For that very reason Jesus is exalted. This seems to be a "reality" that the Anabaptists of the sixteenth century grasped so readily and so fully, but a reality that proves so very difficult for us to fathom today. Since the resurrection of nonviolent power is at the heart of the Christian faith, Christians, if indeed that is who we are, know the power of nonviolence. This, we should understand, is not a creedal or dogmatic declaration: it is rather a claim based on the testimony and practice of those earliest followers of Jesus. Our participation in the kind of life Jesus lived, the kind of vulnerability he endured, the kind of death he died, will determine our capacity to experience resurrection.

A dramatic shift in the understanding of power from violence to nonviolence was in the purview of the earliest followers of Jesus, including Paul.[81] Resurrection for those first believers was the defeat of violence. But the Jesus-event—the life, death, and resurrection of Jesus—had barely been registered on the map of history, much less had the fullness of it been grasped by the early church, until it began to be reconceptualized. The repackaging of the resurrection continued not simply and not primarily through the early apostolic community, but largely through the intelligentsia who mirrored the wisdom of the pagans more than the carpenter of Nazareth; and who early on became more concerned that the "faith" of the Messiah be communicated in respectable, non-revolutionary terms than that the daily life of its adherents be transformed by it. The most dramatic changes occurred in a culture that understood less about Abraham, Amos, and Jesus than about Plato and Plotinus. In this milieu the hypothesis that "Plato is nothing else than Moses speaking Greek"[82] found ready acceptance. Those Anabaptists who identified with Abraham, Amos, and Jesus through their lives are thus the Anabaptists who belong in our "canon."

In conclusion, I can perhaps do no better than to raise a set of second-level questions that will emerge almost immediately were we as a congregation or a group of colleagues to discuss with some seriousness of intent the gradual implementation of the Anabaptist "canonical guidelines" I have offered in this essay. Here is but an initial set of so-called "practical issues" randomly selected. Consider them simply as conversation starters. The reader will surely immediately add her or his own to the list.

1. What kind of vision is this then that we have of Anabaptism? Is Anabaptism best grasped by placing it all under the umbrella of "church," as I have implicitly done? Or is Anabaptism also—at least the Anabaptism that we envision for us today—a *movement*, less structured than the church, less under the tutelage of an institution that readily slips into an establishment—a sustainer of the status quo?

2. What kind of leadership is best fitted for Anabaptism for today? Is the professional Protestant model—the kind that our seminaries are structured to produce—the kind of leadership best suited for Anabaptist congregations? H. S. Bender skirted this issue in his vision. So have I. Although we have made our institutions, foremost among them our seminaries, sacrosanct, dare we avoid the hard questions? For we shape our institutions, and they in turn powerfully shape us. I wonder what has happened to an earlier concept of part-time pastoral teams in which each team member also has a tent-making job. Does the need to specialize and be "professional" rob us of creativity and the ability to take a prophetic and vulnerable stance?

3. What should be the nature and structure of our worship services? Will the current trends toward formality and the sacramental continue? Were our Anabaptist foreparents simply misguided in their emphasis on a participatory peoplehood as opposed to the sermon and the sacraments? Or have we as Mennonites of today become more sophisticated, with a different set of "needs?"

4. How is the church to engage the "world"—governments and that larger society that are not church? Are our current mechanisms serving us well? Should we have more Mennonite Church Committee Washington Offices and MCC Peace Sections? This opens the delicate conversation between activism and quietism, between political engagement and a more withdrawn posture, between nonviolent resistance and nonresistance.

5. Finally, the questions of material possessions and wealth: Are our communal structures in any way capable of providing structures of accountability that will include our businesses and professions? If not, is Anabaptism, after all, passé?

NOTES

1. Harold S. Bender, "The Anabaptist Vision," *Church History* 13 (March 1944): 3-24

2. Bender's Mennonites "needed" an Anabaptist identity that would bring the church a sense of self-respect and dignity and would be slightly ahead of where the church itself was—a prophetic challenge without threat. In his Anabaptist Vision he gave the Mennonite church a respectable past (the Anabaptists were not the weirdoes they had for centuries been made out to be), a biblical heritage that was neither Fundamentalist nor Liberal but offered a third way (following Jesus), a theological heritage that was orthodox but underscored pacifism as integral to the faith (i.e., nonresistance, which allowed Mennonites to keep their basic quietism), and retained a middle-class work ethic and economic outlook (Bender's vision did not pick up on Anabaptist economics nor on mission).

3. James M. Stayer, *Anabaptism and the Sword* (Lawrence, Kan.: Coronado Press, 1972). See also James M. Stayer, Werner O. Packull, and Klaus Depperman, "From Monogenesis to Polygenesis: The Historical Discussion of Anabaptist Origins," *Mennonite Quarterly Review* 49/2 (April 1975): 83-121.

4. Claus-Peter Classen, *Anabaptism: A Social History 1525-1618, Switzerland, Austria, Moravia, South and Central Germany* (Ithaca, NY: Cornell University Press, 1972).

5. Peachey, *Die soziale Herkunft der schweizerischen Wiedertäufer in der Reformationszeit: Eine religionssoziologische Untersuchung* Schriften des Mennonitschen Geschichtsvereins, no. 4 (Karlsruhe: Buchdruckerei und Verlag Heinrich Schneider, 1954). Though the tabulations in themselves may be correct, astonishingly, in this "sociological" work neither Peachey nor his advisory team ever seem to have asked how the illiterate peasants were presumed to have written about themselves, or where Western European academics in the twentieth century might find non-self-scripted evidence, other than in the mainline academic archives and libraries.

6. Fritz Blanke, *Brüder in Christo: Die Geschichte der ältesten Täufergemeinde, Zollikon 1525* (Zürich: Zwingli Verlag, 1955). Later translated into English as *Brothers in Christ* (Scottdale, Pa.: Herald Press, 1966), among Anabaptist Mennonites this book was for the ensuing twenty-five years probably the most frequently quoted book of all times on Anabaptism. It is not clear how strong American Mennonite influence was on Blanke at the time.

7. *"Wie es eigentlich gewesen ist"* (Leopold von Ranke, a leading figure in nineteenth-century historicism).

8. For example, American Mennonites had great difficulty seeing sixteenth-century Anabaptism's close ties politically, chronologically, and geographically with the peasants' unrest of the times.

9. A case in point here is "spirituality," if by that is meant a form of mysticism rather than an ethically observable quality of life. Introducing medieval mysticism into twenty-first-century secularism may well make for a less secularly oriented and spiritually devoid community, but this should hardly be done in the name of Anabaptism any more than in the name Martin Luther or Thomas Müntzer.

10. However much scholarship may disagree on the nature of Schleitheim (*Brotherly Union of a Number of Children of God Concerning Seven Articles*)—Was it quietist, apolitical (so say Stayer and Martin Haas)? Was it prototypical

Anabaptism (a position rejected by Snyder)?—there is common consensus that it represents at least one group's effort to find a normative position for themselves and, most likely, for the larger body of scattered Anabaptist groups. For a lively, well-researched and well-argued position against polygenesis (*a la* position five below), see Gerald Biesecker-Mast's chapter on "the Schleitheim Brotherly Union" in *Separation and the Sword in Anabaptist Persuasion* (Telford, Pa.: Cascadia Publishing House, 2006), 97-132.

11. Here should be mentioned the positive work of C. A. Cornelius and Ludwig Keller. This stands in contrast to Karl Holl and Heinrich Boehmer, who continued to advocate a traditional interpretation linking the Anabaptists with Thomas Müntzer. See George H. Williams' brief overview in the *Introduction to Spiritual and Anabaptist Writers*, ed. George Huntson Williams and Angel M. Mergal (Philadelphia.: Westminster Press, 1957), 19-28.

12. Although this is not what H. S. Bender actually did, it is what he assumed he was doing. The term regional is important inasmuch as Bender considered Anabaptism to have a single geographic origin and hence to be all one larger geographic movement across Europe—with, of course, powerful intervening influences from both charismatic leaders and various socio-political conditions entering the stream and, at times, significantly altering the course.

13. John Howard Yoder's analysis of dialogues of Hans Pfistermeyer in 1531 and the Anabaptists at Bern in 1538 is perhaps the best representation of this stage. See John Howard Yoder, *Täufertum und Reformatoren im Gespräch: Dogmengeschichtliche Untersuchung der frühen Gespräche zwischen Schweizerischen Täufern und Reformatoren* (Zürich: EVZ-Verlag, 1968), esp. 44ff. The term *selective* is descriptive of what Yoder himself claimed to do.

14. Stayer, *Anabaptism and the Sword*. "Non-selective," or more strongly stated, "objective," is how Stayer at the time understood himself to be working. Some years later it was easier for him to see that at least on some points he was overly reactionary against the "Goshen School."

15. To the degree that Stayer was discriminating (i.e., selective in the subjects he chose), he selected specific figures and movements that documented his case against the Goshen School.

16. Here I include William Klassen's reading of Marpeck—*Covenant and Community: The Life, Writings and Hermeneutics of Pilgrim Marpeck* (Grand Rapids, Mich.: Wm. B. Eerdmans, 1968)—as well as John Rempel's reading of Hubmaier, Marpeck, and Philips—*The Lord's Supper in Anabaptism: A Study in the Christology of Balthasar Hubmaier, Pilgrim Marpeck, and Dirk Philips* (Scottdale, Pa.: Herald Press, 1993)—and C. Arnold Snyder's work with Hubmaier, using Hubmaier as the keystone or primary model for an Anabaptist theology. See Snyder, *Anabaptist History and Theology: An Introduction*. As is frequently the case, perhaps even most commonly, a key aspect of the subject under study reflects the scholars' own interests and disposition. It should therefore come as no surprise that as Mennonites became more amalgamated with mainstream society and become more closely aligned with Protestant orthodoxy, the subjects of Hubmaier and Marpeck—the two major early Anabaptist leaders with theological positions most compatible with Luther's—

became (based on an unscientific survey) the two Anabaptist figures attracting the most attention within Mennonite thought of the past fifteen years.

17. James M. Stayer, Werner O. Packull, and Klaus Depperman, "From Monogenesis to Polygenesis: The Historical Discussion of Anabaptist Origins," *Mennonite Quarterly Review* 49/2 (April 1975): 83-121.

18. Gerald Biesecker-Mast, in his recently published work, *Separation and the Sword in Anabaptist Persuasion,* has throughout his work carefully traced the particular arguments within the variety of historical interpretations. Worthy of special note is his lead chapter, *"The Anabaptist Vision* and the Polygenesis Historiography," 35-67. A spin-off chapter, perhaps equally illuminating, that has yet to be written, would be "The Polygenesis of Anabaptist Historiography"—that is, careful documentation supporting the thesis that the reality of polygenesis has its origins not merely in the sixteenth-century events of reform and revolution, but equally within the perception and conception of *modernist* twentieth-century historians.

19. Pneumatology, the activity of the Holy Spirit, is the most significant aspect of Anabaptism, according to C. Arnold Snyder in his *Anabaptist History and Theology* (Kitchener, Ont.: Pandora Press, 1995). Throughout this volume, "spirituality" finds its way into the text under other topics. But not until the epilogue is the point explicitly and conclusively made: "It is not an overstatement to say that early Anabaptist pneumatology was the *sine qua non* of the movement" (379). A more recent work of Snyder's, *Following in the Footsteps of Christ: The Anabaptist Tradition* (Maryknoll, N.Y.: Orbis Books, 2004), advances the same theme.

20. See J. Denny Weaver, *Becoming Anabaptist: The Origin and Significance of Sixteenth-Century Anabaptism* (Scottdale, Pa.: Herald Press, 1987), 116-22, and the 2005 second edition with the same title, 174-75. To say that Weaver held to Bender's basic categories, while affording polygenesis some validity, does not mean that these categories were not nuanced and newly applied. So close was Weaver with Bender in the first edition that he continued to use the traditional terminology of "nonresistance." The second edition reflects a deeper awareness of structural violence and the need for more engaged, radical terms, but fully as committed to pacifism and nonviolence.

21. The search for an Anabaptist identity was a key driving force behind a colloquium held at Bethel College in the summer of 2000 in which about thirty Mennonites shared their vision. See Dale Schrag and James Juhnke, eds., *Anabaptist Visions for the New Millennium: A Search for Identity,* (Waterloo, Ont: Pandora Press, 2000). Many of the contributors to that volume, however, were not involved in Anabaptist studies; for those who were, it was not always clear their "vision" was intended to be informed by our past heritage. The book, with its wide spread of creative ideas, would more appropriately be entitled, "Visions of a People Called Mennonite."

22. Philosophically understood to be the really Real, the paramount reality as opposed to, say, physicalism, which is but a secondary reality.

23. Biesecker-Mast, under the rubric of a "rhetorical interpretation," addresses this issue. See, for example, his carefully nuanced statement on interpreting Article IV of the *Brotherly Union* (Schleitheim) *within the political con-*

text of the times and not as an ahistorical doctrinal statement. See *Separation and the Sword*, 107. What Biesecker Mast fails to address forthrightly, and only occasionally skirts, are the epistemological issues acutely encountered in bridging the gap between the sixteenth century and our current postmodern era. Furthermore, although I appreciate Biesecker-Mast's category of "passion" for the *Bloody Theater of the Martyrs Mirror*, it is not at all clear to me that his use of passion and commitment will provide the social fabric and the intellectual acumen necessary to bridge the gap between the era of Anabaptist martyrs and the times we are currently living in. (I have begun to address this very large ethical and epistemological topic elsewhere under the rubric of "worldviews" but am unable to pursue it further in this essay.)

24. James Stayer's somewhat later work, *The German Peasants War and Anabaptist Community of Goods* (Montreal: McGill-Queen's University Press, 1991), in which Stayer relies quite heavily on the neo-Marxist oriented research of Peter Blickle, *The Revolution of 1525: The German Peasants' War from a New Perspective* (Baltimore: Johns Hopkins University Press, 1981), reflects a significant shift in research methodology.

25. The pioneering example of Anabaptism as orthopraxis is John Howard Yoder, *The Politics of Jesus* (Grand Rapids, Mich.: Wm. B. Eerdmans, 1973). Yoder, however, did not attempt to publish a full-orbed Anabaptist vision, but did a theological ethics through the lens of Anabaptist orthopraxis. During one of my post-seminary visits with Yoder, I commented that an Anabaptist theology in the English language had yet to be published. He responded by calling my attention to *The Politics*.

26. This "Anabaptist" nomenclature of church as the new-community-at-the-edge-of-the-old comes from an insightful contemporary application of the Gospel, *The Geography of Faith: Conversations between Daniel Berrigan [when underground] and Robert Coles* (Boston: Beacon Press, 1971). Of the post-Vietnam era Berrigan notes: "It is a chapter of history which, we hope, will see the center of the Church's concerns located at the edge of society—where human lives are involved in a really tragic struggle for survival and human dignity" (129).

27. The confusion that can emerge within an individual who was sacrally conditioned within the Reformed tradition and then becomes "Anabaptist" without grasping this groundswell shift, including the epistemological fault line, is depicted in a recent essay in *The Mennonite* by Arthur Paul Boers: "Sharing," he says, "is a non-native invader that distorts worship and becomes impossible to dislodge." Boers, "Thank you for Zebra Mussels, Asian Ladybugs, and Sharing?" *The Mennonite* (Feb. 27, 2006), 9.

28. *Normative*, as I am using the term, is less the representation of a phenomenon to be continued in unbroken sequence through time and place than the core values and the embryonic social expressions that are ever and again to be recreated. Normative, as I wish to use the term, is by nature dynamic. Justice-with-peace is normative to the Anabaptist movement as Jesus of Nazareth is normative to the Christian.

29. Cf. John Driver, *Radical Faith: An Alternative History of the Christian Church* (Waterloo, Ont.: Pandora Press, 1999). In Driver's words: "This is the

story of . . . the 'little ones,' as Jesus called them in the Gospels; the 'heretics,' as they have been called since the time of Constantine; and the minority movements, those who follow the models patterned by the Abrahamic and Messianic minorities of biblical history. . ."(Preface, 7). As is suggested here, the common theme shared by each of these groups is "marginalized peoplehood" or "the new-community-at-the-edge-of-the-old" rather than nonviolence, or "just-peace."

30. Anabaptism shows conclusively that where the life of the church is gone, it will not be restored through sacrament and ritual. What is *not* conclusive is what role symbols and rituals play in maintaining vibrant fellowship within healthy congregations.

31. Arnold Snyder, after underscoring what he sees as an apparent lack of pacifist depths at nearly every stage of development within early Swiss Anabaptism, comes to a rather surprising summary statement in *Anabaptist History and Theology*, 62-63: "Swiss Anabaptism was unique . . . in that it moved to a sectarian position [i.e., "separation from the world, . . . limits of involvement in the world and society, and . . . limits of sword bearing (or participation in government)"] in a very short time. All surviving Anabaptist groups eventually arrived at similar affirmations, but the path leading there was filled with inter-Anabaptist discussions, testing and dissension. . . ." I affirm Snyder's assessment that in the end that Anabaptism which survived was for the most part pacifist. See my dissertation, "The Mission Impulse of Early Swiss and South-German-Austrian Anabaptism" (Vanderbilt University, 1980), 228-267, 322-336, for an understanding of Swiss Anabaptism that is less "withdrawn."

32. Mysticism was the traditional medieval form of "spirituality," usually built on neo-Platonism. There is no correlation between this mystical form of spirituality and a higher social ethic. For every historical instance where a positive correlation might be drawn (e.g., St. Francis of Assisi), an alternative negative instance can be found (e.g., Bernard of Clairvaux, who blessed the weapons of the Second Crusade).

33. If we search for the broadest, least delimiting, most characteristically normative language to express God's movement toward peace-with-justice, I would simply call it "life-giving" (as opposed to death-dealing), referring neither explicitly to God nor to peace and justice. By casting the Anabaptist movement in the larger frame of the historic Judeo-Christian faith and into a *specific expression* of that which is life-giving, the particularity of sixteenth-century Anabaptism is in continuity with the prophetic Judeo-Christian faith.

34. It was quite the opposite of retributive justice, and it was far more than distributive justice. We can best describe this phenomenon as: a) the justice of being able to participate in one's own destiny; b) the justice that strove for sufficiency and equity among all; c) a justice that promoted the dignity of self and one's people; and d) the justice experienced in solidarity with the oppressed.

35. Not even if we rename mysticism, calling it "spirituality."

36. See additional comments on this in Part II, item 5 below. Cf. Arnold Snyder's *History and Theology of Anabaptism*, in which Hubmaier—the non-

pacifist leader—is Snyder's prototypical (orthodox) Anabaptist. Spirituality, for Snyder, constitutes the core of the movement, and nonviolence (under the rubric of nonresistance, mentioned in a discussion of the Swiss Anabaptists and Menno Simons), is passed over quickly, then dismissed as very fragmented and quite insignificant. But in the end, as Snyder notes: "All surviving Anabaptist groups eventually arrived at similar affirmations [to those of the pacifist Swiss]" (63).

37. By traditional theology I include all those theological streams, whether fundamentalist, evangelical, or liberal, that have their roots in scholasticism and in the Platonic-Aristotelian philosophical stream of "realism." In most instances these groups maintain the traditional creedal commitments, hence are "orthodox."

38. Or by that which serves as a functional equivalent of the Corpus Christianum, knowing, of course, that church and state are not *officially* in the same relationship as they were in either the fifth or the sixteenth century.

39. Whether Republican or Democrat in party alignment matters increasingly less.

40. See Walter Wink, *Unmasking the Powers: The Invisible forces that Determine Human Existence* (Minneapolis: Fortress Press, 1986). Wink develops these earlier thoughts further in "The New Worldview: Spirit at the Core of Everything," in *Transforming the Powers: Peace, Justice and the Domination System*, ed. Ray Gingerich and Ted Grimsrud (Minneapolis: Fortress Press, 2006), 17-28.

41. See also my comments on Hubmaier and Marpeck, esp. note 16 above.

42. See my essay on "Resurrection: The Nonviolent Politics of God," available on file. An earlier version of this essay was presented as "Resurrection: God's Nonviolence Made Known," at the "Teaching Peace Conference: Nonviolence and the Liberal Arts Curriculum," Bluffton College, May 26-28, 2004. A much abbreviated and popularized rendition was published "Resurrection: The Nonviolent Politics of God," *Vision* 5/2 (Fall 2004): 71-78. For additional reading see N.T. Wright, *The Resurrection of the Son of God: Christian Origins and the Question of God*, vol. 3 (Minneapolis: Fortress Press, 2003). I consider Wright's book the most valuable book on the resurrection that I have ever read. But in the end, Wright does not, in my opinion, follow through on his own argument. The human perception that violence is power is extremely binding.

43. Hannah Arendt, *On Violence* (New York: Harcourt, Brace and World, Inc., 1969, 1970), 56. Arendt categorically distinguishes between violence and power: "Power is indeed of the essence of all government, but violence is not. Violence is by nature instrumental; like all means, it always stands in need of guidance and justification. . . . Peace is an absolute. . . . Power is in the same category; it is, as they say, 'an end in itself'" (51).

44. This is the case in whatever terms we think of this dualism—sharp and separatist (*a la* Stayer, Packull, Snyder) or mediated (*a la* Yoder, Weaver, Biesecker-Mast).

45. Cf. the Apostle Paul: "see, everything has become new!" (2 Cor. 5:17, NRSV). For a socio-cultural analysis, see Thomas S. Kuhn, *The Structure of Sci-*

entific Revolutions (Chicago: University of Chicago Press, 1970).

46. Although the Anabaptists expressed their convictions in terms of "lordship" rather than "power," their willingness to die rather than to take up weapons of violence is an incredible witness to their understanding that nonviolent power (biblically speaking, the lordship of the nonviolent Jesus) will ultimately reign.

47. I have no interest in using this term as hyperbole. I do, however, want the term to connote imperialist dimensions of the state. Hence, Empire is a state (whether a dictatorship, democracy, or some other form) that attempts to "go it alone," that conceives itself to be beyond the bounds of negotiating out of political necessity. In Machiavellian style Empire holds that "might makes right" both politically and morally—politically, since to have the potential, that potential must be manifested through action; morally, inasmuch as winning a war or conflict is evidence of being aligned with God.

48. Walter Wink, *Engaging the Powers*, esp., 46-47. Wink's focus on the "inner spirit" does not always allow him to do justice to the socio-political structures.

49. *Engaging the Powers*, 47.

50. Every political system (secular or otherwise) needs and uses religion, for political systems in the end have multiple modes of operation, the chief one being neither logic nor law but, for want of a more conventional term, I will call it "religious persuasion." That this applies particularly to those political regimes that over-extend themselves is a topic that needs to be addressed at greater length.

51. In some ways "Empire" is the new slogan for what some of us were introduced to under the rubric of "Constantinianism," for Empire, like Constantinianism, seeps into the marrow of our religious bones. Yet Empire focuses more distinctly on the dominating nature of the State and on its goals—not merely to rule but to be Ruler of all by whatever means deemed necessary.

52. "Instinct" as used here should be understood less as a genetic characteristic and more as cultural conditioning so profound that it creates a reflexive action.

53. In the "Letters to Thomas Müntzer by Conrad Grebel and his Friends," the authors of the letters warn against sacramentalism in regard to the Lord's Supper: "The server from the congregation should pronounce them [the words of blessing] from one of the Evangelists or from Paul. They are words of the instituted meal of fellowship, not words of consecration. Ordinary bread ought to be used without idols and additions." *Spiritual and Anabaptist Writers*, 76. See also Walter Klaassen, *Anabaptism: Neither Catholic nor Protestant*, 3rd. ed. (Waterloo, Ont.: Pandora Press, 1981, 2001).

54. "Getting in the way" is the slogan adopted by Christian Peacemaker Teams. To be engaged in "violence reduction," not to mention promoting justice, gets in the way of the politics of Empire. "Getting in the way" as a slogan is a wonderful discussion starter. Only when it is placed into a larger context (such as "getting in the way like Gandhi or Jesus got in the way") can it become the basis of a theology.

55. Biblical prophetic "justice" may also be translated as "righteous-

ness"—the righteousness of God (Rom. 1:17). It includes the following dimensions: sufficiency for all; dignity, individually and collectively; participation in one's own destiny; solidarity/accompaniment with the poor and oppressed.

56. Spirituality in many different expressions and perceptions—mysticism, belief in witches and demons, hyper-apocalypticism, the immediacy of the living God—filled the medieval/reformation atmosphere and was quite literally the stuff of breath in every village. Spirits were approached in many different ways through highly developed rituals, and presumed to be so very different from each other in function. Nevertheless their identities were often confused from one group to the next and viewed from opposing perspectives, so similar were the phenomena called "spirits" and the moral quality referred to as "spirituality."

57. I am a believer in an open canon, and I would not want my usage of the term *canon* to be understood otherwise. An open canon implies that God may yet reveal new truth and make old wisdom come to new life.

58. The presuppositions and the distinctives are not in parallel arrangement.

59. Mennonite first cousins, the Bruderhof communities, may have given this more thought than have we Mennonites. A good place to begin may be observation of and dialogue with the Bruderhof's various communities and manufacturing operations.

60. It is dubious that many current Mennonite institutional structures could survive under the standard of "incarnational quality." For example, advancement divisions could no longer solicit donors for building projects with the lure of having donors' names engraved on a bronze plaque by the entrance door. Mennonite Mutual Aid Association would most likely need to find an entirely new basis for investment of savings and retirement funds, dropping not merely those manufacturing corporations whose products are of spurious value, but all companies whose highest goal is profit-making rather than providing life-giving services to humanity.

61. Gingerich, "Missional Impulse," esp. 129-172.

62. John Howard Yoder, *For the Nations: Essays Public and Evangelical* (Grand rapids, Mich.: Wm. B. Eerdmans, 1997), 241n.4.

63. Theologically referred to as "forensic justification"—a religious evisceration of discipleship.

64. By this I do not mean to suggest that we should be doctrinal separatists, nor do I wish this to be a divisive issue. Nevertheless, we must address it openly.

65. This is not the place to make a case for a rejection of substitutionary atonement, particularly since the case has already been made at considerable length by J. Denny Weaver in his important work, *The Nonviolent Atonement* (Grand Rapids, Mich.: Wm. B. Eerdmans, 2001).

66. This third statement may correctly be thought of as a restatement of H. S. Bender's "discipleship" and "nonresistance." Bender's statement, however, left intact the implicit dualism of Schleitheim. With an emphasis on nonresistance, rather than nonviolent resistance, for a people (North American

Mennonites) who were no longer being persecuted, peace for Mennonites became largely passive.

67. Gingerich, "Mission Impulse," 129-172.

68. This central theme in Yoder's *Politics of Jesus* is one of Yoder's seminal contributions to biblical and Anabaptist understanding. John Howard Yoder, *The Politics of Jesus: Vicit Agnus Noster* (Grand Raids, Mich.: Wm. B. Eerdmans, rev. ed. 1994), 95; see also 53.

69. The prime example of one who was in conflict to the end is Hans Hut, for whom it was extremely difficult to believe that God was nonviolent. It was therefore difficult for Hut to affirm and maintain a nonviolent practice. Hut, after all, to his end, held to a chiliastic eschatology.

70. This is not an attempt to outline a theology of mission, but only to indicate the centrality of *mission* to Anabaptism.

71. See Laverne A. Rutschman, "Anabaptism and Liberation Theology," in *Freedom and Discipleship: Liberation Theology in an Anabaptist Perspective*, ed. Daniel S. Schipani (Maryknoll, N.Y.: Orbis Books, 1989), 51-65.

72. I know of no place in the primary literature of Anabaptism where the concept of "mission in reverse" is approached (i.e., those who would be the redeemers become the redeemed, those who would be the bearers of salvation find themselves being saved); nevertheless the epistemology of discipleship (see above) is also present in mission.

73. James M. Stayer, *The German Peasants' War and the Anabaptist Community of Goods* (Montreal, Ont.: McGill-Queen's University Press, 1991). See also my theological analysis of the Anabaptist community of sharing in "The Economics and Politics of Violence: Toward a Theology for Transforming the Powers," in *Transforming the Powers*, 113-126.

74. This is to say, "spiritual" was not an escape from the physical as it overwhelmingly tends to be in our culture (and within the worldview of modernity). See Wink, *Unmasking the Powers*.

75. See my dissertation, "The Mission Impulse." The entire first chapter is devoted to the "Incarnational Community: Desacralization of the Sacraments," (20-110), and the second chapter to "The Incarnational Community: Desacralization of the Word," (111-177).

76. See my essay on "The Nonviolent Politics of God."

77. For a careful documenting of biblical references to an *inversion of status* in God's reign, with special attention given to the early church, see Hans-Ruedi Weber, *Power: Focus for a Biblical Theology* (Geneva: WCC Publications, 1989), 134-137.

78. What Arendt argues philosophically (*On Violence*), the early church through the Gospel writers and Paul stated in "narrative theology" by describing the Jesus-event culminating in the resurrection (also "exaltation," Philippians 2). For a more comprehensive listing of power types—"power with" versus "power over"—consult Wink, *Engaging the Powers*, 46-47.

79. A typical "Yoderian" phrase which over the years I have come to appreciate.

80. As is the case with Mennonites and other pacifists when they thank God for a strong military to protect their freedom.

81. A raging Saul (Paul) persecuting those "belonging to the Way," was transformed when he encountered Jesus, the resurrected Lord. What Paul experienced was a revolutionary new way of perceiving power. The violence of persecution was an exercise of weakness and fear. Visions of the resurrected Jesus and Paul's being "filled with the Holy Spirit" were demonstrations of God's nonviolent politics (Acts 9:1-19). It is not an exercise in eisegeses to interpret Paul's writings on the resurrection in this context. I owe this insight to a sermon preached by André Gingerich Stoner. See also Gil Bailie, *Violence Unveiled: Humanity at the Crossroads* (New York: Crossroad Classic, 1996), 232-33.

82. The quote comes from Numenius of Apamea (second century CE) who came from Syria, and as suggested by Robert Doran, may have been the impulse behind Plotinus's desire to investigate Persian and Indian philosophy. *Birth of a Worldview: Early Christianity in Its Jewish and Pagan Context* (Lanham, Maryland: Rowman & Littlefield Publishers, Inc., 1999), 47.

Part 4
THE WORK OF JESUS ON THE CROSS

CHAPTER TEN

ATONEMENT: BEING REMEMBERED

Harry J. Huebner

We can say that the word ["truth"] has at least three different meanings; but it is mistaken to assume that any one of these theories can give the whole grammar of how we use the word, or endeavor to fit into a single theory cases which do not seem to agree with it.
—Ludwig Wittgenstein[1]

The worst form of idolatry is not carving an image; it is the presumption that one has—or that a society has, or a culture has—the right to set the terms under which God can be recognized.
—John H. Yoder[2]

For in hope we were saved.
—Romans 8:24a

For God's foolishness is wiser than human wisdom, and God's weakness is stronger than human strength.
—1 Corinthians 1:23

INTRODUCTION

The atonement debate is often cast as if one is compelled to choose from a set of competing languages or theories. This raises all the dangers of reductionism in ways that both Yoder and Wittgenstein warn against in their words above. Both know that concepts such as atonement are rooted, not first of all in ideas, but in events and are appropriated into real lives in ways that require language that opens up a world in which we can participate. Or to put it more generally, theology is not a choice between different theories but a set of linguistic skills that helps the seeing of and the participation in a world that understands events like creation and redemption as vistas that can become real for us.

My purpose in this essay is to emphasize that the biblical view of atonement cannot be adequately understood with a single metaphor or theory—or better, it requires multiple languages and images to uncover the diversity of God's redemptive activities. That we find multiple atonement images in our Scriptures should not surprise us, for sin also takes on many forms. Each metaphor adds a layer of meaning uncovering an aspect that other images do not adequately expose. Each is a way of entering into an eternal mystery, a way of being taken up into wholeness and purpose, whether individually or corporately, to redeem what is broken and rebirth that which is marked by death.

Biblical atonement imagery hence seeks to uncover the richness of human existence veiled by the brokenness of human sin. Its "understanding," in other words, does not admit of a narrow "linear" logic, for, as Stanislas Breton puts it, "The Logos of the cross is indeed a logos, a saying: but this saying disconcerts our thoughts to the point that it can only be folly, and it is as folly that it is power of God."[3]

To say this another way, it is precisely in its vitiation of theory that atonement language and imagery can help us participate in salvation. For theories truncate and reduce, or totalize and foreclose, while metaphors unveil and disclose what is not immediately evident to the naked mind.[4] When we see atonement as an intrinsically revelatory event permitted to stand as gift and into whose variegated strangeness we are asked to place our own existence, we are at once caught up in a drama of hope (Rom. 8:24a) and in the existential moment of fear and trembling (Phil. 2:14). The gaze of revelation is wonder and awe.

Saying it this way, of course, is singularly unsettling for most moderns since, as the life of Jesus that culminated in the cross and resurrection shows, when you can't put a message into a framework of meaning, which not even the disciples were able to do according to the gospel narratives that relate Christ's foretelling of such events (e.g., Luke 9:45), our accepted understanding of moral agency is put in question. That is, when you can't find a "handle" on your own story, or explain it with a theory, or domesticate it, it stands there as a terrifying promise because we know not where it will take us. When the only true disclosure of life's meaning comes through invitation ("O taste and see . . ." or "Come and follow me . . ."), then its true response—participation in what we do not own—dislodges us from our comfortable modern perches.

This does not mean, however, that the Christ event is unintelligible; it speaks instead of how its intelligibility is found. David Bentley Hart, an Eastern Orthodox theologian, speaking of Christ as "the supreme rhetoric of the Father,"[5] suggests that in Christ we find intelligibility not because his language and practice are ordinary, since Christ came into a world messed up by human sin which rendered God's creation barely recognizable, but because his embodied rhetoric is the original language of creation, and it is that very beauty that is being made visible again by the process of being drawn into what we already are in Christ. For Hart, atonement is incarnation. As he puts it,

> [Christ] is not an impalpable and unworldly redeemer, a ladder for souls, rising up out of the quagmires of flesh and time, but the Lord who saves precisely because he can be grasped, precisely because of his concrete particularity, his real and appearing beauty, which draws others on into history, into the contingencies and particularities of time, into the concrete community of the church.[6]

The task before us then is not to craft a framework (theory) that shows how Christ "fits into" God's "plan of salvation," but a language able to point to ways God in Christ is restoring people, nations, and the entire cosmos to their created intent. In other words, to make atonement intelligible requires clarifying how the biblical language shows us that in Christ God's reconciling work is evident and how being in Christ—participating in the venture—can save us.

METAPHORS

He is the image of the invisible God, the firstborn of all creation, for in him all things in heaven and on earth were created, things visible and invisible, whether thrones or dominions or rulers or powers—all things have been created through him and for him. He himself is before all things and in him all things hold together.
—Colossians 1:15

This passage from Paul's letter to the Colossians uses multiple images (metaphors) to give an account of who Jesus is. And the picture is not simple; the images are even in tension with one another (like the one who is was the firstborn). Yet in it all we gain an understanding. Paul here does not present an argument or expound a theory but gives a metaphorical account—a "thick description"—of what he saw in Christ.[7] In effect he is painting a picture where he places Christ within the same picture frame as God and as human beings. He emphasizes that in Christ all things were created. This is, of course, Trinitarian language, language necessary for anyone who, like Paul, has come to see Jesus as Messiah. The Trinitarian idiom continues, saying that in Christ "all things hold together." And this is but a way of saying that Christ necessitates another look at creation, not that the first creation was flawed but that it has been so distorted by sin that it is difficult to see it in focus. We see as through a fog—dimly.

What Paul is getting at here, I believe, is that to make our lives and our worship intelligible we must recognize that our creator is our redeemer and our redeemer is our creator. The biblical discourse on atonement is an attempt to capture this refocusing for us, not only in gaining a clearer understanding of who we are and what abundant living entails for us, but how life can be seen in a manner that sustains wholesome, peaceful existence, despite the distortions of sin—that is, how we can participate in the activities of the creator redeeming.

Biblical images of atonement abound.[8] We find images of redemption, for example: setting free, liberation, ransom, being bought with a price, redeemed from the curse of the law. Sacrifice images are numerous: Jesus is a Passover sacrifice, a covenant sacrifice, a sin offering, a sacrifice to God, or, as stated in Hebrews, "without the shedding of blood there can be no forgiveness of sins" (Heb. 9:22). Other passages speak of Jesus as the true light that enlightens everyone (John 1:9), that is, atonement is revelation. Paul speaks of God's reconciling activities in the crucifixion of Jesus, reconciliation not only for human beings but for the whole cosmos (Rom. 8:22-23). And he explains what Jesus did to the powers in his death and resurrection: "He disarmed the principalities and powers and made a public example of them, triumphing over them in him" (Col. 2:15).

The challenge for Christians is to find ways of letting these images open up God's redeeming presence among us.[9] The temptation, however, is to squeeze them into a single theory where one of the images dominates the rest. We then get either the substitutionary (satisfaction) theory, or the moral influence theory, or the Christus Victor theory, or different variations of one of these. But in virtually all cases these theories get crafted at the expense of reducing or collapsing other images into a favored one. And that has had the unfortunate effect in the history of theological discourse of truncated reductionisms or of setting up debates that are based on distinctions without substantial differences.

But nor is it helpful to simply grant all metaphors the same significance just because they are there, or, on the other hand, to attempt to develop a master theory using all the images. All three options—particular theories, exhaustive aggregation, universal theory amalgamation—are themselves driven by an ontology foreign to the biblical story, the singularity of being. Perhaps uncovering a biblical ontology will help us incorporate difference through a depiction that is at once biblical, theological, and able to open up new vistas of both understanding and participation.

The suggestion of an alternative ontology once more pushes us back to the Trinitarian image that is evident in Colossians 1:15. The biblical and orthodox view of God is trinity, the modern language is being. Scholars like John Milbank and Romand Coles have argued that these are significantly different views leading to different ways of conceiving the theological enterprise itself. The former (trinity) casts ultimate existence in terms of relationality, community, and plurality (harmonious difference) and the latter (being) in terms of singularity and the reduction of difference.[10] Moreover, the movements of understanding are different. The biblical/orthodox view invites seekers into an understanding of the unity of a threefold existence—creator, redeemer, and sustainer. That is, it is faith seeking understanding of how the Creator in endlessly creative ways redeems and sustains. The modern view, on the other hand, begins with the assumptions of the singularity of being as given by scientific reason where paradox, analogy, and mystery[11] give way to consistency and singularity, such that understanding is sought through the rationality of faith on the basis of universal principles of reason. How one casts intelligibility has broad implications in other arenas of the Christian life like power, violence, agency, and ecclesiology, all topics beyond the scope of this paper. But the tensions here are not unrelated to the tensions that express themselves in the contrasting view of atonement that is evident between the *ecclesia* and the *imperium*.[12]

Ecclesia is a body called forth not by an idea, but by a person. Its identity is therefore not held in place by a philosophy or a theory but by a dynamic, a dynamic that is able to bring into unity diverse individuals and peoples, a unity that embraces diversity, a harmonious difference rooted in the trinity itself. For the Christian life to be intelligible requires an imagination in which we see our "improvised performances" as participating in a drama that is not under our own direction, but one which addresses our deepest human desires in ways that show us our beings as gifts of the creator who redeems.[13] That is, we are invited into the givenness of the world, not merely as we see it in its current marred/sinful state, but principally in its fundamental ontological givenness—as peaceful, good, beautiful—the way it was freely, lovingly willed into existence by divine trinity; a givenness in which we may find at once our own sinfulness and our own redemption. But to say it this way requires that we recapture the somewhat neglected notion of participation. After all, to become part of the givenness of reality requires cultivating the kinds of habits that place us in it, habits that allow it to remain gift to us. Just as one cannot become part of the world of baseball without playing it, so one cannot become part of the God's divine givenness without finding ways of participating in it. For as Milbank puts it, "Because gift is gift-exchange, participation of the created gifts in the divine giver is also participation in a Trinitarian God."[14]

PARTICIPATION

For our sake he made him to be sin who knew no sin, so that in him we might become the righteousness of God.
—2 Corinthians 5:21

One of the limitations of non-sacramental theologies and church practices, like Mennonite theology and practice, is that they have a narrow understanding of participation in divine being. We tend to be afraid of the phrase "in Christ!" We remember Christ, we reflect on Christ, we follow after Christ, but we are nervous about participation in Christ. We invite Jesus into our hearts, but we resist entering into the heart and mind of Christ. It is hard to know what all the factors are for this reticence, but it may well be a fear of mysticism or sacramentalism, or perhaps it is a particular casting of discipleship. I raise the question of whether we may have rejected too much. I want to suggest that participation imagery may well help us in our Christian self-understanding, precisely at the point where atonement intersects with ethics. I suggest this especially in light of having advocated above a renewed consideration of a biblical ontology. For the notion of atonement is intertwined with the matter of being, and we know all too well that not all ontologies are equally redemptive.[15]

Consider four illustrative examples, each focusing the poverty of participation in different ways, and each highlighting the important dialectic between atonement and ethics. They are: command-obedience, self-sacrifice, Holy Communion, and aesthetics.

First, discipleship ethics, which I take to be thoroughly biblical, is often cast in the language of command and obedience. Jesus commands and we obey! I do not wish to argue that this language is wrong so much as that it tends to distort precisely in its nuance of distance. The gospel narratives suggest that Jesus invited people to follow after him—to leave behind what they were doing and join him in his life and agenda—that is, he invited them into an activity heading in a direction the end of which was undefined; a drama performed not to *tight* scripting but by improvisation. While the life of Jesus is clearly unintelligible without script (Scripture, tradition), nevertheless Jesus' own practice of "non-identical repetition" led him to do and say the same things that every Jew was familiar with, differently.

Command-obedience is militaristic language and hence is distancing in its assumption of the authority/subject relationship. On this metaphor one is told what to do and is not invited into anything. In fact, the authority lies precisely in the otherness and distance of the commander.

The contrasting metaphor of participation looks different. Here one is invited (taken up, as it were) into Christ and in this way empowered to do as he did—bear the cross with Christ and receive new life in Christ. It is therefore not surprising that the disciples were okay as long as they were with Christ, but when they were alone they had problems, for example, Peter's denials. In effect the disciples were invited to become an extension of Christ's activities—the very body of Christ, which, of course, is precisely Paul's way of speaking about the church. This language presents the matter of authority as participation within the being of another, not just any other, but one who is the author of life itself. For Christ is more than a teacher, or a model, or an authority, but one who has created and hence can recreate, a healer, one who wills to carry us within his own being to give us divine worth, take upon himself the pain that is ours, take into himself even our sins. For alone we are nobody, with others we are somebody, but in Christ we become human.

Second, this suggests an understanding of what it means to enter not only into the life and ministry of Jesus but also into the cross-resurrection. For the cross-resurrection is not different in kind from the rest of the Christ event (his whole life was a form of taking up the cross), for it too is invitation and has special importance for the linkage of atonement with discipleship. For as Christ offered his faithful obedience to God which led him to the cross and then received his life back as blessing through God's resurrection gift, so we are invited to participate in obedience to God awaiting God's blessing of new life.[16] It is therefore not an accident that Jesus instructed his disciples to take up the cross daily and follow him (Luke 9:23).

It is at the point of "taking up the cross," however, where the temptation to go awry is strong. John Milbank, for example, is concerned that atonement and ethics too often have to do only with the cross and not with the resurrection. As he puts it, "I am arguing that resurrection is an inseparable moment of atonement, or that sacrifice is only ethical when it is also resurrection."[17] Milbank is critical of the tendency to see Christian ethics primarily in terms of "self-sacrifice for the other; without any necessary 'return' issuing from the other to oneself."[18] To guard against this misreading, he proposes an understanding of the Christian life as free gift exchange, or feast, or marriage, all of which are participatory metaphors.

Milbank's suggestion is an especially helpful reminder for those advocating a discipleship pacifism, for such pacifism is beset by the danger of making one of two false turns: one emanating from seeing Christian ethics primarily as self-sacrifice for the other, and hence showing indifference regarding the redemption (change) with respect to both one's own suffering as well as that of others;[19] and the second sees Christian pacifism as a Gnostic-type secret knowledge and strategy which, once known, contains all the necessary features for the establishment of the new kingdom on earth.[20] These are but two sides of the same stained shekel. It is important to acknowledge that the notions of self-sacrifice and dying for the other have neither instrumental nor intrinsic value. Christian sacrifice is misunderstood in both cases and, as Milbank argues, is made intelligible only with a language like free gift-exchange, where it is seen as an act made complete in "asymmetrical reciprocity." This is but another way of emphasizing the necessity of divine-human participation in coming to see how, properly understood, atonement and ethics are one.

Third, a church practice that highlights participation as a mode for seeing the unity of atonement and ethics is the Eucharistic feast or Holy Communion. For sacramental churches the Eucharistic feast is an event in which church members are invited to participate in the saving activity of Christ. For non-sacramental churches—perhaps especially those from the historic peace church tradition—it is often seen primarily as a memorial feast. There is a difference. The former invites church members into a re-enactment of God's grace and hence into a re-living of the original event of fellowship with Christ. In this way participants become part of the picture, that is, they experience it, by placing themselves into an act of recreating what sin has distorted. In other words, the Eucharist is not merely a memorial service commemorating the past but its "remembrance" is a display of God's atonement among God's community called church.

Holy Communion is hence also more than a love feast where we celebrate the love we have for one another (although it is that); it is an act of opening up to God who can make us the kind of people we were created to be. Communion is a feast that celebrates the activity of God among us wanting to make our holiness visible. As Hauerwas reminds us again and again, the holiness of the church is necessary for the redemption of the world.[21] Perhaps even more poignant are Dietrich Bonhoeffer's comments emphasizing that belief and remembering the past simply cannot cut it when it comes to the Christian story. Instead, what is crucial is the presence and activity of God. He puts it as follows:

> Belief in the Resurrection is not the solution to the problem of death. God's beyond is not the beyond of our cognitive faculties. The transcendence of epistemological theory has nothing to do with the transcendence of God. God is beyond amid life. The church stands, not at the boundaries where human powers give out, but in the middle of the village. [22]

The sacrament of the Eucharist can, of course, take a variety of forms. I am reminded of the Mennonite practice of communion as an act of forgiveness and social cleansing in the congregation of my childhood at the Crystal City Mennonite Church. In its own way (a common practice in the Mennonite churches in those days) it was a participation in Christ's redeeming activity; it recognized that when we come into the presence of the Holy One we ourselves become concretely transformed through the forgiveness of sin. As such it is a profound participation in the Christ event, albeit its style as sacrament is unusual.

It spanned several weeks of activity, which is why communion was practiced only a few times per year. Two weeks before the Sunday morning celebration the minister announced the event and encouraged all in the congregation to "make things right" with God and neighbor. I recall one day when my father was "visiting" in the car with a neighbor for what seemed like a long time, especially since the family was waiting for him to come in for supper. I asked my mother why he was taking so long, and she said simply, "There is communion on Sunday." That was enough for me to understand: "things needed to be made right."

During these weeks God was at work sanctifying the body. Then on Sunday came the feast, the celebration, the participatory remembrance of the renewal of the body. This celebration had its own rituals. For example, everyone had a white hanky to hold the bread (as symbol of its holiness) until all had been served, and then we ate together. The common cup was then passed from one person to another and before partaking, a nod of approval was given by the person who passed the cup, indicating that all had been made right. After drinking, the white hanky was used to wipe the rim of the cup so as not to pass on germs. This was a sacramental event in that it brought together the incarnation (remembrance of Christ), the crucifixion (the agony of repentance and seeking forgiveness), and the resurrection (celebration of God's blessing). That is, it held atonement and ethics in unity.

Fourth, to highlight a different emphasis on participation, I turn to a somewhat unusual source, Slavoj Zizek, a Slovenian philosopher and psychoanalytic theorist. Protestants and churches like the Mennonites in particular have not made a happy peace with aesthetics other than music. It is in fact somewhat puzzling why for Mennonites music, both performance and participatory singing, has been so central in their worship service when other art forms have not been. Whatever has been the reason for this, it is clear that visual art, drama, and dance have been suspect.

Zizek has recently described the tension between the Object and the Void, the subject matter of visual art, in emphasizing the importance of the redemption of place.[23] (He gets many of his insights here from the French psychoanalyst, Jacques Lacan.) For humans to be at peace with themselves, they must participate in beautiful, that is, appreciated, spaces. In this connection he makes the distinction between different modalities of suicide, because suicides normally occur when there is loss of meaningful participation in comfortable places, or, if you like, where the very possibility of participation in the space provided becomes impossible, for whatever reason.[24]

A suicide of which the "suicide bomber" is the most popular example is one where the person dies for a cause; that is, it is "imagined" that the death will bring about a state of affairs or a new place that is desired both by the person committing suicide as well as a number of important others. A death of this nature has meaning (is appreciated) and hence has value and importance insofar as these others see it as significant in promoting the larger cause. To put it differently, the person is given a place of importance, meaning, appreciation (like an object in a piece of art) through the instrumentality of the person's death. In fact, it is the death that ironically produces the "aesthetic" expression of worth.

Another modality is "symbolic suicide." This is the opposite kind of death, in that it has no instrumental value whatsoever; in fact, it is an escape from a life of instrumentality precisely because nothing matters. It is deemed necessary because all symbols of personal identity have ceased to be meaningful and no "appreciated places" any longer exist. It is because the person cannot see him/herself in the mirror of life (as it were) when all else is there as it ought to be, that place can no longer be imagined as real. All functionally real worlds have collapsed, and life is a mere "missing in the picture" existence. Death comes, but as a pronouncement of the nothingness of existence, because participation can no longer be imagined.

The death and resurrection of Christ raises the notion of occupying significant space not because his death is a suicide but because the "atoning" power of Christ makes both modalities of suicide "unnecessary." This is so because in the first case it shows that we no longer need to die for just causes, since justice is itself a gift (resurrection), not an acquisition or a possession. This does not ensure that we will not die, but that our death will not serve as an instrument to advance a cause. And in the second case, it shows that there can never be a time when "place in life" is no more because creator/redeemer God gives life eternally. The loving God assures us of an ongoing "appreciated place" through God's gift of life to us. God's redeeming work in the resurrection restores moribund existence to life.

In God's picture frame we are beautiful objects, whether we can see ourselves in life's mirrors or not. For just as bringing about peace is not up to us, neither is sustaining our own existence. Both are gifts. Hence, irrespective of whether or not our own weaknesses prevent us from seeing beyond a solution that requires death (our own or others), such a solution can never be required, because in the death of Christ we have the final repudiation of sin—resurrection. Sin is not the last word, for the most it can do is kill us, and even in this it is unable to make death permanent. The life/death/resurrection of

Christ is therefore the sufficient gift that can heal all human brokenness.

It may be hard to see how Zizek's comments on suicide highlight the importance of the unity of atonement and ethics; these few comments barely point to a proper Christian aesthetic. But as life's experience tells us all, meaningful existence and participation in the beautiful are co-extensive human appetites. In unpacking atonement imagery, we do well to remember how failure to appreciate aesthetic participation limits the Christian view of atonement, and how goodness and beauty are separable only at peril to the fully given human life.

At this point I must sum up how I believe these four illustrations help us to understand atonement. At one level it is very simple—atonement is living in Christ. Karl Barth is right in saying that "Jesus Christ is the atonement," which is but to say that Christ is the realization of God's recreation/redemption for the whole human race and the entire cosmos.[25] Christ is thus the one in whose life our own is made complete, and in whose life our lives collectively find fulfillment. Of course, if Jesus Christ is the atonement, then the practices of the church—the body of Christ—are its appropriation. It should not, then, surprise us that a search for a Christian understanding of atonement should lead us to ecclesiology. I know no better summary of this claim than the one given by Rowan Williams, who responds to the common notion that "the church is essentially a lot of people who have something in common called Christian faith and get together to share it with each other and communicate it to people 'outside.'" Such an ecclesiology may appear "harmless enough" at first,

> but it is a good way from what the New Testament encourages us to think about the church—which is that the church is first of all a space cleared by God through Jesus in which people may become what God made them to be (God's sons and daughters), and what we have to do about the church is not first to organize it as a society but to inhabit it as a climate or a landscape. It is a place where we can see properly—God, God's creation, ourselves. It is a place or dimension in the universe that is in some way growing toward being the universe itself in restored relation to God. It is a place we are invited to enter, the place occupied by Christ, who is himself the climate and atmosphere of the renewed universe.[26]

If the church is really Christ's place, it is a reality shaped by what Christ has done and continues to do. To narrate this properly requires the language of sacrifice; it requires the language of what Christ has done and continues to do *for us*—substitutionary language. Yet such language often clashes with our sensibilities about notions such as justice, violence, and power. I turn now briefly to that discussion.

SACRIFICE AND VIOLENCE

But as it is, he has appeared once for all at the end of the age to remove sin by the sacrifice of himself.
—Hebrew 9:26b

So if anyone is in Christ, there is a new creation: everything old has passed away; see, everything has become new! All this is from God, who reconciled us to himself through Jesus Christ, and has given us the ministry of reconciliation
—2 Corinthians 5:17-8

It is impossible to read the biblical account of atonement without coming face to face with the language of sacrifice. And this language creates stark reactions by some scholars because it is sometimes seen as a legitimation of violence. For example, Joanne Carlson Brown states, "Christianity is an abusive theology that glorifies suffering" and "it must itself be liberated from this theology. We must do away with the atonement, this idea of a blood sin upon the whole human race that can be washed away only by the blood of the lamb."[27] Others have made the point that God's requirement of the death of a son justifies child sacrifice and patriarchy.

There are also those who are more discriminating in their choice of atonement imagery and argue instead for care in selecting the proper kinds of atonement metaphors, capitalizing on the development of a nonviolent atonement. That is, as J. Denny Weaver puts it, we should rejects theories like Anselm's satisfaction theory because it "depends on a divinely sanctioned death as that which is necessary to satisfy the offended divine entity, whether God or God's law or God's honor. Satisfaction atonement depends on the assumption that doing justice means to punish, that a wrong deed is balanced by violence."[28] So Weaver advocates a revised Christus Victor model which he finds most open to Christian pacifism.

There is much to be said for Weaver's interesting argument, but there is also a danger here in that his argument tends to put the nonviolence cart before the biblical horse. Why, one wonders, should the measuring stick be nonviolence? If there is a credible biblical teaching on nonviolence it should grow out of the language of atonement and not be an assumption that determines which atonement images to select and which to reject, or how to modify the understanding of atonement to be consistently nonviolent. That is to say, Anselm should be judged not on whether his analysis justifies violence but on whether it gets atonement right. If he does and that happens to justify violence, so be it. Christian pacifists then have a problem. My point here is merely that our concern should be to understand the biblical/theological view of atonement. Anselm should then be judged by that standard.[29]

While I am not a particular fan of Anselm's satisfaction-substitutionary account of atonement because I believe it to be reductionistic, I do think that it has some significant merits if it is understood properly. And my fear is that in rejecting him we may again, as with sacramental and participatory language, be rejecting too much. In fact, perhaps ironically, I believe that Anselm can help us precisely at the point of getting Christian pacifism right. For I do not believe that Christian pacifism has much to do with the notion that we can, in all cases, without violence and bloodshed achieve the just ends we all want. In other words, even in peacemaking it is important to emphasize what Christ has done and is doing *for us*. Anselm, I believe, helps us to understand the sense in which peace and salvation are gifts and not commodities, something that Christian peacemakers in a capitalistic world are prone to forget.

First, a brief rehearsal of the theory as often caricatured. Human sin has brought disharmony and injustice into the world which so offended the honor of God that a debt payment had to be made to restore God's honor. Since humans owed the debt, due to their sin, they could not make restitution, so Jesus, who was human but free of sin, paid with his death on our behalf and God was satisfied. The most frequent criticisms of this caricature are then as follows: a first criticism suggests that Anselm falsely depicts God's nature, dividing God's mercy from God's justice and presupposing that God orchestrated the death of his son to satisfy his own ego. Such a view of God is in tension with the larger conception we get from reading the Scriptures. Second, Anselm's approach to the atonement is faulted for making salvation universal: if God is now satisfied, the reasoning goes, then all of humankind is saved from God's wrath. Third, Anselm's critics charge that he renders the resurrection irrelevant to atonement.

But caricatures are not yet the whole truth. David Bentley Hart has written a defense of Anselm I find compelling.[30] This is not the place to give a detailed account of Hart's argument, but his simple point is this: Anselm's language of satisfaction does not presuppose a division betweens God's mercy and justice, nor does he ignore the resurrection. Scholars like Vladimir Lossky and Gustav Aulén are wrong in their reading of Anselm precisely at this point. Hart reads Anselm deploying satisfaction imagery in a way that ends up not being in tension with other biblical images of redemption, but in fact enlightens them.

I present now a very cursory summary of Hart's defense of Anselm. First, Hart stresses that it is right to argue that sin has messed up this world, and Anselm correctly points out that this sin violates the integrity of God's creation.

Second, of course sin offends God's honor, but not in the sense of a wounded pride in need of ego restoration. The traditional notion of honor is foreign to most contemporaries and hence difficult to comprehend. But Hart's point is simply that for Anselm God's honor is inseparable from God's goodness.[31] When God's good gifts are squandered, of course God takes offense. Rightly so, because God's taking offense is but an expression of care for the goodness and beauty of creation gone awry. For offense not to be taken in such cases would be the equivalent of a disregard for the defilement of what was created good and beautiful. But in the incarnation God is doing precisely the opposite—restoring the creation which humans have defiled.

Third, Anselm is right to assume that given the nature of the sinful state of this world, the cross (that is, suffering and even death) is the way of reconciliation. For when love, beauty, and goodness meet sin, suffering is unavoidable. The only issue is whose suffering will do. Will God destroy the defilers, or will God absorb the very need for that destruction within God's *own being*? And clearly in Christ the latter road is taken.

Fourth, Anselm understands the cross in essentially non-economic terms; that is, "Christ's death purchases nothing, but his obedience to the Father calls forth a blessing."[32] Hence, God receives no price from Christ's death, but his satisfaction (the restoration of his honor) stems from a non-identical repetition of the re-giving of creation in the form of resurrection—a gift and not a purchase.

Fifth, there is therefore no division between God's mercy and justice, since in the free gift of resurrection God's justice is seen as God's mercy; that is, in the resurrection God again gave boundlessly of God's creative self in the very way God gave bountifully in the original act of creation.

Hart does not seek to advance Anselm's theory of atonement as the definitive orthodox version, but nor does he want to lose the power of this imagery. To do so, he believes, would mean a distortion of the biblical account of salvation. For Hart, perhaps more than some, given his Eastern Orthodox background, atonement is incarnation, and the cross-resurrection is but the culmination of the incarnation. What is right in Anselm is his way of upholding the blessing received and bestowed upon the obedience of the son. For his disciples to be in Christ is for them to live life as a gift from God, as did Jesus Christ, open to the same re-creative blessing.

Herein lies Anselm's importance for a Christian understanding of pacifism. The insight we receive in the cross does not assure us that the path from suffering to peace can be wrought through nonviolent obedience. That is at least heresy and perhaps blasphemy, for it assumes we have solved the mystery of God's ways and gained the controls. It would be a rejection of the relevance of God. Rather, the relationship between our obedience and our peace is most profoundly seen in the resurrection blessing given freely by God. This relationship informs both our understanding of atonement and discipleship.

We have then with Hart's rendering of Anselm another image of atonement as participation in the life of Christ as sacramental gift—the one who recreates what is broken and blesses what is good and beautiful. Hence in our own daily interactions with others—through reconciliation, risk, gift, forgiveness; instead of through ownership, control, and manipulation of outcomes—we participate in the cross-resurrection activity of God. In other words, we participate in the body of Christ. Such life in Christ saves precisely because it is sacrifice, a giving up—meaning that in Christ the future, the world's and our own, is not in our hands but in God's. This might indeed include violence, but if it does we will be not its intentional perpetrators but its victims. Such a life is possible because we know that even so God remembers the faithful, and in God's remembering we are saved.

CONCLUSION: BEING REMEMBERED

"Jesus, remember me when you come into your kingdom." [Jesus] replied, "Truly I tell you, today you will be with me in Paradise."
—Luke 23:42-3

The last days of Jesus' life are all about abandonment. His friends deserted him in the Garden, denied knowing him; he died being rejected and was not even recognized in his post-resurrection encounter with his disciples. Milbank suggests that "he suffered thereby the worst extremity of human agony," yet "he still did not endure ontological desertion." Why not? Because "Jesus only submits to be handed over because he is in himself the very heart of all transition as really loving gift, and thereby able to subvert every betrayal and abandonment."[33]

If atonement is the presence of God in Jesus Christ, abandonment is its antithesis. We have in the biblical teaching the notion that God will never abandon us, that is, we are being remembered. Of course, the fundamental act of being remembered by God is the incarnation itself. God did not abandon the world even as it abandoned God. In the incarnation we hear the words: "I am with you always . . ." (Matt. 28:20b). Our stance therefore is one of receptivity. For this receptivity we do not need theories of atonement as much as we need rich language and images that help us to receive, images and language that lift us into the very being of Christ's presence.

In an important sense Jesus' death was not a sacrifice.[34] It was itself a gift, for its prevention would have required a taking. In saying "Father, into your hands I commend my spirit" (Luke 23:46), Jesus uttered not the words of defeat but the words of sacramental gift. The act of giving over his life to God is not an act of final desperation but the act of placing it into its true home. For that giving is a giving up of what he could not have had without a taking (an owning). In the words of the Roman centurion, "Certainly this man was innocent," (Luke 23:47b), we (perhaps ironically) find not only the recognition of the horridness of the moment but also a way of saying that what is happening here is not a transaction capable of description in terms of natural justice but an act of gift exchange, an act of true human giving and true divine receiving—a delicate moment of the meeting of God and humanity.

Remembering and being remembered are not the same. To remember something is to recall it to mind. To be remembered, as the phrase is used biblically, is to be brought into the other's realm of consciousness, concern, and even action. That is, when God remembers someone, God deals with the person from the standpoint of who God is. To say it from the other end, from the perspective of the ones being remembered, we are brought into the very being or character of the other, and we experience the effects upon us of that person's character. That is why being remembered can be both horrifying and saving. To be remembered by someone evil, for example a serial killer, is a very bad thing and can mean death. To be remembered by someone who truly wills your well-being and fulfilment as a human being can save you. Being remembered makes intelligible the possibility of being drawn into the character of the other.

This may well be part of what is going on in the gospel of John when Christ speaks about being one with the Father. "Do you not believe that I am in the Father and the Father is in me? The words that I say to you I do not speak on my own; but the Father who dwells in me does his works" (John 14:10). Perhaps even more important for us—his disciples—being remembered may well be what makes intelligible Christ's comments in Matthew 25, where Jesus says to those who have acted mercifully to the dispossessed, "Truly I tell you, just as you did it to one of the least of these who are members of my family, you did it to me" (Matt. 25:40b). In showing mercy to the oppressed we are doing what God does; we are being remembered by God; we are drawn into the character of another.

I entitled my essay "Atonement: Being Remembered" because I believe that atonement is all about casting ourselves into the care of God, as did the thief on the cross. We cannot save ourselves precisely because we cannot know ourselves as we are known by the One who created us. We cannot save ourselves because as selves we are lost; and in becoming an other—God's other—we can be found. We are saved only by being remembered by God, for being so remembered we are pardoned for our guilt, forgiven for our sins, and drawn into our true humanity in Jesus Christ. In this way we are able to give our lives over to the One who wills to make of it a blessing.

> Remember, I am with you always, to the end of the age. (Matt. 28:20b)

> Justice is to be found where God, the one supreme God, rules an obedient city according to his grace, forbidding sacrifice of any being save himself alone.[35]

NOTES

1. Quoted in Ray Monk, *Ludwig Wittgenstein: The Duty of Genius* (New York: Penguin Books, 1990), 322.

2. John Howard Yoder, "Walk and Word: The Alternatives to Methodologism," in *Theology without Foundations: Religious Practice and the Future of Theological Truth*, ed. Stanley Hauerwas, Nancey Murphy, and Mark Nation (Nashville: Abingdon Press, 1994), 89.

3. Stanislas Breton, *The Word and the Cross*, trans. Jacquelyne Porter (New York: Fordham University Press, 2002), 64.

4. Robert Scholes in his 2004 presidential address of The Modern Language Association of America has summarized two quite different reasons for the heavy reliance on theory currently evident in the humanities: one represented by John Guillory in *Cultural Capital* (Chicago: University of Chicago Press, 1993) and the other by Terry Eagleton in *After Theory* (New York: Basic, 2003). Says Scholes, "For Guillory theory was an attempt to bring the humanities into alignment with an increasing technobureaucratic culture. For Eagleton, on the other hand, theory was an attempt by the humanities to think their way out of a co-option by military and industrial structures that had already taken place" ("Presidential Address 2004: The Humanities in a Posthumanist World," *PMLA*, 120 [2005]: 726). Scholes remains skeptical that we will be able to theorize our way out of the failure of the humanities to humanize and instead advocates a renewed attention to the use of poetry and rhetoric to enable the heart and mind to meet in language (733). Although he addresses a different concern, his comments resonate with our discussion on atonement.

5. See David Bentley Hart, *The Beauty of the Infinite: The Aesthetics of Christian Truth* (Grand Rapids, Mich.: Wm. B. Eerdmans, 2003), e.g., 320.

6. Ibid.

7. For a further understanding of the notion of "thick description" see, for example, Clifford Geertz, "Thick Description: Toward an Interpretative Theory of Culture," in *The Interpretation of Cultures* (New York: Basic Books, 1973).

8. One can find these images rehearsed in many books on the subject, but I will cite only two: Joel B. Green and Mark D. Baker, *Recovering the Scandal of the Cross: Atonement in New Testament and Contemporary Contexts* (Downers Grove: InterVarsity Press, 2000), esp. 100ff and J. Denny Weaver, *The Nonviolent Atonement* (Grand Rapids, Mich.: Wm. B. Eerdmans, 2001), esp. 14ff.

9. Karl Barth has it right when he begins his discussion of atonement with a chapter called "God withUs." See his *Church Dogmatics*, "The Doctrine of Reconciliation," vol. 4, part 1, trans. G.W. Bromiley (Edinburgh: T&T Clark, 1956).

10. One could of course cite many modern thinkers here who argue for the understanding of God as ultimate being, but among the earliest are William of Ockham and René Descartes. Space does not permit to recite the debate here. I refer the reader instead to sources where it is given, to wit, John Milbank, *Theology and Social Theory* (Oxford: Blackwell Publishers, 1990), e.g., 14-20, and Romand Coles, *Rethinking Generosity: Critical Theory and the Politics of Caritas* (Ithaca, N.Y.: Cornell University Press, 1997), e.g., 8ff.

11. By "mystery" I do not mean secrecy and flight from reality but metaphorical language and imagery that attempt to capture the notion of participation in the life of another.

12. For a helpful discussion of the distinctions between *ecclesia* and *imperium*, see John Milbank, *Being Reconciled: Ontology and Pardon* (London: Routledge, 2003), esp. his chapter, "Atonement: Christ the Exception," 94-104.

13. For further discussion of the notion of "performance" and "improvisa-

tion" see the essay by James Fodor and Stanley Hauerwas, "Performing the Faith: The Peaceable Rhetoric of God's Church," in *Performing the Faith: Bonhoeffer and the Practice of Nonviolence* (Grand Rapids, Mich.: Brazos Press, 2004), 75-109, and Sam Wells, *Improvisation: The Drama of Christian Ethics* (Grand Rapids, Mich.: Brazos Press, 2004).

14. John Milbank, *Being Reconciled*, xi.

15. One needs to be careful not to imply that there are many ontologies, even though there are certainly many constructed worlds. It is important to understand the world in which the redemption wrought in Jesus Christ is made intelligible. For the rendition of this world is not general, but particular, not constructed but revealed. For as Karl Barth reminds us, "The Word did not simply become any 'flesh,' any man humbled and suffered. It became Jewish flesh. The Church's whole doctrine of the incarnation and the atonement becomes abstract and valueless and meaningless to the extent that this comes to be regarded as accidental and incidental."—*Church Dogmatics*, Vol. IV, Part 1, 166.

16. This is perhaps a slight recasting of the way John Howard Yoder has put it since he remains characteristically Barthian in retaining the language of command-obedience. However, it is important to emphasize that the "blessing" relationship (as opposed to the cause-effect relationship) of cross-resurrection is precisely Yoderian and Barthian. What reading John Milbank is able to help us with is to see more clearly the dangers in the non-explicit emphasis on participation. It is fascinating to note that the Augustinian theology of Milbank and the Barthian theology of Yoder arrive at very similar conclusions even if via different routes. See esp. John Howard Yoder, *The Politics of Jesus: Vicit Agnus Noster*, 2nd. ed. (Grand Rapids, Mich.: Wm. B. Eerdmans, 1994), 232; and Milbank, *Being Reconciled*, especially his chapter entitled, "Atonement: Christ the Exception," 94-104.

17. John Milbank, *Being Reconciled*, 154.

18. Ibid.

19. This is but a way of raising a caution against the tendency to narrate the faithfulness-effectiveness dichotomy in unhelpful ways. It might be thought that Milbank is here in direct tension with Yoder, who uses the dichotomy to caution against a Niebuhrian Christian realism, but that would be a mistake. For both want to emphasize that human ownership of the moral project and control of outcome are perversions of the gospel precisely because they fail to recognize the gift-nature (blessing) of the redemptive activities of God. And this is only intelligible by holding together the cross and resurrection in ways that overcome the language of causal connection.

20. This is the particularly pernicious perversion of Christian ethics seen in a type of conflict resolution theory which has every bit as much interest in imposing its will upon the other and controlling outcomes as do violent forms of social change, only it wishes to do so nonviolently.

21. See, for example, Stanley Hauerwas, *Performing the Faith*, 44.

22. From his *Letters and Papers from Prison*, quoted here from Hauerwas, *Performing the Faith*, 47.

23. Slavoj Zizek, *The Fragile Absolute or Why is the Christian Legacy Worth*

Fighting For (London: Verso, 2000), 27ff.

24. Zizek actually discusses three modalities of suicide, but for purposes of brevity I highlight only two.

25. Karl Barth, *Church Dogmatics*, Vol. IV, Pt. 1, 34.

26. Taken from the official website of Rowan Williams, Archbishop of Canterbury. From "'The Christian Priest Today': Lecture on the Occasion of the 150th Anniversary of Ripon College, Cuddesdon," 2. The web address is www.archbishopofcanterbury.org/sermons_speeches.

27. Quoted in Richard J. Mouw, "Violence and the Atonement," in *Must Christianity be Violent? Reflections on History, Practice and Theology*, ed. Kenneth R. Chase and Alan Jacobs (Grand Rapids, Mich.: Brazos Press, 2003), 162.

28. J. Denny Weaver, *The Nonviolent Atonement*, 225.

29. I want to make sure I am being understood. I have a great respect for Weaver's work, and I am, I believe, as committed to pacifism as he is. If Anselm's view of atonement challenged my view on Christian pacifism, I too would think it necessary to sort that out. This sorting out would lead to the following three possibilities: Anselm's view could prove unfaithful to the biblical tradition and mine could be vindicated, or his could be proven faithful to that tradition and mine would need to be rethought, or we could both be wrong. All I am arguing here is that the measuring stick for our theological convictions should not be a preconceived view of nonviolence, but the biblical/theological tradition itself.

30. See David Bentley Hart, "A Gift Exceeding Every Debt: An Eastern Orthodox Appreciation of Anselm's *Cur Deus Homo*," in *Pro Ecclesia* 7/3 (Summer 1998), 333-349.

31. Ibid., 346.

32. Ibid., 345.

33. John Milbank, *Being Reconciled*, 98-9.

34. Milbank, relying on Giorgio Agamben, makes this point. For Milbank see *Being Reconciled*, 99; for Agamben, see his *Homo Sacer: Sovereign Power and Bare Life*, trans. Daniel Heller-Roazen (Stanford: Stanford University Press, 1998).

35. Augustine, *The City of God*, trans. David Knowles (Harmondsworth, U.K.: Penguin, 1972), 890.

CHAPTER ELEVEN

"WHO DURST DEFY THE OMNIPOTENT TO ARMS": THE NONVIOLENT ATONEMENT AND A NON-COMPETITIVE DOCTRINE OF GOD

J. Alexander Sider

*T*heology is centrally a reading of Scripture, and Scripture is the primary imaginative resource for Christian theology. While theology is often viewed as a heady enterprise, it is in the first instance merely the practical discipline of learning to read Scripture well. Yet reading Scripture well is not as simple a task as one might often like it to be: It involves not only close attention to "the way the words go," to Scripture's internal patterns of cross-reference and discontinuity, but also to the presuppositions that allow canonical texts to function as Scripture in the life of the church. Thus, one might say, the primary function of Christian theology is to reflect on how Scripture is read in church.

No one who is familiar with J. Denny Weaver's theological work could comfortably suggest that he has failed to pay close attention either to Scripture or to the life of the church. Indeed, I think, his "narrative Christus Victor" theology of the nonviolent atonement should be understood primarily as an attempt to describe how Scripture should function within the church. For Weaver, the good news that the church is called to proclaim is the creation of a people capable of continuing Scripture's story, that is, of Christ's making the reign of God visible and effective in the world. However, while the prominence in Weaver's work of such themes as the ongoing story of Scripture and the disclosure of God's reign places him alongside many other "apocalyptic," "postliberal," and "narrative" theologians of the second half of the twentieth century, in a key respect Weaver diverges from most of these theologians. An important aspect of postliberal narrative theology has been to show how a philosophically articulate and robustly ecclesiological contemporary rendering of Christian theology can exist in deep continuity with the so-called "creedal" theologies of the patristic era. By contrast, Weaver has been an ardent "non-Constantinian" critic of patristic theologies and a chronicler of their allegedly deleterious effects on Christian faith.

One of the central facets of Weaver's non-Constantinian reconfiguration of theology consists in undoing what he calls "Anselm's deletion." In Anselm's satisfaction theory of the atonement, Weaver contends, the theological role of the devil is eclipsed so that the essential conflict in the drama of salvation occurs *in God*. Not to put too find a point on it, for Anselm it is almost as though human sin triggers a schizoid episode in God, causing a collision between God's benevolence and God's justice. For Anselm, atonement is reduced to a scheme that heals God's personality disorder. That scheme is itself traumatic, in that it requires the sacrifice of Christ, the "God-man." God's enduring beneficence is contingent upon the bloody satisfaction of God's wrath.

While I would contend that this representation of Anselm's theology fails to do justice to the trinitarian character of Anselm's argument (and, furthermore, does not adequately engage the patristic emphases with which Anselm interacts), my present interest lies in exploring Weaver's rehabilitation of the devil's theological role in the story of salvation, a rehabilitation played out in Weaver's theology of the "powers." His account of the powers, I argue, tends in a nominalist direction, one that both refuses a radical account of divine transcendence and fosters a voluntaristic conception of human participation in God's reign. I will go on to suggest, however, that a recovery of certain patristic and pro-Nicene emphases concerning power can help create the conditions under which a theology of the powers may be employed for a contemporary theological account of salvation that avoids the nominalist reduction of God to the level of a mere thing with which humans can compete.

'THE POWERS" IN CONTEMPORARY THEOLOGY

Weaver's most concise account of his theology of the powers appears in an important paragraph near the end of *The Nonviolent Atonement*:

> I follow Walter Wink in understanding the devil or Satan as the accumulation of earthly structures that are not ruled by the reign of God. This devil is real, but it is not a personified being who may or may not have rights in the divine order of things. Wink argued that the principalities and powers, demons, and so on of the Bible are not independent entities that inhabit a place. Instead, they are the "spiritual" dimension of material structures. All powers in the world—the state, corporations, economic structures, educational institutions, and so on—have inner and outer, or spiritual and material dimensions. Power does not exist independent of a material incorporation or system. The inner essence is the collective cultural ethos that surrounds a specific outer manifestation. Thus, the powers are real, although not separately existing, independent entities; and their moral identity and character depend on whether or not they assert their existence over against or under the lordship of Christ. None of the powers is good in and of itself, since they all exist in a system of domination in which they are accomplices. But as fallen powers, all are also redeemable and thus potentially good to the extent that they submit to the lordship of Christ.[1]

Such a theology of the powers has become tremendously popular among left-leaning contemporary Christians. While it is largely motivated by a desire to read the Bible realistically, it also has roots in post-World War II Europe.

The primary architect of the theology of the powers that Weaver and others employ was Hendrik Berkhof. His short book, *Christ en de Machten*, first appeared in 1953 as an extension of lectures Berkhof presented to a German audience in 1950. In the preface to the second English edition, Berkhof noted, "Whoever knows anything of the situation of devastated and divided Germany in the early years of the cold war can hear an echo of that in the book."[2] The story goes a good deal deeper than that, however, for *Christ and the Powers* deserves to be read in continuity with Berkhof's earlier work, *Kirche und Kaiser*, first published in 1946.³ While it was primarily a historical work, *Kirche und Kaiser* also had a constructive agenda, that of bringing to light a number of striking parallels between fourth-century imperial Christianity and the *Deutsche Christen* movement of the Third Reich. Sadly, this constructive agenda has been all but ignored in theological appraisals of Berkhof's work, and theologians who have used Berkhof since have rarely paused to ask whether and how Berkhof's biography shaped his theological historiography. Of course, there is no question of the work being invalidated on the basis of Berkhof's history, but equally there ought to be no question that his work is something other than naïve as-it-happened historiography.

The same holds true for Berkhof's theology of the powers, especially insofar as it claims to represent "what Paul really thought."⁴ Theologians, by and large, are not nearly startled enough by such claims: In contrast to the more cautious pronouncements of biblical scholars, theologians display surprising temerity in appropriating "Pauline" thought as if innocent of coloration by our own polemical agendas. In the next few pages, therefore, I investigate some of the coloration I think a theology of the powers receives in the wake of Berkhof.

NOMINALISM AND ATONEMENT: DOES GOD COMPETE?

As a young teenager I stumbled across two battered blue volumes on my parents' bookshelves. I took the books down, sat on the floor beside the shelves, opened the larger book to a page near the beginning, and began to read:

> . . . Him the almighty power
> Hurled headlong flaming from the ethereal sky
> With hideous ruin and combustion down
> To bottomless perdition, there to dwell
> In adamantine chains and penal fire,
> Who durst defy the omnipotent to arms.
> Nine times the space that measures day and night
> To mortal men, he with his horrid crew
> Lay vanquished, rolling in the fiery gulf
> Confounded though immortal.

I have never, before or since, experienced anything remotely like these words in print. The lines in question are, of course, 44-54 from Book I of *Paradise Lost* by John Milton.[5] They describe the devil's fall from heaven, which Christians have imagined in epic terms ever since Luke recorded Jesus' words to the seventy after they returned to him saying, "Lord, in your name even the demons submit to us! He said to them, 'I watched Satan fall from heaven like a flash of lightning'" (10:17-18).

Paradise Lost, it hardly needs to be said, is one of the greatest epics of the English language, and one of its chief attractions is Milton's charismatic—even sympathetic—portrayal of the devil. In *Paradise Lost* Satan is possessed of heroic qualities, such as courage and eloquence, that many of us hope to find in ourselves. By nearly all accounts Milton's Satan is high romance, which prompted William Blake, upon whom Milton exerted immense influence, to comment that he "was a true Poet and of the Devil's party without knowing it."

Philip Pullman, the Oxford children's fiction author and one of Milton's recent interpreters, recounts in his introduction to *Paradise Lost* a story he heard secondhand (at best):

> A bibulous, semi-literate, ageing country squire two hundred years ago or more, [sits] by his fireside listening to Paradise Lost being read aloud. He's never read it himself; he doesn't know the story at all; but as he sits there, perhaps with a pint of port at his side and with a gouty foot propped upon a stool, he finds himself transfixed.
>
> Suddenly he bangs the arm of his chair, and exclaims, "By God! I know not what the outcome may be, but this Lucifer is a damned fine fellow, and I hope he may win!"[6]

While Pullman shares the old squire's sentiments exactly, I cannot say that I do, despite Milton's overwhelming craft. I find myself nagged by a question: Could God have lost? Could God have lost the battle with Satan? Or evil? Or sin? Or death? Or, in the idiom with which I am most concerned in this essay, the powers? I think that the answer to this question must be "No, or else, we aren't talking about God." Albert Einstein, who authored the theory of relativity, is supposed to have complained about Heisenberg's Uncertainty Principle that "God doesn't play dice." I wish to add to Einstein simply that this is not at all because God and chance are incompatible, but because God, if God is God, does not compete.

Yet much Christian theology, contemporary and otherwise, seems to me to be conducted under precisely the opposite premise, namely, that God and the world God created are locked in an apparently interminable struggle for power, a struggle God has already won in Christ but which has not yet been brought to fullness. Weaver makes a similar argument from a variety of scriptural texts, placing "the teaching and life of Jesus from an earthly perspective . . . within the framework of Christus Victor." "In many ways the teaching and acts of Jesus pose the reign of God in conflict with the powers that oppose it," Weaver argues. "When Jesus was executed, the powers of evil enjoyed a momentary triumph—Jesus' very existence is removed. However, God raised Jesus from death, thereby revealing the reign of God as the ultimate power in the cosmos."[7]

In this passage, Weaver explicitly places God's power in competition with created powers, with the effect that only God's victory in Christ vindicates God's superior power. Such a comparison, however, implies that God and creatures exercise the same kind of power, and so in some sense are the same kind of things; such comparison is a conceptual symptom of nominalist theology.[8]

Nominalism developed in the intellectual climate of late medieval mendicancy, primarily among the English Franciscans.[9] Its theological "cash-value" is difficult to summarize in any comprehensive and accessible way. At its simplest, however, nominalism is the view that all speech about things is purely a matter of convention. Rowan Williams summarizes this perspective nicely in *The Wound of Knowledge*. He writes that for nominalism, "[t]here could be no certain (that is, experiential) knowledge of realities outside the realm of sense experience. Knowledge was seen as 'acquaintance,' pragmatic contact. Religious knowledge, therefore, was, from a purely natural point of view, impossible."[10] Like many philosophical and theological programs throughout history, nominalism has a variety of modern expressions that influence our churches and cultures. A few of its salient features, therefore, deserve notice.

First, in terms of its rational psychology, nominalism tends to concentrate on the primacy of the will. Because intellectual knowledge is certain only to the extent that knowing subjects similarly constitute their thought worlds, all knowledge is ultimately a matter of one's willed assent to propositions (propositions of one's own devising or ones adopted from others). Such nominalist assumptions, incidentally, provide both the intellectual climate and polemical context for Immanuel Kant's critical philosophy. To some extent, this strand of nominalism remains ambient in the later Wittgenstein as well.

Second, and accompanyingly, nominalism tends to reinforce the division of faith and reason. At this level, Williams comments, "Either we suppose that faith has nothing to do with the knowing of the rational subject and is exclusively a matter of will (responding to some incalculable divine agency); or else we hold that true and certainly knowable propositions are miraculously delivered to the Church and promulgated as authoritative dogma."[11] Ernst Troeltsch and Karl Barth were, in very different ways, the twentieth-century's legatees of this aspect of nominalist thought, though I might just as easily cite a host of fundamentalisms, Catholic and Protestant alike.

Finally, and this aspect of nominalism remains underappreciated, nominalism tends toward "associative" forms of human community. If knowledge is to be construed as a matter of willed assent to propositions, and the only available alternative to this is personal (that is, subjective) experience, then people will tend to congregate in groups of like-minded individuals. Robert Bellah demonstrated this thesis amply in *Habits of the Heart*, but Max Weber and Friedrich Nietzsche each made similar claims over a century ago.[12]

Throughout *Paradise Lost*, Milton's vision of God's power flirts constantly with nominalism, and in a way that illustrates nominalism's chief effect on theological speech, namely, the non-analogical comparison of God to creatures.[13] Again, near the opening of the poem, Satan, while roiling in the wreck of hell, discerns another fallen angel, "One next himself in power, and next in crime / . . . Beelzebub."[14] Satan addresses Beelzebub at length and notes that though once they were joined "in glorious enterprise,"

> . . . now misery hath joined
> In equal ruin: into what pit thou seest
> From what height fallen, so much the stronger proved
> He with his thunder: and till then who knew
> The force of those dire arms?[15]

Milton's Satan, at least, believes that God's power is of a sort that could be opposed by something that is not God. Thus, he proposes "To wage by force or guile eternal war / Irreconcilable, to our grand foe / Who now triumphs, and in the excess of joy / Sole reigning holds the tyranny of heaven."[16] Satan thinks that his action may in some way challenge God's activity—he dares "defy the omnipotent to arms." He behaves as though, by introducing Sin and Death into the world, he might diminish God's glory. The more he wages war against heaven, the more difficult it will be for God to achieve God's perfect plan of providence. Milton's Satan is thus a wonderful example of nominalist theology, because his every action is dictated by the belief that God and God's creatures cause things to happen in the same way. They exercise the same power; the only issue is quantity: How much power do they have at their command?

From the claim that God and God's creatures have the same kind of power flow two further ideas: first, that God and creatures compete, or at least potentially do so; and second, that God's transcendence is not radical. For Milton's Satan, as for nominalism generally, God is simply one more thing with which to interact. Satan's view of God's power is, however, mistaken, for if God *is* the "metafertile" source of all, as the Christian teaching of *creatio ex nihilo* suggests, then God's power is not univocal with creaturely power. The old joke about God's conversation with a geneticist puts the point well:

A geneticist met God. Eager to prove that God isn't so special, he challenged God to create the perfect human. After all, now that the secrets of the human genome were laid bare before him, he could accomplish anything.

God said, "Okay. I accept your challenge. You go first."

So, the geneticist took God to his lab and began the process. "One drop of this ... two drops of that ... recombine them like so, and ... voila! I have it!"

God stared at the geneticist, surrounded by all his scientific apparatus, and said, "But you cheated. I thought you said creation."

God's power is not to be thought of as simple sameness as or difference from creaturely power. Rather, any comparison of God's power to creaturely power ultimately founders on the infinite qualitative divide that distinguishes creator from creature. Consequently, Satan's determination to resist God's power is not only ineffective, but also false, *not because God will always win but because Satan is comparing incomparable things*. If God is God, then God's qualities are incomparable. God, as Kathryn Tanner puts it, is "the giver of all kinds of things and all manner of existence," but God is not a thing and therefore relates to creatures in an incomparable, that is to say, noncompetitive, way.[17]

Many of the theologians who employ scriptural terminology like "the powers" as a way to consider the reality of evil in the world tend to personify them in much the same way as Milton personified Satan: at least, they characteristically speak about power in reifying ways. There is little to draw on today by way of a theology of the powers that takes adequate account of either realist or postmodern understandings of power, the likes of which can be found in the works of Carl Schmitt, Michel Foucault, Gilles Deleuze and Felix Guattari, or Michael Hardt and Antonio Negri.[18] A theology of the powers today needs to confront very vexed questions of agency and accountability, which current theological writing tends to sidestep with vague references to complicity, cooperation, and culpability that invoke but refuse to examine concepts like action, agency, and responsibility.

Weaver, Wink, Berkhof, Yoder, and others have helped to uncover the extent to which contemporary technologies of power regularly disguise and reify its pathways.[19] Thus, "the powers" in the guise of mega-states and corporate transnationalism appear godlike—omnipresent, omnipotent, omniscient, and basically impersonal realities which we have to find ways of resisting. But hand in hand with the task of naming such institutions must go renewed reflection on the way that the individual is not only the product of but also produces these powers. Thus, a theology of the powers today needs to recognize that power is personal without culminating in voluntarism. Because every interpersonal encounter occurs as a manifestation of power(s), an adequate theology of the powers needs to trace the patterns of responsibility for the shapes, directions, limits, exclusions, and openings of various power encounters. In other words, a theology of the powers needs to attend to what Foucault called power's "microcapillary" distillations. If it can do so, then we will have moved a step closer to (re)constituting a set of "spiritual exercises" regarding power that yield prospects for more positive relationships than contemporary theologies of the powers acknowledge.

Here at least, undoubtedly, we should listen to Anselm's warning, "Nondum considerasti, quanti ponderis sit peccatum."[20] As Peter Dula and I put the case in a recent article on radically deliberative democracy, we need frank recognition that

> [T]hose of us who want to see past/through/into the ideologies of megastates and transnational corporations also feel and embody the "noetic effects of sin," or rather of power (the two are not to be equated), all the way down. By habituating ourselves to the knowledge that we too, local communities too, grass-roots activist movements too, are all shot through with lived equivocations concerning the very forms of power we decry, we can learn to see movement and fluctuation, intensifications and displacements of power where before we saw only sedentary and external uniformities.[21]

It is in this spirit that I wish, in the final section of this essay, to begin exploring scriptural and philosophical conceptions of power, with a view toward laying a groundwork for further conversation on a theology of the powers.

RETHINKING THE POWERS: WHAT EXISTS AFFECTS

Early in my divinity school career at Duke University, I enrolled in a seminar course with Richard Hays called "New Testament Ethics." During the course of the semester my attention focused on the language of power, *dunamis*, and its corollary terms in the New Testament.[22] I had been prepared to think of these issues as prominent by having read Berkhof's *Christ and the Powers* and John Howard Yoder's *The Politics of Jesus* during college, so I wrote my seminar paper for Hays on these themes, basically parroting Berkhof and Yoder. While Hays' comments on the paper were characteristically gracious, one sharp sentence stuck out: "There's a lot more to the word *dunamis* than Yoder or Berkhof ever considered."

A few years later, during my doctoral coursework, I studied fourth-century Trinitarian theology in earnest. Lewis Ayres directed our attention to a largely unexplored summary of the Christian faith in Gregory of Nyssa's *On the Holy Trinity*, where Nyssa says that he believes in "three Persons . . . one Goodness, one Power, one Godhead. . . ."[23] This is hardly the standard "substance," "essence" or "nature" terminology that scholars generally associate with pro-Nicene fourth-century theology's ways of talking about what there is one of in God. For Gregory, however, it is absolutely critical, if one is to have a robustly Trinitarian theology, that God is conceived insofar as possible as *one active power in three persons*. Unsurprisingly, the word at stake in Gregory's text is dunamis. More surprisingly, Gregory's attention crystallizes around power because it is a scriptural term that concentrates on God's activity in the economy of salvation. Gregory is thus a strong counter-example to the argument that patristic theologians were more concerned with Hellenistic philosophical conventions than they were with reading Scripture.

To approach the link between pro-Nicene Cappadocian and scriptural uses of dunamis, one must understand something of the word's resonance and use in pre-Christian Greek philosophy and literature.24 While dunamis appears in Hesiod, Homer, Herodotus, Pindar, and Parminides, among others, the most decisive philosophical use of dunamis in pre-Christian Greek thought occurs in the Hippocratic Corpus of the early fifth century BCE.[25] Because the Hippocratic Corpus is first and foremost a literature of medical philosophy, the Hippocratic writers were chiefly concerned to demonstrate the reliability of causal relations between events and things. This is the principle on which medical diagnosis and therapy was (and to a large extent, remains) based.

Power figured heavily in this philosophy because a thing's dunamis, its power, was conceived of as its capacity to influence other things. Whatever is affects other things, and its capacity to do so is its power. As Michel Barnes says, "A dunamis is the distinctive capacity ... of any specific existent, that is, those causal capacities that belong to an object because it is specifically what it is: the hot (heat) is the dunamis of fire, for example, and anything which lacks the dunamis of the hot is not fire."[26] So, a thing's dunamis is not distinct from what it is; there is no fire without heat. Moreover, the principle of causality involved can be summarized as "like from like." When fire affects another thing, it acts by imparting its dunamis (heat) to that thing—think of boiling a kettle of water on a stovetop. Similarly, adding salt to food makes it salty, and adding water to sand makes it wet—these are standard examples of the effects of powers on other things. The dunamis of one thing produces a similar effect in something else.

From very early on, Greek philosophy divided being into a set of relations between opposites. The Hippocratics merely added that the oppositions in question were relations between the powers. The dunamis of hot was opposed (and potentially cancelled) by cold; wet and dry opposed each other as *dunameis*; sweet and sour, and so forth. Obviously, this conception of power has cosmological ramifications, but it also has psychological ones. While these oppositions are not "ethical" in any straightforward way—it would not make sense in an ancient Greek milieu to speak of the dynamic opposition between hot and cold as good or evil—because the oppositions do not exist in the abstract, that is, apart from their effects, then insofar as they characterize a thing's way of being in the world, they can be spoken of as good or evil.

In other words, it is misleading to understand the entire skein of oppositional relations as "metaphysical," in the currently fashionable and pejorative sense of the word: power is an *active* concept, a way of talking about how whatever is affects other things, which effects can be good, bad, or indifferent. In consequence, one way of conceiving of much ancient philosophy, from that of the Hippocratics up to and including that of the later Stoa, was as sets of spiritual exercises designed to cultivate the proper *tonos*, or tension, among the powers (and their related concepts) active in the soul.[27]

POWER IN A NON-COMPETITIVE THEOLOGY

Where does this basic conceptual sketch of powers-language in Hellenistic philosophy leave us with respect to Scripture and Christian theology? In terms of interpreting the New Testament, it paints a rather different picture of what is at stake in speaking of dunameis than that given to us by Berkhof, Weaver, and others. Berkhof, for his part, appears to have assumed that the primary literary backdrop for Scripture's use of dunamis was apocalyptic rather than philosophical. He argued:

> Research . . . in recent decades has indicated that Paul's thought was not isolated from his intellectual and religious environment. Not that we find useful parallels in contemporary Greek philosophy . . . : but we do find a very distinct relatedness to certain lines of thought in the Jewish apocalyptic writings of Paul's time and the immediately preceding years. These writings, devoted to the exposition of heavenly mysteries, conceive of the "powers," "thrones," and the like as classes of angels located on higher or lower levels in the heavens. For that matter, all Jewish thought on the period was deeply interested in angels and their influences on terrestrial events.[28]

I am not suggesting that Berkhof was entirely mistaken about the literary heritage of scriptural references to power. However, I see little reason to conclude with him that apocalyptic and philosophical thought-patterns should be opposed. As I maintained above, it is quite possible for a concept like dunamis to play a crucial role in both the cosmology and the rational psychology of many philosophies in the ancient world. Indeed, I suggest, after Plato's extended series of analogies among the soul, the city, and the sacred that we call *The Republic*, this is the normal run of affairs in ancient philosophy.[29] Neither, incidentally, is there sufficient reason to assume that Paul's Judaism insulated him against ancient philosophy. Philo and Josephus are both contemporary testaments to the contrary.

With respect to pro-Nicene patristic emphases in theology, this sketch of the philosophical background to dunamis offers a way of avoiding the nominalist overtones present in contemporary theologies of the powers. It is becoming increasingly widely acknowledged that the Trinitarian controversies of the fourth century centrally concerned the nature of God's power and its relationship to the economy of salvation revealed in Scripture. This, and not an abstract (that is, non-soteriological) account of Trinitarian unity and diversity is the context in which Nicaea's *homoousion* is best understood. Ever since the nineteenth-century renaissance in the history of dogma, it has been commonplace to observe that the original polemical context for the first council of Nicaea in 325 CE concerned the disagreement between Arius and Alexander over whether or not there are effective degrees of divinity. Arius is generally assumed to have argued that there are: while the Father is "true God," the Son is simply god. In this context, homoousion simply declares against the "arian" position that whatever the Father is, the Son is that also—at least this seems to be the interpretation of Nicaea that became dominant by the end of the fourth century.

This is the textbook account, and it clearly "rules out" readings of Scripture that concentrate on certain kinds of subordinationist language.[30] By the late fourth century, however, terminology like homoousion had already been displaced to some extent by other terminologies, including dunamis, with the effect that the "same-substance" debate acquired a more expansive function than it had through the 340s. This refiguration of Nicene issues can perhaps best be seen in Gregory of Nyssa's theological work, which, as Lewis Ayres put it, forces "upon us a deliberate and focused *askesis* of the imagination, insisting that the logic of ineffable natures known through the activity of their intrinsic powers is fundamental to the structure of the creation itself."[31] In other words, Gregory's reflections on Nicene theology in the late fourth century creates an imaginative façade upon which Scripture's demand that we conceive of a unitary divine power can be explored for its soteriological resonance, yet without placing God in an implicitly competitive relation to creation. How so?

In keeping with his education, Gregory understood dunamis as a thing's capacity to act in a way that distinctively manifests its nature (or "thingness," what it is that makes it different from other things). In *Against Eunomius* he based his main argument in favor of pro-Nicene theology on such an understanding of the unity that exists between natures and powers. There, he argued that because God reveals Godself in Scripture as one power, the persons of the Trinity must share the same nature, and he supported this argument with numerous examples from Hellenistic power (meta)physics of the kind that I enumerated above. In *On "Not Three Gods": To Ablabius*, he made a similar argument regarding divine unity:

> Since among [humans] the action of each in the same pursuits is discriminated, they are properly called many, since each of them is separated from others within his [or her] own environment, according to the special character of his [or her] operation. But in the case of the Divine nature we do not similarly learn that the Father does anything by Himself in which the Son does not work conjointly, or again that the Son has any special operation apart from the Holy Spirit; but every operation which extends from God to the Creation, and is named according to our variable conceptions of it, has its origin from the Father, and proceeds through the Son, and is perfected in the Holy Spirit.[32]

In this understanding of creation's relationship to God, nothing created can be limitless, so everything that is has limited power. Yet for Gregory, Scripture demands that we conceive of God's power, power common to the Father, Son, and Holy Spirit, as unlimited and "a sufficient cause to the things that are, for their coming into existence out of nothing."[33] Put as simply as possible, this means just that because God creates everything that is, God is not one thing among others. Such a radical theology of divine transcendence provided Gregory with the basis for a non-competitive theology of salvation that draws together an economy of infinite divine plenitude and an understanding of God's salvific restoration of creation in Christ.

While it remains possible in a sense to speak of this restoration in terms of God's "victory"—indeed Gregory does so and recognizes that Scripture does so as well—Gregory also argues that salvation should more properly be conceived as the possibility of human participation in God's activity and power. Gregory's "three persons one power" theology says that Jesus acts with God's power in such a way that God constitutes Jesus' identity—this is his reconfiguration of Nicaea's same-substance language. Because we know God in God's power, Jesus is what there is to say about God.[34] Yet what is present for Gregory that is lacking in later appropriations of dunamis is his clear assumption that God's power cannot be compared to any other power. For Gregory, this assumption sets the stakes for pro-Nicene theology: it is the very incomparability of God's power that allows human participation in God's life. Gregory, it is generally recognized, reoriented discussion of the concept of participation in the divine from a concern with who God is to what God does. Salvation is thus to be construed as a matter of acting as God acts—in charity, humility, and compassion. Yet this participation cannot be thought of in voluntaristic or decision-based terms, as willed assent to propositions or doctrine, because, for Gregory, true knowledge of God cannot be captured conceptually. Furthermore, if true knowledge of God is not conceptual, then the Christian life is a journey into the infinity that characterizes the triune life. This is no abstract "absoluteness" in the Hegelian-Troeltschian sense, but rather, "an infinity of what Gregory simply calls 'goodness,' an infinite resource of mercy, help and delight."[35] There is thus, for Gregory, no sense in which such an infinite resource could be encountered competitively, just as there is no sense in which God's power could be contemplated as something that could be defied. The Christian life is always marked by an ecstatic desire for this goodness—to which it will never be adequate—and this desire characterizes (insofar as we can say) the resurrected life as well.

While these reflections could be extended, the point here is simply that we are not finished wrestling with a theology of the powers. A contemporary theology of the powers must pick up where Berkhof, Yoder, and Weaver left off by insisting it is not a simple thing to conceive power in Scripture and the ancient world as external, corporate, or structural; power, moreover, should not be equated with the form of evil in the world. As I said before, Gregory of Nyssa is one strong counter-example to this trend. For him, power is both an important limiting concept that directs our attention to Scripture's insistence on a basic distinction between creator and creature and, accompanyingly, the condition of possibility for our salvation. Theology today, perhaps especially Mennonite theology with its inadequate and underdeveloped understanding of the way in which we are both products of and producers of power, needs to draw on the nuanced reflections of theologians such as Gregory if theology is to avoid bland moralism and continue to provoke fresh encounters with Scripture.

NOTES

1. J. Denny Weaver, *The Nonviolent Atonement* (Grand Rapids, Mich.: Wm. B. Eerdmans, 2001), 210.

2. Hendrik Berkhof, *Christ and the Powers*, trans. John H. Yoder (Scottdale, Pa.: Herald Press, 1977), 8.

3. Hendrik Berkhof, *Kirche und Kaiser; eine Untersuchung der Entstehung der byzantinischen und der theokratischen Staatsauffassung im vierten Jahrhundert*, trans. Gottfried W. Locher (Zollikon-Zürich: Evangelischer Verlag, 1947). Berkhof also wrote *Die Theologie des Eusebius von Caesarea* (Amsterdam: Uit-

geversmaatschappij Holland, 1939), in which he anticipates the argument of *Kirche und Kaiser*.

4. "We must read from the words of Paul himself what the Powers meant to him; only then may we say whether and to what extent he shared current conceptions." Berkhof, *Christ and the Powers*, 17.

5. Unless otherwise noted, all references are to John Milton, *Paradise Lost*, Intro. Philip Pullman (Oxford: Oxford University Press, 2005).

6. Pullman, "Introduction," *Paradise Lost*, 1.

7. Weaver, *Nonviolent Atonement*, 43.

8. The literature on analogy, univocity, and equivocity is already vast but keeps growing nonetheless. The clearest treatment I have encountered can be found in chapters 7-11 of Nicholas Lash's *Theology on the Way to Emmaus* (London: SCM Press, 1986). Regarding nominalist theologies of the univocity of being, see now Conor Cunningham, *Genealogy of Nihilism: Philosophies of Nothing and the Difference of Theology* (London: Routledge, 2002).

9. It is not a mistake, I think, that nominalism has been associated with the theologies of the radical reformation. See, e.g., David C. Steinmetz, "Scholasticism and Radical Reform: Nominalist Motifs in the Theology of Balthasar Hubmaier," *Mennonite Quarterly Review* 45 (April 1971): 123-144. The Anabaptists of the sixteenth century traced their theological heritage through the anticlerical and antifraternal debates of the fourteenth and fifteenth centuries: Wyclif, Hus, and the so-called mystics of late-medieval Europe, all of whom were the progenitors of the reformation maxim *sola scriptura*, are but one philosophical step removed from Ockham. Cf. David Knowles, *The Evolution of Medieval Thought*, 2nd. ed. (Harlow: Longman, 1988), 298-306.

10. Rowan Williams, *The Wound of Knowledge: A Theological History from the New Testament to Luther and St John of the Cross* (Atlanta: John Knox Press, 1980), 138.

11. Williams, *Wound of Knowledge*, 138.

12. Robert N. Bellah et al., *Habits of the Heart: Individualism and Commitment in American Life* (Berkeley: University of California Press, 1985).

13. It is generally a bad idea to attribute consistent philosophical positions to poets, and one could also argue that *Paradise Lost* thoroughly criticizes nominalism; thus, I say that Milton "flirts" with nominalist positions, at least, because in Satan they look both attractive and commonsensical.

14. Milton, *Paradise Lost*, Book I, lines 79-81.

15. Ibid., I. 81-94.

16. Ibid., I. 121-124.

17. Kathryn Tanner, *Jesus, Humanity and the Trinity: A Brief Systematic Theology* (Minneapolis: Fortress, 2001), 4.

18. James P. Mackey's *Power and Christian Ethics* (Cambridge: Cambridge University Press, 1994) and Oliver O'Donovan's *The Desire of the Nations: Rediscovering the Roots of Political Theology* (Cambridge: Cambridge University Press, 1996) are each interesting cases of texts that deal with power in a Schmittian fashion without taking serious account of contemporary Continental thought.

19. Cf. Michel Foucault, "Truth and Power" in *The Foucault Reader*, ed. Paul

Rabinow (New York: Pantheon, 1984), 66.

20. *S. Anselmi Cantuariensis Archiepiscopi Opera omnia*, vol. 2, *Cur Deus Homo* I:21, ed. F. S. Schmitt (Edinburgh: n. pub., 1946), 88. "You have not yet considered how heavy a weight sin is."—Anselm of Canterbury, *Why God Became Man* I:21, in *The Major Works*, ed. Brian Davies and Gillian Evans (Oxford: Oxford University Press, 1998), 305.

21. Peter Dula and Alex Sider, "Radical Democracy, Radical Ecclesiology," *CrossCurrents* 55/4 (Winter 2005/2006): 490.

22. Related arguments can be made concerning *stoicheia* and *arche*.

23. Gregorii Nysseni Opera 3:1a, 5:18ff.

24. In contrast to Berkhof (and Yoder, following Berkhof), who assumed that the background of dunamis and its corollaries in Hellenistic philosophy were largely irrelevant to New Testament and theological studies. Cf. Berkhof, *Christ and the Powers*, 16.

25. An excellent account of this literature can be found in Wesley Smith, *The Hippocratic Tradition* (Cornell: Cornell University Press, 1979).

26. Michel Rene Barnes, *The Power of God: Dunamis in Gregory of Nyssa's Trinitarian Theology* (Washington, D.C.: Catholic University of America Press, 2001), 28-29.

27. The current revival of spiritual exercise as a concept with which to understand ancient philosophy (as well as philosophy since) owes much to the efforts of Pierre Hadot. See his *Philosophy as a Way of Life: Spiritual Exercises from Socrates to Foucault*, ed. Arnold I. Davidson (Oxford: Blackwell, 1995) and *What is Ancient Philosophy?*, trans. Michael Chase (Cambridge, Mass.: Harvard University Press, 2002). See also John M. Cooper, *Reason and Emotion: Essays on Ancient Moral Psychology and Ethical Theory* (Princeton: Princeton University Press, 1999), especially "Part III: Hellenistic Philosophy" and Martha C. Nussbaum, *The Therapy of Desire: Theory and Practice in Hellenistic Ethics* (Princeton: Princeton University Press, 1994).

28. Berkhof, *Christ and the Powers*, 16.

29. Cf. Gillian Rose, *Mourning Becomes the Law: Philosophy and Representation* (Cambridge: Cambridge University Press, 1996) for an extended reflection on Plato's analogies under the conditions of postmodernity.

30. See Ben C. Ollenburger, "Mennonite Theology: A Conversation around the Creeds," *Mennonite Quarterly Review* 66/1 (January 1992): 57-89, for an excellent account of the hermeneutically regulative function of patristic conciliar formulations.

31. Lewis Ayres, *Nicaea and Its Legacy: An Approach to Fourth-Century Trinitarian Theology* (Oxford: Oxford University Press, 2004), 361.

32. Gregory of Nyssa, *On "Not Three Gods": To Ablabius*, Nicene and Post-Nicene Fathers II:5, ed. Philip Schaff and Henry Wace (Grand Rapids, Mich.: Wm. B. Eerdmans, 1994), 334.

33. Gregory of Nyssa, *On the Making of Man*, NPNF II:5, ed. Philip Schaff and Henry Wace (Grand Rapids, Mich.: Wm. B. Eerdmans, 1994), 414.

34. Rowan Williams, *On Christian Theology* (Oxford: Blackwell, 2000), 157; cf. Nicholas Lash, *Theology on the Way to Emmaus*, 167-185

35. Williams, *Wound of Knowledge*, 55.

CHAPTER TWELVE

NEEDLES NOT NAILS: MARGINAL METHODOLOGIES AND MENNONITE THEOLOGY

Malinda Elizabeth Berry

*D*enny Weaver's work in *The Nonviolent Atonement* has produced "creative controversy" in Mennonite theological circles. Rather than get caught up in questions about the orthodoxy of his position, though, I prefer to focus on what Weaver has done methodologically for Mennonite theology.

By making the claim that we are in one way or another "marginal" to the larger Western Christian tradition (theology in general), Weaver asks Mennonites in North America to consider the multi-colored, -textured, and -layered fabric of Christian life. He does this by offering a survey of the other voices on the peripheries of theology in general, particularly the voices from liberationist traditions in contemporary theology: black, feminist, and womanist.

Even in his most comprehensive engagement with these voices in *The Nonviolent Atonement,* Weaver brings these marginal voices into the discussion primarily because they offer their own thoroughgoing critiques of Anselmian atonement and share points of compatibility with his proposal for a Narrative Christus Victor approach to atonement. What might happen if we moved the conversation to some other aspects of soteriology in addition to atonement? For example, what might feminist, womanist, and Mennonite theologians have to say to one another about the tension between violence against women and love of enemies and neighbors? How do we need to modify our peace position to consider black theology's demand for justice in order more fully to love our disenfranchised neighbors and even end Mennonite capitulation to white supremacy and racial enmity? These questions, present in Weaver's work in cursory ways, need to be revisited because they are connected to the social dimension of salvation and redemption that Mennonite theology considers to be integral to a holistic (i.e., social and spiritual) view of the good news of Jesus Christ.

My essay engages this task by considering the way feminist and womanist theologies might bring Mennonite theology to a Christology that considers patriarchy/demonarchy/kyriarchy[1] to be one of the structural powers that holds us all—men and women alike—in its bonds. Our redemption and salvation include being freed from the lies, deceptions, dualisms (domination/subordination, strong/weak, tempted/temptress, etc.), and alienation that plague so many of our relationships as women and men. So this redeemed human nature—the divine transformation of human relationships—is often the subject and object of feminist theology.

In the literature of feminist theological discourse, metaphors are often invoked to describe women's experience, critical theological reflection, and feminist consciousness. The choice of metaphor is intentional, connecting theological method with women's work and heritage. Whatever the choice of metaphor, the analogous relationship emphasizes a *reconstructive* move in theology. Such a move makes it plain that there is something about the way generations of Christians have constructed doctrine and other church teachings that does not resonate with women's ways of knowing, being, and doing. Moreover, those constructions have given men a sense of superiority and normativity that are false and hubristic. Whatever the way forward, feminist theological proposals share a common goal of integrating experiences into wholeness. As a result, metaphors like quilting and weaving abound in feminist writing.

To proceed, I want to build on the coincidence of Denny's surname, Weaver, by linking the weaver's task to the quilter's work. We know that it takes a weaver to produce fabric that is then cut or salvaged and pieced to create a quilt top. Then the intricate needlework begins. Mennonite women representing the European ancestry of our tradition have been quilters for generations. When we look past our own European diasporic reality, we find that for peoples from diverse cultures and ethnicities, quilting has historically been a global, functional, and decorative art form among women (and even some men) for generations. There is another connection between Weaver's work and the feminist theologian/quilter: any quilter can tell you, once the quilt top has been placed in the frame, you must begin at the edges and work your way toward the middle. So I take my place with Weaver at the edge of the Christian theological frame and begin to stitch, joining together patterns and layers of fabric.

QUILTING: FEMINIST METHODOLOGY

Rebecca Chopp describes the texture and qualities of the quilting metaphor in her book *Saving Work: Feminist Practices of Theological Education*. Her comments on feminist theological work identify how that work changes when women use their experience as a primary source for the tasks they face. "Theology no longer uncovers unchangeable foundations or hands down the cognitive truths of tradition or discloses the classics or even figures out the rules of faith, as suggested by modern and contemporary metaphors of doing the work of theology," Chopp points out. She extends this observation by citing the work of feminist theorists and theologians like Elaine Showalter, Judith Plaskow, and Carol Christ: "Quilting, weaving, and constructing become the focus of theological work as a communal process of bringing 'scraps' of materials used elsewhere and joining them in new ways."[2] The richness of these textile metaphors, Chopp says, represents three distinct and related dimensions of feminist theological work: first is the work itself, second are the symbols and narratives of theology, and third is concern for how theology is done. I will briefly summarize Chopp's discussion of these three dimensions and elaborate on the quilting metaphor.

First is the task of theology. When we think of feminist theology as quilting (as well as weaving and/or reconstructing), we affirm the need for "empancipatory praxis," Chopp argues. This praxis is concerned with removing political, cultural, and even personal obstacles and structures that oppress, repress, and generally stifle us as human beings. "All theology speaks of God, Christology, and ecclesiology, and in turn this discourse directs the praxis of the community. Within feminist theology the discourse of God directs the praxis of Christian community to emancipation: to be set free from sin and into new life."³ Here I add that we know that quilting requires patience, ingenuity, creativity, and discipline. Quilting cannot be done haphazardly, otherwise the end product does not serve its purpose: being aesthetically pleasing in its functionality. Theology done in a feminist mode is similar. If it is done haphazardly, it does not serve its purpose either: setting Christian believers free from patriarchy's bonds and snares so women and men can be co-workers in building community as God makes all things new.

Second, there are the symbols and narratives of Christian tradition. Tradition is a dynamic part of Christianity because it is comprised of symbols, patterns, and stories whose meanings are always being (re)interpreted. In concrete terms, tradition (the collection of religiously significant symbols, practices, and texts) is represented by church doctrine. Feminist theology, Chopp argues, capitalizes on the dialectical nature of the interpreting process. While we view reality through the "symbolic lenses" of Christianity, reality may very well turn around and cause us to reconsider what those symbols mean. Chopp points us to the improvisational side of interpretation, something with a corollary in quilting. Quilting is also about working with patterns, and a number of traditional quilt patterns build on optical illusions like Tumbling Blocks, Axe and Churn, and the Double Irish Chain. With these quilts, the pattern seems to move; there is flux in what is static.

But there are other ways to deploy the metaphor in relation to patterns. For example, the resourceful quilter may have to deal with what to do if there is not enough fabric of the right color to complete the pattern. Other quilters use patterns to chronicle events so that not only does the final product look nice and provide warmth, it also tells a story that changes with each telling as the quilt is passed on from generation to generation.⁴ Finally, the innovative quilter may experiment with age-old patterns to create a new pattern or use different color combinations with the same pattern to different effect.⁵

Third is the question of method, or how theology is done. Chopp's understanding of feminist theological method points to Elisabeth Schüssler Fiorenza's work with rhetoric.⁶ Schüssler Fiorenza outlines what she calls four rhetorical movements based on feminist consciousness-raising amongst women and men.⁷ These four movements come together as a process of interpretation that is non-linear so that the movements are not prescriptive or formulaic but descriptive and theoretical: a hermeneutics of ideological suspicion, historical remembrance and reconstruction, proclamation or ethical and theological evaluation, and creative imagination and ritualization.[8] These hermeneutics, like quilting, require a thoughtful, careful, creative selection of materials "for the patterning of the symbols of emancipatory praxis."[9] A brief word about each of these movements is in order.

Hermeneutics of Ideological Suspicion

Schüssler Fiorenza advocates a feminist understanding of the Bible as androcentric, that is, male-centered. Therefore a feminist reading of Scripture lays bare the ideological foundations of the Bible and the generations of commentary that explicate the biblical text. The feminist critic's goal is to become a sleuth who detects and analyzes the "androcentric presuppositions" that 1) we have as readers and 2) the Bible contains because of the contexts in which the Bible and we as readers have been produced.[10]

Hermeneutics of Historical Remembrance and Reconstruction

Here readers take the biblical text's sociopolitical context seriously so that the marginalized (especially women) become central and thus visible. Schüssler Fiorenza likens this movement to the work of a quilter who takes the scraps and pieces of biblical history that we have and stitches them together into a new pattern. That new pattern ("memory and heritage for the *ekklesia* of women") replaces the old androcentric pattern ("reified artifact") of early Christian history.[11]

Hermeneutics of Proclamation or Ethical and Theological Evaluation

In this movement, the interpreters are reading in a way that "transforms our understanding of Scripture as 'the foundation stone of truth' to that of 'nourishing bread and food.'" This involves evaluating any given passage of the biblical text asking if and/or how it may inspire communities to struggle against injustice or allow injustice to persist. This kind of scrutiny, Schüssler Fiorenza observes, is like the work of a health inspector who "attempts to test which foods are poisoned and which are not," and "seeks to judge to whom and under what circumstances such 'food' can be given." Proclamation comes into the movement when a preacher or minister is confronted with how to present scriptural injunctions such as "love thy neighbor."[12]

Hermeneutics of Creative Imagination and Ritualization

This movement focuses on retelling and dramatizing Bible stories. I see this movement as the culmination of Schüssler Fiorenza's hermeneutics. Here readers tap their creative powers to "elaborate and enhance the textual remnant of liberating visions" that we have in the Bible. Here we celebrate and honor our spiritual foresisters' and foremothers' stories of triumph and suffering.[13]

This is what it means to do feminist theology. Such a methodology calls us as Mennonites to wonder collectively how our theological rhetoric and biblical hermeneutics help us embody emancipatory praxis. Since we are likely caught up short by such a question or perhaps ready to detail how we give faithfully to Mennonite Central Committee or other charitable church organizations, let me offer an example of how the quilting theologian is ready to shake the foundations so that traditional theological constructions are shattered and then re-pieced like so many Broken Dishes.

QUILTING: WOMANIST APPLICATION

Womanist theology is a theological mode that uses feminist methodology with some clear qualifications, particularly narrowing the scope of women's experience to the space defined as black women's experience.[14] To be sure this is often a fluid space, but nonetheless, it is a space where Schüssler Fiorenza's hermeneutical movements are evident. Delores Williams' womanist reading and interpretation of Hagar's story from Genesis is one example of what feminist and womanist theological reflection and discourse can offer Mennonite theology.

Scholars often cite Williams' book *Sisters in the Wilderness: The Challenge of Womanist God-Talk* as the most comprehensive constructive womanist theological text in part because this work provides womanist theology with its primary symbol, narrative, and pattern for reconstructing black women's experience theologically. In her deconstruction and reconstruction, Williams takes apart some old quilts and from their remnants creates a quilt that uses familiar shapes but original patterns: wilderness, the story of Hagar, and Jesus' ministerial vision.[15]

We are familiar with the story of Abram/Abraham, Sarai/Sarah, and their clan. Recall that after God made a covenant with Abram in Genesis 15, Sarai offers her Egyptian slave-girl Hagar to Abram as her surrogate. Hagar's pregnancy, however, stirs up enmity between the women so Hagar decides to flee Abram's compound. God then sends a messenger to her offering her words of comfort and covenant. Remarkably, Hagar names rather than invokes Yahweh: El-roi (a God of seeing), "the God who sees and the God who is seen."[16] Hagar eventually gives birth to a son named Ishmael. Thirteen years later, God affirms the previous covenant, renames Abram and Sarai, and announces that Sarah is pregnant. Not long after Isaac is born (Gen. 21), Sarah decides that it is time for Hagar and her son Ishmael to be sent away. She tells Abraham, "'Cast out this slave woman with her son; for the son of this slave woman shall not inherit along with my son Isaac'" (Gen. 21:10).

The text tells us that Abraham is distressed, but God reassures him that a nation will also rise up from Ishmael because he too is Abraham's child. Hagar and Ishmael are sent away with a few provisions, and they travel into the wilderness of Beersheba. They fall on desperate times. God, hearing Ishmael's cries, sends a messenger to assure the boy and his mother of their continued divine protection and provides a well for them to drink from. The text concludes their story by telling us, "God was with the boy, and he grew up in the wilderness" (Gen. 21:20a).

It does not take a scholar in early American history to discern the similarities between Hagar's experience in Abraham's family system and the slave/slave-owner relationship in particular or plantation culture in general. Williams carefully pieces together historical and sociological data, slave narratives, and spiritual song lyrics to show a pattern of exploitation Williams names "coerced surrogacy" that mirrors Hagar's experience.

> The American slavocracy was an all-encompassing legal, political and economic system that affected every relationship in the slave community. Therefore the social process in the antebellum slave community turned black motherhood into something totally different from what was thought to be the model of motherhood in white society.... The antebellum black mother had no real power. The power above her and her family was the white antebellum slave master and his family.[17]

This power encompassed the slave master's ability to include in his "white" family his slave children who could pass.

The shape of black women's exploitation shifted from coerced surrogacy of the antebellum period into voluntary surrogacy of the postbellum era (voluntary in that the formal slave/master relationship ended with emancipation). This voluntary surrogacy manifested itself, and still does, in the role of many black women as domestics in white homes. Williams groups both types of surrogacy in the category of "social-role surrogacy." History (the field woman's experience of working both inside and outside the home), economic precariousness, racial stereotypes (Mammy's childrearing patterns of disciplinarian with her children and comforter with "Massa's" children), classism, and the image of black motherhood described above come together to create the space where black womanhood is just as confined as it is defined. Williams writes:

> Whatever may be the case with regard to the style of power and authority black women exert in their homes and beyond, one thing is certain. Surrogacy has been a negative force in African-American women's lives. It has been used by both men and women of the ruling class, as well as by some black men, to keep black women in the service of other people's needs and goals. By appropriating the biblical Hagar stories, African-American people have kept the issue of surrogacy alive in the community's memory. Thus generations of African-Americans can understand the struggle black women wage against the devaluation of their womanhood that social-role surrogacy supports.[18]

Having gone through the movements of historical reconstruction and remembrance, Williams begins the work of theological evaluation. First, she identifies the four constituent parts of black liberation theology (the horizontal encounter, the vertical encounter, transformation of consciousness, and epistemological process) and reads them with a hermeneutics of suspicion.

Second, she follows Jacqueline Grant's critical observation that black theology, like much of "theology in general" is androcentric, albeit black androcentrism. Her response to this reality is to assert "wilderness experience" as "a more appropriate name... to describe African-American existence in North America," in part because it is inclusive of men, women, and children.[19] Wilderness points to both Hagar's story and the Hebrews' forty years of wandering after their emancipation from Pharaoh. Williams explains that "the biblical wilderness tradition also emphasizes survival, quality of life formation with God's direction, and the work of building a peoplehood and a community."[20]

The christological turn in Williams' work moves us to the center of her theological perspective, but that turn is away from classical atonement theories (ransom, substitution, satisfaction, and moral influence). These theories each offer an explanation of Jesus' crucifixion as redemptive for humanity because he died in our place, taking our sin upon himself. This raises a deep theological problem for "any theology significantly informed by African-American women's experience with surrogacy."[21]

While Williams' assertion may trouble some of us for its theological implications, we cannot deny the validity of her point: The theologians who outlined atonement theories did so using the "language and sociopolitical thought of the time to render Christian ideas and principles understandable." As a womanist theologian, Williams is doing the same thing.

What are the theological implications of Williams' christological turn? She explains that our salvation, as black women and otherwise, "does not depend upon any form of surrogacy made sacred by traditional and orthodox understandings of Jesus' life and death." Instead, she continues, "salvation is assured by Jesus' life of resistance and by the survival strategies he used to help people survive the death of identity caused by [an] exchange of inherited cultural meanings for a new identity shaped by the gospel ethics and world view."[22] Jesus' salvific value is found in his ability, as the Christ, to make all things new in ways other than surrogacy.

Elaborating on Jesus' salvific value, Williams turns from notions of redemptive suffering to places in the New Testament that tell us the incarnation was about "redemption through a perfect *ministerial* vision of righting relations." As Weaver's chapter on womanist theology in *The Nonviolent Atonement* points out, Williams eloquently and persuasively articulates the ways this ministerial vision is demonstrated in the Gospels. "The resurrection of Jesus and the flourishing of God's spirit in the world as the result of resurrection represent the life of the *ministerial* vision gaining victory over the evil attempt to kill it," she writes. Her sermonic reflections on this vision culminate in the following passage.

> [We] are intelligent people living in a technological world where nuclear bombs, defilement of the earth, racism, sexism, dope, and economic injustices attest to the presence and power of evil in the world. Perhaps not many people today can believe that evil and sin were overcome by Jesus' death on the cross; that is, that Jesus took human sin upon himself and therefore saved humankind. Rather, it seems more intelligent and more scriptural to understand that redemption had to do with God, through

Jesus, giving humankind new vision to see the resources for positive, abundant relational life. Redemption had to do with God, through the *ministerial* vision, giving humankind the ethical thought and practice upon which to build positive, productive quality of life.[23]

In summary, Williams' reconstruction of soteriology and atonement calls us neither to forget the cross nor to glorify it. "Jesus did not come to be a surrogate. Jesus came for life, to show humans a perfect vision of ministerial relation that [we] had very little knowledge of" before the incarnation. Glorifying Jesus' suffering sacralizes exploitation, particularly the exploitation of black women, which is tantamount to glorifying the sin of defilement, Williams concludes.

Returning to Williams' point about the deep theological problem classical atonement presents, honesty requires we admit that Mennonite theology is not a theology that has been significantly informed by black women's experience. This admission is quickly followed with a question: Exactly whose experience has significantly informed our theology? My guess is that most of us would answer this question by filling in the proverbial blank with our favorite sixteenth-century Anabaptist(s), hardly a compliment to our theological method! I suggest that we allow a question from the back-and-forth between Jesus and the lawyer in Luke 10 to guide our response to the question of whose experience *ought* to shape our theology. The lawyer asks Jesus, "And who is my neighbor?"

The fact is, in our current political climate, black women are not just Mennonites' neighbors, they are our sisters and friends. If we review the activity of the U.S. Congress, we will find that black women are the people who have consistently stood up and spoken against the various wars the U.S. military is waging around the globe. Moreover, they are the people who see the linkages between public policy and quality of life with prophetic clarity. If the primary objective of Mennonite theology, wherever it is being done in the world, is to faithfully interpret and explicate God's message of reconciliation as embodied by and manifested in Jesus' ministry among us, then black women's experience has everything to do with Mennonite theology.

QUILTING: SATISFACTION

But what of sin, evil, and human selfishness? Does this feminist and womanist discourse erode all understanding of personal responsibility for our unjust and destructive actions? Is there no need for divine intervention into human affairs? No and yes, respectively. Let me reiterate that feminist and womanist theological work invites us to first put aside traditional construction tools like hammers and nails. As Chopp notes, we are not bound to tradition just because that is what it is. Then we can have a seat and pick up another set of traditional tools, a needle and thimble, to consider how we can rearrange the traditional piecing and patterning of theological reflection in a way that takes women's experiences seriously. Theologians who share Williams' concerns are still Christian and are still faithfully looking for ways of putting the pieces of Christian tradition together in ways that bind up the brokenhearted rather than keeping old wounds open and even creating new ones: We favor needles over nails.

"Without a doctrine of atonement," Jane McAvoy writes, "we are left with the conclusion that we are responsible for our own salvation."[24] Many are under the impression that this is what feminist and womanist theologians do, tear apart atonement doctrine and replace it with a generic unitarianism. I agree with McAvoy that taking such a dismissive view of feminist and womanist critiques of classical atonement theories is an inadequate response to perspectives that uncover real abuses and pastoral concerns that faithful Christian theology cannot condone.

McAvoy's work in theology has taken her into the realm of atonement by way of the world of medieval women mystics. Her decision to examine texts written by women (and in many instances for women), is another example of Schüssler Fiorenza's hermeneutical movements at work. "A theology based on women's writing," McAvoy observes, "is particularly suited to respond to the feminist critique of abuse and has the added bonus of allowing one to incorporate feminist hermeneutics of analysis" as these primary sources are considered. She points out that the "abundance of writings [on atonement] by women in the medieval period is second only to that of our current day."[25]

By bringing medieval texts written by women to our attention, McAvoy is helping us all reconsider the androcentric interpretations of biblical texts and themes used to build the Christian tradition of atonement. Furthermore, McAvoy's work reminds us of two important things. "Feminist theology did not invent the question of whether self-sacrifice and self-negation are the solution or the problem of the Christian life. Neither is it unique in criticizing Anselm's understanding of satisfaction as the meaning of salvation."[26]

Before I elaborate on McAvoy's proposal for a feminist theology of atonement, I need to briefly summarize both Anselm's theological perspective and those who critique him. Anselm's view of the relationship of Jesus' crucifixion to our salvation, described as the satisfaction theory of atonement, is summed up in a parable that is part of his dialogue with Boso in *Why God Became Human*.[27] In this story, a servant is given a task to complete by his master. Before being sent on his way, the servant is told that he should not jump into a nearby pit from which there is no escape. In an act of rebellion, the servant proceeds neither to complete the assigned task nor stay clear of the pit. Anselm asks Boso, "Do you think that his incapacity serves in the slightest as a valid excuse for him not to perform the task assigned to him?" Boso replies, "Not at all. It serves, rather, to increase his guilt, since he has brought the incapacity upon himself. For indeed he has sinned in two ways: in having not done what he was told to do, and in having not done what he has been told to do."

Anselm proceeds to interpret the parable theologically. "A person's incapacity to repay to God what he owes—an incapacity which brings it about that he does not make repayment—does not excuse him, in the event that he does not make repayment." He adds further on in the text, "It is mockery for mercy of this kind to be attributed to God . . . mercy of this kind is absolutely contrary to God's justice, which does not allow anything to be given in repayment for sin except punishment."[28] These are the terms under which Christ came into the world. Anselm continues to instruct Boso (and the reader) in soteriology by explaining "how the life of Christ is recompense paid to God for sins of [humankind]; and how Christ was obliged, and was not obliged, to suffer."[29] Anselm's explanation of Jesus' self-sacrifice is that it was completely voluntary because his righteousness made him blameless before God.[30] This sacrifice, then, satisfied the debt of human sin allowing God's mercy to be extended to humanity.

With Williams' concerns about surrogacy registered above, it is not difficult to see why some of us refuse to adopt Anselm's theological position. In *Introducing Redemption in Christian Feminism*, Rosemary Radford Ruether surveys and summarizes a variety of approaches to understanding redemption within Christian frameworks that take women's experience and the evil of patriarchy/demonarchy/kyriarchy seriously (including Williams). As she takes a close look at the way the warp and woof of Christian tradition have been woven together, Ruether finds the fabric formed is "a complex synthesis of human self-blaming and a view of God who is both omnipotent and yet a compassionate savior.... Both God's power and goodness are vindicated in the face of suffering by teaching that God voluntarily takes on human suffering and pays for the primal sin that is its cause." Unraveling the threads of suffering and silence is not an easy task.

Ruether's concluding observations offer some provocative theological assertions as she considers the refashioning of old patterns that feminist theologies offer Christian communities. Suffering and death do not convey the full message of Jesus' gospel, let alone the meaning of salvation and redemption, Ruether argues. "Redemption happens through resistance to the sway of evil, and in the experiences of conversion and healing by which communities of well-being are created.... We follow [Jesus] by continuing this same struggle for life against unjust suffering and death." For Ruether, how we think about Jesus' death on the cross is directly connected with our view of God: "If God wills Jesus' death, if God wills the unjust violence of poverty, sexism, racism, and anti-Semitism, then God is a sadist and a criminal."[31] Resurrection becomes the primary symbol of Christianity for theologians working in a feminist mode because this is the moment in which death is defied. It is the space where the Living Christ is found; the living cannot be found among the dead.

Returning to McAvoy's discussion of atonement engages the messages we receive from much of Western popular culture (including "Christian culture"): "through discipline, hard work, and sacrifice we can reach happiness and personal satisfaction." McAvoy responds to these messages with a provocative question: "Does satisfaction come through sacrifice?" For Christians, this is where atonement enters the conversation. "Christians assume," McAvoy observers, "that the path to personal satisfaction has something to do with Jesus Christ, who overcomes whatever it is that keeps us from being satisfied."[32]

This brings McAvoy to the conclusion that, at their core, atonement theories are grappling with the reality that we do not save ourselves. Indeed, this is the gospel message from a variety of New Testament theological viewpoints, but within both the biblical text and Christian tradition no consensus exists regarding the answers to such questions as "How are we saved?" and "What are we saved for?" McAvoy shifts the focus from such questions to the one she is interested in addressing: Who or what are we saved by?

In turning to the writings of women like Julian of Norwich, Mechtild of Magdeburg, and Hildegard of Bingen, McAvoy uncovers another tradition of satisfaction.[33] A singular definition of satisfaction as appeasement or compensation, as in Anselm's work, is not tenable when we consider other medieval Christian theological writings. For medieval women mystics, satisfaction also means resting in assurance. My use of McAvoy's work will focus on Julian of Norwich as the former interprets and the latter describes what it means to be satisfied.[34]

In the fiftieth chapter of the "Long Showings," Julian relates an aspect of her vision that is very much like Anselm's parable above, but the outcome and interpretation is quite different.[35] There is again a servant and a master who dispatches the servant on an errand. This servant is so eager to do his master's bidding that he is a bit careless, falls into a dell, and is seriously injured. No matter what he does, he cannot help himself. What hurts the servant most, though, is that he cannot "turn his face to look on his loving lord." Julian reports the master's response to the servant's plight:

> Then this courteous lord said this: See my beloved servant, what harm and injuries he has had and accepted in my service for my love, yes, and for his good will. Is it not reasonable that I should reward him for his fright and his fear, his hurt and his injuries and all his woe? And furthermore, is it not proper for me to give him a gift, better for him and more honorable than his own health could have been? Otherwise, it seems to me that I should be ungracious.

Julian is overcome by the lord's response to his servant: The lord's goodness and honor require that he bless and reward the servant forever "above what he would have been if he had not fallen."[36] I would connect Julian's vision and the parable of the Lost Sheep. God, represented in Julian's vision by the courteous lord, is primarily concerned about the well-being of the beloved servant, not that he has fallen or wandered away from his lord. The clear theological implication is that, in McAvoy's words, sin is not disobedience. "The problem is that blame"—which is critical in the logic of Anselm's parable—"is a very real human experience. It is an injury to human nature that is manifested in the physical separation of the lord and servant" in Julian's vision. While this separation is the source of pain and longing, it is not the source of offense to the lord's honor.[37]

As Julian contemplates the words and actions of the "courteous lord" in subsequent chapters of *Showings*, what begins to come together is quite remarkable. McAvoy's reading of Julian's work is persuasive and has important theological implications. "To say that God honors us for our sin is to tear at the social order of our universe," McAvoy claims. "It mocks Anselm's notion of justice and breaks down the hierarchy of master and servant." Julian discerns that our understanding of atonement creates a social fabric. In a "saved world of courteous relation" we are able to recognize the image of God in us and thereby catch a glimpse of what God sees. "We are not saved by satisfying God's honor," McAvoy stresses, "but by being satisfied that God loves us." McAvoy writes that for Julian

> the reward of salvation is to grow into the fullness of our humanity. Julian calls this "oneing," and it is the process of growing into one-ness with God.... Like most mystics who talk about union with God based on love, Julian imagines a "oneing" that is not a dissolving of self, but a meeting of the soul in God. Her phrase for this is "knitting" to God ... and Andrew Sprung notes that by this Julian means a weaving of one's soul to God.[38]

Julian gives us a theology of atonement that "responds to the social injustice of our world" by showing us that the "oneing" of atonement is the recognition that we are called to be satisfied that God loves us. This salvific message affirms God's omnipresence and omniscience because "God can see beyond the limited vision of the servant and see creation in its created, fallen, and redeemed states." Christ comes into the world "to empower us with a glimpse of eternal love." This love is found in restored relationships, especially friendships.[39]

In the end, McAvoy argues that satisfaction is a human need; feeling dissatisfied in God's love is our sin. "To be satisfied is to realize that salvation is accomplished by divine initiative, not human effort." She adds, "The satisfied life will take us down many roads that counter our individualized, privatized notions of comfort and satisfaction. It will call us to challenge our cultural limitations. It will challenge us to speak up despite the criticism of the church. It will inspire us to follow the mad love of God wherever it will lead."[40]

Building on the work of feminist and womanist theologians, I have laid out some new ways we might piece together the patterns of Mennonite theology as we consider soteriology and atonement. This proposal is not particularly new, because I make it in the tradition of the women and men who gathered at Associated Mennonite Biblical Seminary in 1987 and 1992 to consider feminist perspectives on biblical hermeneutics and peace theology.[41] I am grateful for Denny Weaver and the way his theological imaginings and convictions have brought him into the company of women who have been laboring for generations to create works, theological and otherwise, that meet the demands of Jesus Christ and bring wholeness and satisfaction without the high price of pointless self-sacrifice; there is another way to live into the meaning of Christianity's symbols and stories than the traditions of dominant, "malestream" theologies.

In addition to academic theological work awaiting us, there is also Schüssler Fiorenza's challenge to use our creativity to re-image and retell the liberating stories of God's people using a feminist hermeneutic; this means preaching sermons and designing rituals that challenge the traditional rendering of Christianity's symbols. She joins Williams and McAvoy in inviting us to a realization of *ekklesia* that is interested in the ministerial vision of God's *baselia*.

If you know anything about quilting, you know how satisfying the work can be. How can the leftover bits of life—a piece of silk from last year's Easter dress, some denim leftover from a jacket made for a nephew, calico from Grandma's old aprons, some linen from a bridesmaid's dress altered for a sister—be pieced together in new ways? Work like this requires patience, wisdom, vision. This is the power of reconstruction with needles, not nails.

NOTES

1. This trio of terms is used by feminists and womanists to describe the character of the social forces and systems that impair human development, especially that of women of various colors. Demonarchy is defined by Delores Williams "as the demonic governance of black women's lives by white male and white female ruled systems using racism, violence, violation, retardation, and death as instruments of social control." It is rooted in the history of American slavery and creates a matrix of oppression and victimization so that black women are not simply trying to get out from under the thumbs of their husbands but also white supremacy. See Delores S. Williams, "The Color of Feminism: Or Speaking the Black Woman's Tongue," *The Journal of Religious Thought* 43/1 (1986), 52-56. Kyriarchy is Schüssler Fiorenza's neologism referring to the rule of the emperor, master, lord, father, and husband over his subordinates. "With this term I mean to indicate that not all men dominate and exploit all women without difference and that elite Western educated propertied Euro-American men have articulated and benefited from women's and other 'nonpersons' exploitation." See Elisabeth Schüssler Fiorenza, *Jesus: Miriam's Child, Sophia's Prophet: Critical Issues in Feminist Christology* (New York: Continuum, 1994), p. 46 and n. 46 and 47.

2. Rebecca S. Chopp, *Saving Work: Feminist Practices of Theological Education* (Louisville, Ky.: Westminster John Knox Press, 1995), 54.
3. Ibid.
4. Faith Ringgold's work stands out here. She is a New York-based African-American painter and quilter who combines media to create works that tell stories. This is a particularly important part of the aesthetic among quilters from the racial minority traditions of North America.
5. My mother owns a quilt that combines Jacob's Ladder and Grandmother's Fan patterns into what is now called Jacob's Fan. Similarly, the Christmas Star and Odd Fellows Chain are the same pattern but when the colors are changed produce a dramatically different effect.
6. In her book *Bread Not Stone: The Challenge of Feminist Biblical Interpretation* (Boston: Beacon Press, 1984), Schüssler Fiorenza proposes four reading strategies that she theorizes in *But She Said: Feminist Practices of Biblical Interpretation* (Boston: Beacon Press, 1992).
7. Schüssler Fiorenza is clear that "feminist movement in biblical religion is not just a civil rights but also a liberation movement. Its goal is not simply the 'full humanity' of women, since humanity as we know it is male-defined. The goal is women's (religious) self-affirmation, power, and liberation from all patriarchal alienation, marginalization, and exploitation." She goes on to describe the difference between conversion for men and for women in feminist theology: "like other liberation theologies, feminist theology explicitly takes an advocacy position.... Whereas in a feminist conversion *men* must take the option for the oppressed and become women-identified, in such a conversion *women* must seek to overcome our deepest self-alienation ... our position of advocacy must be articulated not as an 'option for the oppressed' but as self-respect and self-identification *as women* in a patriarchal society and religion" (emphasis hers). Elisabeth Schüssler Fiorenza, *Bread Not Stone: The Challenge of Feminist Biblical Interpretation*, xv.
8. Ibid., 52. Schüssler Fiorenza has also summarized these movements in her essay, "The Bible, the Global Context, and the Discipleship of Equals," in *Reconstructing Christian Theology*, ed. Rebecca S. Chopp and Mark Lewis Taylor (Minneapolis: Augsburg Fortress Press, 1997). I am using language from both the book and the essay.
9. Chopp, *Saving Work: Feminist Practices of Theological Education*, 74.
10. Schüssler Fiorenza, *But She Said*, 53.
11. Ibid., 54.
12. Ibid. The references to stone and bread are Schüssler Fiorenza's provocative play on the Ten Commandments written on stone tablets and Jesus 'question to those whom he is teaching, "Is there anyone among you who, if your child asks for bread, will give a stone?" (Matt. 7:9, NRSV). Schüssler Fiorenza uses the all too common example of a woman battered by her spouse. Pastoral counseling that uses "love thy neighbor" to make a case for the woman to remain in the destructive marriage, she argues, serves patriarchy. I would add that in this situation community members (including clergy) are called to show "compassionate love" to the victim and "tough love" to the batterer.

13. Ibid.

14. I do not want to gloss over or make light of ongoing conversation between (white) feminists and womanists. The debates and discussions are well-documented and my own appropriation of feminism is done with full acknowledgement that the wounds of racism, prejudice, and injustice leave nasty scars when and if they heal. Therefore I want to be clear that my bringing together feminist and womanist theologies is a political choice on my part. The rationale for my choice is two-fold: first is my experience as a biracial woman and second my agreement with bell hooks' analysis of the dynamic between black and white women spelled out in her essay, "Black Women and Feminism." See bell hooks, *Talking Back: Thinking Feminist, Thinking Black* (Boston: South End Press, 1989), 177-182.

15. Delores S. Williams, *Sisters in the Wilderness: The Challenge of Womanist God-Talk* (Maryknoll: Orbis Books, 1993).

16. Phyllis Trible, *Texts of Terror: Literary-Feminist Readings of Biblical Narratives* (Philadelphia: Fortress Press, 1984), 18. Williams also points out that the symbolism of the eye and eyesight in Egyptian myth is at work in Hagar's name choice: "Though El may also be, as Roland de Vaux contends, an altered form of 'Baal' in the text 'under the influence of Yahwism,' the name of Hagar's God (pointing to sight and therefore eyes of the deity) recalls certain Egyptian myth associated with the God Ra, his eye, and the creation of humans." For other significant parallels, see *Sisters in the Wilderness*, 23-26.

17. Williams, *Sisters in the Wilderness*, 39. She also points out that this motherhood dynamic "extended beyond the mere limits of female role activity into areas of control that should have belonged to the black man (according to American standards of male role functioning)." This demonstrates my earlier argument that patriarchy/demonarchy/kyriarchy contribute to the alienation that puts women and men at odds with each other.

18. Ibid., 81.
19. Ibid., 159.
20. Ibid., 161.
21. Ibid., 162.
22. Ibid., 164.
23. Ibid., 164-65. (Emphases hers.)
24. Jane McAvoy, *The Satisfied Life: Medieval Women Mystics on atonement* (Cleveland: Pilgrim Press, 2000), 2.
25. Ibid., 5-6.
26. Ibid., 25.
27. Most translations of Anselm's Latin title, *Cur Deus Homo*, are translated as "Why God Became Man" or "Why the God Man." When I look *homo* up in my Latin dictionary, the first English term listed is "human being."
28. Anselm of Canterbury, "Cur Deus Homo," in *Anselm of Canterbury: The Major Works*, ed. Brian Davies and G.R. Evans, *Oxford World's Classics* (Oxford: Oxford University Press, 1998), 310-11.
29. Ibid., 348.
30. Ibid., 351. Anselm explains, "Indeed [Christ] is both God and man, so consequently, where his human nature was concerned, from the time when

he became human, he received from his divine nature . . . the circumstance that whatever he had was his own. As a result, there was nothing which he 'ought' to give, except what he wished."

31. Rosemary Radford Ruether, *Introducing Redemption in Christian Feminism* (Cleveland: Pilgrim Press, 1998), 107.

32. McAvoy, *The Satisfied Life*, 1.

33. McAvoy also includes Margery Kempe, Hadewijch of Brabant, and Catherine of Siena in her study. Ruether notes that within Christian tradition, Julian and Hildegard, through their references to divine Wisdom, "began to undermine the androcentric theology that made women incapable of being theomorphic and Christomorphic" (see *Introducing Redemption*, 12-13).

34. Julian lived in England during the fourteenth century. She was an anchoress living her life enclosed in a chapel in Norwich, where she engaged in solitary prayer, counseled other Christians, and on May 13, 1373, when she was thirty years old, received a series of revelations from God. She spent the rest of her life interpreting and contemplating the content and meaning of these revelations.

35. McAvoy notes that while Julian lived three centuries after Anselm, we do not know if she was familiar with his theology, making this parallel quite intriguing.

36. Julian of Norwich, *Showings* (New York: Paulist Press, 1978), 267-69.

37. McAvoy, *The Satisfied Life*, 17.

38. Ibid., 19-21.

39. Ibid., 61.

40. Ibid., 118, 20.

41. See Gayle Gerber Koontz and Willard Swartley, eds., *Perspectives on Feminist Hermeneutics* (Elkhart, Ind.: Institute of Mennonite Studies, 1987) and Elizabeth G. Yoder, ed., *Peace Theology and Violence against Women* (Elkhart, Ind.: Institute of Mennonite Studies, 1992).

CHAPTER THIRTEEN

Notes for Nonviolent Eschatology

Jane Thorley Roeschley

. . . . and through Christ to reconcile for Christ all things, whether on earth or in heaven, making peace by the blood of the cross.
—Colossians 1:20 (Throckmorton)

For God has made known to us in all wisdom and insight the mystery of God's will, according to God's purpose set forth in Christ as a plan for the fullness of time, to unite all things in Christ, things in heaven and things on earth.
—Ephesians 1:9-10 (Throckmorton)

I don't remember when I first encountered J. Denny Weaver's theological works, but, surveying his writings, I recognize that his thinking about a theology of nonviolent atonement runs parallel to my own questions and struggles with the atonement. Weaver's focus on a nonviolent atonement has been stimulating to me, particularly in this past decade as I have been called into the pastoral ministry. I have benefited from engagement with Weaver's reading of Scripture, a reading in which the biblical concept of God's *shalom* extends through the entire Christ event.[1] Weaver's work has contributed to giving me hope—a hope I have needed.

I NEEDED HOPE

I was not raised Mennonite, but as a child I was introduced to a God who is love and loves all. I discovered my "Mennonite identity" as a young adult at Bluffton College because the Anabaptist peace theology articulated there resonated so clearly with my own. This Mennonite peace identity deepened during a three-year overseas service assignment with Mennonite Central Committee (MCC) following college. My formation as a Mennonite Christian happened, then, in the wider Mennonite church ethos, with an energetic and intense exposure to Christians who were thinking about peace and how to pursue it.

Upon arrival back to North America in the early 1980s and re-entry into middle class rural Mennonite churches, a difficult adjustment awaited me. The theologically invigorating perspectives and lifestyle of the MCC context seemed almost completely to disappear for me. For the local North American churches, understandings of peace, justice, citizenship, and service seemed very different from the ones that had shaped me. Religious ideas, language, and teachings in the local churches seemed to reflect an early twentieth-century pietism rather than the radical, New Testament thinking, speaking, and living I wanted to embrace. So, while I settled in and got on with life in the United States, there was part of me that grew increasingly restless.

That inner restlessness led me to seminary and to recognize, in midlife, a calling to pastoral ministry. While some of the restlessness has subsequently faded, something else, theologically, has not. Something else, theologically, has in fact worsened with the years and become more confounding and disturbing.

THE ATONEMENT . . . AND BEYOND

Part of my theological struggle has been encountering the seeming glorification of divine violence in some of the images of the atonement. Related to this struggle are a whole host of questions about the nature and biblical revelation of God, the meaning of Christ's life, death, and resurrection, the way God is at work in the world, and how the church participates with God in that work. These questions include the following:

- Who is God? Is Jesus the complete revelation of God? What do Jesus' ethics reveal (or not reveal) about God? Is God nonviolent?

- Who caused the death of Jesus? Was Jesus' death a necessary result of God's anger and violence? Was it self-given? Does our theology grow out of an understanding of God as a God who seeks *revenge* or who *reconciles*?
- Does God's ministry of reconciliation, healing, and shalom function only on earth or does it extend into eternity? Is it possible that God's ministry of reconciliation, healing, and shalom might—at some distant point in eternity—allow for a *complete reconciliation* of all persons and of the whole creation with God? Is it *biblically* possible there might be a nonviolent eschatology?
- If one reads Scripture as revealing God as loving, reconciling, and nonviolent, is one ignoring other essential aspects of God's character and casting God in the image one wishes?[2] What does one do with the parts of Scripture that present a seemingly violent picture of God? How does one reconcile those parts of Scripture with the understanding of God as on a divine mission to restore the whole of creation?
- Does one dare voice questions like these in a church where one default theology[3] seems to assume a God of violence and a framework of "redemptive violence"?[4]
- What would the church's understandings of the atonement look like if *both* women and men had been part of the development (and articulation) of atonement theology throughout the past centuries? Would the atonement be understood as a father's sacrifice of his son to satisfy the father's honor if women had been part of the conversation?[5]
- Is there a relationship between a "default" view of a violent atonement and the church's subsequent willingness (or unwillingness) to engage in dismantling injustice, resisting violence, and building shalom?
- As a pastoral leader, is it spiritually responsible or irresponsible to offer hope for an eternal, complete reconciliation—to offer hope that all might be saved?

This is a *long* list of questions. They reflect challenging issues for me in my relationship with God, in my call to follow Jesus, and in my desire to be in authentic Christian community with other believers in living out the church's mission of being a visible sign of the reign of God. These questions have forced me to wrestle with the theological concepts of evil, suffering, conflict, estrangement, judgment, punishment, torment, hell, and death, both in particular lives now here on earth and also in the eternal realm of souls. I've needed to become a student of Christology and atonement theology. What *is* the meaning of Christ's life, ministry, death, and resurrection for the church? For the world? For the entire creation? Does it matter how we think, teach, and preach about that?

These questions trace an important thread that leads me to ask what is at the spiritual core of Anabaptist-Mennonite peacemaking: divine peace (nonviolence) or divine violence? What impact does this violent or nonviolent spiritual core have on us as Anabaptist Christians day-to-day? If God's greatest act of salvation, the atoning work of Jesus Christ, reveals a God who wills or acts with violence, is it not inevitable that persons describing themselves as Christians will become violent too?

CORE MATTERS

A relationship exists, I contend, between our core beliefs about God and if we choose to fully engage the nonviolent divine power of the Risen Christ. It matters where we "start" with God. If we start with a God who exercises divine violence, then it should not be surprising that followers of God will come to rely on violence in their personal responses as well.

These questions I have raised are ones for which no simple, clear, even straightforward biblical answers can be found. Fine minds through the ages have wrestled with them systematically and still we do not have unquestioned consensus about them in the church.[6] The work of Denny Weaver and others on a nonviolent atonement has been a welcome source of some guidance for me, but I confess I am still struggling. Indeed, much remains a mystery—a mystery and a struggle of faith.[7]

Yet, as I embrace the midlife milestones of my spiritual quest, I have a growing, energizing hope in God's never-ending love and God's nonviolent power to transcend my many questions. I have hope in God's ability, in the fullness of time, to "gather all things up in" Christ (Eph. 1:10). *All* things. I am coming to hope in a complete and full reconciliation and restoration of all of creation: biblical *shalom*. I am even coming to a hope in a nonviolent eternity: a nonviolent eschatology. I take inspiration from the letter to the Colossians: God worked "through Christ to reconcile for Christ all things, whether on earth or in heaven, making peace by the blood of the cross" (Col. 1:19-20).[8]

The reader may find this hope overextended. At the very least, I recognize it as a minority viewpoint within the Christian tradition, though there is evidence that some theologians of the early church subscribed to what might be called "universal reconciliation."[9] The Anabaptist theologian Hans Denck (1495-1527) may have considered universal reconciliation a possibility: "Since love in him was perfect," Denck reasoned, "and since love hates or is envious of none, but includes everyone, even though we were all his enemies, surely he would not wish to exclude anyone. And if he had excluded anyone, then love would have been squint-eyed and a respecter of persons. And that, God is not!"[10]

THE REIGN OF GOD: AN ORIENTING REALITY

My hope in the ultimate reconciliation of all things to God is grounded in my understanding of God's present but still arriving reign. I think of it as God's shalom endeavor: God's creation goodness, now fallen into sin, for which God's love is relentlessly working to one day completely restore.

The Old Testament reveals the reign of God as the coming day of God's shalom—a future day of complete well-being for all the people of God. The Gospels, in turn, narrate the life, death, and resurrection of Jesus as the ongoing action of God to fulfill this Hebrew vision of God's shalom. In that sense, the coming of Jesus is a supreme act of shalom. The Gospels, however, are not only writings about Jesus, the gospel is this shalom endeavor of God that Jesus models and preaches. Jesus' teaching centers on proclaiming the reign of God. It shapes his mission and is the main task he gives his followers: "As you go, proclaim the good news, 'The kingdom of heaven is near'" (Matt.10:7). Even in Paul's brief notes about the reign of God, the vision is there, too: "For the kingdom of God is not food and drink but righteousness and peace and joy in the Holy Spirit" (Rom. 14:17).

However, differing understandings of the timing, nature, and purposes of this reign of God have historically caused deep divisions among Christians. Is God's kingdom temporal only, spiritual only, or both? Does it have ethical implications for us now or only for some future, completed time? What is the nature of its power? How does love behave? How is justice viewed and enacted? Does it operate with violence?

This diversity of viewpoints on the nature of God's reign has led to immense historical misunderstandings and conflicts for the church. Perhaps this diversity is some mysterious part of the genius of God. However, as a result of these differing understandings of the reign of God, the church has a legacy that is tragically marked with hurt, harm, violence, rejection, exclusion, and death, seemingly taking God's people further away from God's intended *shalom* purposes rather than nearer to them. The Crusades, religious wars, anti-Semitism, persecutions, and Christian support of slavery and segregation come to mind.

For Christians, struggling with the meaning of the reign of God also means grappling with the nature of the atonement, of God's work in Jesus Christ. We confess that through Jesus Christ come healing, reconciliation, redemption, and restoration in God's relationship with a flawed and broken world. The witnesses of Jesus' life, death, and resurrection make testimony to this work in our Scriptures. God's Reign has been experienced in the lives of God's people and the saints across the ages. We experience it in our own lives. How we understand the reign of God is linked to how we understand the atonement. The church has wrestled for two millennia with how to express the mystery of the atonement, and the results of this struggle are multiple images, theories, and metaphors of it.[11]

Denny Weaver's *The Nonviolent Atonement* joins in this ecclesial wrestling with the atonement by clearly anchoring the work of Jesus in the overarching reign of God.[12] In conversation with black, feminist, and womanist theologies, Weaver develops his "narrative Christus Victor" model of the atonement. Most significantly, from my perspective, his model eliminates the divine violence characteristic of other models.[13] Furthermore, he stresses that narrative Christus Victor atonement also calls the church to accept the corollary challenge of *being* a visible sign of the reign of God. The church, Weaver stresses, is "the earthly instrument that continue[s] Jesus' mission of making visible the reign of God."[14]

How the church understands this overarching shalom endeavor of the reign of God is, I argue, critical for the church. In contrast to a view of the reign of God as arriving only in some distant eschatological age, an embrace of the present, inbreaking reign of God—and the meaning of Christ's life, death, and resurrection as a pivotal part of that reign—means Jesus' teachings have contemporary ethical significance for the Christian church *here and now*. We are not simply waiting on some apocalyptic "left behind" event that will establish the reign of God for a future eon, initiated by a violent overthrow of the world by Christ. The reign of God is coming, but it is also *now*. Jesus said, "the kingdom of God is among you" (Luke 17:21; see also 10:9). It is spiritual, but it is not only spiritual. It is also temporal, with present relational and ethical realities. James Mulholland explains:

> We are not the first to be confused about the timing of God's kingdom. Jesus was asked when the kingdom of God would come. He replied, "The kingdom of God does not come with your careful observation, nor will people say, 'Here it is,' or 'There it is,' because the kingdom of God is within you" (Luke 17:20-21). The kingdom of God is not something external that we await. It is within us, waiting to be born as it is in heaven. When we pray "Thy Kingdom come," we are not making a request. We are taking a vow. We are pledging our willingness to allow God's kingdom to be established in and through us.[15]

Nonviolent atonement theology contributes to our understanding of God's present and inbreaking reign and our ethical participation in it. It highlights that we are called to embody the same ethic and nonviolence of Jesus.

A HOLISTIC PARADIGM

Weaver's narrative Christus Victor offers a needed corrective, an alternative paradigm of the atonement, one that draws deeply from the Old Testament and New Testament. According to Weaver, "Narrative Christ Victor atonement . . . is story in which the death and resurrection of Jesus definitively reveal the basis of power in the universe, so that the invitation from God to participate in God's rule—to accept Jesus as God's anointed one—overcomes the forces of sin and reconciles sinners to God."[16]

Weaver's revisioned, holistic, nonviolent atonement paradigm emerges at a critical time for the North American church. As a pastor in congregational ministry since the September 11, 2001 tragedies, I have become increasingly appalled at what I see as an insidious and foundational embrace of violent atonement theology in North American Christianity. Violent, "default" sacrificial atonement theology bolsters the notion of redemptive violence and feeds into a devastating patriotic rhetoric that consequently supports militaristic initiatives of the U.S. government. Too often the church, called to be an *alternative* community and a sign of the reign of God, supports war and violence. Some preaching in pulpits and on the airwaves since 9/11, connecting Christianity with a fear-driven American civil religion, makes it seemingly shameful and un-Christian, as well as unpatriotic, not to provide uncritical support for U.S. foreign policy and its deadly military rhetoric, spending, and initiatives.

The church is called to challenge, not to support, the myth of redemptive violence, to expose it as a deceptive temptation ultimately based on fear. The church's embrace of the myth of redemptive violence represents a tragic failure of the church to be true to its calling to be a sign of the reign of God by loving mercy, doing justice, and walking humbly with God (Mic. 6:8). The 9/11 event infused this generation of Americans with an understandably heightened sense of vulnerability, magnified by subsequent fear-mongering. My pastoral concern is that the church unwittingly contributes to a fear-based, nationalistic mindset by an unexamined embrace of the violence of its atonement theology and thus propagates a (perhaps reluctant) embrace of war and violence, based on the faulty notion that it mirrors the character of God with violence that is "redemptive."

How we understand God's character *is* formational, for individuals and for the church. We become like the God whom we worship. "In every aspect of our lives, we become like the God we adore," argue Matthew, Dennis, and Sheila Fabricant Linn.

> For example, in a time when we have the capacity to annihilate one another with nuclear weapons, many churches have issued pastoral letters on peace. Our church's pastoral letter says that we can never use nuclear weapons against our enemies. However, if my God can send God's enemies to a hell inferno, then I can send a nuclear inferno on my enemies. But if my God doesn't treat people that way, I can't either. We find a key to personal and social healing is healing our image of God.[17]

If the Christian church sings, teaches, preaches, models, and prays the classic violent atonement that God needed Jesus to die a violent death for us so that we could have eternal life, something powerful is happening that forms us in that image as well. If we sing, teach, pray, model, and preach that God needed a violent death to do a good thing, then is it a surprise to find ourselves as a society "needing" other deaths—the enemy's, or even those of our own sons and daughters!—to bring about a "worthy" outcome, too? Our image of the God we worship, and our subsequent church practice, "forms" us. Therefore, we must, according to Ray C. Gingerich,

> examine more carefully the sociopolitical sources of our theology. We would not anticipate fresh water to be drawn from a

brackish well (cf. James 3:11); why should we expect a consistent peace theology, including a nonviolent understanding of God and power, to come from a theological tradition that does not follow the nonviolent way of Deutero-Isaiah and Jesus? How we live determines in great measure the "reality" we perceive and the thoughts we are capable of formulating systematically.[18]

Narrative Christus Victor's vision of divine nonviolence, Jesus' self-giving love, and Jesus' triumphant resurrection power over death, sin, and evil, provide a deep and necessary corrective to part of the church's flawed theological thinking, its ethical compromises, its diminished hope, its impotent confrontations with evil, and the apathy that tempts the church away from its core ministry of reconciliation and transformation. Much vital work needs to be done in the church to renew our understanding of the atonement as the nonviolent continuation of God's shalom initiative to heal and save the whole world. There must be a renewed understanding of the church's call to be a visible, nonviolent sign of the reign of God as well as a renewed understanding of being "ambassadors for Christ" through whom God spreads "the message of reconciliation" (2 Cor. 5:18-20a).

A FURTHER STEP: TOWARD A NONVIOLENT ESCHATOLOGY

In carrying out [God's] mission, Jesus was killed by the earthly structures in bondage to the power of evil. His death was not a payment owed to God's honor, nor was it divine punishment that he suffered as a substitute for sinners. Jesus' death was the rejection of the rule of God by forces opposed to that rule.[19]

Just as violent understandings of the atonement have compromised the church's mission and witness, an embrace of the nonviolent atonement will give renewed, life-giving shape to the church's witness and ethics. God's love of enemies, including us, modeled in Jesus' nonviolent work, enables us to trust in God's redemptive, restorative justice and power. We are called to trust in God's power, not in our own. This requires a trust in the ultimate victory of the resurrection, and a willingness to be creative in the church's active (but non-lethal) resistance to evil. This trust is an incredible challenge for the church in today's culture of personal and global violence. Pastors and church leaders must wrestle with how to help the church in living as an alternative community, as a visible sign of the nonviolent reign of God.

I would also argue, however, that the nonviolent atonement has even further implications, implications beyond our lives on earth. What does the nonviolent atonement mean for a nonviolent eschatology? "In narrative Christus Victor," according to Weaver, "individuals as well as the world are saved, although we still await the culmination of that salvation in the eschaton."[20] Weaver claims that approaching atonement from a nonviolent perspective "produces a wide-ranging discussion with implications for a wide array of doctrines in Christian theology."[21] What are the *eternal outcomes* of this holistic new paradigm articulated by Weaver? We need discussion about how to take nonviolent Christus Victor a logical, critical step further—to a full and complete visioning of the eternal outcomes of this nonviolent theology.

NONVIOLENT ESCHATOLOGY

Weaver says that narrative Christus Victor is more than an atonement motif. He considers it to be a comprehensive way of seeing God working in the world. Narrative Christus Victor "has no place for a relationship to God that is based on retributive justice or the idea that [restorative] justice means to punish."[22] What are the theological implications of this claim? If God's purposes are not premised on retribution and violent punishment, then is it not credible, and logical, to envision a nonviolent eternity—based on a nonviolent eschatology? Wouldn't anything other than imagining a complete reconciliation of the *entire* creation and of *all* souls be a failure of God's divine intention? "For he must reign until he has put all his enemies under his feet," Paul writes in his first letter to the church at Corinth that

> The last enemy to be destroyed is death. For "God has put all things in subjection under his feet." But when it says, "All things are put in subjection," it is plain that this does not include the one who put all things in subjection under him. When all things are subjected to him, then the Son himself will also be subjected to the one who put all things in subjection under him, so that God may be all in all. (1 Cor 15:25-28)

Is imagining a nonviolent eschatology going too far? A pastoral colleague of mine noted in a discussion about how many congregants believe in a violent, eternal torment for some souls that "We can't know what actually becomes of such souls, but we do know that God is in control and that Jesus is present. I choose to trust Jesus." I do not disagree! It is because I trust Jesus that I have difficulty accepting that God's resurrection power and never-failing love are, in the end, thwartable, and might fail to reach people suffering in hell.

How we understand the end of history is critical for our self-understanding, for the decisions we make and actions we take. If the church witnesses to an inclusive and completely reconciled future in history, our manner of evangelistically joining God now in God's mission and inviting others to "joyfully follow Jesus"[23] with us will be markedly different than evangelism and conversion motivated by a fear that earthly death before personal salvation results in eternal condemnation to hell.[24] If we act on the belief that in the end all persons and the entire creation are being gathered up in Christ, then triumphalist worldviews and politics have no place in Christian thinking. We can approach others who are different, or who are yet without the completion in their lives of God's shalom through Jesus Christ, with a commitment to loving them as God loves them and participating with God in God's healing, restoring initiatives in their lives.

Developing a nonviolent eschatology as a logical outgrowth of a nonviolent understanding of the atonement requires consideration of three interrelated issues: the divine regard for human freedom; the nature of God's justice; and the hope we can have in the eternal victory of resurrection power. I address these now in turn.

ETERNAL HUMAN FREEDOM

Divine love and power respect human freedom and choice. God does not coerce. God even permits us to choose against the abundant life God desires. This same divine, loving power, meanwhile, also allows us the full consequences of any such choice. God's loving power honors the integrity of humanity even when we choose against God. Just like Jesus suffered as a result of the sinful choices of mankind, God's love suffers as it allows us the difficult consequences of the fallen, compromised, and misguided choices we make.

Being permitted to experience the full and painful consequences of our choices is also an experience of hell. Hell *is* real. As a pastor, I see the realities of the hell that people experience, both from their own fallen choices, and as a result of the fallenness of others and of creation. This world is not as God originally intended or designed it. In one way or another, all of us experience shades of hell as we struggle with sin and withstand the consequences of the sin of others.

However, choices that lead to hellish consequences—choices that destroy life within ourselves and others and result in suffering, pain, hurt, and harm—need to be understood as choices that are made before one is truly "free" as God intends it. Choices that diminish God's best within ourselves and others are, in fact, in logical terms, not even fully rational choices. "If someone does something in the absence of any motive for doing it and in the presence of an exceedingly strong motive for not doing it, then he or she displays the kind of irrationality that is itself incompatible with free choice," argues Thomas Talbott.

> A necessary condition of free choice, in other words, is a minimal degree of rationality on the part of one who acts freely.... If I am ignorant of, or deceived about, the true consequences of my choice, then I am in no position to embrace those consequences freely; and similarly, if I suffer from an illusion that conceals from me the true nature of God, or the true import of union with God, then I am again in no position to reject God freely. I may reject a caricature of God, or a false conception, but I would be in no position to reject the true God himself. Accordingly, the very conditions that render a less than fully informed decision to reject God intelligible also render it less than fully free.... So if a fully informed person should reject God nonetheless, then that person ... would seem to display the kind of irrationality that is itself incompatible with free choice.[25]

A choice isn't truly rational, or a "free" choice, if its consequences lead to pain and harm. That kind of choice must be understood to have been made when *true* freedom is compromised by ignorance, brokenness, bondage, oppression, illness, or illusion. Choices that result in pain and harm do not, in the end, represent *free* choice. Ignorance, deception, illusion, oppression, sin, and bondage are characteristics of decisions that reject God and lead to harmful, hurtful consequences. Such decisions, compromised as they are, are not in fact free choices and represent a need for healing.

Thus, obstacles to true freedom must be removed. "God," Talbott asserts, "should be able to remove the conditions—the ignorance, the illusions, the bondage to unhealthy desires—without in anyway interfering with human freedom."[26] Such divine action is what the shalom endeavor biblical writers envision—making all well and whole. God's shalom requires a transformation of all ignorance, brokenness, bondage, oppression, illness, illusion, deception, and sin in order that persons will truly be "free" to choose. There is need for the complete wholeness that only God's healing love can give. That transformation is ultimately completed through Jesus Christ, whose life, death, and living resurrection presence are the pinnacle expression of God's transforming love. Talbott presents a compelling vision of how God's love in Christ overcomes all obstacles to reconciliation:

> I assume that God permits no evil, however horrendous it may appear to us in the present, that he cannot eventually turn to good; and he permits no harm to befall his loved ones that he cannot repair in the end. I also assume that, given a long enough stretch of time, the Hound of Heaven can overcome all of the obstacles that our wrong choices can present and can thus achieve all of his redemptive purposes; in that respect, he is like the grand chess master who, though exercising no direct causal control over the moves of the novice, is nonetheless able to checkmate the novice in the end. . . . God's love will eventually triumph; he will destroy evil completely and thus remove every stain from his creation.[27]

God's healing mission is to "free" all for a true choice for God. Because God's overarching shalom mission is the complete healing and full restoration of all that is broken, wounded, suffering, and oppressed—all that is evil—and because God's unstoppable power is demonstrated in the life, death, and resurrection of Jesus—it can be hoped that that, in the end, all souls will come to their own authentic and clearly "free" choice *for* God![28] In the words of Julian of Norwich: "It is sooth that sin is cause of all this pain; but all shall be well, and all shall be well, and all manner of thing shall be well."[29]

ETERNAL RESTORATIVE JUSTICE

The expectation that all souls will eventually find a way to reconciliation with God does not ignore, discount, or conflict with God's justice. God's justice demonstrates God's respect for human integrity and freedom when it allows us to experience the consequences of all choices, even the hellish ones. In fact, being permitted to experience the full outcome of all choices is the first part of God's justice at work. The consequences of choices that take us away from God—that participate with evil—justly bring about pain, suffering, and torment in our lives and in the lives of others. Biblical writers have used the concepts of the "wrath of God" and "punishment of God" as apt descriptions of the genuine experience of hell that comes from choices made that separate us from God or participate in evil.[30]

But God's justice isn't content to let suffering and torment continue endlessly. God's justice is, finally, not *punitive* justice. God's justice is shalom justice. It gives what it needed despite what is merited. It offers what is *not* deserved to bring what is divinely intended: wholeness.[31] Building on the work of Raymund Schwager, Denny Weaver helpfully outlines the contours of God's justice:

> Jesus' mission was to make present and visible the reign of God. That mission meant witnessing to and presenting God's unmerited forgiveness and the reconciliation of sinners to God.... In his preaching about judgment Jesus did not teach that the goodness and the justice of God were two consecutive stages, as that at a point in time the goodness and mercy of God end and then the judgment of God begins. Rather, Jesus made it clear that statements about the retribution of God were really a declaration of what those who reject the rule of God bring on themselves. Declarations of judgment make clear the consequences of rejecting God. But God remains a God of love and grace, whose offer of forgiveness always remains open.[32]

To speak of God's "anger" and God's "wrath" are human attempts to describe what it is like when God's just and loving power is strong enough, and firm enough, to allow us to experience the consequences of sin and idolatries to their fullest extent. Such consequences do take us to hell. "Hell" is a very real description of what is faced when we choose separation from God's purposes and ignore the call of Christ in our lives.

But hell is not unending. It is not eternal. "Punishment," experiencing the consequences of choices, and "judgment of sin," recognizing the truth about wayward choices, will, it is my hope, eventually lead not to eternal rejection but to reconciliation with God. Along with God's shalom initiatives toward healing in our lives, what we perceive as punishment and judgment can be understood as a purifying form[33] of God's mercy because they eventually lead to restoration and a choice for God. "The wrath of God and the love of God," Weaver argues,

> represent the two stances from which we view the salvation drama, the two perspectives from which we view the act of God in Christ—as an act of judgment as long as we continue in bondage to the powers of evil that enslave us, and as an act of

love that frees us from the powers of evil. These are not the consecutive stages of God's attitude toward humankind, but differing stages in humankind's perception of God.³⁴

God's love, in Jesus, even comes to us in hell. Matthew, Dennis, and Sheila Fabricant Linn build on the work of Hans Urs von Balthasar's discussion of Holy Saturday to signify "Jesus' utter solidarity with sinners":

> As the expression of God's infinitely merciful love for sinners, Jesus identifies completely with them, to the point of dying on the cross as one of them [and seemingly being abandoned by God.] Then, on Holy Saturday, Jesus goes to be with sinners in still another way, in what we call his descent into hell. If we define hell as the adamant choice to close one's heart to God, then it would seem that hell is the one place that God cannot be. By going there anyway, Jesus refuses to accept that [adamant] choice and expresses God's adamant unwillingness to leave us to our own worse selves.... Jesus' descent into hell is his refusal to accept our choice of destruction... and being with us there until his healing presence renews us enough to rise with him on Easter.³⁵

It is not suffering that satisfies the demands of a just God. God's righteous justice requires something else. God's justice requires repair. God will not settle for brokenness and division, oppression and destruction. God will settle for nothing less than perfect justice, for repaired wholeness. If that which is broken, divisive, oppressive, destructive (and more) is sin, then what will cancel sin? What will defeat sin? Will punishment cancel sin? No, what will cancel sin is not *separation* but *reconciliation*. The consequences of sin reveal to us our true separation from God and thus help us see through the self-deception that makes evil choice possible. The freedom to experience the full consequences of our sin leads us to see truth. The painful-but-purifying consequences, in time, strip us of our illusions. Our false ways and our false selves are unmasked and destroyed.

What happens to us—to our world—in this shattered condition? God embraces. God heals.³⁶ God saves. That's what God's mission is: to save all creation and all people from every kind of hell, now and in the future. God's mission is to restore what is broken and reconcile what is alienated. God's shalom endeavor is to bring wholeness to creation even though it is not merited.

God's justice is *restorative* justice. It is not retributive, nor is it unendingly punishing. God's justice offers what is needed rather than what is merited. It acts to bring wholeness. God's action in history has not been to settle the score of an offended divine honor with violent punishment. God's overarching activity through the sweep of biblical history has been to bring healing, restoration, wholeness, and shalom. God does not *do* violence; God *condemns and redeems* the violence that evil and sin have done and are doing.[37]

God raised Jesus from the dead as a sign that Jesus' way of suffering love leads to real victory over the powers of evil and death. Reconciliation is at the heart of God's restoration (2 Cor. 5:18-19). Reconciliation is God's restorative justice as seen in Jesus Christ. Though for a time hell may describe the consequences of sin, we are not abandoned to that experience forever. The gates of hell will not prevail. God's restorative justice and loving power—as demonstrated in the resurrection of Jesus—will heal, reconcile, redeem, and restore all. There is all of eternity in which for God to accomplish this restorative mission.

ETERNAL RESURRECTION POWER

Narrative Christus Victor theology puts the resurrection squarely at the center of God's shalom, of God's victory of *life* over evil and death. "The resurrection as the victory of the reign of God over the forces of evil constitutes an invitation to salvation," according to Weaver. "It is an invitation to enter a new life, a life transformed by the rule of God and no longer in bondage to the powers of evil that killed Jesus. . . . The resurrection reveals the true balance of power in the universe whether sinners perceive it or not. Sinners can ignore the resurrection and continue in opposition to the reign of God, but the reign of God is still victorious."[38]

God's power is life-affirming. It is proactive and takes the initiative. It is a power that moves toward relationship despite sin and separation. In his letter to the Romans, Paul reasons that "if while we were enemies, we were reconciled to God through the death of his Son, much more surely, having been reconciled, will we be saved by his life" (Rom. 5:10).

In the story of Jesus, God's power is most fully demonstrated in the resurrection. God's loving power was *not* thwarted by a grave. In fact, the most spectacular movement of God's loving power in the whole life of Christ was executed in a grave: restoring Jesus to life! God's power triumphed over the earthly death of Jesus. Is this divine resurrection power any less able to work in any other grave? Is God's loving power capable of being thwarted by any other earthly death?[39] We find hope, Randy Klassen explains,

> in the assurance that God is not finished with us when we die. If Christ is Lord "both of the dead and the living" (Rom 14:9), then God's justice will still be revealed to those who missed it on earth. Peter is quite specific in affirming the ongoing action of God for those who have died. "For this reason the gospel was proclaimed even to the dead, so that, though they had been judged in the flesh as everyone is judged, they might live in the spirit as God does" (1 Pet 4:6). How God's grace and mercy will work for the people after they die, we cannot fully understand, but we can affirm that God will be just and, as always, God's justice will be immersed in mercy. The traditional view of hell fails the test of justice.[40]

The resurrection power of Jesus demonstrates that, though it may look impossible, we can trust God to achieve what God intends. Though it may take an eternity, the power of the risen Christ is the power that will bring an end to that which is destructive, diseased, harmful, and evil. Everything separated from God will be reconciled. The resurrection power of the risen Christ will complete God's endeavor of shalom for healing the whole creation and all that is in it. God will provide what is needed for wholeness despite what is truly deserved. The resurrection power of the risen Christ will fulfill God's intentions and God's purpose. "Love never ends" (1 Cor 13:8).

ALL THINGS GATHERED UP IN CHRIST

Narrative Christus Victor theology presents an alternative reading of the Bible, one that offers a corrective to traditional atonement theologies by illuminating the nonviolent victory of the Anointed One over evil and death. My hopeful conviction that God will reconcile all things to God is also based on a valid, though less common, reading of the Bible. It takes the narrative Christus Victor reading and extends it into eternity. It visions a nonviolent eschatology.

There is hell, to be sure, as long as there is sin. Choices that take us away from God's intended best bring about consequences that God's love rightfully permits us to experience in full. These consequences become teachers, eventually leading us on the journey for which we were created: relationship with God. In the course of that journey, we will meet Christ, and nothing "will be able to separate us from the love of God in Christ Jesus our Lord" (Rom. 8:39). God's love reaches us with healing and liberation. We are freed and fully reconciled to God in Christ and will safely come home in the perfect reign of God. The "defeat" of sin will not be more separation. It will be reconciliation, total and full. Thus, taken to its logical and ultimate end, God's unfailing love means that *no thing* and *no one* will fail to be reconciled or restored. We dare to dream a nonviolent eschatology and hope in the fulfillment of Ephesians 1:10 that all things will be gathered up in Christ.

THINKING AND LIVING IN HOPE

At the nadir of my own theological struggle with questions about God and violence, I had a pivotal encounter in prayer. On a Good Friday I was reflecting upon the meaning of the day. I was in despair over what seemed like divine violence in the crucifixion. I was in lament over the human violence that had killed Jesus and that kills yet today.

Into the midst of that despair, I sensed God saying, "Jane, it is well and good to try to get your atonement theology sorted out. That is not a waste. BUT... what is it you are *doing*, each day, to dismantle injustice and build the shalom in which you say you believe?" In a single moment I realized that my long list of questions suddenly took second place to a more critical, more pivotal question asked of me by God. What *am* I doing each day to build shalom? I needed to move beyond my conflicted, intellectual immobility and theological angst. Rather that trying to get all the theological ideas sorted out, my call is to living that commitment to shalom, and building it with my life. That is the evidence that must be seen in a life that longs to believe in a nonviolent atonement and a nonviolent eschatology.

What, then, might a commitment to nonviolent atonement and eschatology look like in our lives and in congregations? How does it go beyond a mere pursuit of ideas and become embodied in the ways the congregation joins God in God's purpose to heal and restore the entirety of creation?

NONVIOLENT ESCHATOLOGY AND THE CONGREGATION

Hope in a nonviolent atonement and eschatology empowered by faith in the Risen Christ will manifest itself in the lives of congregations and individuals in the way we worship, teach, preach, heal, care, support, prophetically confront, serve, and witness to life, life over all death.

Congregations who live this life over death are communities that both enter into suffering in solidarity with others and also refuse to relinquish joy. We are people of the cross *and* the Resurrection. This is a seeming paradox, an exercise in embracing ambiguity. On the one hand, we are clear-eyed and honest about the "not yet" parts of the reign of God: We dare to see and respond to the horrific pain, suffering, turmoil, abuse, oppression, evil, and death in our world and in ourselves, and we dare to come alongside one another and all of those who suffer to enter it with them for the purposes of transformation and shalom. We do that because we know there is no hell in which there is also not the presence and power of the Risen Christ.

We are also adamant, however, that because nothing separates anyone from the love of God in Christ, there is room for joy alongside the sorrow. As we learn, teach, and testify to the story of God's shalom endeavor, we claim and stubbornly hold on to capacity for joy even amid despair, because our certain hope always is that "all shall be well, all manner of things shall be well."

I have experienced the transformative power of this nonviolent eschatology in pastoral ministry. When fear of hells of *all* kinds is healed by the perfect love that casts out fear, and when persons have an enlarged sense that God's love, both personally and eschatologically, restores *all* the brokenness the world can create, then something transformational takes place at a core level: at a spiritual, emotional, psychological, relational, and even cellular level. Anxiety and ruts of reactivity start to be reprogrammed. Love and trust are allowed to flourish and to do their healing, reconciling, and building work. When the Christian congregation can envision and understand itself as part of God's shalom endeavor in the world, as part of the ultimate victory in Christ even if as yet unseen, then its energy is projected toward life. This movement with God toward life ultimately transforms persons, families, their communities, and the world.

We also are the church differently when our vision includes an eternally nonviolent God. Worship, preaching, spiritual formation, Christian education, mentoring, catechism, spiritual direction, evangelism, and pastoral care are ministries and practices that take on different, life-affirming dynamics when we image a loving, nonviolent God. If we preach, sing, teach, counsel, model, and give witness to a God who is ultimately nurturing and restorative, then the love that casts out fears starts to become real. The congregation becomes a community that embodies God's reconciling mission at every level of people's lives. It becomes a place in which, and through which, the Spirit will produce fruit, a place where good news is preached, freedom is proclaimed and experienced for prisoners of all of life's woes, sight is given to see the powers of God at work, the oppressed released, and the Lord's favor extended to all. Compassion, gentleness, humility, openness, trust, and faith form and grow more abundant in lives within the congregation and in lives beyond it.[41]

Since "we become like the God we adore," this kind of transformation actually has subversive and radical implications for the congregation. It will be counter-cultural within the wider ecumenical community and acutely so within the social civil religiosity of American culture today. Christian congregations will be communities of "grace, joy and peace"[42] that are healing and transformative through worship, community, and mission—not out of avoidance of seeing or responding to sin, but with an integrity that continually and persistently invites people to recognize God's love in their lives, to confront their sins and addictions, to turn toward healing and wholeness in deep and authentic relationship with Jesus, and to share their story with others. Congregations that grow in love with an eternally nonviolent God will help bring God's healing, transformational restoration and hope to individual lives, to their communities, and to our world. They will, in short, "joyfully follow Jesus into the world" as part of God's eternal shalom endeavor.

NOTES

1. For another reading of the biblical story in which God's work for shalom is central, see Perry B. Yoder, *Shalom: The Bible's Word for Salvation, Justice and Peace* (Nappanee, Ind.: Evangel Publishing House, 1987).

2. Rachel Reesor writes: "Any attempt to explain how Calvary is related to our communities and the cosmos must not domesticate God." See Reesor, "Atonement: Mystery and Metaphorical Language," *Mennonite Quarterly Review* 68/2 (April 1994): 218.

3. It is my perception after worshipping in Mennonite settings for three decades that the "default" way that some Mennonites understand the atonement is that God's anger is the issue and that this anger is/was appeased by killing God's son—God "sending Jesus to die in our place." It is surprising to me how often I have heard churched Mennonites speak about God as if God is turned away from people in righteous perfection and wrath over sin and that God seemingly must stay that way until sinners crawl to God in prostrate repentance and confession that "God loved me enough to send Jesus to die for me." The idea is that only a substitute death can appease God's anger.

Then God can turn toward people in the grace and love God actually has—but which God could not convey until this anger was appeased. Still, doubts linger. I've heard senior Mennonites preface thoughts about anticipating eternal life with, "Well, if I get to heaven. . . ." The default theology seems to be that God is understood as so angry and full of wrath that even after lifelong Christian living and a confession that "Jesus died for me," people still cannot be sure there is an eternal home with God.

4. Walter Wink offers a helpful discussion of the deep roots of humankind's devotion to violence and the manner in which the biblical story is "diametrically opposed to all of this." Wink claims that we are not aware that our cultural "devotion" to violence is a form of religious piety and that the myth that violence might be redemptive is pervasive. "The myth of redemptive violence," Wink argues, "is the simplest, laziest, most exciting, uncomplicated, irrational and primitive depiction of evil the world has even known." See Walter Wink, "Babylon Revisited: How Violent Myths Resurface Today," *Media and Values* 62 (Spring 1993).

John D. Roth also critiques the notion of redemptive violence: "In the end, redemptive violence is a myth for Christians because there is nothing Christian about its logic. If every human being is indeed made in the very image of God, then what argument can possibly justify one of God's creatures—especially one who has come to know and claim the love of God—to take the life of another human?" *Choosing Against War: A Christian View* (Intercourse, Pa.: Good Books, 2002), 60.

5. While we do not know for certain that no materials in the canon are written by women, tradition assumes exclusively male authorship. This would also be true of the early church writings. For one look at Medieval women mystics on atonement, see Jane McAvoy's *The Satisfied Life* (Cleveland, Oh.: Pilgrim Press, 2000), where she constructs a feminist theology of atonement that is not dismissive of atonement as a non-redemptive theological doctrine. She draws on the insights of six medieval women mystics to reveal alternatives to a theology of oppression and blindness to God's love, which leads to self-blame and the projection of self-wrath onto God. See also Rachel Reesor, "Atonement: Mystery and Metaphorical Language," in which Reesor maintains that understandings of the atonement must be opened up rather than narrowed down. Finally, see Mary H. Schertz, "God's Cross and Women's Questions: A Biblical Perspective on the Atonement," *Mennonite Quarterly Review* 68/2 (April 1994),194-208, where Schertz responds to feminist arguments that resist the notion that suffering is or can be redemptive, and to other feminist impulses to reformulate a theology of the cross from the resource of women's experience (i.e. birthing). Schertz uses Luke to offer a textual basis for a way of thinking about the atonement that contributes to feminist thinking about suffering and about what is liberating for women.

6. Willard Swartley, in a groundbreaking way that systematically exegetes the scores of references to peace in the New Testament, energetically addresses some of the critical questions with which I struggle. See Swartley, *Covenant of Peace: The Missing Peace in New Testament Theology and Ethics* (Grand Rapids, Mich.: Wm. B. Eerdmans, 2006), particularly chapter 14,

"God's Moral Character as the Basis for Human Ethics," and chapter 15, "New Testament Peacemaking in the Service of Moral Formation."

7. See Ronald Rolheiser, "A Spirituality of the Paschal Mystery," in *The Holy Longing: The Search for a Christian Spirituality*, (New York: Doubleday, 1999): 141-166. Rollheiser writes: "Hence, Christian spirituality does not apologize for the fact that, within it, the most central of all mysteries is the paschal one, the mystery of suffering, death and transformation. In Christian spirituality, Christ is central and, central to Christ, is his death and rising to new life so as to send a new Spirit. This is the central mystery within Christianity . . . also . . . one of the great misunderstood and ignored mysteries . . . we seldom really try to understand what [it] means and how we might appropriate it within out own lives" (142).

8. The translation of Colossians is taken from Burton H. Throckmorton Jr., *The Gospels and the Letters of Paul: An Inclusive-Language Edition* (Cleveland, Oh.: Pilgrim Press, 1992). Jesus death on a cross was brutally, undeniably violent, and Jesus' obedience "to the point of death—even death on a cross" (Phil. 2:8) is a pivotal part of the work God enacted in the atonement. My struggle in how to understand the atonement is whether or not there is *divine* violence being done in this death. Or is God's action nonviolent transformation—that of turning death into life through the resurrection?

9. See the material gathered together in Phillip Gulley and James Mulholland, *If Grace is True: Why God Will Save Every Person* (San Francisco: Harper, 2003), including discussion of St. Clement of Alexandria, Origen, Didymus, Diodore of Tarsus, Gregory of Nazianzus, St. Jermone, St. Gregory of Nyssa, Theodore of Mopsuestia, Theodoret the Blessed, and Peter Chrysologus.

10. Quoted in Frances F. Hiebert, "The Atonement in Anabaptist Theology," *Direction Journal* 30/2 (Fall 2001): 122-128.

11. See John Driver's *Understanding the Atonement for the Mission of the Church* (Scottdale, Pa.: Herald Press: 1986) for a discussion of multiple scriptural images and an articulation of a non-Constantinian, biblically-grounded, missionary-oriented vision of the atonement.

12. J. Denny Weaver, *The Nonviolent Atonement* (Grand Rapids, Mich.: Wm. B. Eerdmans, 2001).

13. For two different viewpoints regarding the atonement and divine violence, which argue that human nonviolence is not premised on divine nonviolence, see A. James Reimer, "God Is Love but Not a Pacifist," in *Mennonites and Classical Theology: Dogmatic Foundations for Christian Ethics* (Kitchener, Ont.: Pandora Press, 2001), 486-492 and Miroslav Volf, "Violence and Peace," *Exclusion and Embrace: A Theological Exploration of Identity, Otherness, and Reconciliation* (Nashville: Abingdon Press: 1996), 275-306.

14. J. Denny Weaver, *The Nonviolent Atonement*, 81.

15. James Mulholland, *Praying Like Jesus: The Lord's Prayer in a Culture of Prosperity* (San Francisco: HarperSanFrancisco, 2001), 52-53

16. Weaver, *The Nonviolent Atonement*, 45.

17. Matthew, Dennis, and Sheila Fabricant Linn, *Good Goats: Healing Our Image of God* (Mahwah, N.J.: Paulist Press, 1994), 7.

18. Ray C. Gingerich, "Reimagining Power: Toward a Theology of Nonvi-

olence," in *Peace and Justice Shall Embrace: Power and Theopolitics in the Bible*, ed. Ted Grimsrud and Loren Johns (Telford, Pa.: Pandora Press, 1999), 192-216.

19. Weaver, *The Nonviolent Atonement*, 44.
20. Ibid., 227.
21. Ibid.
22. Ibid., 226.
23. Mennonite Church USA identity statement, Charlotte 2005.
24. See J. Nelson Kraybill, *Four Spiritual Truths of a Peacemaking God* (Elkhart, Ind.: MCUSA, 2004), in which Kraybill uses Christus Victor as a "useful and timely way to explain salvation in our day when conflict is so prominent in the world."
25. Talbott, *The Inescapable Love of God* (Boca Raton, Fl.: Universal Publishers, 1999), 184, 186, 187
26. Ibid., 187.
27. Ibid., 183.
28. My thinking here is rooted in the eternal life of Christ that exceeds earthly existence. For a valuable discussion of the nature of that cosmic Christ, and our participation in that life, see Thomas Yoder Neufeld's *Believers Church Bible Commentary: Ephesians* (Scottdale, Pa.: Herald Press, 2003), specifically Ephesians 1:5-23 and 2: 1-10. I would also argue that God's healing continues beyond the earthly grave (like it did in the work of resurrecting Jesus), so that persons who have not yet made their free choice for God at the time of earthly death will continue that journey toward reconciliation with God in eternity. This complete reconciliation may even include Satan. As Madeleine L'Engle writes: "No matter how many eons it takes, he will not rest until all of creation, including Satan, is reconciled to him, until there is no creature who cannot return his look of love with a joyful response of love."— *The Irrational Season* (San Francisco: HarperSanFrancisco, 1984), 97.
29. This was the answer given to Julian in her visions of Christ when she protested that all could not be well if sinners were eternally punished in the flames of Hell.
30. Talbot, 81-106
31. Yoder, *Shalom: The Bible's Word*, 45.
32. Weaver, *The Nonviolent Atonement*, 41.
33. Talbot, 197.
34. Ibid., 78.
35. Linn, Linn, and Linn, 33.
36. Randy Klassen argues thus: "Understandably a holy God will not ignore sin, not only because it mars [God's] plan but also because it hurts the creatures God loves. Yet the prophets have spoken, the justice of God is intended to heal not destroy, even though the path toward healing may include some destruction and pain." Klassen, *What Does the Bible Really Say about Hell? Wrestling with the Traditional View* (Telford, Pa.: Pandora Press U.S. and Scottdale, Pa.: Herald Press, 2001), 87.
37. Swartley explains: "To attribute violence to God is a misnomer, a misplaced indictment from Scripture's point of view. Rather, judgment is what characterizes the sovereign, holy God who punishes humans for sin and vio-

lence. God's redemptive acts stand in the service of bringing violence to an end! Only then can God's shalom cover the earth as the waters cover the sea. To attribute violence to God is to undermine the moral character of God, God's redemptive purposes, and confuse human perversity with the divine prerogative to establish justice and shalom by punishing human violence. To put it bluntly, God's vengeance, however executed, stands against human violence. Scripture rarely speaks explicitly about God being violent or nonviolent, but depicts God as one who condemns human violence in order to establish divine justice and shalom." Swartley, 395.

38. Weaver, *The Nonviolent Atonement*, 45.
39. Randy Klassen, *What Does the Bible Really Say About Hell*, 87.
40. Ibid., 87
41. Philip and James Mulholland, *If God Is Love: Rediscovering Grace in an Ungracious World* (San Francisco: Harper, 2005). Universalist in orientation, Gulley and Mulholland offer a compelling view on how the world could look if the church took seriously God's unthwartable love for all people.
42. "Vision: Healing and Hope," available at www.mennolink.org/doc/vhh.html. Viewed Dec. 29, 2006.

Part 5
THE WORK OF JESUS IN THE CHURCH

CHAPTER FOURTEEN

"The Tongue is a Fire": On the Dangerous Missiological Vocation of the Theologian

Alain Epp Weaver

"**N**ot many of you should become teachers, my brothers and sisters," warns the letter of James, "for you know that we who teach will be judged with greater strictness. For all of us make many mistakes. Anyone who makes no mistakes in speaking is perfect, able to keep the whole body in check with a bridle." The author of James' epistle cautions that "the tongue is a fire," "placed among our members as a world of iniquity." "No one can tame the tongue," James adds, for it is a "restless evil, full of deadly poison." Human speech is prone to intemperance and arrogance, and so teachers—or, indeed, any Christian—must be ever vigilant, checking to see if they use their tongues to "bless the Lord and Father" or to "curse those who are made in the likeness of God." Teachers must learn to control their tongues so that they are conformed to the "wisdom from above" that is "first pure, then peaceable, gentle, willing to yield, full of mercy and good fruits, without trace of partiality or hypocrisy" (James 3:1-18).

James' words sit uncomfortably with those of us whom the church grants the title of "theologian," and they should sit uncomfortably with all Christians who, by virtue of their calling, are compelled to proclaim that Jesus Christ is Lord, for we know that our mission, be it expressed in teaching, worship, or proclamation, requires us to speak and so requires that we embroil ourselves in the danger of using our tongues, of using language. We are (or should be) aware that, as John Howard Yoder observed in his discussion of James' understanding of the teacher's vocation, "language has a dangerously determinative function," and must therefore be treated with great care.[1] The theological task—which, by its nature, is the missiological task of confessing Christ's lordship in new contexts—is thus inherently a risk-filled venture.

THEOLOGICAL RISK, ECCLESIOLOGICAL FRAGILITY

Much contemporary theologizing can, I would suggest, be viewed as an attempt to avoid theological risk, an attempt doomed to failure, for no matter how careful we are in crafting particular theological formulations, words can always be distorted and can always leave room for diverse interpretation and appropriation. Take, for example, Reinhard Hütter's critique of Karl Barth's ecclesiology and pneumatology. Barth's "newly recovered understanding of theology as a public enterprise normative for the church," Hütter warns, "remains inherently unstable if the church to which it belongs fails to recover itself as a public." Hütter continues: "Can there be a church in the New Testament sense if it is not a public that is defined and circumscribed in an *unambiguously binding* way?" (italics in the original).[2] For an "unambiguously binding" authority, Hütter joins other ecumenically minded theologians such as R. R. Reno, Ephraim Radner, and the multiple authors of *In One Body through the Cross: The Princeton Proposal for Christian Unity*, in turning to the ecumenical creeds.[3]

Such an approach has its appeal, of course, in that it appears to secure the stability of the theological enterprise by grounding it in authoritative dogma. The problem with this approach, as explained insistently by J. Denny Weaver, is that it masks ecclesial division and instability more than reconciles it. Why? Insofar as the creeds jump from Jesus' birth to his death and resurrection, they omit reference to Jesus' authoritative life and teachings. Weaver is convinced that pacifist Christians, such as Mennonites, who believe that confession of Christ's lordship goes hand in hand with a renunciation of all violent force, have reason to worry about appeals to Nicaea-Chalcedon as the "central," "unambiguously binding" teachings that will stabilize the church's witness. The worry is that this approach marginalizes the church's commitment to a christologically focused nonviolence.

The danger, from this perspective, of taking the creeds as unambiguously binding lies in the fact that, on the question of violence, the creeds are themselves ambiguous. They are open to the interpretation that Jesus' lordship does not consist in his binding call to his disciples to put away the sword and to follow him.[4] One can argue, as John Howard Yoder did so masterfully in *The Politics of Jesus*, that creedal logic, when combined with submission to the rule of Scripture, *should* issue in a commitment to nonviolent discipleship. To say, however, that the creeds can be appropriated in defense of Christian pacifism does not mitigate the fact that, taken by themselves, the creeds are ambiguous and can, like other linguistic artifacts, be appropriated in a variety of ways.[5]

Denny Weaver, however, appears to share Hütter's desire to delineate an unambiguously binding teaching for the church, to shore up the stability of the church's witness. The problem with the creeds, from Weaver's perspective, is that they say too little. What is needed, Weaver seems to imply, is a doctrinal formulation that will clearly and unambiguously underscore the essential connection of confessing Jesus Christ as Lord and a life of nonviolent discipleship. But note: just as Nicaea-Chalcedon can be appropriated by theological defenders of violence, so can critiques of the ecumenical creeds, such as Weaver's, be appropriated by those who simply reject the notion of binding authority *tout court* or who reject the creeds' strong christological affirmations. Such rejections, of course, are not Weaver's intent, but the inherently risky character of the theological enterprise (its fragility, its instability) means that such appropriations of Weaver's work are inevitable.[6]

My point here is not to question the idea of binding doctrine but to problematize the assumption that theologically we can easily arrive at unambiguously binding doctrine, with the lack of ambiguity serving as a safeguard against theological and ecclesiological instability. Hütter, I suggest, is mistaken in his critique of Barth's ecclesiology. For Barth, as for his student John Howard Yoder, the inherent *instability* of the church is not something to which we should react in horror—but an essential mark of the church.

As the church engages in patient, non-defensive, missiological encounters in the ever-new contexts in which it finds itself, it is sustained completely and solely by God's gift of the Spirit. Among the

Spirit's gifts are to be counted not only the teachings and learnings of our ancestors but also the in-breaking of new wisdom from beyond the walls of the church. The church, to be true to her calling to embody a nonviolent gospel, must cultivate a radical receptivity to voices outside herself. Christian witness, that is, the shape of Christian mission, Barth and Yoder made clear, takes the form of patient conversation; if such is the shape of Christian mission, then ecclesiological instability and fragility are inevitable.[7] Theological projects to secure some dogmatic or liturgical touchstone free from the possibility of corruption inevitably fail, for they do not adequately account for the pervasive character of human sinfulness, for the dangerous fire that is language.

Again, my point is not that the church should not have binding doctrine, for surely the church must proclaim Jesus as the Christ if she is to be faithful. Rather, I simply wish to stress that as the church engages in this proclamation she will inevitably find herself confronted with the ambiguities of language. She will find her words coming up short, or find her words being appropriated in ways that she did not intend, and so will have no choice but to engage in patient, dangerously fragile, conversations to explain her confession of Jesus as Lord in greater detail. Contending with such inevitable risk is the dangerous missiological vocation of the theologian.

MISSIOLOGICAL RISK: PRACTICAL REFLECTIONS

As I reflect on a decade of work with Mennonite Central Committee in the Middle East, *danger* and *fragility* come quickly to mind as words to describe the nature of MCC's missionary presence. Not, I should be quick to add, danger and fragility in a physical sense; for the most part, MCC takes great care to minimize physical dangers to its workers. I do not wish, by speaking of danger and MCC work in the same breath, to attribute heroic characteristics to MCC workers (especially myself). Rather, I refer to theological dangers that arise as MCC workers seek to serve, in word and deed, "in the name of Christ" in contexts such as Palestine/Israel and Iraq. Theological danger is not, one should stress, only to be found in "exotic" locations such as the Middle East, but is an unavoidable part of Christian mission, be it in Bluffton, Ohio; North Newton, Kansas; or Jerusalem. Bound up as it is with the use of language, Christian mission is simply an inherently dangerous task.

I am most familiar, however, with the dangers and fragilities of Christian mission in the Middle Eastern context, and so in the remainder of this essay I propose to explore some of the ways in which Mennonite mission work in the Middle East has placed the church in productively precarious (and thus fragile, dangerous, and unstable) positions. Specifically, I will examine four ways in which MCC work in the Middle East is fruitfully fragile: MCC's relatively implicit missiology of accompanying Middle Eastern churches in their witness; grappling with theological understandings of election, promise, and the land as they relate to the Palestinian-Israeli conflict; the promise and peril of coalition-building in peacebuilding work; and the promise and limits of promoting nonviolent action as an effective tool in the struggle against dispossession.

A Missiology of Accompaniment amid Broken Communion

In the Occupied Palestinian Territories, Jordan, Iraq, Lebanon, Syria, and Egypt, MCC works in close partnership with churches with which Mennonite churches are not in communion. In Syria and Egypt, in particular, MCC's presence and work exists and continues at the invitation of Orthodox (Syrian and Coptic, respectively) churches in which Mennonites cannot join in the Eucharistic feast. The Syrian Orthodox church welcomes MCC teachers at its seminary and its schools and the Coptic Orthodox church hosts MCC volunteers in its evening language classes for adults, but this welcome does not extend to the altar. The same could be said for the Roman Catholic (Latin) schools where MCC workers teach in the West Bank and Jordan.

MCC and the Mennonite mission boards, by deciding not to establish Mennonite churches in the Middle East, countered an all-too-typical colonialist pattern in which Western churches have come to the Middle East with the intention of witnessing to Muslims but have ended up fracturing the divided body of Christ still further by starting new churches that have drawn away members from existing communions.[8] Mennonite work with the indigenous churches of the Middle East has, at its best, served as an alternative to the Western Christian antagonism (and, at various points in history, violence) toward the Eastern churches.

For the Mennonite mission boards (e.g., Mennonite Board of Missions, now Mennonite Mission Network, and Eastern Mennonite Missions) the decision not to try to plant Mennonite churches in the Middle East led for the most part to partnerships with evangelical, "free" churches in the region and with the foreign evangelical mission boards that had started them (e.g., the Southern Baptist mission board, the Assemblies of God, etc.).[9] Most of MCC's church partners in the Middle East, in contrast, have been Orthodox, Catholic, and the "established" Protestant churches (Lutheran and Anglican). MCC's vision during its nearly six decades of presence and witness in the Middle East has been less about building up its own institutional presence and more about supporting and encouraging the various forms of Christian witness already undertaken by Middle Eastern Christians, be they Orthodox, Catholic, or Protestant. This assessment holds particularly true for the past two decades in which MCC has moved explicitly in the direction of being a partnership agency that supports projects carried out by churches, church-related organizations, and NGOs, and away from being an implementing agency that designs and carries out its own programs.[10]

Given that MCC serves as the peacebuilding, relief, and development organization for several churches that would typically be classified as "free" or "evangelical" churches, MCC's tendency to join in partnership with the "establishment" churches in the Middle East might appear incongruous. Surely, one might suggest, the most natural missiological fit for MCC would be with the small evangelical churches of the region, some of which share traditional Anabaptist concerns about infant baptism.

To my mind, however, MCC's inclination to seek out partnership possibilities with Catholic and Orthodox churches of various types has been laudable and productive, a reflection of an anti-colonialist determination not to import our own ecclesiological projects to the region but rather to follow the lead of the Chaldean Catholic, the Syrian Orthodox, the Coptic Orthodox, and the Latin (Roman) Catholics (among others), to support their ministries and mission to their societies. At its best, MCC has sought to divest itself of the need to control projects, of the desire to establish a particularly Mennonite "brand" in the Middle East. At their best, MCC workers have opened themselves to be instructed by the ways in which the liturgies, polities, and doctrines of Middle Eastern Christians express the gospel confession of Christ's lordship.

The danger in MCC's posture, however, lies in the possibility of MCC workers minimizing the reality of ecclesial division, of viewing doctrinal, ecclesiological, and liturgical differences as simply superficial. MCC's posture of accompaniment, of supporting the ministries of the Middle Eastern churches, will only be a radical form of witness if Mennonites through these partnerships open themselves up to ecumenical challenge. Mennonites must be prepared both to give a witness to our understanding of the Christian faith and to receive a witness from those with whom we work. Partnership with Middle Eastern churches should not lull Mennonites into a relativistic ecumenical pluralism. Rather, Mennonites should allow such partnerships to underscore the enduring scandal of ecclesiological division, to call into question any separatist inclinations we might have that suggest to us that we can be faithful without seeking to learn from and to be reconciled with those Christians from whom we remain divided.

Election as Promise and Danger

For many Palestinian Christians, the very idea of a "chosen people" has become deeply problematic. Reacting against theologies that equate God's election of the Jewish people with divine justification for the establishment of the state of Israel, many Palestinian Christians struggle with the concept of chosenness.[11] The late Roman Catholic priest, Fr. Michael Prior, explored how throughout history claims of being a chosen people have translated into colonialist violence against indigenous peoples, a pattern Prior traced to the Old Testament narratives of the conquest of the land of Canaan. Concepts of the United States of America as a chosen nation and of Manifest Destiny went hand in hand with justifications of violence and genocide against Native American peoples, while Afrikaners viewed themselves as a chosen people who were entitled to rule over the tribes of southern Africa. The Israeli dispossession of the Palestinian people, Prior argued, must be understood in the light of this pattern of claims of election being used to justify colonialist ideology and its violent mechanisms.[12]

That the theological-political concept of election is a dangerous concept cannot be denied. Time and again various peoples have used the claim to be a chosen people, to be graced with a peculiar mission, as a divine *carte blanche*. One can certainly understand the struggle many Palestinian Christians have with appropriating as Scripture, as good news, biblical texts that urge the slaughter of native peoples such as the Canaanites and that promise God's chosen people that they will inherit houses they did not build and vineyards they did not plant (Deut. 7 is particularly harrowing). Not only Palestinian Christians find election theologically and morally troubling. Some of my MCC colleagues, dismayed by the ways in which the ideology of election is deployed to support Palestinian dispossession, rejected the category.

In my writing on Jewish-Christian relations and the Palestinian-Israeli conflict, however, I have tried to sketch a different approach to the question of election. For Christians to abandon the notion of election is, it seems to me, problematic both scripturally and theologically. Is not God eternally faithful to his covenant promises (e.g., Romans 9-11)? Does not the church claim to be grafted onto Israel, and as such does not the church claim to be "a chosen race, a royal priesthood, a holy nation, God's own people" (1 Pet. 2:9-10, echoing Exodus 19:6)? As much as we might decry the ways in which triumphalist Christendom has failed to be a "holy nation," can we reject the calling to be a holy nation and to be faithful? Can we abandon the Old Testament story of God choosing a people, Israel, to be a light to the nations, without ramifications for our understanding of Jesus and the church continuing this story of election for a divine mission?

Certainly, the rhetoric of election is dangerous, susceptible to various forms of abuse and distortion. Such is the case with all theological language of interest and depth. Rather than trying to cut off the danger by abandoning all potentially dangerous theological concepts, however, I suggest that the path of trying to articulate life-giving understandings of election consonant with Christ's lordship over all of creation has greater theological integrity. In the case of election and claims to land, such an approach would stress that the various theologies and narratives about land in Scripture, in addition to including ideologies of violent conquest, also point toward the possibility of security in the land that is not reducible to nationalist models of sovereignty, that is compatible with, even dependent on, a shared life of justice and reconciliation in the land with other peoples.[13]

Israel's election (which now includes the church's election through Jesus Christ) as a light to the nations should not, I have argued, be used to justify Zionist ideology and practice, but should rather serve as a goad to creative thinking about shared life in the land, a shared life that should not be constrained by nationalist models of sovereignty. Struggling with Palestinian Christians over these matters has been a risk-filled venture. How does one share one's convictions about the ongoing importance of election as a theological category without being naïve about ways in which the rhetoric of election has been coupled with violent ideologies and practices? How does one maintain a commitment to listen to and learn from the Palestinian churches? These have been challenges, but, at least for me, productive challenges.[14]

Peacebuilding Coalitions: Enhanced or Diluted Witness?

How should a Christian organization such as MCC understand partnerships with non-Christian organizations? In its peacebuilding work in Palestine/Israel, MCC not only supports initiatives by Christian organizations, such as the Sabeel Ecumenical Liberation Theology Center, but also assists pioneering work carried out by avowedly secular organizations like the Palestinian Badil Center for Residency and Refugee Rights in Bethlehem, or the Israeli Zochrot Association in Tel Aviv, two groups that develop nonviolent initiatives to promote discussion of Palestinian refugee return and restitution. Critics of MCC might suggest that partnerships with groups like Badil and Zochrot dilute MCC's Christian witness. By joining with secular organizations to advocate for particular rights, for particular forms of justice, does not MCC, the argument might go, run the risk of substituting a general concept such as "peace" or "justice" for Jesus?

This potential critique is misguided to the extent that it rests on an assumption that God's reconciling Spirit is not at work beyond the walls of those who name Jesus Christ as Lord. Karl Barth used the phrase "parables of the kingdom" to describe those non-Christian words, actions, and signs that point to Jesus even without naming his name.[15] Groups like Badil and Zochrot that work for peace and reconciliation built on the foundation of justice embody such parables.

This defense of collaboration between Christian and non-Christian organizations, however, should not obscure the fact that such partnerships are inherently risky. Discerning what non-Christian words and actions are "parables of the kingdom" requires careful process. MCC must continually ask itself whether or not a particular partnership with a secular organization, an Islamic charitable society, or a Jewish peace group glorifies God, whether or not such a partnership moves with God's boundary-breaking Spirit of reconciliation.

For such discernment to take place, MCC workers must conceive of their work in explicitly Christian terms. As MCC workers engage in various forms of joint work with non-Christians, and as MCC, to ensure accountability to donors and partners, adopts the language and methods of results-based management, the risk will always be present that MCC workers will come to conceive of their work in terms of seemingly abstract categories such as "humanitarianism," "peace," or "conflict resolution." The only way to safeguard against this inevitable risk is an institutional commitment to placing workers who approach MCC work missiologically, who understand MCC's development, relief, and peacebuilding work as an integral part of the church's mission to the world.

Nonviolence, Tragedy, and the Fragility of Hope

The disciples of Walter Wink confidently preach that if only we expend sufficient creative effort we will discover nonviolent solutions to the injustices that give rise to violent conflict. Just as Jesus' admonitions to turn the other cheek and to go the extra mile suggested creative responses to violence and occupation in their day, so too today can nonviolent initiatives be created that address dispossession and military oppression. The Palestinian struggle against Israeli military occupation and against forced dispossession from their lands will, the reasoning goes, be more successful, more effective, if Palestinians concentrate on developing nonviolent forms of collective and individual action against the matrix of military, geographic, and economic control that circumscribes Palestinian daily life.

Many Palestinians, both Christian and Muslim, have made this very argument over the past several decades. MCC has been privileged to support creative nonviolent initiatives carried out by groups such as the Palestinian Center for Rapprochement between Peoples, the Wi'am Center for Conflict Resolution, the Holy Land Trust, and many others. Furthermore, the primary form of Palestinian struggle since the *Nakba* (catastrophe) of 1948 has not been armed struggle, but rather the obstinate steadfastness of Palestinians remaining on their land in the face of pressures to leave (in Arabic, *sumud*). Palestinians have not needed international peace teams to come "teach" them nonviolence, as nonviolence has been adopted of necessity by many people as a means of carrying on the daily struggle to make ends meet (for example, by finding one's way around checkpoints and roadblocks to get to work). During the past few years of the second *intifada* (uprising) against the occupation, Palestinian interest in nonviolence as a collective strategy has steadily increased.

Despite my sharing the conviction that the Palestinians' best hopes are in pursuing nonviolent forms of struggle, the optimism of many Winkian proponents of nonviolence often strikes me as naïve, a failure to grapple with the pervasive tragedy of human existence. My concern for MCC and for other outside actors to the Palestinian conflict (such as Christian Peacemaker Teams or the International Solidarity Movement) is that we avoid a hubristic promotion of the supposed benefits of nonviolence, that we soberly face up to the limits of nonviolent action, that with clear heads we acknowledge that sometimes no effective nonviolent solutions unveil themselves. Consider again the experience of Palestinians in the Occupied Territories. Alongside various forms of armed struggle, average Palestinians have engaged in a variety of nonviolent responses to Israeli military occupation, including strikes, boycotts, protest marches, the planting of trees to try to protect land from confiscation for the construction of illegal settlements, sit-ins in front of bulldozers coming to uproot olive trees, and more. Yet year after year, decade after decade, the Israeli colonization of the Occupied Territories has continued and intensified, leaving the Palestinian body politic geographically and socially fragmented and Palestinian towns and villages increasingly strangled economically and socially by rings of settlements, settler-only bypass roads, and (most recently) the walls and fences of the separation barrier.[16]

In the face of Israeli military and political might (backed more or less uncritically by the United States), Palestinian struggle (be it armed or nonviolent) has recorded very limited success. Take the case of Aziz Armani from Khirbata, a village near the West Bank town of Ramallah that lost much of its farmland to the separation barrier. Armani suggested the limitations of nonviolent direct action in his description of the protest marches in front of armed bulldozers as the barrier went up. "The main thing," Armani reflected about the protests, "is that we feel we are doing something—if not for ourselves then for the coming generations. Even if we are able to get the fence moved two meters and save a few meters of our land, that will be something."[17]

From a *Realpolitik* perspective, Armani's assessment of the protests at Khirbata point to the weakness of nonviolence. A few meters of land might have been saved, but meanwhile the separation barrier went up, dispossessing thousands of farmers, cuttings thousands of people off from water, school, and medical resources, and dismembering the Palestinian body politic for years to come. To imagine that if only Armani and his fellow Palestinians had been more creative, had only exercised their nonviolent imaginations with greater vigor, the walls and fences of the separation barrier would not have been erected, strikes me as unfair. Rather, it seems more realistic to conclude that, in the face of overwhelming Israeli power and the Israeli determination to construct the barrier as a unilateral way of demarcating future boundaries and of staving off the perceived Palestinian demographic "threat," Palestinian resistance, be it armed or nonviolent, was likely to fail.

Does being sober about the limitations of nonviolent action mean abandoning a commitment to nonviolence in desperation? By no means. What it does suggest, however, is that the most important function of nonviolent action in Palestine/Israel is its role as a proleptic sign of possible future reconciliation. When Israeli Jewish peace activists joined Armani and others in Khirbata to sit in front of Israeli bulldozers clearing the way for the separation barrier, they did chalk up some concrete successes. As Armani noted, the path of the barrier might have been moved a few meters, thus saving a few meters of farmland. However, the most important aspect of such joint Palestinian-Israeli actions, to my mind, was the way they served as glimpses into a possible future of peace and reconciliation based on the solid ground of justice.

The walls, fences, and legal barriers carving up the Occupied Territories and dividing Palestinian from Israeli and Palestinian from Palestinian may last for decades, as they did in Berlin or apartheid-era South Africa. One day, however, these barriers will fall. When that happens, the experience of Palestinians and Israeli Jews struggling for justice together now will serve as a positive example for Palestinians and Israeli Jews in the future as they search for ways of living in a reconciled co-existence. This understanding of nonviolent action means that it must be viewed within a long-term framework. The temptation (one that might properly be termed Pelagian) for outside actors such as MCC and other proponents of nonviolence is to imagine that, if only people were more creative, faster solutions might be found. The challenge for outside actors and agencies is to have a commitment to long-term presence alongside Palestinians and Israelis as they work toward justice and reconciliation.

The church's mission to the world calls Christians into risky situations, into relationships and events in which words and actions will always be open to a multiplicity of interpretations. As they engage in such mission, whether they are university professors teaching undergraduate theology courses, MCC administrators, or pacifist Christians sharing their faith with a co-workers who ardently support U.S. military action, Christians quickly discover the dangers of the tongue, of communication. Learning, with God's grace, to discipline our tongues, while also being graced with the confidence to proclaim Christ's lordship, thus constitutes our dangerous missionary calling.

NOTES

1. John Howard Yoder, *The Priestly Kingdom: Social Ethics as Gospel* (Notre Dame, Ind.: University of Notre Dame, 1984), 32.

2. Reinhard Hütter, *Bound to be Free: Evangelical Catholic Engagements in Ecclesiology, Ethics, and Ecumenism* (Grand Rapids, Mich.: Wm. B. Eerdmans, 2004), 21.

3. See R. R. Reno, *In the Ruins of the Church: Sustaining Faith in an Age of Diminished Christianity* (Grand Rapids, Mich.: Brazos Press, 2002); Ephraim Radner, *The End of the Church: A Pneumatology of Christian Division in the West* (Grand Rapids, Mich.: Wm. B. Eerdmans, 1998); and *In One Body through the Cross: The Princeton Proposal for Christian Unity*, ed. Robert W. Jenson and Carl E. Braaten (Grand Rapids, Mich.: Wm. B. Eerdmans, 2003).

4. Among the many essays in which Denny Weaver has addressed the ecumenical creeds, see "Nicaea, Womanist Theology, and Anabaptist Particularity," in *Anabaptists and Postmodernity*, ed. Susan Biesecker-Mast and Gerald Biesecker-Mast (Telford, Pa.: Pandora Press U.S.; copublished with Herald Press, 2000), 251-279, and "Christology in Historical Perspective," in *Jesus Christ and the Mission of the Church: Contemporary Anabaptist Perspectives*, ed. Erland Waltner (Newton, Kan.: Faith and Life, 1990), 83-105.

5. Yoder famously asserted that the political picture of Jesus he offered in *The Politics of Jesus* was "more radically Nicene and Chalcedonian than other views."—Yoder, *The Politics of Jesus: Vicit Agnus Noster* (Grand Rapids, Mich.: Wm. B. Eerdmans, 2nd. ed., 1992), 102. Craig Carter has argued forcefully that Yoder's theology should be viewed as a deliberate, logical outworking of Nicene-Chalcedonian assumptions. See Carter, *The Politics of the Cross: The Theology and Social Ethics of John Howard Yoder* (Grand Rapids, Mich.: Brazos Press, 2001). For a more nuanced assessment of Yoder's relationship to creedal orthodoxy, see my article, "Missionary Christology: John Howard Yoder and the Creeds," *Mennonite Quarterly Review* 74/3 (July 2000): 423-39.

6. Similarly, Denny Weaver's critique of the Anselmian substitionary atonement model can be appropriated by those who wish to reject all notions of God's wrath or of Jesus Christ's unique and sufficient salvific efficacy. Again, such is clearly not the intent of Denny's work on the atonement. [See especially *The Nonviolent Atonement* (Grand Rapids, Mich.: Wm. B. Eerdmans, 2002).] My point is that by risking a critique of substitionary atonement Denny inevitably finds himself facing the possibility of his work will be appropriated by persons who do not share his own high christological affirmations.

7. For a discussion of missiological patience, see John Howard Yoder, "'Patience' as Method in Moral Reasoning: Is an Ethic of Discipleship 'Absolute?'" in *The Wisdom of the Cross: Essays in Honor of John Howard Yoder*, ed. Stanley Hauerwas, Chris K. Huebner, Harry J. Huebner, and Mark Thiessen Nation (Grand Rapids, Mich.: Wm. B. Eerdmans, 1999), 24-42.

8. For an overview of Mennonite work in the Middle East, see LeRoy Friesen, *Mennonite Witness in the Middle East: A Missiological Introduction* (Elkhart, Ind.: Mennonite Board of Missions, 1992; rev. ed. 2000).

9. Mennonite Board of Mission work with Messianic Jews, ongoing since

the early 1950s, has typically operated in partnership with other Western mission agencies.

10. One should not impose too rigid a schema on MCC work in Palestine, however. MCC was integral in providing personnel and financial support for the establishment of the Bethlehem Bible College, the leading Palestinian evangelical institution. I discuss the shifting shape of the MCC Jordan-West Bank-Palestine program in my article, "Mission and Dialogue in Palestine: A Case Study," *Criterion* 38/2 (Spring 1999): 26-34.

11. For English-language articulations of Palestinian theology, see Naim Stifan Ateek, *Justice and Only Justice: A Palestinian Theology of Liberation* (Maryknoll, N.Y.: Orbis Books, 1989) and Mitri Raheb, *I Am a Palestinian Christian* (Minneapolis: Fortress Press, 1995).

12. Prior developed his critique of colonialism in the Bible and the use of the Bible in colonialism in his study, *The Bible and Colonialism: A Moral Critique* (Sheffield: Sheffield University Press, 1997).

13. The posthumously published study by John Howard Yoder, *The Jewish-Christian Schism Revisited* (Grand Rapids, Mich.: Wm. B. Eerdmans, 2003) contains some tantalizing insights into a theology of land based on the recognition that God is the ultimate owner of the land. See also Marlin Jeschke's perceptive discussion of biblical land theologies in *Rethinking Holy Land: A Study in Salvation Geography* (Scottdale, Pa.: Herald Press, 2005) and *Under Vine and Fig Tree: Biblical Theologies of Land and the Palestinian-Israeli Conflict*, ed. Alain Epp Weaver (Telford, Pa.: Cascadia, 2007).

14. I have sought to develop a "non-supersessionist" theology of land and of the Palestinian-Israeli conflict in a variety of articles, including "John Howard Yoder's 'Alternative Perspective' on Christian-Jewish Relations," *Mennonite Quarterly Review* 79/3 (July 2005): 295-328; and "On Exile: Yoder, Said and a Theology of Land and Return," in *A Mind Patient and Untamed: Assessing John Howard Yoder's Contributions to Theology, Ethics, and Peacemaking*, ed. Gayle Gerber Koontz and Ben Ollenburger (Telford, Pa.: Cascadia, 2004), 161-186.

15. I discuss Barth's understanding of "parables of the kingdom" in my article, "Parables of the Kingdom and Religious Plurality: With Barth and Yoder towards a Nonresistant Public Theology," *Mennonite Quarterly Review* 70/3 (July 1998): 410-441.

16. The Israeli "disengagement" from settlements and military bases in the Gaza Strip and parts of the northern West Bank has not changed the overall reality in Palestine-Israel, as the disengagement process has been about solidifying Israeli colonization of the West Bank and East Jerusalem (while keeping tight control over the Gaza Strip by maintaining sole jurisdiction over the Strip's borders).

17. Quoted in Aviv Lavie, "Back to the Grassroots," *Haaretz Friday Magazine* (April 16, 2004), 7.

CHAPTER FIFTEEN

An Anabaptist Theology of Youth Ministry

Randy Keeler

"*I* don't like theology." Students in my practical theology courses on youth ministry, Christian education, and spiritual disciplines consistently make such comments. What my students are trying to express is that they do not like having historical analysis put their minds in a whirlwind as they seek to make sense of complicated subjects such as patristic and medieval dialogues about particular doctrines, such as the doctrine of the atonement. The young men and women do not always concur when I tell them that they must learn to appreciate theology because every action in their lives either reflects an act of theological reflection or a failure to apply faith to life experience. Whether they realize it or not, I stress to them, they do theology every waking moment of their lives by implementing or not implementing what they believe about God in their lives lived with God.

Any person who undertakes the task of ministry must be attentive to the discipline of theology, particularly how theology relates to specific ministerial tasks like youth ministry. Pete Ward, for example, correctly observes that "A theology of youth ministry . . . seeks to demonstrate how our understanding of God shapes and influences the practice of youth ministry."[1] Students and practitioners of youth ministry must be attentive to theology to be true to the gospel proclamation of Jesus Christ. Recent works by youth ministry veterans affirm the need for more serious theological reflection among the ranks of youth ministry practitioners.[2]

Most youth ministry is practiced by individuals with little to no theological training; even if youth ministers have theological training, they often feel so overwhelmed by organizing one activity after another that they do not feel like they have adequate time to think theologically about why they do what they do in ministry. Even if youth ministers had the time for some serious theological reflection, would they then have the time and energy to integrate with integrity that theology into their youth ministry? Ministers, of course, will always feel the pressure of time constraints. I contend, however, that youth workers must take the time to think theologically about why they believe what they believe and then have that theology shape their ongoing ministry practice. Time for theological reflection should not be viewed as an optional supplement to youth ministry; it must be built into the youth minister's weekly routine.

Youth workers may be surprised to hear me urge them to read the work of J. Denny Weaver on atonement theology as they reflect on their ministries theologically. They would likely respond that Weaver did not have youth ministry in mind when he wrote books like *The Nonviolent Atonement*.[3] Has Weaver practiced youth ministry or ever even thought of how his theology would impact the congregational youth ministry in a given location, they might ask?

Weaver obviously is not a youth ministry practitioner, but his view of atonement, I contend, raises serious questions that those in youth ministry need to consider. Does the view of Jesus we present to the youth with whom we work remain consistent with our Anabaptist convictions? Is there a particular Anabaptist approach to inviting young people to follow Jesus that qualitatively differs from the approach of the youth ministry down the street? When we invite young people to a saving knowledge of Jesus Christ, what does that mean and what does it look like practically? Does the way we invite youth to a life with Christ influence their subsequent life of discipleship?

How we invite youth to experience salvation through Jesus Christ, I would argue, is profoundly shaped by our theological perspectives on what being a Christian means. Even the way the invitation to faith is offered affects the life of discipleship. Is the act of following Jesus propositional or is it relational? Is choosing to be a Christian assenting to certain beliefs about Jesus, or is it instead choosing to walk the path that Jesus walked?

ANABAPTIST-MENNONITE THEOLOGICAL CONSIDERATIONS

Some Christian youth workers have made concerted efforts to articulate a theology of youth ministry, but these efforts have often been fairly generic, providing minimal guidance for developing a specifically Mennonite theology of youth ministry. For example, in a recent issue of *Youthworker Journal*, Kenda Creasy Dean proposes to set out a "practical theology" of youth ministry, with "practical theology" understood as the study of "that messy arena of human action, where our practices embody our deepest convictions about God."[4]

The deepest convictions she identifies, however, do not touch on Mennonite concerns about nonviolence. *Youthworker Journal* has a wide ecumenical readership; one wonders how possible it would be in that context to articulate with passion one's deepest convictions. How free, for instance, would someone be to state that the deepest convictions one holds for a theology of youth ministry must include the rejection of violence? Such an assertion would likely generate numerous letters to the editor from military veterans who themselves currently serve in full-time youth ministry positions. Another way of posing the question about theological influences from outside the Anabaptist tradition on youth ministry would be to join Bob Yoder in asking, "will the 'how-to' practical books published by non-denominational businesses such as Youth Specialties and Group continue to theologically influence our adult leaders?"[5] Have our adult leaders been theologically trained to discern between Anabaptist and other theological traditions? I would suggest that the answer is no, because an Anabaptist theology of youth ministry has never been adequately defined or articulated.

Many involved in Mennonite youth ministries have hungered for both theological and practical help in their work. They have digested non-Mennonite resources, failing to develop an approach to youth ministry emerging from the theological roots of Anabaptism. I am not the first, of course, to express concern that Anabaptist theology has not sufficiently shaped contemporary Mennonite engagements in the growing field of youth ministry.[6] Lavon Welty, for example, in his 1988 manual, *Blueprint For Congregational Youth Ministry*, worried about Mennonite failure to think about youth ministry from a distinctly Mennonite perspective. His study, a project of the Integrated Congregational Youth Ministry Council (a group of youth workers from the Church of the Brethren, General Conference Mennonite Church, and the Mennonite Church) sought to fill this gap, "to develop a broad framework for youth ministry in congregations that have a particular understanding of faith, that of a 'believers church' perspective."[7]

Youth ministry from an Anabaptist perspective, Welty claims, should be congregationally focused. Welty proceeds to advance a conceptual model for youth ministry closely aligned with the inclusive-congregational approach advocated by Malan Nel.[8] Often youth ministry only happens in the context of what is called "youth group," a dynamic that can lead to the development of a "parallel congregation,"[9] or what Kenda Creasy Dean describes as a "one-eared Mickey Mouse" approach to youth ministry, one in which the congregational ministries and the youth ministry are clearly separate entities, and at best only marginally connected. Dean clearly captures the unhealthy dynamic that develops: "the congregation gathered on Sunday mornings; youth gathered on Sunday nights. The congregation listened to sermons; youth heard 'youthtalks.' The congregation had Bible study; youth had devotions. The congregation had a budget; youth had a bake sale."[10]

Welty suggests an alternative paradigm for congregational youth ministry, one that maximizes interaction between adults and youth. Welty envisions a congregational youth ministry in which the congregation is "the primary context for youth to discover their identity as persons created in God's image who are called to be unique expressions of God's love in the world."[11] In this model youth are included in congregational life, and the congregation develops a consortium of adult mentors for youth across a broad intergenerational spectrum to help them discover their identity as Christians. In Welty's model, youth and adults interact in seven intentional settings (worship, family life, Sunday school, youth group, catechism, mentoring relationships, and peer ministries), settings in which youth and adult together grow as Christians.

The intentional search for community as a key component necessary in adolescent development is one that also intersects with a key theological tenet of Anabaptism. But is "community" the only key tenet of Anabaptism? When a youth is invited to become a believer in Jesus Christ, is the main component of that invitation only to join a community of believers? What other theological components for an invitation to salvation are necessary for a holistic Anabaptist understanding?

I would argue that discipleship and the rejection of violence must be vital parts of ministry with youth. Welty's paradigm of youth ministry rightly centers on community, but a clear and central emphasis on discipleship and the rejection of violence must be present in a youth ministry paradigm to make it distinctively Anabaptist. A youth ministry growing out of the Anabaptist heritage will be missional, inviting others to walk with Jesus as a disciple, to join the community of faith, and to participate in the nonviolent reign of God on this earth. Keeping discipleship and nonviolence central in our thinking will help us evaluate youth ministry models prevalent in our communities. I turn now to a critical consideration of one particular youth ministry paradigm that has influenced many Mennonite churches, that of Youth for Christ (YFC).

A CRITIQUE OF A CONTEMPORARY PARADIGM

Youth For Christ (YFC) operates a popular North American ministry with youth. In my community in northwest Ohio, the YFC area chapter has a meeting place and office right across from the high school. Youth have easy access to its facilities after school in the afternoons and evenings. YFC has been effective in our community in establishing relationships with youth and encouraging them in their faith in Christ. My own three sons have been and are currently active as participants in the ministry of YFC. In my congregation, as in other Mennonite congregations, YFC has been influential.

One can trace the beginnings of the YFC movement to a series of youth rallies held throughout the United States in the 1940s, during and shortly after World War II. These rallies had different names in different geographic locations: Singspiration (Kansas City), Victory Rally (San Diego), Voice of Christian Youth (Detroit), Word of Life (New York), Jubilee (Los Angeles), and Youth For Christ (Indianapolis).[12] By the end of World War II, hundreds of weekly youth rallies across the country attracted hundreds of thousands of people. Soldiers and sailors organized similar rallies across Europe, the Pacific, and East Asia. Jack Wyrtzen, a young evangelist, who headed up the Word of Life organization in New York, emerged as a leading personality of this movement.[13] Wyrtzen used the slogan, "Youth For Christ," for the rallies he held in New York Times Square in 1940. He was not the first to use that slogan for these nation-wide rallies, but he was perhaps the first to popularize it as a trademark slogan of the movement.[14]

The YFC movement officially organized as a result of a meeting held at Winona Bible Conference at Winona Lake, Indiana, in 1944. By 1945, YFC International had officially formed, with Torrey Johnson elected as its first president. By 1949, Jack Hamilton in Kansas City became the first full-time Bible Club staff member of YFC after he challenged the YFC organization to participate in high school campus ministry. His efforts to spread YFC's high school program to cities around the U.S. resulted in the establishment of 3,600 clubs within a few short years.[15]

Identifying exactly when Mennonites became involved in YFC is difficult, but some indications exist that Mennonites early on participated in the movement first through the rallies and then through the community club program, later called Campus Life. In the 1940s and 1950s, the place for many young Christians, particularly young evangelical Christians, to be on a Saturday night was at the large youth rallies held in urban centers.[16] A group of youth from the Deep Run Mennonite Church East of Bedminster, Pennsylvania, attended a "Word of Life Youth Rally" in Philadelphia in 1961, led by Jack Wyrtzen.[17] There is little reason to imagine that they were alone among Mennonite youth participating in YFC rallies.

Willie Yoder of the Bethel Mennonite Church, West Liberty, Ohio, took leadership roles in the area's local YFC organization. Willie began his work with YFC by accepting a position on the youth rally board. An early part of his ministry included coaching Bible quiz teams sponsored by YFC, with his 1961 quiz team taking sixth in the nation. By 1983 Campus Life chapters had opened at five area high schools thanks in large measure to Yoder's efforts, and Yoder aimed to start a Campus Life chapter in each of the remaining high schools of Logan and Champaign counties. The Bethel congregation evinces a fair amount of pride that one of its members played such a prominent role in this community youth ministry.[18]

Undeniably, the YFC movement has had a far-reaching impact within the North American Christian youth culture. The Mennonite church has not been exempt from the impact of YFC's ministry. We must ask, however, whether or not the YFC ministry vision is compatible with the Anabaptist vision of faith.

On the face of it, the YFC vision statement has broad ecumenical appeal: "As a part of the body of Christ, our vision is to see every young person in every people group in every nation have the opportunity to make an informed decision to be a follower of Jesus Christ and become a part of a local church."[19] Certainly Anabaptist Christians can affirm many elements of this vision. The goal of seeing every youth become a part of a local church also resonates strongly with the community dimension of the Anabaptist vision. The emphasis on making a decision to be a follower is language compatible with discipleship. The use of the word *follower*, rather than *believer*, is perhaps intentional as a way of saying that it is expected that there will be evidence in youth of a changed life focused on the resurrected Christ. But what kind of follower of Jesus is YFC trying to mold and shape?

Jon Pahl's critique of the YFC movement is compelling. Pahl notes that one searches in vain for anything critical of American culture in early YFC publications. YFC, to be sure, critiqued individual moral standards like premarital sex, and alcohol and drug use, but did not launch a broader social critique. "Youth for Christ leaders found plenty of ways for individual youths to ruin their lives," Pahl observes, "but saving them was simple: accept Jesus as an individual, and accept American social norms and national policies."[20] There was a concern for "moral fitness" and a desire to revive American civic faith, and the answer that YFC gave was a "personal faith in Christ, tied to devotion to the Allied cause and to world evangelization."[21] YFC leaders were troubled that so many young military men had indulged in a party life filled with alcohol and sexual encounters during their years of service but were not concerned that these same men also killed other human beings. Rejection of violence did not constitute part of YFC's understanding of discipleship.

That YFC's youth ministry in its inception accommodated (and today accommodates) military service, and has been from its beginnings relatively uncritical of American culture means that it will stand in an uneasy relationship with an authentically Anabaptist vision of youth ministry. Does this tension with Anabaptist theology mean that Mennonites should refuse to participate in YFC? Discernment is obviously demanded before any congregation or individual embarks on any particular ministry. The strong militaristic overtones are not as evident in YFC's ministry today as they were after WWII, but a whole generation of youth has been affected by the civil religion and national pride promoted by the youth rallies of the 1940s and 1950s. No doubt YFC ministries have strengthened the faith and piety of many Mennonite youth. Yet one wonders if concerned Mennonites raised their voices during the 1940s and 1950s about how involvement in YFC might affect Mennonite youth in their understanding of Jesus' call to nonviolence. Are we concerned today about our youth participating in youth ministries that might not share Mennonite peace convictions?

INVITATION TO WHAT?

My first summer after college, I served as counselor and recreation director at a Mennonite summer camp. During the two weeks of staff orientation we received training in numerous facets of the camping program, one of which was how to lead a child to Christ. Trainers gave staff members a number of models to help us in this task, one of which was the Four Spiritual Laws written by Bill Bright of Campus Crusade for Christ. In the training leaders told us that if we led the campers through these four spiritual laws by explaining each of them by way of their scriptural references, then invited the campers to own the laws for themselves, they would be "saved" and be "Christians." I remember after leading a camper through these laws, he responded, "Is that it? Is that all I have to do to be a Christian?" My answer, as I understood it at that point, was, "Yes." "I don't feel any different," the camper rejoined.

The "Four Spiritual Laws," as articulated by Bright, proclaim:

> God LOVES you, and offers a wonderful PLAN for your life. (John 3:16; 0:10)
> Man is SINFUL and SEPARATED from God. Therefore, he cannot know and experience God's love and plan for his life. (Rom. 3:23; 6:23)
> Jesus Christ is God's ONLY provision for Man's sin. Through Him you can know and experience God's love and plan for your life. (Rom. 5:8; 1 Corinthians 15:3-6)
> We must individually RECEIVE Jesus Christ as Savior and Lord; then we can know and experience God's love and plan for our lives. (John 1:12; Ephesians 2:8-9; John 3:1-8)[22]

In Bright's framework, faith in Christ involves affirming particular propositions. If you assent to certain beliefs about Jesus, then you are considered a follower of Jesus. No wonder, then, that the camper asked me, "Is that it?" Nothing within these laws assumes an ethical dimension of faith, or that a life of discipleship within the context of community emerges as a natural consequence of faith. As Nelson Kraybill remarks in his critique of the Four Spiritual Laws, "... in light of Anabaptist convictions and early church witness, the Four Spiritual Laws omit essential parts of salvation. They place too much emphasis on the individual, as if salvation is a personal and private transaction apart from God's plan to redeem all of creation."[23]

For an Anabaptist youth ministry paradigm, following the nonviolent Jesus will be central. To support such ministry, we need to draw on efforts in recent years to articulate a Christology that takes into account the ethical dimension of following Jesus. The early Anabaptists spent more time reflecting on the ethical dimension of following the risen Christ than trying to develop a systematic theological paradigm for understanding the atonement. Their lifestyles and ethical stances are what set them apart from the rest of Christendom. The early Anabaptists may have been "orthodox" in one sense, holding creeds such as the Apostles' Creed as part of the tradition, but they did not give the creeds any final authority. As John Howard Yoder has stated, "They gave no special importance to the fact that the church had made decisions about phrasing in the fourth or fifth century. . . . the creeds are helpful as fences, but affirming, believing, debating for, and fighting for the creeds are probably things on which a radical Anabaptist faith would not concentrate."[24]

While it may be true that the early Anabaptists used language similar to the early creeds from the first centuries of the church, and may have even quoted from them during times of persecution, some recent Mennonite theologians have found that the creedal language is inadequate for taking the ethics of Jesus seriously for living a life of consequence in the world. "The various forms of the apostles' Creed," argues Gareth Brandt, "go directly from 'born of the virgin Mary' to 'suffered under Pontius Pilate.' There is no mention of the life and teachings of Christ nor of the exemplary and ethical dimension of his death."[25]

An Anabaptist youth ministry model will also stand in tension with the substitutionary model of the atonement as developed by Anselm of Canterbury. As Denny Weaver explains, this view of the atonement assumes that "a debt payment was necessary to restore God's honor or to restore justice in the universe. Since humankind owed the debt and could not pay it, Jesus paid the debt by dying in their place."[26] Taken by itself, this understanding of the work of Christ does not provide adequate ethical direction for the believer. Salvation becomes an event by which we Christians are passive bystanders observing all that God is doing with no accountability on our part to live a life of ethical discipleship.

Bill Hull, in his study, *The Disciple-Making Pastor*, illustrates well the dangers of operating solely with a substitutionary model of the atonement. Hull makes a clear distinction between Christians and disciples.[27] The role of the pastor is to encourage Christians in the church to take the next step in their faith by becoming disciples of Jesus. By making this distinction, Hull assumes that salvation has no ethical dimension; salvation comes first, through an acknowledgment of Jesus' payment of our debt to the Father; ethics and discipleship are secondary. An Anabaptist understanding of the atonement, in contrast, would insist that salvation cannot be reduced to a verbal assent to Jesus' lordship; rather, salvation is holistic, including a life lived in accordance with the reign of God. The kingdom of God is among us because God's people live out that kingdom ethic in the here and now.

J. Nelson Kraybill has articulated what an invitation to faith involves when ethical considerations are given prominence in his "Four Spiritual Truths of a Peacemaking God." Kraybill suggests that communicating with an individual considering faith in Jesus should involve describing what one does when one becomes a follower of Jesus. Kraybill's four truths describe a faith relationship with Jesus and of a life of discipleship; they are less propositional in character than the "Four Spiritual Laws."

> (1) A God of love made you and me in his image as a good part of creation. God wants us to live at peace with our Maker, our world and one another.
>
> (2) Sin destroys harmony in creation when we try to run our own lives apart from God. Suffering, greed, violence and broken relationships result.
>
> (3) Jesus died on the cross because he confronted the powers of sin that fracture our world. Jesus healed the sick, forgave enemies and lived in the joy of the kingdom of God.
>
> (4) You can have a new beginning by the same power that raised Jesus from the dead. God forgives when we confess our sin, and the Spirit of God enables us to follow Jesus in all of life.[28]

Bright's "Four Spiritual Laws" are individually focused, inviting the believer to consider what God has done for them through Jesus dying on the cross. Kraybill's "Four Spiritual Truths," in contrast, are more community-focused, inviting us to be involved in the world the way God is involved in the world with the rest of God's people. The former are more inward-looking. The latter focus our attention outward to service in God's good creation.

The narrative Christus Victor model of the atonement developed by Denny Weaver meshes well, I believe, with Kraybill's Four Spiritual Truths. According to Weaver's atonement model, we experience salvation when we join with God in establishing the rule of God on earth:

In narrative Christus Victor, individuals as well as the world are saved, although we still await the culmination of that salvation in the eschaton. In the intermediate time, Christians participate in that salvation when they accept God's call and are transformed from creatures aligned with evil to those who become co-laborers with Jesus in making God's rule present and visible on earth.[29]

The Scriptures tell the story of God redeeming the world through the people of Israel, through Jesus, then through the church. Inviting others to faith in Jesus is not seeking their acceptance of certain propositions about who Jesus is or what the nature of their relationship with him is, but rather consists of an invitation to walk with Jesus in life by joining a committed community of followers who seek to live out the reign of God on this earth. We are invited to make the story of God our story, to join with God as God continues to redeem the world.

YOUTH MINISTRY IN A POSTMODERN CULTURE

Postmoderns, argues Leonard Sweet, value experience. "Postmoderns," he asserts, "are not willing to live at even an arms'-length distance from experience. They want life to explode all around them."[30] Moderns want their information straight and quantifiable, but postmoderns want to receive their information through experience, the more extreme the better. Postmoderns enjoy accumulating experiences and will sacrifice most things for it. The burgeoning tourism industry reflects the need and desire for experience. The rise of reality television shows is another demonstration of the increasing infatuation with what is perceived to be "real-life" experience.

The desire for experience is not in itself bad. Christian educators like Thomas Groome have long advocated for experience-based education.[31] Postmoderns desire to be participants because they want to have a role in the story of life. They understand a given story best when they see where they fit in that story. In his critique of the "Four Spiritual Laws," Brad Kallenberg suggests that presenting Christian faith as particular principles to which one should adhere involves a modern misunderstanding of how language works, a misunderstanding that has caused frustration for those who have tried to use them in evangelistic settings. It has "produced despair among kingdom workers when presentations of the four laws appear to be losing effectiveness as they fall on the ears of a culture that has grown increasingly deaf to biblical propositions."[32]

Employing storytelling in evangelism, in contrast, invites others into the kingdom by giving them opportunities for first-hand engagement in the life of the community as it lives out the reign of God on earth. Such an invitation assumes there is a community worth getting involved in. The zeal and excitement of those sharing the gospel message must not be "limited to simple proclamation of the message; it must be broadened to include a passion for increasing the health of the community into which would-be converts will be invited."[33]

Weaver's narrative Christus Victor understanding of the work of Jesus in the world fits well, I suggest, with this type of narrative-based, postmodern evangelism. Inviting youth to give their "lives" to something, and not just their metaphorical "hearts," gives them something to stir their imagination as to how they can become part of something that makes a difference in the world. Instead of inviting youth into an individualistic relationship with Jesus with no communal embodiment, we must begin to see our inviting others to faith as "a zeal for forming communities capable of embodying the story of Jesus."[34]

A while back I had a conversation with a college student trying to explain to me why he was not going to major in youth ministry. He had recently had a conversation with one of his friends who had not attended college yet was very active in his congregation's youth ministry. The student deduced from this encounter that a college degree or advanced theological study was not necessary for doing youth ministry. This conversation drove home for me the reality that a very shallow understanding of youth ministry still exists in our church culture. Unfortunately, youth ministry is viewed by many as merely keeping our youth busy in "Christian activity" so they are not as tempted by immoral vices. Had this student ever gotten to the point that he would have sat in on one of our youth ministry courses on campus, he also would have likely begun asking, "Why is all this theology so important?"

To be involved in youth ministry at a level where serious theological reflection supports the very foundation of the ministry, extensive study is necessary and vital. Thorough preparatory and ongoing theological study by those in youth ministry is necessary because we want to be true to who we are called to be as believers in Jesus Christ. We do not want to water down the gospel to a merely propositional assent, but we desire to "make disciples" as Matthew 28:19-20 calls us to do. If we are true to what we believe about "making disciples," then we will be intentional about the nature of the communities of faith that we are forming, the method and definition of discipleship, and the rejection of violence. These three foci of our faith will then be integral to the missional task of inviting others to join in what God is doing in our world and of joining in the reign of God on this earth.

NOTES

1. Pete Ward, *God At the Mall* (Peabody, Mass.: Hendrickson, 1997), 33.

2. Recent works by Dean Borgman, *When Kumbayah Is Not Enough: A Practical Theology of Youth Ministry* (Peabody, Mass.: Hendrickson, 1997) and Kenda Creasy Dean, Chap Clark, and Dave Rahn, *Starting Right: Thinking Theologically About Youth Ministry* (Grand Rapids, Mich.: Zondervan, 2001), are leading examples of attempts to get youth ministry practitioners to think more about the theology that motivates their work.

3. J. Denny Weaver, *The Nonviolent Atonement* (Grand Rapids, Mich.: Wm. B. Eerdmans, 2001).

4. Kenda Creasy Dean, "Getting Out of God's Way: Freeing Our Inner Theologian," *Youthworker Journal* 21/3 (Jan./Feb. 2005): 32.

5. Bob Yoder, "A Historical Review of Mennonite Youth Ministry in the Past 120 Years," unpublished term paper (Western Theological Seminary, May 6, 2005), 29.

6. See, for example, Gareth Brandt, "A Radical Christology for a Radical Youth Ministry," *Direction* 31/1 (Spring, 2002): 26.

7. Lavon Welty, *Blueprint For Congregational Youth Ministry* (Newton, Kan.: Faith and Life Press, 1988), iii.

8. Malan Nel, "The Inclusive Congregational Approach to Youth Ministry," in *Four Views of Youth Ministry and the Church*, ed. by Mark H. Senter, III (Grand Rapids, Mich.: Zondervan Publishing, 2001), 2-22.

9. Welty, *Blueprint*, 2.

10. Kenda Creasy Dean and Ron Foster, *The Godbearing Life* (Nashville, Tenn.: Upper Room Books, 1998), 30.

11. Welty, *Blueprint*, 65.

12. *Operations Manual*, 4th. ed. (Denver: Youth For Christ, rev. May 1997), 2.

13. Joel A. Carpenter, *Revive Us Again: The Reawakening of American Fundamentalism* (New York: Oxford University Press, 1997), 161.

14. Mark H. Senter, III, *The Coming Revolution in Youth Ministry* (Wheaton, Ill.: Victor Books, 1992), 110-111.

15. *Operations Manual*, 2-3.

16. Ibid., 2.

17. Timothy Rice, *Deep Run Mennonite Church East: A 250-Year Pilgrimage, 1746-1996* (Morgantown, Pa.: Masthof Press, 1996), 108.

18. James O. Lehman, *Uncommon Threads: A Centennial History of Bethel Mennonite Church* (West Liberty, Oh.: Bethel Mennonite Church, 1990), 189.

19. *Operations Manual*, 6.

20. Jon Pahl, *Youth Ministry in Modern America: 1930 to the Present* (Peabody, Mass.: Hendrickson, 2000), 64-65.

21. Carpenter, *Revive Us Again*, 168.
22. Available at www.crusade.org/fourlaws/law4.html. Viewed June 8, 2005.
23. J. Nelson Kraybill, "Four Spiritual Truths of a Peacemaking God," *The Mennonite* (Nov. 4, 2003), 10.
24. John Howard Yoder, *Preface to Theology* (Grand Rapids, Mich.: Brazos Press, 2002), 222-223.
25. Brandt, 28.
26. J. Denny Weaver, *The Nonviolent Atonement*, 16.
27. Bill Hull, *The Disciple-Making Pastor* (Grand Rapids, Mich.: Baker Book House, 1988), 31.
28. Kraybill, 11.
29. Weaver, 227.
30. Leonard Sweet, *Postmodern Pilgrims* (Nashville, Tenn.: Broadman & Holman Publishers, 2000), 28.
31. Thomas Groome, *Christian Religious Education* (San Francisco: HarperCollins, 1980).
32. Brad J. Kallenberg, *Live To Tell: Evangelism for a Postmodern Age* (Grand Rapids, Mich.: Brazos Press, 2002), 115.
33. Ibid., 118.
34. Ibid., 126.

CHAPTER SIXTEEN

Hanging up Our Harps, Taking up Our Harps: Worship in the "Already, Yet Not Yet" Church

Janeen Bertsche Johnson

As a religion major at Bluffton College in the 1980s, I took all but one of the courses that J. Denny Weaver offered. In most of those nine theology, history, and ethics courses, Denny started with the same lecture. He began with the end—a theology of eschatology. Denny proposed that what we believe about the end times shapes everything else in our belief system.

Over twenty years later, I can still remember Denny's opening lecture. Denny's insistence that God's kingdom has already come in Jesus but is not yet fully revealed articulated the theology I had come to know but had never explicitly named. God's kingdom is not just for the future—some long-awaited "pie in the sky." It is a present reality, inaugurated by Jesus, and we are invited to live in kingdom ways now. We do not yet see, however, God's kingdom in its final, complete expression. The book of Revelation affirms that Jesus has already won the crucial battle over the powers of evil, but Jesus' followers wait in an unfaithful world until all things are put under Jesus' feet (1 Cor. 15:25-27).

The church lives in the in-between time, experiencing not only the ongoing reality of evil and death in our world but also the victory of Jesus over evil and death. We live in the tension between being exiles and citizens. We are foreigners, resident aliens, in the nations of our birth. These nations, however loved, can never be our true home, and thus can never be our ultimate loyalty. For when we are baptized into Jesus' church, we are reborn, with a new citizenship in God's kingdom.

This theology of the "already, yet not yet" kingdom should have a deep impact on the worship life of the church. Our worship must proclaim the hope and joy of Christ's victory over evil, yet also the reality of sin, death, and pain which we still face in our daily lives in this in-between time. I suggest that Psalm 137 and the worship texts of Revelation describe these two poles of our experience and offer models for our worship life in the church.

HANGING UP OUR HARPS

Psalm 137 expresses the lament of the people of Judah, after the city of Jerusalem and its temple had been destroyed in 586 BCE by the Babylonians, and the Jews were now living in exile:

> By the rivers of Babylon—
> there we sat down and there we wept when we remembered
>   Zion.
> On the willows there we hung up our harps.
> For there our captors asked us for songs,
> and our tormentors asked for mirth, saying,
> "Sing us one of the songs of Zion!"
> How could we sing the Lord's song in a foreign land?
> If I forget you, O Jerusalem, let my right hand wither!
> Let my tongue cling to the roof of my mouth, if I do not
>   remember you,
> if I do not set Jerusalem above my highest joy.
> Remember, O Lord, against the Edomites the day of
>   Jerusalem's fall,
> how they said, "Tear it down! Tear it down! Down to its foundations!"
> O daughter Babylon, you devastator!
> Happy shall they be who pay you back what you have done
>   to us!

> Happy shall they be who take your little ones and dash them against the rock!

The poignancy of this text is palpable. We are transported to the banks of the Tigris and Euphrates rivers, and we observe the exiled Jews weeping there, as devastated spiritually as their beloved city and temple had been physically.

This was not, however, just a lament for the loss of buildings. The Israelites believed that God had resided among them in the ark of the covenant, in the Jerusalem temple. With the destruction of the temple, where was God? What was left of faith?

The Babylonians knew the Jews were facing a spiritual crisis in their captivity, and they taunted the Jews by asking them to sing their songs of faith. Psalm 137 expresses the response of the exiles. Perhaps in defiance, perhaps in defeat, they hung their harps in the trees, and refused to sing the glad songs of their faith for their tormentors. But perhaps they sang instead the words of lament and rage of this psalm, pretending to honor their captors' demand while (in a foreign language) actually engaging in an act of resistance.

There is much in this psalm that disturbs us: the brutal desire for revenge against the Babylonians, the seeming loss of faith in God. Yet, there is also something in this lament with which we resonate. We have a sense of the uneasiness of living in a land that is not our true home, among people who sometimes scorn our faith. We know what it is like to be surrounded by a culture whose values are foreign to us, constantly tempting us to assimilate. Psalm 137 expresses in the most extreme way the "not yet" of our experience as the people of God. It names the realities we still face in our lives: evil and exile, loss and longing.

TAKING UP OUR HARPS

Woven throughout the worship texts of the book of Revelation are several references to the saints of God taking up their harps:

> When [the Lamb] had taken the scroll, the four living creatures and the twenty-four elders fell before the Lamb, *each holding a harp* and golden bowls full of incense, which are the prayers of the saints. They sing a new song: "You are worthy to take the scroll and to open its seals, for you were slaughtered and by your blood you ransomed for God saints from every tribe and language and people and nation; you have made them to be a king-

dom and priests serving our God, and they will reign on earth." (Rev. 5:8-10, emph. added)

And I heard a voice from heaven like the sound of many waters and like the sound of loud thunder; the voice I heard was like the sound of harpists *playing on their harps*, and [the 144,000] sing a new song before the throne and before the four living creatures and before the elders. (Rev. 14:2-3, emph. added)

And I saw what appeared to be a sea of glass mixed with fire, and those who had conquered the beast and its image and the number of its name, standing beside the sea of glass *with harps of God in their hands*. And they sing the song of Moses, the servant of God, and the song of the Lamb: "Great and amazing are your deeds, Lord God the Almighty! Just and true are your ways, King of the nations! Lord, who will not fear and glorify your name? For you alone are holy. All nations will come and worship before you, for your judgments have been revealed." (Rev. 15:2-4, emph. added)

The harps are first taken up by the twenty-four elders, then by the 144,000 who had been redeemed, then finally by all who have conquered the beast.

What is the significance of the harps? It is clear from the symbols John chooses (Rev. 17:9) that he identifies the beast as Rome, the seat of power that has been persecuting the Christians. In the text of Revelation, however, he names the beast as Babylon. In doing so, he not only avoids naming Rome directly (to avoid further persecution), but he also reminds the Christians of their connection to the Jewish people who lived in exile in the hated Babylon. In describing the fall of Babylon (Rome) in Revelation 16-19, John is declaring that the Lamb (Jesus) has won the victory over the forces of evil which killed him and are now persecuting his followers. Those who have stood firm in their faith, who have refused to worship the beast, and who have faced persecution because of their faithfulness now take up the harp in celebration of Jesus' victory, and they sing the songs of God's triumph over evil and death. John's description of the taking up of the harps functions as a reversal of Psalm 137.

These texts from Revelation anticipate the fulfillment of the kingdom of God, when the victory of Jesus is brought to completion and the people of God no longer live as exiles in the world, but gather around the throne of God in their true homeland. The message of

Revelation, however, is not just a promise for a future day. It is also encouragement to those still living as resident aliens in any Babylon that demands their loyalty and worship today. All who take up the harp in praise of God's victory proclaim that Christ has already defeated the powers that try to make us captive to sin and death.

WORSHIP IN THE "ALREADY, YET NOT YET" CHURCH

Psalm 137 and Revelation 15:2-4 express the exile and victory which Christians experience, and offer models for our worship in the "already, yet not yet" kingdom of God. Christian worship can provide both a place of lament and a place of eschatological hope.

Lament is an essential element of worship, because it allows us to acknowledge our experiences of exile and captivity. We "hang up our harps" when we confess that sometimes God seems distant or absent, and yet vow not to forget God's presence with us in the past. We hang up our harps when we name the ways we are held captive to sin in our lives. We hang up our harps when we acknowledge that our culture tempts us to worship the idols of power and wealth and scorns our allegiance to the Prince of Peace. We hang up our harps when we enter into intercessory prayer on behalf of those who do not experience the shalom God intends. We hang up our harps when we call on God to hear our rage at all that is wrong in this world and to set things right again.

Our worship must also express our eschatological hope. We "take up our harps" when we retell the story of God's mighty acts throughout history to redeem God's people. We take up our harps when we proclaim that Christ, in his life, death, and resurrection, has won the battle against sin and death and is Lord of all. We take up our harps when we claim Christ's resurrection power against all the powers which threaten us now. We take up our harps when we name our allegiance to God, when we "set Jerusalem above our highest joy" (Psalm 137:6). We take up our harps when we encourage one another to "come out of Babylon" and not participate in her sins (Rev. 18:4), but also when we "seek the welfare of the city" of our exile and pray to God on its behalf (Jer. 29:7). We take up our harps when we remind each other what it means to live in the kingdom which is already here. We take up our harps when we rejoice together over the signs of God's kingdom becoming evident in our lives and our world. We take up our harps when we affirm, even in the face of death, that one day we will live in the presence of God, and that death, mourning, crying, and pain will be no more (Rev. 21:4). We take up our harps and we sing:

> Blessing and honor and glory and pow'r, wisdom and riches and strength evermore,
> offer to Christ who our battle has won, whose are the kingdom, the crown, and the throne.
> Give we the glory and praise to the Lamb! Take we the robe and the harp and the palm.
> Sing we the song of the Lamb who was slain, dying in weakness but rising to reign.[1]

NOTE

1. Text by Horatius Bonar, 1866, alt, #108 in *Hymnal: A Worship Book* (Scottdale, Pa.: Herald Press, 1992).

Part 6

THE WORK OF JESUS IN THE WORLD

CHAPTER SEVENTEEN

The Gift of Creation and Interpretation

Trevor George Hunsberger Bechtel

A certain sense of mystery accompanied my first college class with J. Denny Weaver. Denny had come north to Canadian Mennonite Bible College to teach on a sabbatical from his home institution, Bluffton College. Why, I wondered, is this Mennonite interested in understanding the atonement? And why is he convinced that the language of Christus Victor is appropriate for discussing the atonement? After all, the atonement is the most violent moment in the Christian story, and the interpretation offered by Christus Victor makes the story about winning and losing, something that deep in my Mennonite bones seemed problematic. Was this the impact living in the United States had on someone? Was he just wrong?

    I came to appreciate his approach to Anabaptist theology and the importance of a Mennonite attempting to theologize in an area that had not received satisfactory attention from within our tradition. I invited him to my regular lunch of Kraft Dinner one day to press him on a side concern surfaced by his course on the atonement. Just what was Jesus doing during those three days from crucifixion to resurrection? Were these the days that Jesus battled Satan in hell?

    A bit more than a decade after being Denny's student, I became his colleague at what is now Bluffton University. I have learned more about what it means to live in the United States. I also now know that in the United States people dine on Kraft "Macaroni and Cheese Dinner," and that that my lunch hour questions were malformed. I should have asked Denny what the nature of God and God's good creation were so that an account of atonement was necessary, and about what possibilities existed for rendering that account nonviolent. I realize now that I should have asked Denny, "Is God nonviolent?"

To honor my teacher, colleague, and friend, I propose in this essay to suggest a way forward on this last question, the question of God's nonviolence. It is very much my way forward, one that does not directly engage Denny's work on the atonement, salvation, or peace. It is, however, representative of the kind of theology which has grown up and flourished at Bluffton during Weaver's tenure—a theology which works with tradition in a light, edgy, perhaps even heterodox way, producing new visions that can serve the church.

I will not address the question of God's nonviolence directly; rather I will explore two conditions of possibility for God's nonviolence—creation and interpretation. I offer here a reading of creation and interpretation that links the two together and links them both to the way in which the nature of God is revealed in how God shows Godself to creation. Finally, I show how this approach to creation and interpretation works its way out in the Anabaptist trope, "The Gospel of All Creatures."

I choose creation and interpretation because both are often assumed to be sites of natural violence. The created order, in some accounts, is at its root violent: Nature shows us this in the paradigm of the ecosystem. The need for interpretation, others contend, results from unavoidable violence in the structure of speech which assumes a viewpoint which does damage to the other and creates further violence in the plurality of possible interpretations, itself a cause of violent disagreement. My account grounds creation and interpretation in God's embodied self-revelation. Throughout I assume that God's self-revelation continually undercuts the possibility of violence without doing violence in itself; this may result in suffering, but it need not result in violence. The connection between creation and interpretation is primarily an embodied one; recognizing this connection causes us to consider the role and revelation of God's body in creation. I begin this exploration of God's self-revelation in creation and interpretation by outlining an ethics of interpretation that builds on the work of James K. A. Smith.

JUDGMENT AND DIFFERENCE: AN ETHICS OF INTERPRETATION

Within the limits of charity, there is room for plurality which, Augustine admonishes, ought to issue in a hermeneutical humility that makes room for difference but that does not eliminate criteria. The ethics of interpretation, for Augustine, is a hermeneutics of love.[1]

Smith's work offers a good entry point into the ethics of interpretation. The question of interpretive difference first arises for Smith in his essay, "Fire From Heaven: The Hermeneutics of Heresy," in which he attempts to sketch a phenomenology of judgment. Smith locates himself in the phenomenological tradition of Merleau-Ponty, attempting to "uncover the unconscious inferences and criteria which lie behind our judgments."[2] Smith details the approach of the church to heresy, and notes that while the church, "allowed some room for interpretive difference,"[3] it quickly connected its infallibility with the need to burn heretics. Smith's critique of infallibility is not an argument for "toleration"—toleration, for Smith, is impossible because it presupposes a normative interpretation. Any theological position or doctrine (the trinity, *homoousious,* anti-Semitism), because it is theoretical and removed from lived faith, is always someone's interpretation. Therefore, no given interpretation can, without extreme danger, be equated with God's interpretation.[4] While Smith wishes to honor theological difference, the necessary absence of theological normativity in his schema sets him against toleration. In Smith's phenomenology of judgment the criteria of authority is found "insufficient (though sometimes deadly) because [it is an] illusory universal."[5] Orthodoxy becomes only the most successful heresy.

With reference to the possibility of a theology after Auschwitz, Smith insists that it is still important to judge, but he seeks to relocate the site of heresy from theory to action. Drawing on Edith Wyschogrod's *carnal generality* and Emmanuel Levinas' *corporeal sensibility,* Smith suggests that the criteria to judge exist "in my guts, in my bones, my body, my flesh. So it is not that judging is without criteria but rather that it is from different criteria ... [which] are disturbing even haunting criteria because they cannot be theoretically disclosed."[6] Following Levinas, Smith asserts that these pre-theoretical criteria bind him and extract an obligation to which he did not consent—they bind him to his own body and to the bodies of others.

In his first book-length treatment of these questions, *The Fall of Interpretation: Philosophical Foundations for a Creational Hermeneutic,* Smith examines the connection between interpretation and fallenness and argues that for much of history, interpretation has been viewed as a necessary sin. Hermeneutics either occurs as a result of the Fall (Pannenberg, Gadamer, Habermas, Lints, and Koivisto) or is a structurally violent part of human be-ing (Heidegger, Derrida).[7] Against these hermeneutical strategies, Smith argues that

> The hermeneutical structure of creation is good; it produces goods: a plurality of interpretations and a diversity of readings. The sin of Babel was its quest for unity—one interpretation, one reading, one people—which was an abandonment of creational diversity and plurality in favor of exclusion and violence.... Plurality in interpretation is not the original sin; it is, on the contrary, the original goodness of creation: a creation where many flowers bloom and many voices are heard, where God is praised by a multitude from "every tribe and language and people and nation."[8]

Smith repeats here his critique of normative interpretations, but then argues more strenuously on behalf of interpretive norms. He introduces a phenomenological criterion for judgment—the world as limit. The world is binding on our interpretations of it. Every interpretation is an *interpretation* of the world—but also an interpretation *of the world*. The world functions as a universal but not in the sense of an *a priori criterion*, rather as an *empirical transcendental*. The world is transcendent—given and outside of me—and it needs interpretation.

This is good, and I can interpret the world in many ways. However, the world also limits my interpretations by imposing itself on me. Smith's example is the tree outside his window: "If I interpret the tree as a chimera and attempt to run through its trunk, my interpretation will quickly prove itself wrong."[9] This interpretation of the tree upon Smith is equally binding upon anyone who would offer a similar *bad* interpretation. The world becomes a rule limiting or bounding interpretation and all interpreters are similarly bound.[10] Smith's *empirical transcendental* exists before interpretation and resists misinterpretation just as the tree exists before I decide to run at it and resists the same. The *empirical transcendental* is exactly the face of the Other found in Levinas' work. However, since the Other is real[11] it cannot be contained by consciousness. Coupled with its inherent resistance of distortions, the Other places an ethical demand on any interpreter—to interpret justly without manipulation.

In *Speech and Theology*, Smith builds on insights from his earlier work to approach the gap between pre-theoretical experience and conceptual understandings in both theology and philosophy. Smith carefully formalizes the problem of incommensurability through a study of Husserl, Heidegger, Levinas, Marion, and Derrida. Key to this work is the rejection, in Levinas and Marion, of the traditional privileging of immanence over transcendence in phenomenology.[12] In a brilliant inquisition of Husserl on the question of God's possible appearance in phenomenology—a right which Husserl denied to God since God can be neither simply immanent nor worldly—Smith avers that a "worldly God" is in fact all that we have. The appearance of God is only possible in the incarnation.[13] The incarnation thus establishes the condition of possibility for both speech about God and for language in general.[14]

The gaps between God and humanity, the transcendent and the immanent, the pre-theoretical and the conceptual, are overwhelmed by this incarnational paradigm. The incarnation is what allows us to stop opposing transcendence to immanence and instead to speak about God. Furthermore, understood incarnationally, concepts

> relinquish any attempt to grasp or encompass, and thus must be accompanied by a certain "humility" attentive to the play of signifiers and the elusiveness of transcendence. Such an employment of concepts will find its *telos* in an ethical methodological modesty.... An incarnational concept, while "embodying" transcendence, denies any claim to domesticating or rigidly determining such transcendence. Rather, it opens itself to the Other.[15]

This ethical modesty regarding the incarnation parallels the ethical demand Smith articulated earlier in regard to creation and heresy. The openness to the other and the embodying of transcendence both indicate that speech is not *prima facie* violent. I believe that Smith is correct about the incarnation, but I would not limit God's appearance to the incarnation. A worldly God is all we have, but God's appearance in the incarnation is not the only possibility for God's appearance. God, for example, appears as a body to Moses. The gift of speech, of return to our origins, is also made possible in creation.

CREATION

Following the instincts of her mentor Gordon Kaufman, who has suggested that God be understood as serendipitous creativity,[1] Sallie McFague provocatively suggests that we think of the world as God's body.¹⁷ McFague recognizes that this is a radical idea, although not without precedent in recent thought.¹⁸ What is it that makes the idea of the world as God's body so foreign to us?

One reason for the foreignness of McFague's understanding of a God so intimately bound up with the world that it makes sense to speak of that world as God's body is this: McFague connects this theological claim with a creation story that puts the scientific, evolutionary ecosystem at the heart of how this world/body works.¹⁹ To people comfortable thinking of God in personal or transcendent terms, an ecosystemic God will seem strange and disconcerting. However, I would suggest a second reason for our discomfort, namely, that McFague's description of the world as God's body irritates our sensibilities because we have become so comfortable thinking of the world and God in oppositional terms. One can cast this opposition in multiple ways: history vs. nature, male vs. female, or perfection vs. fallenness. The binary oppositions created by this way of thinking about the relationship between God and world are dangerous for numerous reasons and make it difficult for us to think about God as a body. McFague contends that,

> As long as we refuse to imagine God as embodied, we imply (as we do when we refuse to allow the female to serve as a metaphor of God) that the body is inferior. We imply that bodies, because of how "our world" is constructed, do not merit divine validation. But in "another world," in another construction of reality, one that took the ecological context as the primary one, the body would be an appropriate model of God. . . . the model of the universe as God's body suggests both an anthropology and a theology . . . [with] God as the inspirited body of the whole universe.²⁰

To understand how thought about creation came to be plagued by such a dualistic structure we must turn to an essay which has served as the genesis for modern thinking about creation, "The Theological Problem of the Old Testament Doctrine of Creation."²¹ In suggesting in this essay that there is no independent doctrine of creation in the Old Testament, Gerhard von Rad successfully, if unwittingly, initiated a period of theologizing about creation that reduced its importance in the overall scheme of theology and pitted history against nature. Von Rad began by delineating the relationship between Yahweh as Creator and God's redemptive function: "The Yahwistic faith of the Old Testament is a faith based on the notion of election and therefore primarily concerned with redemption."²² He probed the possible independence of the theological doctrine of creation from that of redemption, which he took to be the dominant theme of the Old Testament. Against those who suggested that the doctrine of redemption presupposes a doctrine of creation as its indispensable theological basis, von Rad contended that the Hebrew Bible does not support an independent doctrine of creation.

Ted Hiebert argues von Rad thus reduced nature to a stage of the drama of salvation.[23] Hiebert finds four simple conceptions underlying the view of nature in biblical scholarship following von Rad:

> 1. nature and history are distinct categories, 2. biblical religion was grounded in history rather than nature, 3. in this regard biblical religion was distinct from other ancient religions that were grounded in nature, and 4. the Bible's historical consciousness was an advance in the evolution of human thought.[24]

The division between nature and history, between Yahwistic faith and the faith of Israel's neighbors, and the elitism and chronology of this viewpoint represent a progression of alienation between God and the world. I find Hiebert's simple diagnosis of the situation compelling, but his explanation of the underlying assumptions that support these dichotomies even more so.

The history vs. nature dichotomy has often been related to the landscape or physical environment in which it has been assumed it came into being—desert nomadism. This standard view is based on several crucial conceptions. The environments and cultures of the Ancient Near East can be divided into two separate spheres, the desert and the sown, representing a division between the nomadic and agrarian life. Biblical culture is associated with the desert, and other Ancient Near East cultures with sedentary agricultural life. Nomadic pastoralism is a more primitive stage of societal development, so that even though Israel when it settled Canaan was agrarian, its real roots were nomadic.

Hiebert finds suspect this strong distinction between desert and the sown. In early anthropological study a three-stage theory of social development dominated: from hunting and gathering to herding to cultivation. It now seems much more likely that farming provided the condition of possibility for nomadic pastoralism. Hiebert quotes Emmanuel Marx: "The more specialized pastoral nomadism becomes the more it is integrated into the social fabric of a complex urban civilization."[25] If this separation between desert and sown is suspect, then the division between nature and history also comes under suspicion.

Indeed, von Rad himself, late in his career, recognized that

> the Old Testament draws no such distinction between Nature and history, regarding them as one single area of reality under the control of God . . . [they are] merely vast ciphers, so many images projected [therefore] anyone who wishes to see the world in some measure as Israel saw it must first rid his mind of both mythical and philosophical ways of thinking. It is much easier said than done.[26]

There are multiple beginnings in the Hebrew account of creation, but traditional orthodox theological ideas like the notion of creation *ex nihilo*; the idea of a single, total creation; the notion of absolute vs. relative beginnings; the idea of a point-like beginning, followed by a subsequent series of events; the idea of creation happening in human time; or creation by generation or progression are not among them. While some of these ideas, like *creatio ex nihilo*, are easily traced to Hellenistic, rather than Hebrew contexts, others seem to our eyes to be grounded in the biblical text. The idea of a beginning to the world, for example, seems to find more support in the biblical creation story than the thought worlds inhabited by either Greek philosophy or other Ancient Near Eastern religions. The remarkable resurgence of six-day Creationism in the United States today shows the lasting popularity of the idea of a historical beginning for nature.

The question of the relative weight to be assigned to soteriology and creation is a high-stakes discussion for Christian communities, scholars, and all those who think about beginnings and origins. Paul Ricoeur asserts that when we think about creation from a biblical perspective, what counts is creation by God. Creation happens all at once as in a single outburst, but this must be thought of as *il illo tempore*, outside of human time. We must address the relationship between this pre-history and human history if we want to think about creation, and the best way to think of creation, according to Ricoeur, is to imagine creation as a primordial history (or even better: many primordial histories). It is better to speak of many primordial histories running alongside many primordial narratives than to focus on one, since creation is rendered in the Old Testament by many different literary genres at many different times.

Ricoeur contends that "The bond that unites the primordial history . . . and dated history . . . still has to be thought through."[27] This relation between primordial and dated history is a relationship that has nothing to do with historical continuity or chronological anteriority. Precedence is not the simple linear passage of time. However, precedence must also have some inaugural value, some foundational significance. Rather than simply oppose "precedence as not chronological" and "precedence as inaugural," Ricoeur seeks a broader definition under the headings by paying attention to the themes of separation and inauguration.

Ricoeur wants to read the histories of the creation of humanity and its fall together as one progressive separation, a separation that distinguishes the Creator and the creature. "Guilty and punished, humanity is not cursed."[28] This move of separation is one of moving from creation "in itself" to being "for itself." Ricoeur carefully tracks this theme, insisting again and again that humanity is subject to limits across the entirety of the biblical narrative and that (at least) three types of separation characterize the human: "separation between the Creator and the creature, separation of the human within what is created, (and) separation of evil humans from their good creaturely depths."[29] This logic of separation is very different from the logic of dualism.

Creation has the role of the inauguration of history itself, and of Israel in particular.[30] Most importantly, Ricoeur avers that despite their multiplicity, the stream of beginnings (including those of Genesis 4-11) should be all thought of as primordial. This wipes out any distinction between absolute and relative beginnings. The question then becomes one of the connection between beginning and continuing. Ricoeur argues that "We do not speak of beginning except after the fact of continuing. The inaugural function of the beginning is recognized in this 'after the fact'-ness."[31] I take Ricoeur to mean here that we only understand what it means to begin something in light of our already having continued it. Creation is a question, for both scientists and the biblical narrator, of "projecting the origin." We can then only ever speak of an origin which has always already happened for us. To speak of an origin we already need to know how it happened. Ricoeur puts it this way:

> What is important for any thought or language relative to the beginning, to the origin, is the conflict between these two movements.... The latter movement starts from a present, self-centered awareness, seeking its own beginning; the former starts from the beginning itself, which decenters consciousness and imposes itself as being there already before consciousness starts to look for it. The religious presupposition here is that the origin itself speaks in letting itself be spoken of. The origin of things

and that of speech coincide at this point. This coincidence has to be taken as a gift: a gift of being and of speaking of being. Starting from this gift, every return toward the origin is possible, allowed, required, even if they do end up at the ungraspable.[32]

This gift, the gift of creation, is also a gift about creation, and a gift of self-revelation of the divine. At one moment humanity is separated from the divine decisively in the acknowledgment that any speech, any sight, feeling, action, or disposition aims at an ungraspable origin. But we don't just fail at approaching God's body. Instead, we do see God, we are able to talk about the divine, we do act and dispose ourselves in ways that are sometimes more, rather than less, holy.

The ethics of interpretation developed above by Smith and the resolution of dualism in this account of creation both indicate our ability to speak and the possibility that we can do so according to the logic of gift, a logic that is nonviolent. This does not mean we will speak nonviolently, but it does highlight the possibility of nonviolent speech.

CREATION AND INTERPRETATION

Ricoeur is willing to follow von Rad and acknowledge that creation is indeed separable from salvation (and therefore thinkable as an ordered reality) only if we acknowledge several caveats. We must recognize that thinking creation is not the same as thinking in terms of the idea of order. Order and creation both have the character of an event. Therefore, especially when we attend to justice, order does not designate a completed work but rather a work in process.[33] This event character of creation and order is that of an *originary* account. There is then an analogy between the gift of speech about creation and the *empirical transcendental*. Both are pre-theoretical, yet reliable, in similar ways.

Creation suggests the idea of fragility intrinsic to order itself. Resistance to order is not about rebellion or sin but inherent in creation. Limits and finitude are part of who we are. However, the origin of evil is not about the fragility of creation. Creation cannot capture evil because the theological field cannot be totalized. For Ricoeur, creation, revelation, and redemption constitute separate strata of reality.

Creation is always already there. Redemption is always in the future. Between the two is the eternal now of the "You, love me!" or "I am the one who is," found in the revelation of God to God's people.

Finally, the three must be held together so that creation is neither an appendix to redemption nor a separate theme. Creation is separable from redemption, but it is a separation that, while remaining distinct, is still always part of one, whole, integral body, the body of God.

This sedimentation found in creation, redemption, and revelation also occurs in the body that interprets. Every moment of a process of interpretation or performance can be seen along this same sedimentary model. Processes of interpretation or performance involve three levels—pre-theoretical, intentional, and reflective, three levels logically related in turn to creation, revelation, and redemption. These strata can never be separated or picked apart. A given strata is never necessarily present, but we can never expect that any are not present.

For example, there is the potential for intentionality across the interpretive/performative process. The writer has an intention, though mostly occluded. The text has intentionality, although a strange intentionality of particular orderings and trajectories. The writer's intention and the text's intention are interdependent, but they are not identical. During interpretation, intentionality as fore-understanding and prejudice plays on the text. The interpreter or actor is intentional both with respect to the text and with respect to the audience. The process of performance intends certain goals, while the audience with respect to itself and the performer intends certain changes or feedback. Every moment in this interpretive/performative process is shot through with both pre-theoretical and theoretical elements, voluntary and involuntary dimensions, tacit and explicit understanding.

One cannot, I stress again, enter the interpretative/performative process at a specific point at a given stratum and penetrate through to deeper or other levels. Again, these strata should instead be thought of as tightly coiled, constantly rotating, matrically sedimented layers, so that one can never determine from the outside at which point or into which stratum one will first plunge. When looked at this way, *interpretation is analogous to God's own process of creation, revelation, and redemption.* God reveals this in the revelations of God's name and God's body throughout the story of God's relationship to God's people.

THE REVELATION OF THE DIVINE NAME

When Moses asks after God's name in Exodus 3:14, his query is at least partly an attempt to bind God with philosophy. The question includes a challenge to God. Moses, the Egyptian-raised leader of God's people, knows all about the binding power of names from the myth of Ra and Isis.³⁴ Moses (and Moses' people) is not unaware of God's name, but instead seeks the power of God's name, God's magic name. Moses' intention is not entirely pure or nonviolent. In seeking the power of God's name Moses at least partly seeks to snare the excesses of divine existence in his question, *mah šemô* (what is God's name?)³⁵ God's revelation of the divine name exceeds and frustrates Moses' question.

God is asked for God's name, a special powerful revelation that binds God and contains God's demise, dismissal, and demotion. God exceeds this request both by refusing to acquiesce to its demands and by offering a revelation more powerful, more descriptive, and more relational. The name God gives Moses offers more information about God, promises a closer relationship—and therefore more effective revelation—than a magic name could offer. Following Gese, André LaCocque argues that the tetragrammaton is connected to the semantic field of the Hebrew root *hyh* through the paronomasia *ehyeh ašer ehyeh*. Translated as "I shall show myself in that I shall show myself, as the one who will show himself,"³⁶ *ehyeh ašer ehyeh* ensures in its circularity that the demand for a magic name goes unmet but still offers a name for a personal, invocable God who discloses in this name God's committed openness to the future. LaCocque describe the implications of this kind of a name beautifully:

> Hence the Name is *theophanic* and *performative;* it elicits recognition and worship as the recipients are not just made privy to a divine secret but are the objects of an act of salvation.... It is not a question of divine essence, but it is a promissory statement that God, as it were, "stands and falls" with his people, and in the first place with Moses about to return to Egypt where a price is set upon his head.³⁷

God *shows* in God's name that God will act to save God's people. God *shows* that God is with Moses. The name is then just as much a name that shows salvation as it is a name which reveals a being or an essence.³⁸

If God's name only makes sense in a context before ontology and open to revelation, where does this leave us at the end of the twentieth century? Ricoeur is surely right in insisting that we cannot return to a moment in which this hellenization of the Name had not yet occurred. Furthermore, even if we seek to tell differently the story of God's relationship to God's people on the other side of modernity, do we not need to realize that it is on this side of modernity, with all that that means for thought and our conception of the body, from which we gaze toward God? The core of any inquiry is not to deny any individual determinant of being, showing, thinking, or speaking, but only to insist that these inquiries can proceed along multiple trajectories simultaneously, in an underdetermined, differential fashion. Therefore we can ask, what if the gift of origins, that gift of being and speech, is also received as a gift of a name *and* a body? Is not the origin of God's name connected to God's body?

To answer yes to these questions is to assert that God's name is not just *theophanic* and *performative* but also *embodied*. The emphasis on salvation found in the *showingness* of the divine name is tied to an emphasis on judgment and condemnation, especially in texts from Ezekiel in which God judges Israel for the sake of God's name.[39] Just as my body is both fallible and capable, so God seeks both to judge and save me. However, God also shows me that this salvific interest knows no end in visions like the one found in Ezekiel 37, where dry bones are re-embodied and resurrected. It is this relationship which is determinative for both of our existences—God's and mine—at least from the human perspective. For LaCocque, "The sharpest paradox is that the only One who is really entitled to say 'I,' and who is the unique *ehyeh*, has a Name that includes a second person, a 'you.'"[40]

God's name expects a relationship. In a very different register, Gordon Kaufman makes a similar point:

> Each of the constitutive metaphors of the traditional image/concept of God (creator, Lord, father) is a *relational* term; these metaphors thus identify and characterize God in terms of God's relatedness to and significance for the world of human experience.[41]

In showing Godself in the revelation of the divine name, at the same time that God frustrates Moses' question, God exceeds Moses' expectations.

The excesses of God's existence are not intended to be captured by language. Instead, language about God is in itself excessive. It flows beyond the "bounds of every translation."[42] Nor are these excesses intended to be captured by an encounter with the whole of God's being. The demand of the other[43] is not the demand of God, for God doesn't reveal God's face. The showing of God in the gift of the divine name is also a hiding of God's face. Human perception remains in this encounter both transcendent and fallible. To Moses, God reveals not only a name which is not a name but also a glimpse of God's back. Gordon Kaufman's reflection on this passage highlights that

> For the biblical traditions in the main, God is simply not the sort of reality that is available to direct observation or experience. For the most part subsequent theological reflection has taken the same line: it has held that all knowledge of God is analogical or symbolical; that is, it is never unmediated or direct but is based on likenesses drawn from ordinary objects of experience.[44]

Kaufman notes that God's revelation is found in analogy to the ordinary. God does not reveal Godself—instead, God should be thought of as a symbol for that reality which best shapes human flourishing. The role of the Bible in such an endeavor is conflicted. Kaufman suggests that even when theologians have considered their task to be essentially hermeneutical or one-dimensional, theology

> has, in fact, always involved much more than this. Since God was portrayed in the Bible essentially as a person or agent—an active being conceived on a political and personal model—who was working creatively and redemptively in the world; it seemed reasonable to assume that knowledge of God could be acquired in a variety of ways.[45]

Theology has always been two-dimensional, negotiating the tensions between revealed and natural theology, special and general revelation, and reason and revelation.[46] Furthermore, theologians have found that any attempt to balance these two dimensions is inherently unstable. An ethics of biblical interpretation, or even the Bible itself, will only ever occupy a small contributing role in Kaufman's larger constructive theological project. While many Mennonites have been appreciative of Kaufman's work, he has not been readily accepted in either the Mennonite academy or the Mennonite church. Harry Huebner offers an explanation of why Kaufman's work has not found a welcome reception among Mennonites:

> Unless our theological imaginations can "explain" the "continuity of God-language" convincingly in light of the biblical text and the tradition which has given us our understanding of God to begin with, they cannot be meaningfully said to be Christian theology. But perhaps even more important, the "explanation" ought to be sought... in the lives of the ones who have remained traditional enough to be able to open themselves to the trans-

forming power of God who has spoken through texts the church considers authoritative.[47]

Although I believe Huebner overstates his case at this point, many Mennonite thinkers and churchgoers do not. Unless the Bible occupies a central place in the working out of any ethics or construction of a picture of God, Mennonites will not be able to accept it. Any body of God will need to have been sketched first in a thoroughgoing way in the Bible. It seems this constrains Mennonites to words, at least the words found in the Bible. Is there a body in the body of words that compose the text of the Bible? Or is it that we have not worked out, despite some impressive statements in a variety of our confessions of faith, the relationship between natural and divine revelation?

However, as Sallie McFague (building directly on Kaufman's project) reminds us, God does reveal God's back. Backs are indeed ordinary, but theology has paid precious little attention to what the importance of God's back might be for either the knowledge of God or the image of our own bodies. In Kaufman, the mind's analogy based on ordinary experience shapes our knowledge of God, not any decisive revelation either in word or body. For McFague, the body's analogy based on ordinary experience shapes our knowledge of God in every available body:

> Everything can be a metaphor for God, because no one thing is God. The body of God is not the human body nor any other body; rather, all bodies are reflections of God, all bodies are the backside of divine glory.[48]

Bodies, according to McFague, are a kind of indirect metaphor or analogy. The body reflects God, but no body decisively reflects God, since all bodies are reflections of God. Still, embodiment is decisive for our encounter with God, and this occurs in a non-metaphorical fashion. The body is not incidental to human relationship with God: "God is available to us only through the meditation of embodiment. We are offered not the face of God, but the back. God is neither enclosed in nor exhausted by the body shown to us, but it is a body that is given."[49]

God offers us the gift of speech, God's name, and God's back. Each of these gifts ground our existence as humans. However, God's self-revelation does not end as God passes by Moses in the cleft of the rock. God reveals Godself even more decisively to Ezekiel.

THE GLORY OF YHWH IN EZEKIEL

And above the dome over their heads there was something like a throne, in appearance like sapphire; and seated above the likeness of a throne was something that seemed like a human form. Upward from what appeared like the loins I saw something like gleaming amber, something that looked like fire enclosed all around; and downward from what looked like the loins I saw something that looked like fire, and there was a splendor all around. Like the bow in a cloud on a rainy day, such was the appearance of the splendor all round. This was the appearance of the likeness of the glory of the Lord. When I saw it, I fell on my face, and I heard the voice of someone speaking.
—Ezekiel 1:26-28

Like the theologians who have taken the restrained revelation of the body of God to Moses as theologically normative, biblical scholarship is typically chary about this theophany and Ezekiel's depiction of it. Zimmerli, with the characteristic care of the biblical scholar, notes restraint in the description of the human figure seen on the throne in Ezekiel 1:26.[50] Block insists that Ezekiel sees not a representation, but rather a reflection, of deity.[51] Greenberg is similarly circumspect when he states that the terms used in this passage act as 'buffer terms' so that, "It looked like torches, sapphire, a human being, but that is not to say that torches, sapphire, and a human being were actually there."[52]

However, amid this caution, Zimmerli is also careful to state unambiguously that Ezekiel did not simply encounter a "vague presence of deity" but instead had his expectations shattered, and the future course of his performances and preaching shaped, by the glory of YHWH, the God of Israel.[53] Kutsko acknowledges that the language of appearance and likeness is cautious, but at the same time emphasizes that Ezekiel "is talking about the physical appearance of God."[54] Even more decisive for our argument is the fact that the physical appearance that God takes in Ezekiel is the form of a human (*adam*). Blenkinsopp adroitly illustrates the significance of the use of adam in both Genesis 1:26-27 and Ezekiel 1:26-28.

At this point we might recall the creation of humanity in Gen. 1:26-27, from the same preistly tradition mentioned earlier. There humanity (*adam*) is created in the likeness (*demût*) of God. Here [in Ezek. 1.26-28] God appears in the likeness of humanity (*demût kemareh adam*). Humanity is in God's image, God is in humanity's image—a mysterious connaturality, not confined to the superior faculties (as

Augustine), encompassing in some mysterious way the entire person, corporeal, psychical, and spiritual.[55]

God's body, like—that is, in the likeness of—a human body, is here disposed across every aspect of what it means to be human. Both the anthropomorphism and the gripping physical nature of God's theophany to Ezekiel are intensified in Ezekiel 8. Here Ezekiel reports that God "stretched out the form of a hand, and took me by a lock of my head; and the spirit lifted me up between earth and heaven, and brought me in visions of God to Jerusalem."[56] Throughout the book of Ezekiel, the hand of God is upon him, and in most instances it is a heavy hand. It is as if Ezekiel could not move even if he willed it.[57] In this vision it is clear that this hand is not (or at least not just) metaphorical. This is a hand that can identify where to best grab a human, even if in the moment the human seems more like a cat. Ezekiel's words carry with them a palpable sense of the physical presence of God.

The connection made here between heaven and earth through God's embodiment in Ezekiel in many ways inverts, for the purpose of again unifying, God's creative and redemptive purposes. Ezekiel's call was to be a sentinel warning the people of their unfaithfulness. It was never a call away from what faithfulness demanded in the concrete reality they found themselves in during the Babylonian exile. Instead, just as Ezekiel is asked again and again to make God's Word come alive in new ways for a lost people, so God first shows Godself to Ezekiel for God's people. This imaginative showing, while being a creative activity which in many ways brings together creation, revelation, and redemption, is entirely at God's initiative.

MARPECK AND THE "GOSPEL OF ALL CREATURES"

In addition to biblical descriptions of creation revealing God's body, the Anabaptist tradition also offers a fruitful resource for reflecting on God's self-disclosure in the world. Specifically, the Anabaptist "Gospel of all Creatures" offers an account of the revelation of God's order in creation which is simultaneously scriptural and natural, an account, moreover, which connects the incarnation's disclosure of God's suffering with a proper understanding of creation. This trope originates in German Mysticism and is treated most fully in five German radicals: Müntzer, Hut, Schiemer, Schlaffer, and the Tyrolean engineer-theologian, Pilgram Marpeck. This theme is important to my study because it shows both the sedimentary process detailed above and a non-dualistic approach to the question of embodiment and interpretation. I will focus on Marpeck because I think that much of Marpeck's genius in treating the topic comes from the way he calmed the apocalyptic tensions so central to this curious way of thinking.

While the Gospel of all Creatures received a more systematic treatment from Hans Hut, and was discussed more often in Marpeck's writings, it clearly has its genesis and was most creatively phrased in Thomas Müntzer's thought. Müntzer may have drawn on influences as diverse as the *Theologia Deutsch*, Tauler, Suso, Hildegard of Bingen, Raymond of Sabunde, Le Fevre, and Nicholas of Cusa, in formulating his Gospel of all Creatures, but, using these diverse influences, Müntzer developed his own distinctive theological idiom.[58]

> I have not heard from a single scholar about the order of God implanted in all creatures, not the tiniest word about it; while as to understanding the Whole as a unity of all the parts those who claim to be Christians have not caught the least whiff of it—least of all the accursed priests.[59]

The Gospel of all Creatures was more than a clever way to undermine the lofty thoughts of Luther and the princes. It was central to Müntzer's thought, for he rests all of his argument on God's order, an order implanted in the creatures. The content of the Gospel of all Creatures in Müntzer is clear, for "Holy Scripture shows nothing else—as all the creatures bear witness—than the crucified Son of God."[60] For Müntzer, the Gospel of all Creatures revealed suffering, divine order, and Scripture. There is an analogy between the relationship of the creatures to humanity and between humanity and God.

Hut appropriated many key elements of Müntzer's thought, albeit in a more systematic and thorough fashion. If in Müntzer the genre of the Gospel of all Creatures was divine order, in Hut it became a divine parable. Hut's parables were all about divine order so the connection in content is close, but when one reads Hut's "On the Mystery of Baptism" the distinction between order and parables becomes clear. Hut spent pages talking about Christ's parables, about Paul's parables, about how David spoke in parables, about how "Christ always preached the gospel, the kingdom of God, by using the creatures and parables."[61] "For all that can be shown in the Scriptures is already shown in the creatures," wrote Hut. "Christ had no need of Scriptures unless he wanted to prove something from it to the soft scholars."[62]

Here the Gospel of all Creatures contains the egalitarianism and anticlericalism which are characteristic of Anabaptism. Furthermore, the world that is created in the Gospel of all Creatures is not purely spiritual, political, or economic. In Hut it was also a material, natural world. This is a gospel about and in creation. A positive appraisal of the created world permeated Hut's Gospel of all Creatures:

> When, according to the Lord's command, the "Gospel of all Creatures" is preached, a person is then brought to understanding in a reasonable and natural way. He sees it in his own work, that which he does in relation to the creatures.[63]

The main theme of the Gospel of all Creatures remains unchanged from Müntzer to Hut. The main parable the Gospel of all Creatures conveys involves suffering:

> If one wants to use an animal, it must first be dealt with according to human will—it must be prepared, cooked and roasted. That is, the animal must suffer. And God does the same with human beings. If God has use of us or will have benefit of us, we must first be justified and made pure by Him, both inwardly and outwardly; inwardly from greed and lust, outwardly from injustice in our way of living and our misuse of the creatures.[64]

Such imagery was readily appropriated by an apocalypticism like that which fueled the massacre at Frankenhausen in which Müntzer drove 6,000 people to futile deaths in a hopeless armed rebellion against Philip, the Landgraf of Hesse, who lost only six soldiers.[65]

Must the Gospel of all Creatures be linked to a violent apocalypticism in which the life of the slaughtered animal is considered normative for human existence? Other Anabaptist and related writers developed this theme in more productive, life-giving ways. Stephen Boyd, for example, follows how thinking about the creatures in the *Theologia Deutsch* and the writings of Leonhart Schiemer and Hans Schlaffer all articulate a Gosepl of all Creatures distinct from that of Müntzer.[66] An emphasis on divine order and suffering permeates the thinking about the creature in the *Theologia Deutsch*. The relationship of creature to God in divine order is based solely on the creature's participation in the perfect being of God. When the creature turns away from this participation, not only is the relationship to God damaged, but the relationship to other creatures and the neighbor is disrupted as well. Schiemer, Schlaffer, and Marpeck all developed their doctrines of the creatures in ways similar to the *Theologia Deutsch*.

Schiemer, for example, maintains a strong emphasis on divine order and suffering, but in a way in which suffering does not appear as something God requires for assuring human purity. Schiemer writes:

> God created all creatures in five days so that they can be used by the human, who was created on the sixth day. Then the creature has its rest. But the human being was not created to remain a human being on the sixth day, but that he would come to the seventh day, indeed that he become godly, or divinized, and come to God. That is then the appropriate human rest or true day of celebration. And indeed the means by which all creatures come to be useful to the human is suffering. One kills, cuts and cooks and the creature holds still and suffers for the sake of faith. And just as an animal is not useful to the human for food unless the body dies, so no human becomes blessed, who does not die for Christ's sake.[67]

The apocalyptic tone, so present in Müntzer and Hut, seems less evident in Schiemer. Suffering occurs as right relationships, balances, and order are again established by God in humans. Suffering is the response to human separation from the divine will. As humans purify themselves of selfish reliance, dependency, pain, and suffering occur, here in graphic proportions. But this suffering is necessary for humans in a world of confused priorities, not a prerequisite for our use by God.

For Hans Schlaffer, in contrast, suffering is also key to faith, but the emphasis is again on God's role in preparing the human through suffering. Schlaffer reasoned as follows:

> with a hen or fish or other animal, that you want to eat, it is clear that it (according to its own will or pleasure) cannot prepare itself, that is, it may not lay itself out, open itself, clean itself and boil or fry itself. But you must do it according to your own will, which it must suffer.[68]

Schlaffer was by no means apocalyptic, so it seems in some ways curious that he picks up this aspect to the Gospel of all Creatures that proved so tragic at Frankenhausen. One reason for his doing so could have been his concrete, physical notion of participation in Christ's life. The positive approach of the Gospel of all Creatures to the natural world is strongly evident in Schlaffer. Boyd says that for Schlaffer the

> reality of Christ and his justness in something in which one participates; it reorders the human being's mode of existence. It does not remain outside, embodied in bread and wine; rather it is embodied and mediated by real, flesh and blood people.[69]

The Gospel of all Creatures reaches in Marpeck a more mature development. The Gospel of all Creatures loses most of the apocalyptic bite it had in Müntzer and Hut and adopts a more apologetic tone, since Marpeck was often responding to the Spiritualists. A good example of Marpeck's treatment of the creatures appears in his lengthy "Judgment and Decision":

> The Gospel of the creatures is that the gospel may be preached through discerning the nature of the divine Creation by which the Creator is known. Carnal reason, however, has no right to use the witnesses of the creatures of the gospel; reason errs in its use, an error which has beset all the philosophers in this world . . . man . . . must first by means of the creature be led to a knowledge of God; Christ talked to the people about the kingdom of God by means of many parables of nature.[70]

Marpeck here delineated a fine line between nature and carnal wisdom. Marpeck provided a positive understanding of the natural world, one uncorrupted by carnal reason. Nature holds an important place in God's order. In a long discourse on Mark 16:15, the verse which inspired the gospel of all Creatures, Marpeck argued that the creatures are not damned with those who can be taught but will not believe.[71] Finally, Marpeck's strong incarnational focus correlated with his positive view of the natural world, as evident in his christological slogan, "The Lord Christ became a Natural Man for natural man."[72]

The Gospel of all Creatures takes on an egalitarian, anticlerical dimension in Marpeck's, "A Clear Refutation":

> Yes, even if a dog or a cat were to proclaim the gospel as a testimony, throughout the unbelieving world and deliver it into repentance an improvement, who could declare it wrong? For everything that leads to godliness is good, and not evil, for all visible creatures are placed in the world as apostles and teachers (Job 12). If such mute creatures could speak, Christ's sending the apostles to elucidate or preach the gospel would have been unnecessary.[73]

The world described by Marpeck through his use of the Gospel of all Creatures motif is natural and good, egalitarian and anticlerical. Marpeck valued suffering, but it does not receive the same kind of ontological priority that it does in the writings of other Anabaptists who expounded a Gospel of all Creatures.

Boyd argues that Marpeck intended to embed suffering into his treatment of the Gospel of all Creatures by reference to Job 12.[74] Job there indicts Zophar for being unable to understand that which even simplest creatures can understand—the hand of God in Job's suffering. *Contra* Boyd, I am unconvinced that suffering plays a central role in Marpeck's treatment of the Gospel of all Creatures. The context of Job 12 is indeed Job's suffering. But, I would suggest, Marpeck deployed a metaphor from Job to strengthen and modify an existing trope in Anabaptism (the "Gospel of all Creatures"). The creatures in Job 12 are not suffering but are rather preaching. In fact they are not just preaching—they are proclaiming the gospel as a testimony throughout the unbelieving world and delivering it into repentance and improvement. The result is not simple purification but the redundancy of Christ's sending of the apostles. Marpeck's use of Job 12 is about preaching the gospel, not about Job or suffering.

The physicality of the Gospel of all Creatures served as a powerful counter to sixteenth-century spiritualism, just as God's appearance to Ezekiel and Moses offered powerful statements of God's presence in times of assumed divine absence and confused loyalties. The Gospel of all Creatures functioned in Anabaptism to create a world in which the natural, created world was viewed positively, one in which God preaches to all through even the simplest creature. This world is a radical mixture of religious influences, at the same time traditional, mystical, and reformed. It is a world in which suffering will often occur due to the clash of divinely ordered creatures and self-obsessed creatures, but this suffering, at least in the thought of Marpeck, is without ontological status.

In conclusion, I would like to respond to one possible critique of my argument. While I do not think that the analogical connections among the revelation of God in God's name, God's body, and the Gospel of all Creatures are weak ones, the question of whether or not these analogies create the conditions of possibility for interpretation does deserve further comment. We saw in our review of Smith that the world is a limit on our interpretation and that interpretation is *of the world*. Smith's categories of the *empirical transcendental* and *corporeal sensibility* shape an ethics of interpretation. But what are we interpreting? If I want to use the arguments presented in this essay, I can only argue that we are interpreting the world. This again connects our thinking about creation and our thinking about interpretation, but Huebner's call that we first and foremost interpret Scripture should still sound a dissonant tone.

My account of creation and interpretation implicitly calls for further work on how biblical interpretation connects to creation. I believe such a connection can be made through the rigorous application of the logic of the body to the whole field of theological endeavor. I believe that those Anabaptists who employed the Gospel of all Creatures were involved in this kind of application. But that is an argument for another time.

In the account of creation and interpretation developed in this essay, I hope to have offered an account of creation and interpretation as revealed in bodies both natural and divine, an account that recognizes the possibility of suffering but denies violence any ontological priority. Violence is the result of the primordial separation from God, not an existential existent inherent in some dualistic structure of creation, some predication forced on the other, or some fall from grace. In this imagination, we are both finite and fallen, but neither of these is connected to each other structurally, so we can acknowledge that fallenness is more about the exercise of the capabilities we have than any structural defect. As Ricoeur says, fallenness—rather than being a ontological existent—grows from "a specific act of preference."[75] Ricoeur clarifies the relationship between the will and the body this way:

> It is my body which introduces this existential note; it is the initial existent, underivable, *involuntary*. Suddenly the entire abstract relation of willing to its motives come to life; the brackets which shielded our description are removed; the "I am" or "I exist" infinitely overwhelms the "I think."[76]

Our bodies (for Ricoeur the *corporeal involuntary*) are always already there in any act of the will, and the will expresses itself only through the body. Ricoeur notes that the body is a "body-for-my-willing" but also insists that willing is "project-based-(in part)-on my body."[77] Ricouer describes this circular movement thus: "The involuntary is for the will and the will is by reason of the involuntary."[78] The body takes on a surplus of meaning here by virtue of its own overwhelming reason, which then gives shape both to our will and our fallenness. The body shapes the will and our potential for separation from God. However, this fallenness is, in the biblical world, always spoken of in the context of salvation from sin. Just as questions of finitude and fallibility must be considered in the context of the transcendence of finitude and fallibility, so sin must be considered in the context of salvation from sin. On this account, our fallen flesh, a category which cuts across both body and soul, is managed by inclination and preference, liberated from bondage to sin, but still subject to preferences which separate the person from God.

In the revelation of the divine name and the divine body, and in the revelation by creatures of the divine order, God creates, sustains, and redeems the world. Humans receive revelation in a constant process of interpretation. God offers a variety of gifts in a plurality of forms. As creatures in a gifted universe, what we use them for is up to us.

NOTES

1. James K. A. Smith, "Fire From Heaven: The Hermeneutics of Heresy," *Journal of Theta Alpha Kappa* 20 (1996): 17.
2. James K. A. Smith, *The Fall of Interpretation: Philosophical Foundations for a Creational Hermeneutic* (Downers Grove, Ill: InterVarsity Press, 2000), 17
3. Ibid, 20
4. Smith includes this enticing sentence in his longer explication of his argument: "I would even say that all theology is heresy, though I would not go so far as to say that." *The Fall of Interpretation*, 22.
5. Ibid., 24.
6. Smith, "Fire From Heaven: The Hermeneutics of Heresy," 26.
7. Smith, *The Fall of Interpretation*, 23
8. Ibid., 33.
9. Ibid., 169.
10. Ibid., 169-175.
11. Not *Irreal* or *Ideal* in Husserlian terms. See Ibid., 176.
12. James K. A. Smith, *Speech and Theology: Language and the Logic of Incarnation*, (London: Routledge, 2002), 27.
13. Ibid., 55.
14. Ibid., 155.
15. Ibid., 169.
16. Gordon D Kaufman, *In the Beginning—Creativity* (Minneapolis: Fortress Press, 2004), ch. 2.
17. Sallie McFague, *The Body of God: An Ecological Theology* (Minneapolis: Fortress Press, 1993), 20.
18. Grace Jantzen, *God's World, God's Body* (Philadelphia: Westminster Press, 1984).
19. McFague, *The Body of God*, ch. 2.
20. Ibid., 21-22.

21. Gerhard von Rad, *The Problem of the Hexateuch: And Other Essays* (Edinburgh: Oliver & Boyd, 1966).
22. Ibid., 131.
23. Theodore Hiebert, *The Yahwist's Landscape: Nature and Religion in Early Israel* (New York: Oxford University Press, 1996), 5.
24. Ibid., 7.
25. Ibid, p. 20.
26. Ibid., p. 18.
27. André LaCocque and Paul Ricoeur, *Thinking Biblically: Exegetical and Hermeneutical Studies* (Chicago: University of Chicago Press, 1998), 32.
28. Ibid., 39.
29. Ibid., 46.
30. Ibid., 47.
31. Ibid., 51.
32. Ibid, 53-54.
33. Ibid., 57.
34. Ibid., 309.
35. Ibid., 310.
36. Gese's German translation of *ehyeh ašer ehyeh* is "*ich erweise mich als der ich mich erweisen werde*"; see LaCocque and Ricouer, *Thinking Biblically*, 361.
37. LaCocque and Ricouer, *Thinking Biblically*, 316.
38. Ibid., 313-314.
39. Ibid, 323.
40. Ibid., 315-316.
41. Gordon D. Kaufman, *In Face of Mystery* (Cambridge, Mass.: Harvard University Press, 1995), 323 (emphasis in the original).
42. LaCocque and Ricouer, *Thinking Biblically*, 361
43. For Emmanuel Levinas this demand is contained in the implicit command found in the face of the Other, "Don't kill me."
44. Kaufman, *In Face of Mystery*, 323.
45. Ibid., 20.
46. Ibid., 20-21.
47. Harry Huebner, "Imagination/Tradition: Disjunction Or Conjunction?," in *Mennonite Theology in Face of Modernity: Essays in Honor of Gordon D. Kaufman*, ed. Alain Epp Weaver (North Newton, Kan.: Bethel College, 1996), 78-79.
48. McFague, *The Body of God*, 134.
49. Ibid., 134.
50. Walther Zimmerli, *Ezekiel : A Commentary on the Book of the Prophet Ezekiel*, ed. Frank Moore Cross and Klaus Baltzer, trans. Ronald E. Clements (Philadelphia: Fortress Press, 1979), 122.
51. Daniel Isaac Block, *The Book of Ezekiel* (Grand Rapids, Mich.: Wm. B. Eerdmans, 1997), 108.
52. Moshe Greenberg, *Ezekiel 1-20: A New Translation with Introduction and Commentary* (Garden City, NY: Doubleday, 1983), 53.
53. Zimmerli, *Ezekiel*, 124.
54. John F Kutsko, *Between Heaven and Earth: Divine Presence and Absence in*

the Book of Ezekiel (Winona Lake, Ind.: Eisenbrauns, 2000), 67.

55. Joseph Blenkinsopp, *Ezekiel* (Louisville: John Knox Press, 1990), 22.

56. Ezekiel 8:3

57. I am grateful to Hannah Kehr for this insight.

58. E. Gordon Rupp, "The Gospel of all Creatures" in *The Bulletin of the John Rylands Library* 43/2 (March 1961): 493-494.

59. Peter Matheson, ed. and trans., *The Collected Works of Thomas Münzter*. (Edinburgh: T&T Clark, 1988), 357.

60. Rupp, "The Gospel of all Creatures," 498

61. Daniel Liechty, ed., *Early Anabaptist Spirituality: Selected Writings* (Mahwah: Paulist Press, 1994), 69.

62. Ibid., 72.

63. Ibid.

64. Ibid., 70.

65. C. Arnold Snyder, *Anabaptist History and Theology* (Kitchener, Ont.: Pandora Press, 1995), 29.

66. Stephen Blake Boyd, *Pilgram Marpeck: His Life and Social Theology* (Durham: Duke University Press, 1992).

67. Ibid., 32

68. Ibid, 38

69. Ibid.

70. William Klassen and Walter Klaassen, eds., trans. *The Writings of Pilgrim Marpeck* (Kitchener, Ont.: Herald Press, 1978), 352-353.

71. Ibid., 250.

72. Ibid., 85.

73. Ibid., 56.

74. Boyd, *Pilgram Marpeck*, 77.

75. Ricoeur as quoted in Donn Welton, *Body and Flesh: A Philosophical Reader* (Malden, Mass: Blackwell Publishers, 1998), 242.

76. Paul Ricoeur, *Freedom and Nature: The Voluntary and Involuntary* (Evanston, Ill: Northwestern University Press, 1966), 85.

77. Ibid.

78. Ibid., 86.

CHAPTER EIGHTEEN

"Truth Did Not Come Into the World Naked": Some Images, Some Stories, and an Immodest Proposal

Jeff Gundy

When I initially read the invitation to contribute to this volume, with its request to "situate your own viewpoint on Christology in relationship to Denny's work," the first word I wrote down in response was "Yikes."

Let me explain. I have followed J. Denny Weaver's work ever since I became his colleague at Bluffton twenty years ago, and I have learned a great deal from him. We have had conversations (and occasional arguments), alone and with others, on too many subjects to list. Weaver's ongoing theological enterprises, and his many other interests, have influenced and energized my own work in many direct and indirect ways. His determination to construct a thoroughly Anabaptist theology with nonviolence at its center and his trademark energy and conviction have been an inspiration. The series of books and articles through which he has worked out this project, especially the three important studies *Keeping Salvation Ethical*, *Anabaptist Theology in Face of Postmodernity*, and *The Nonviolent Atonement*, provide a model of focused intellectual activity—at once wide-ranging and coherent—that I regard with little short of awe.¹ Weaver's response to my own work, especially his help in shaping my recent book, *Walker in the Fog: On Mennonite Writing,* for the C. Henry Smith Series which he edits, has been generous, rigorous, and constructive.²

So I owe Denny Weaver a great deal. At the same time, I have long been uneasily aware that my own internal processes are far less focused and coherent than his. While I have labored at producing my own texts in more or less academic prose, including a good deal of writing on Mennonite literature, some of which flirts with the boundaries of theology, I have been inclined not toward constructing one consistent, coherent edifice of thought, but toward wandering, exploring here and there, questioning, resisting clear theses and point-by-point expositions. (I say all this as confession, not boast.) For all the attractions of abstraction, I find myself drawn even more strongly toward more concrete language, toward imagery and metaphor and the kind of narrative that resists clear exposition. In the gaps between story and meaning, image and interpretation, exploring what resists being truly or fully known—that is where I feel most alive.

When asked about my viewpoint on Christology, then, what first came to mind was my poem "How the Boy Jesus Resisted Taking Out the Trash":

> O there's not enough to bother with.
> O in a couple thousand years the landfills will be groaning.
> O we're too poor there isn't any trash.
> O what about Naomi what does she do around here.
> O if ever you suspected what's to come you'd put me in the
>   best chair, you'd kill the last goat for supper and feed me
>   the heart and the liver.
> O not now.
> O remember my father's business and all that. Priests and
>   Levites are going to love me, some. Locusts will sing and
>   sizzle. Precious stones will roll toward me like mice.
>   Everybody's pretty daughters will cry because I don't like
>   them that way.
> O I'll change it into figs and honey later, all right?
> O all right.³

This poem is not, of course, a serious effort to envision the actual life of the boy Jesus; it has more to do with memories of my own sons, smart and obstreperous as they were as children, and my guess that even Jesus might have had his moments of resistance to his parents' instructions. The poem suggests that such resistance might be either funny or annoying, depending on your position in relation to it. In the end, though, my boy Jesus says "Oh, all right," recognizing that the familial power structure does have some just claims upon his time and energies. The poem has a kind of implied narrative but does not even tell a completely clear story, let alone state a clear, unified, and precise thesis, and support it. (I spend a lot of my time trying to train students to write clear, unified, and precise prose, which may partly explain why I treasure so much the freedom from such requirements that poems offer.)

While few of the preserved sayings of Jesus are very accurately described as poems, it is no secret that his rhetorical style is often indirect and elusive. At times Jesus even seems to say this elusiveness is deliberate, as in Mark 4:11-12, when he says to the disciples, "To you has been given the secret of the kingdom of God, but for those outside, everything comes in parables; in order that 'they may indeed look, but not perceive, and may indeed listen, but not understand; so that they may not turn again, and be forgiven.'" Biblical scholars tend to be uneasy with what seems the plain sense of this passage—that there are some people Jesus does not *want* to understand his message. Without delving further into that controversy, let me just observe that any quick turn through the Gospels—or a quick contemplation of the last two millennia of Christian history—will confirm that Jesus did not leave an utterly transparent set of teachings behind.

We might also consider these words from the apocryphal Gospel of Philip:

> Jesus took them all by stealth, for he did not reveal himself in the manner in which he was, but it was in the manner in which they would be able to see him that he revealed himself. . . . He revealed himself to the great as great. He revealed himself to the small as small. He revealed himself to the angels as an angel, and to men as a man. Because of this his word hid itself from everyone.[4]

We treasure and trust this indirection of Jesus, however frustrating it sometimes is, because we trust his goals and motives—and, perhaps, because we have little choice but to work with what we have. There are plenty of less honorable indirections and purposeful confusions going on, though, especially in the current alliance of conservative politics with a particular segment of the church.

Recently Mennonite historian John D. Roth, noting the tension between social justice and conservative evangelical elements within the Mennonite church, rather daringly proposed a five-year moratorium on Mennonite involvement in party politics as a way of easing these divisions and encouraging Christian unity: "Mennonites in the United States should commit themselves to a five-year sabbatical from affiliations with any political party. That is, we should resolve to sit out the next presidential election and to consciously abstain from all literature, web sites, organizations and lobbying efforts supported by groups partisan to the Republicans or the Democrats." Roth calls for "serious, sustained church-wide conversation about the nature of Christian witness in the public square" as part of this process.[5]

Though he is right to recognize that current divisions within Mennonites generally reflect the "red/blue" divisions among Americans, Roth may be overly optimistic about the possibility of overcoming these differences through emphasis on unity in Christ. Those on one side of this divide, who generally accept the centrality of nonviolence to the gospel that Denny Weaver has spent his career advocating, believe that refusing to kill, even one's enemies, is an essential and non-negotiable Christian principle. Those on the other side contend that killing the country's enemies is, at the least, a painful necessity and, at most, a glorious duty. Because we differ so radically about what it means to be Christian, it is not clear to me that looking to underscore a common Christian identity accomplishes anything more than concealing the problem.

My proposition, therefore, is somewhat different from Roth's. Instead of (or, if you like, in addition to) a moratorium on partisan political involvement, I propose that for the next span of years we resolve to avoid calling ourselves "Christian" altogether. Let us even keep the general God-talk to a minimum, both here and elsewhere, until and unless that language can be cleansed of the accumulated distortions and misapprehensions—born mostly of fear and greed, hatred and power-lust—that so corrupt it now.[6]

What if we were to leave the term *Christian* to those who want it, and find something better to call ourselves, something less associated in the eyes of the rest of the world with torture camps and foreign invasions? Friends of the poor, perhaps, seekers of truth, refusers of the sword, lovers of our enemies, defenders of beauty and justice, practitioners of radical hospitality, followers of Jesus. You choose, or invent another that suits you better. Maybe it would be best not to name ourselves at all, or to identify ourselves simply by our places. When I hear of moves to rename churches according to some abstract term, something in me rebels. I can't say exactly why, but I would much rather worship at the Big Oak Church than the Neighborly Brother-and-Sisterhood of Missional Outreach.[7]

While I am making outrageous proposals, let me also propose that we let the most familiar stories and verses rest for awhile—not to forget them, but to allow them to be renewed and freshened while we widen our own horizons. Why not abandon the weary round of the lectionary calendar for a stretch and instead seek out the treasures to be found among obscure passages and neglected texts? When did you last hear a good sermon, or even a bad one, on the Song of Songs? Why not spend some Sunday school time reading and discussing the Gospel of Thomas or the visionary "Thunder, Perfect Mind"? While we're at it, why not encourage the whole community, not just those who think of themselves as "creative," to let what they know and believe and hope and pray for flow into new stories, new images, new songs? The result would no doubt be uneven, sometimes awkward or awful, but I predict that many new gems and discoveries would surface during such a process.

I know—all this is crazy and impractical. It won't happen, not while we are so bound to our traditions and conventions, so unaccustomed to speaking new words for ourselves, so bound to bureaucratic and business models of church. No leader of men or denominations myself, I offer these ideas mainly as a thought-experiment, knowing that the good, practical folk will smile faintly and then go back to planning the next committee meeting.

Still, a long thread in our tradition cautions against too much God-talk. St. Francis famously said "Preach the gospel at all times and when necessary use words." Thomas Merton expanded on the idea: "[A] saint is capable of talking about the world without any explicit reference to God," he wrote, "in such a way that his statement gives greater glory to God and arouses a greater love of God than . . . hackneyed analogies and metaphors that are so feeble that they make you think there is something the matter with religion."[8]

When I find myself drifting into the fogs of abstraction, I try to relocate myself in the particular place I inhabit with my physical body. I wrote some of these words in a rented minivan somewhere in Illinois, headed west to my son's college graduation. As we passed through a small town I saw piles of dirt and gravel in a parking lot where a new building was going up. I saw a woman in a yellow vest standing in the middle of an intersection holding a surveyor's stick, yelling numbers to a companion, ignoring the traffic swirling by her on all sides. Soon we were out of town, though, amid ditch grass bushy from the spring rains, not yet laid low by the mowers, and the tender yellowish new corn, two inches out of black earth. Next to me my wife was driving, glancing over to see what I was doing. She didn't ask what I was writing, and I didn't volunteer. Sometimes it's necessary to keep things quiet until their time.

"Jesus said, 'It is I who am the light which is above them all. It is I who am the all. From me did the all come forth, and unto me did the all extend. Split a piece of wood, and I am there. Lift up the stone, and you will find me there.'"
—The Gospel of Thomas[9]

More and more I find myself wanting to leave behind all the human contentions that seem, however crucial, so frustrating and irresolvable, and instead head off to split the wood and lift up the stone, to speak of the world as if it were indeed the habitation of the divine. It would not be so bad, surely, to devote one's time to praise of the earth and our companions living, lost, and to come, and all those beings visible and invisible that lead us toward justice, mercy, and love. Whitman had such business in mind when he offered this wonderful list of what we should do:

> Love the earth and sun and the animals, despise riches, give alms to every one that asks, stand up for the stupid and crazy, devote your income and labor to others, hate tyrants, argue not concerning God, have patience and indulgence toward the people, take off your hat to nothing known or unknown or to any man or number of men, go freely with powerful uneducated persons and with the young and with the mothers of families, reexamine all you have been told at school or church or in any book, dismiss whatever insults your own soul . . . and your very flesh shall be a great poem and have the richest fluency not only in its words but in the silent lines of its lips and face and between the lashes of your eyes and in every motion and joint of your body.[10]

Whitman also wrote beautifully of the patience and calm of animals—though on that subject I must quibble with him. My neighbor has been keeping his daughter's dog, an exotic, energetic animal whose convictions are simple and absolute. Every time I pass by—which I do three or four times a day—Clarence erupts into a utter fury of barking and leaping, dashing along the fence, turning in tight little circles; he doesn't stop until I'm nearly out of his sight, and no matter how many times I pass by his intensity never diminishes. He is quite convinced that I am a deadly threat with whom no compromise is possible, and that only the noisiest and most muscular public hostility will fend me off. My purposes are utterly irrelevant and unthreatening to his, but he's too busy making desperate threats to learn anything about that.

> Truth did not come into the world naked, but it came in types and images. One will not receive truth in any other way. There is a rebirth and an image of rebirth. It is certainly necessary that they should be born again through the image. What is the resurrection? The image must rise again through the image.[11]

Late one fall I visited the Oregon Extension, an intensive study program in the mountains of southern Oregon. Program participants stayed at a sprawling dude ranch nearby, which our hosts said was run by a fervently evangelical family; among its features not visible from the house where we stayed were three gigantic crosses atop a small hill. One chilly but sunny afternoon I went for a long walk around the ranch, with Mount Shasta looming out beyond the closer ranges. This poem was the result.

Contemplation at the Bar R Ranch

Both the owner and his daughter said we'd have to see the crosses
so of course I tried to avoid them. But wandering aimlessly

after sublimity as I do on free afternoons I followed a sign
that said "Baptismal" down a narrow way

and stepped carefully on rocks across the icy creek.
When I looked up there they were, enormous,

big enough to crucify a pteranodon or a giraffe.
As I climbed the muddy path some part of me said

I have to safeguard my doubts and another remembered
how the old picker said to Goodman *I find*

the prettiest woman in the room and play every song for her.
Too edgy to eat, Salinger's Franny tried to pray

the Jesus prayer all the way through homecoming.
With the sun low behind the crosses I could barely look.

Thin grass, lichens, rocks and gravel lay low all around
stunned by some brutal devotion not their own.

Three weeks to solstice. Faint thin birdsong.
So many trees, so many rocks, so many women

whose lives and bodies I will never touch.
The creek rippled on, Shasta glowed in the chilly haze,

a strand of spider silk glinted in and out of sight.
Breathe in: *This is paradise.* Breathe out: *I must go.*[12]

Theology aims to be clear, precise, and straightforward about its propositions, to bring reason to bear on mystery. Is the impulse to theologize somehow related to the impulse to erect larger-than-life-size crosses in a mountain meadow? Or is it related to the impulse to mistrust large public gestures of piety while seeking to register one's own spiritual intimations and quandaries in poetry? I do not mean these as rhetorical questions. As my poem suggests in its own way, the crosses seemed utterly displaced to me there, a kind of poetry doomed by the clumsiness and crudity of its ambitions. True poetry, I believe, seeks to dwell less obtrusively and more lightly within the mysteries of existence. But why should my views of such matters be trusted?

Poetry dwells among the mysteries of language, and what happens to our terms, both abstract and concrete, as we seek to arrange and control them, to use them to speak of phenomena that are not fully contained by any language. Consider what Thomas Merton has to say about one key religious term: "It is a pity that the beautiful Christian metaphor 'salvation' has come to be so hackneyed and therefore so despised. It has been turned into a vapid synonym for 'piety'—not even a truly ethical concept."[13]

Thus far Merton might seem to be on the path Weaver took when he argued that Anabaptists have historically insisted on "keeping salvation ethical" and connected to action in the world, resisting the view that it represents a merely personal exchange between the individual and God. But Merton has a somewhat different dualism in mind. Rather than devaluing the subjective in favor of the ethical, he means to rehabilitate and expand our notions of subjectivity: "'Salvation' is something far beyond ethical propriety. The word connotes a deep respect for the fundamental metaphysical reality of man.... It is not only human nature that is 'saved' by the divine mercy, but above all the human *person*. The object of salvation is that which is unique, irreplaceable, incommunicable—that which is myself alone."[14]

When I recently taught a "spiritual memoir" class, it quickly became clear that I had a diverse group. Some were earnest and devout Mennonites, Catholics, and others; some had little religious background; some came in with traumatic experiences that made them deeply suspicious of "spiritual writing." In the first several weeks we explored what that term might mean—especially, I tried to say that we would be best off not to worry about whether we were being orthodox or not. Rather than concentrating on who was saved and who wasn't, I suggested that we try to write with all the clarity, depth, and openness we could manage about our actual lives, feelings, experiences, thoughts, and convictions.

Once people realized that I actually meant this, the class took off. People found the nerve to talk and write with sometimes astonishing directness and insight about the their lives and their souls, or at least to treat those elements of their lives with more precision, openness, and detail than we were used to. We discovered help in this endeavor in writers like Merton and others such as Anne Lamott, Annie Dillard, Kathleen Norris, and Cynthia Yoder, very different writers who were all quite open about their own doubts and qualms as well as their faith. All of these writers seem (I realize in retrospect) to share Merton's interest in what he calls "the human *person*"—a totality encompassing more than the body, the self, or the soul. Like Merton, they all had a large and generous sense of the "unique, irreplaceable, incommunicable" nature of the human person, and all write as though it is both natural and right that followers of Jesus should cultivate our persons rather than stifling or denying large sections of them.

Not until the class was over did I find a letter from the poet James Wright that touches on similar issues. Wright reflects on the links between his poems and the language of his southern Ohio home town, which he says has been "ringing somewhere in my head all my life":

> I suppose what I'm saying is that a person—like your young poets—should not be afraid to pour into his poetry all the phrases and sayings and rhythms that in truth mean the most to him, the sounds that he can hear outside of himself—because, if he listens, he'll hear them inside of himself, too. Everybody surely hears some kind of song inside of himself. How amazing if he could only be brave enough to sing it out loud. If he does, often he gets back from other people something like an echo—an echo changed and transfigured by the secret songs of the very people who have heard him sing in the first place.[15]

What poems do, perhaps better than any other mode of expression, is delineate those complicated interior and exterior negotiations that make up our lives and our desires. At a conference once I was asked whether poems represent "subjective" truth—the clear subtext being that this sort of thing, while perhaps interesting, is inferior to the "objective" truth to be found elsewhere. I don't remember exactly what I said, except that I resisted the whole notion that truth could be split into such categories and tried to suggest that truth was much bigger than our language for it. This poem by Julia Levine, which dances beautifully among several planes of being and language, helps me think about the subjective and the objective.

On the 12:50 Out of Fairfield
Go ahead.
Say you are not moved by the soul

that looks out of every window,
seven cranes lifted like a train of hours

floating into loss, dusk already sifting down
the splintered rafters of your heart.

Say you don't need Heaven, the fictive afterlife
poured with cirrus blue and saints,

to get you through a rape, two deaths,
every lover that left you all alone.

Or say there is not one God,
but a countless shatter of the sacred,

like rain inside a week of rain,
and all the pearly fragments pour down

like desire, too large and brimming
to be held inside one life,

lust like a holy rush of sea
slapping up against the threatened levies

of your flesh, the conductor
singing out the names where longing dwells,

and all the strangers you will never touch
stepping down to stations

swarmed with light.
So, go ahead. Say you are just fine.

> Say this is enough, right here, right now.
> That you will learn to want
>
> only what you have.
> Go ahead. Try.[16]

The fascination and complication of this poem is mostly in its imperatives, addressed to a "you" who seems to be the poet but is not limited to her. Say this, say that—say that the things and people of the world do not move you, say that there is no "single God," say that you do not yearn for more clarity, more certainty, more ease within this lovely world and all the pain and desire its creatures bear. Crucially, all this "saying" happens not in some realm of abstract ideas, but in a very specific place, on a train with rainy fields and cranes outside and other passengers bearing their own secret lives about with them.

The poem asks radical, fundamental questions. How can the moment—which is always all we have, in one sense—ever be enough? How can we ever find anything more? How do all of our categories and theologies and imperatives and taboos, all our language and rules for engaging this world, intersect with the moment as it passes and keeps passing? All of these things are connected, the poem suggests, but not easily or simply; they cohabit each moment inside of our heads, where the world as we each know it happens.

As the ending reminds us, all the imperatives of the poem are verbal utterances, speech acts not meant to be "true" propositionally but to represent the immediate progression of the speaker's thoughts and feelings. All those imperative "Says," however, do add up to an effort to bring something into being by speaking it—perhaps a fuller acceptance of things as they are, an end to or at least a softening of yearning and desire and lust. At the same time, the poem evokes and recognizes the power of those elemental human realities and how intertwined they are. It is no accident that the poem moves so quickly from God to the "holy rush of sea" to the mysterious bodies of strangers. Equally crucial to the poem is its vulnerability, the poet's recognition of her own ambivalence and uncertainty, her own doubts and lusts. Writing is mysterious this way, because it requires mastery *and* relinquishing, great knowledge *and* greater awareness of one's limits.

"An ass which turns a millstone did a hundred miles walking. When it was loosed, it found that it was still at the same place. There are men who make many journeys, but make no progress toward a destination."
—The Gospel of Philip[17]

I walked home for lunch, as I've done a hundred times before—down the back stairs from my third-floor office, through the sculpture garden, past Shoker Science Center and Marbeck Center, across Riley Creek (still flowing, but low; it's been a dry spring), up the hill past the art building. None of this is new to me, and not for the first time I felt that I've spent my life walking in a pointless circle, moving between my comfortable office and home, wearing the keys on my keyboard shiny, while the bombs explode in Iraq and politicians posture and desperate people suffocate in shipping containers.

How to sum up this world, anyway? Clarence is on the other side of town now, probably still barking at squirrels and any living thing larger than a sparrow. The planet groans as the bonfire that passes for civilization blazes on. My green beans and snow peas are struggling out of the ground, despite little rain. Our aging minivan has a whine in the right rear that starts at 32 miles an hour and disappears at 36. Part of my mind wants to take the tire off and check out the bearing, another to settle on the recliner and read Jacob Boehme on the Unity of the All. Within a few miles of me some of God's children are hungry, terrified, strung out, utterly broke, crushed by depression. None are visible from here. The sun shines softly. The administration led by the most powerful Christian on earth has plans to develop bunker-busting nuclear weapons, lest any place on earth be outside the reach of American power. I try to find something new and inspiring to read, but everything strikes me as either ponderous beyond bearing ("Those in the fourth have forms like human forms and feet like human feet, and wear helmets on their heads, and marble tunics"[18]), or beautiful insights mingled with absurd optimism:

> All movement is a sign of
> Thirst.
> Most speaking really says,
> "I am hungry to know you."
> Every desire of your body is holy;
> Every desire of your body is
> Holy.[19]

Still, the new lilac bush seems to be rooting in, and so do the sunflowers I transplanted from my friend's place in the country. The sun warms the top of my head and all the half-formed desires, fears, and dreams swirling inside, as though all the whole breathing world should answer to that small, dark, teeming space.

"When we get our spiritual house in order, we'll be dead. This goes on. You arrive at enough certainty to be able to make your way, but it is making it in darkness. Don't expect faith to clear things up for you. It is trust, not certainty."
—Flannery O'Connor[20]

I first went on a "poetry night hike" a few years ago, led by my friend Terry Hermsen. I was suspicious about the idea of walking out with a group of people to write poems, but I have now done half a dozen of these hikes, and every one so far has been remarkable in its own way.

Last summer I found myself in charge. I spent days figuring every detail but miscalculated how long the light would last under the trees and got the group—ten of us or so—started much too late. I had planned a fifteen-minute walk past one waterfall and to another, to read a few poems when we got there and then set people loose to write as the dark came on. But as we walked to the upper waterfall, the light already dimming under the trees, I realized that if we pressed on we would be walking back along the rough, root-laced path in more or less total darkness.

It grieved my heart to stop partway and turn around, but everybody seemed relieved when I suggested it. When we got to the lower falls, which are pretty enough in their own right, I read a few poems aloud and we watched the light fade. I stumbled to a sittable rock and got out my little book along with the others.

There's something about writing in a place with trees and rocks and water as the light dwindles. The page gets vaguer and vaguer until you have to rely on muscle memory to avoid writing over your own words and ending up with an illegible scramble. But I always find that as my eyes become less useful, other parts of my being become more alert and more talkative. Still agitated by having messed up, I tried to settle into that twilight state in which all kinds of utterance seem to be possible, the way the sun's absence reveals the stars. As the water murmured along its way I wrote like mad for fifteen minutes or so, paying very little attention to what the others were doing. When I stopped, I realized that many of the others were still at it, and even after everyone had put their pens away we lingered for a while longer, soaking in the sensations of the night.

The way back was quiet, and I still wasn't sure how it had gone. I apologized to everybody, several times, and they were gracious, although my naturalist partner Mike suggested that if I had just listened to him things would have gone better. (He had brought along a fancy little LED headlamp and wandered around sure-footedly as the rest of us stumbled on the rocks and roots.)

On the last night we had an open reading, and I read the poem I had written that night, which has a lot to do with giving up the hope of being too fully in control of anything:

Where Water Finds an Edge
—Blue Hen Falls, June 2004

Nothing like a careful, thorough plan with one large error.
Too dark under the trees, too many roots—

we must turn back. Rocks piled around like bad excuses,
like my father's brow as he gently explains

just how deep and wide my screw-up is. I stumble
for a place to sit, break through a thin sheet of shale.

Even the skin of the earth can't be trusted.
Every splash is a sign; not one is a word.

But we know the light was hiding all these stars.
We need the dark because it makes us clumsy,

because it makes us forget the banks
we are rushing between, muttering about hymns

and women while the falls spill out before us.
We will not need to be ready to tumble down.

We will shine and shout, and all the damage
will be forgotten soon. The water is not wounded

by its breathless journey, it bears its troubles lightly,
it does not falter as the full night arrives.

And the hard ledges glow, long after all else is lost.[21]

The next morning I found myself sitting next to a shy woman I hadn't gotten to know well, although the night before she had put on a marvelous performance of a story she'd written. She said to me "Thank you for your error," so quietly that only later, when the workshop was over, did I understand her words.

NOTES

1. See J. Denny Weaver, *Keeping Salvation Ethical: Mennonite and Amish Atonement Theology in the Late Nineteenth Century* (Scottdale, Pa.: Herald Press, 1997); *Anabaptist Theology in Face of Postmodernity: A Proposal for the Third Millennium* (Telford, Pa.: Pandora Press U.S., 2000); and *The Nonviolent Atonement* (Grand Rapids, Mich.: Wm. B. Eerdmans, 2001).

2. Jeff Gundy, *Walker in the Fog: On Mennonite Writing* (Telford, Pa.: Cascadia Publishing House, 2005).

3. In Jeff Gundy, *Rhapsody with Dark Matter* (Huron, Oh.: Bottom Dog, 2000), 54.

4. Quoted in Willis Barnstone, *The Other Bible* (New York: HarperCollins, 1984), 90.

5. See John Roth, "Called to One Peace: Christian Faith and Political Witness in a Divided Culture," C. Henry Smith Lecture. Goshen College, April 5, 2005. Available at www.goshen.edu/news/pressarchive/photos/JohnDRothlecture.pdf.

6. I once overheard a student telling another that Denny Weaver had made a similar argument in class—something to the effect that the "Christian Right" had so besmirched the word *Christian* that he was not sure he wanted to call himself one anymore—but I have not been able to confirm this anecdote without compromising the clandestine nature of this Festschrift.

7. I must admit that the Big Oak Church on Route 30 east of Bluffton seems to have ceased functioning as a congregation, although the oak tree is apparently doing fine.

8. Thomas Merton, *New Seeds of Contemplation* (New York: New Directions, 1961), 24.

9. Quoted in James M. Robinson, *The Nag Hammadi Library in English* (San Francisco: Harper & Row, 1977), 126.

10. Walt Whitman, *Leaves of Grass and Selected Prose*, ed. John A. Kouwenhoven (New York: Random House, 1950), 446.

11. Quoted in Barnstone, 93.

12. In Jeff Gundy, *Spoken Among the Trees* (Akron, Oh.: University of Akron Press, 2007), 103-3

13. Merton, 37.

14. Ibid., 37-38.

15. James Wright, "Ten Letters," *The Georgia Review* 59/1 (2005): 37.

16. Julia Levine, *Ask* (University of Tampa Press, 2003), 33-34.

17. Quoted in Barnstone, 92.

18. Hildegarde of Bingen, *Scivias*, trans. Mother Columba Hart and Jane Bishop (New York: Paulist Press, 1990), 141.

19. Hafiz, *The Subject Tonight is Love: 60 Wild and Sweet Poems of Hafiz*, versions by Daniel Ladinsky (North Myrtle Beach, South Carolina: Pumpkin House, 1996), 9.

20. Flannery O'Connor, "Letter to Louise Abbot," in *The Habit of Being: Letters of Flannery O'Connor*, ed. Sally Fitzgerald (New York: Vintage, 1979), 354.

21. Gundy, *Spoken Among the Tress*, 25.

CHAPTER NINETEEN

Christus Victor and the Preoccupation with the Concrete in the Work of Christian Peacemaker Teams (CPT)

Kathleen Kern

*I*n 2004, I wrote an article for *The Mennonite* about a war crime that the Christian Peacemaker Team in Iraq had documented.[1] U.S. soldiers had entered the town of Al Jazeera on November 22, 2003, detaining three men as they approached one of the men's homes. The soldiers separated and went into the man's house from different entrances. Soldiers in one group, mistaking men from their squad for enemies, opened fire and killed four of their comrades from the other group. Distraught, the soldiers came out of the house and executed the three Iraqis as they sat on the ground in handcuffs. Helicopters and tanks then destroyed the house with missile fire.

On the same night, five young men had finished prayers at a mosque located about 500 meters from the home where the military operation—in which the four soldiers and three Iraqis died—had just ended. The five got into their pickup and headed away from the operation. A U.S. tank at a neighboring house opened fire on the pickup, killing everyone inside.

In my article, I noted that despite a press conference held by a local Iraqi human rights organization, the American media had not picked up on the story. Members of the CPT's Iraq team repeatedly tried to follow up with U.S. military personnel about this incident as well as other violations of the Geneva Conventions committed by U.S. forces. Each time, the officers dismissed the inquiries, claiming that the team could not trust Iraqis to report stories truthfully. In *The Mennonite* article, I compared this situation with the American experience in Vietnam, by describing American atrocities there that had only recently become known.[2]

I concluded the article as follows:

> [H]istory teaches us that when wars and military occupations happen, atrocities follow. Sometimes they are committed by men enraged and grief-stricken by the death of their comrades; sometimes they are committed by those whom the military has trained to believe that their enemies are less than human.
>
> And what is the job of Christian peacemakers in situations such as these? Listening to victims talk about their trauma is a true ministry, because the belief that anguish has fallen on deaf or uncaring ears is a taproot of violence. Reporting what peacemakers see, hear and experience is also a part of Christian ministry. When the mainstream media ignored the atrocities happening in Guatemala, El Salvador and Nicaragua, Christian missionaries and aid workers informed their constituencies about what was happening in those countries. (The ardently secular Noam Chomsky has often mentioned that he relied more on reports from church workers in Central America for news of the region than he did on the *New York Times*.)
>
> Getting the story out does not mean becoming a news service. It means bearing witness to the truth in whatever context Christians find themselves. The first Anabaptists did it by collecting stories for *The Mirror of the Martyrs*. Bartolomé de las Casas did it when he reported on the genocide of indigenous people in the new world. And of course, the first Christians did it when they described Jesus' death by slow torture at the hands of the Romans, whose military was occupying Palestine at the time.
>
> Matthew 25:40 quotes Jesus as saying "Truly I tell you, just as you did it to one of the least of these who are members of my family, you did it to me." We are honoring Christ, victim of the Great Atrocity, when we refuse to allow Powers and Principali-

ties to suppress news about the brutalization and slaughter of people the world considers disposable.[3]

Since not all members of my family read *The Mennonite*, I e-mailed them the article. The reaction of a much-loved relative, whom I will call L., to my description of Jesus' crucifixion as "The Great Atrocity," plunged me into a six-month theological debate via e-mail. The crucifixion, L. maintained, had been an obviously positive event, given that it made salvation possible for those who believed in Jesus.

In terms I have oversimplified, L. described a Jesus who mainly existed to provide "abundant life" in this world (related to a spiritual state only and not to one's economic circumstances) and guaranteed entry into heaven in the next. L., in response to my assertion that the Gospels showed Jesus standing in solidarity with the poor and those who suffered rather than with the rich and self-satisfied, wrote,

> I think Jesus didn't favor any group of people over the other. In fact, I don't think Jesus really thought about people's outward circumstances at all. I think He was way more interested in their heart and "eternal being" than he was with what conditions they were in. His concern was people having intimate fellowship with their Creator, knowing that from the inward transformation of experiencing utter Father love, fruit would be born that would take care of (or at least relieve) those situations.

I wrote to L. that Satan—or, to use Walter Wink's terminology, the Domination system[4]—found it convenient that Christians had "spiritualized the crucifixion beyond all recognition." I told her that people thought about the cross so much in terms of symbolic concepts—"redemption," "sacrifice," or even "Christian"—that they do not realize the horror of the crucifixion. They do not see Jesus' bravery in pursuing a course he knew could end with his torture and death. They do not see that the Powers have replicated this horror millions of times over by torturing and killing the "least of these" in the centuries since Jesus' crucifixion. I suggested that if people had regarded the cross as an instrument of torture—to which Jesus was subjected because he advocated for the marginalized—rather than as a crusader's banner or jewellery, Christian history might have been different.

As I was reviewing these e-mails recently, I realized that L.'s theological arguments were almost all rooted in abstract concepts: the nature of the Trinity, "abundant life," inner spirituality, personal relationship with God. The work of CPT, on the other hand, is relentlessly grounded in the concrete details of particular situations. The "narrative Christus Victor" model of the atonement championed by J. Denny Weaver fits naturally, I believe, with CPT's focus on the concrete, while substitutionary/satisfaction models too often push Christians toward abstraction.

J. Denny Weaver defines "narrative Christus Victor" as "an image of Christology and atonement that displays the reign of God in nonviolent confrontation of and triumph over evil. This image develops a salvation based on a nonviolent reign of God and separated from the violence of retribution." The Gospels depict this cosmic confrontation between everything that is not under the rule of God and Jesus, as does the book of Revelation.[5]

At first glance, the Christus Victor model of atonement is, of course, also an abstract idea, as are all models. However, Jesus' confrontations with the principalities and powers manifested themselves in concrete ways. Using spit and mud to heal blindness perhaps counts as his most concrete miracle, and the reaction of the religious establishment to this healing certainly shows the Domination System at work (John 9:1-10:21). Weaver notes that Jesus healed on the Sabbath, despite his knowledge that the religious establishment would consider doing so a violation of Jewish law (Luke 6:6-11; 13:10-17; 14:1-6). He spoke frankly to a Samaritan woman about her sex life, when speaking to women or Samaritans was considered shameful (John 4:1-30). He included women among his disciples (Luke 8:1-3) and asserted that education for women was important (Luke 10:38-42). He undertook civil disobedience to prevent commerce in the temple, physically turning over the tables of the moneychangers and sellers of doves whose target market was the poor (Mark 11:15). He rebuked Peter when Peter attempted to defend Jesus with a sword at Jesus' arrest (Matt. 26:51-54; John 18:10-11).[6]

Similarly, the narrative Christus Victor model leads Christians to practical, concrete actions, while the substitutionary atonement model leads some (not all) people to the abstract. This abstraction, which shifts the focus of human beings away from the real miseries at work in the world, can lead to passivity and acquiescence to the Domination System.

The work of Christian Peacemaker Teams shows a preoccupation with the concrete. Teams go to various areas of conflict, describe the forms that violence they have witnessed and intervene physically to deter violence. For example, consider this 2005 CPTnet release about an incident in the southern West Bank:

CPTNET

24 May 2005

AT-TUWANI: Israeli military, police and settlers prevent Palestinians from grazing sheep and goats

by Kristin Anderson

On Thursday, 19 May 2005, Israeli soldiers, police and settlers prevented Palestinians from Jawiyya, a small village in the south Hebron Hills, from grazing their sheep and goats.

Israeli soldiers and a security guard from the Israeli settlement of Ma'on arrived simultaneously about 5:00 p.m. They began interrogating and photographing Palestinians and members of the Christian Peacemaker Teams (CPT). At the same time, four young settlers descended a hill and gathered close to the Palestinian shepherds and sheep, taunting them and picking up rocks. Israeli police proceeded to tell CPTers Kristin Anderson and Sally Britton that they must go to the (Israel bypass) road, because, he said, "The settlers make more problems whenever they see CPTers." Anderson told the policeman that CPTers would not leave because it would not be safe for the Palestinians. The Israeli policeman then took Anderson's passport and threatened her with arrest.

Israeli police proceeded to check the IDs of the Palestinians. They claimed they were verifying ownership of the land where the goats and sheep were grazing. After this, Israeli soldiers corralled the Palestinians and their flocks into a smaller area. The soldiers then began chasing the Palestinians up the hill and physically pushing them. The soldiers were shouting, "This is soldier land—GO! This is soldier land—go home!" The Palestinians moved slowly and verbally refuted soldiers' claims to the land.

One Palestinian defiantly sat on the hillside. The Ma'on security guard continued to drive the goats and sheep roughly up the hillside. Once the Israeli soldiers forced the Palestinians to the top of the hill, just beyond the border of the "disputed" area, the soldiers, police, and remaining settlers left.

In the last week, the settler security guard from Ma'on and/or the Israeli military have interrupted the grazing six times while CPTers and members of Operation Dove, an Italian Christian peace organization, were accompanying the shepherds. Additionally on Saturday, 16 May 2005, between forty and fifty settlers from Ma'on attacked Palestinians harvesting wheat and grazing their animals on this land. A ten-year-old Palestinian boy needed six stitches in his chin as a result of an injury from a rock thrown by a settler. On Monday, 16 May, 2005, twenty settlers attacked Palestinian shepherds and their animals on this "disputed" land, killing three sheep and injuring several others (four of these injured sheep have since died.)

Palestinians from Jawiyya continue to resist nonviolently land confiscation and settlement expansion by grazing their animals on this "disputed" land. While an Israeli soldier was shoving him up the hill, one Palestinian shepherd screamed, "It's a war here every day."[7]

Events in Israel and Palestine usually have numerous abstract overlays superimposed on them. For example, Christian Zionists, using Zechariah 13:7-9 as a proof text, believe that Israel is God's chosen nation and that all Jews must immigrate to Israel to precipitate Jesus' end-times return (at which point two-thirds of them will die horrible deaths and one-third will convert to Christianity). Other partisans of Israel overlay the history of anti-Semitism onto contemporary realities in Israel-Palestine. Jewish suffering is not abstract, of course; too many concrete examples of the torture, murder, and humiliation of Jews throughout history are well documented. However, pogroms in Russia and the Nazi Holocaust have almost nothing to do with Israeli settlers driving Palestinian shepherds from their lands. Another abstract overlay placed on the Israeli-Palestinian conflict by U.S. lawmakers and think tanks is that of "complexity." I remember in high school hearing people describe apartheid in South Africa as "complex" and telling me that we should not rush to judge white South Africans. In fact, of course, apartheid was simple: White South Africans wanted to deny any sort of power to black South Africans. Similarly, the above release about a confrontation in the South Hebron hills describes a simple reality: Israeli soldiers and settlers do not want Palestinians grazing flocks on land for which the Palestinians have legal documents. The CPTers physically placed themselves near living and breathing shepherds to prevent living and breathing soldiers and settlers from attacking them.

My fourteen years with CPT have moved many of my fuzzy beliefs about good and evil, equality and racism, violence and nonviolence, away from the abstract toward the concrete end of the spectrum. One example of this movement involves my attitude toward Satan. The devil personified never factored much into my faith journey before CPT. Now I believe I have seen Satan/the Domination System at work in the world. I have met a few people in the flesh whom I would describe as evil, i.e., they derive joy from observing and causing human suffering. More commonly, and sometimes more distressingly, I meet people who would never shoot a child from their neighborhood but sincerely believe that they ought to shoot children of "the enemy" who are throwing stones at them or should destroy homes in which they know enemy children are living. I know people who would never dream of letting a family in their neighborhood or church starve to death but support economic systems that make starvation inevitable for millions. People who would never torture anyone assent to their government's support of regimes that do torture people. The acquiescence of kind, God-loving people to torture, starvation, and violence for me is the most convincing sign of Satan's work in this world.

Jesus' teachings in the Gospels have also become more concrete for me in the last twelve years. The work has put me amid poor people who connect me to peasants in first-century Palestine. When I hear Jesus telling his first-century followers not to worry (Matt. 6:25-31), I no longer hear it with North American ears. Affluent North Americans abstract these admonitions not to worry by thinking of them in terms of doing well on algebra tests or achieving the workplace promotions they want. Now that I have lived among and worked with nearly indigent peasants in Haiti, Palestine, and Chiapas, Mexico, I realize that a significant portion of Jesus' audience really did not know where their next meal, or their next week's meal, was coming from.

Jesus' teaching on loving enemies became painfully concrete for CPTers who worked on the Chiapas project with a community of Christian pacifist Mayan Indians called the Bees (*Las Abejas*). Once the Bees read the Gospels in their own language, they discerned that they could not follow Jesus' command to love their enemies while taking up arms. Although they publicly supported the reforms that the Zapatista movement called for, referring to the Zapatistas as their brothers, they refused to use violence to achieve these reforms.

On December 22, 1997, paramilitaries slaughtered forty-five men, women, and children from the Bees as they prayed for peace in the Acteal refugee camp. Once CPTers serving on the Chiapas project began to accompany the Bees out of the refugee camps and back to their home villages, members pointed out specific individuals who had assaulted them, killed family members, burned their homes, and stolen their crops. The Bees called the Mexican government to arrest the perpetrators of the massacre but still chose to live among their former enemies who had harmed them in lesser ways, treating them with kindness. Those who repented, they welcomed into their communities.⁸

One of my insights into the concreteness of Jesus' gospel message happened during Lent 1998, when Mark's texts about Jesus' entry into Jerusalem and the woman at Bethany spoke directly to CPT work in the West Bank city of Hebron. Members of the Hebron team were using Ched Myers' *Say to This Mountain*—a book study on the gospel of Mark—as part of our daily worship.⁹ One morning, as I read aloud the passage in Mark describing Jesus' entry into Jerusalem during the last week of his life (Mark 11:1-11), a chilling awareness struck me. Jesus knew. He knew when he entered Jerusalem that what he chose to do would lead to betrayal, humiliation, abandonment, and death by slow torture. In fact, Mark 11:11 indicates that Jesus deliberately chose to commit civil disobedience in Jerusalem for the express purpose of challenging the religious establishment whatever the cost.¹⁰

I finished reading the Scripture in tears as I thought about the conscious decisions our team in Hebron had made to enter into the pain of dozens of Palestinian families facing the demolition of their homes and the confiscation of their land. I wept as I thought about all the families who—despite our best efforts to call attention to what was happening to them—would lose everything they had so that Israeli settlements might expand. I wept because I realized that Jesus knew what it felt like to wonder what people in power would do to us because of our public witness. He knew how it would feel to fail in our efforts to save the homes of Palestinian families whom we had come to love. He knew better than anyone why the idea of entering into dozens more relationships with Palestinian families living under the same circumstances sometimes made me panic.

The story of the woman at Bethany in Mark 14:1-9 also spoke to me in Lent 1998, because it reveals the disciples' unwillingness to look at and name concrete horrors. Three days before the crucifixion, the nameless woman at Bethany visited Jesus at the house of Simon the Leper and poured expensive ointment on his head. Unfortunately, Christians too often point to Jesus' retort to his critics, "For you always have the poor with you" as a justification of their affluence.

But the action of the woman at Bethany represents something gruesome. Jesus told his disciples that he was about to die. The actions he took—especially his very conscious attitude to disrupt commerce in the temple—would lead to his death at the hands of the establishment. And his disciples were in deep denial about it.

John Dominic Crossan, whom I believe too freely imposes contemporary sociological paradigms on first-century Palestine, does get one thing right when it comes to the woman at Bethany.[11] She was the only one of Jesus' followers mentioned in Mark who accepted the reality of what was about to happen. She knew that crucifixion meant torture, public humiliation, pain beyond what most of us can imagine, and ultimately a corpse consumed by carrion birds and dogs. People whom the Roman Empire crucified did not have the benefit of ritual burials, so she showed her love and support for Jesus' courageous decision by giving him the honor of burial before he died. She was there for him in a way that his disciples were not.

In Mark 14:27, nineteen verses after the Woman at Bethany's story is finished, Jesus tells the disciples that they will desert him physically as well as emotionally. Mark 14:50 notes tersely, "and they all forsook him and fled." Mark contains no record of Jesus' male disciples being present for the crucifixion. Mark notes only that "There were also women looking on from a distance; among them were Mary Magdalene, and Mary the mother of James the younger and of Joses, and Salome. These used to follow him and provided for him when he was in Galilee; and there were many other women who had come up with him to Jerusalem" (Mark 15:40-41). These women gave Jesus the tangible things he needed, like food, and were willing to face concrete reality—literally the most horrible reality imaginable—when the disciples were not.

Jesus, Christus Victor, chose to intervene in the lives of people facing illness and contempt from their societies, touching them and eating their food. He chose to disrupt the system that marginalized and humiliated them, even though the consequences were the equivalent of a judicial lynching. Every nerve ending in his human body felt the pain that the Domination System has inflicted on millions of victims over the centuries. His endocrine system pumped the same adrenaline, noradrenaline, and cortisol through his body that floods the bodies of other victims whom the Domination System terrorizes. He wept tears composed of water, salt, enzymes, manganese, and mucus just like the tears that millions of other human beings have wept when they saw their loved ones suffering and could not help them.

Since Lent of 1998, I have wondered whether my main job as a worker for Christian Peacemaker Teams has been to emulate the role of the Woman at Bethany in choosing to face horror, choosing to understand and proclaim that violence and cruelty are at work on people whom God loves, to make people feel that reality as they would feel nails driven through the skin, tendons, muscles, and bones.

There are people working within CPT who believe in the theology of substitutionary atonement, so I do not claim that the substitutionary atonement model necessarily leads to a violent outlook on life or to support for the powers and principalities. However, I do think its focus on abstract concepts enables Christians to support policies and actions antithetical to Christ's teachings in the Gospels.[12] My e-mail correspondence with L. had its roots in a prior, emotional conversation about the incipient U.S. invasion of Iraq. She was teaching her children that the soldiers in Iraq were "fighting for our [Americans'] freedom." When I asked her how that mechanism actually worked, what civil liberties we have under the American constitution that would have been threatened had the U.S. not invaded Iraq, she spoke of how we needed to "take a stand" because of the September 11, 2001, al-Qaeda attacks on the World Trade Center and the Pentagon.

Not surprisingly then, L., once we moved into a cyber-theological debate, kept deflecting the concrete to grasp the abstract. When I asked how one could both love one's enemy or neighbor—clearly commanded by Jesus—and kill them, she said frankly that she did not know, but that was beside the point. More important was my enjoying "abundant life" in Christ (which, to do her justice, she wants me to have). When I said that the central faith question of my life is, "What does it mean to follow Jesus?" rather than "What can Jesus do for me?" she expressed the fear that I did not believe in the Trinity.

The narrative Christus Victor model of atonement articulated by Denny Weaver has the merit of coming a few steps closer to concrete reality than does the concept of substitutionary atonement. Animal sacrifices in the Jerusalem temple (see Hebrews 10) have not taken place for centuries, so the substitutionary atonement model is a theological construct based on a historical reality that has no contemporary relevance for most Jews or Christians.[13] Poverty and oppression, on the other hand, are stark realities in the current world and are becoming worse as corporate profits trump human rights and environmental concerns. Neighbors and enemies—concrete human beings who bleed, laugh, and hope—still exist, and we can make conscious choices to love them or to kill them. We can make choices to confront systems that dehumanize, exploit, torture, and kill people, or we can choose to participate passively in these systems and accept the benefits that accrue to participants.

As Weaver has proclaimed, God, through the teaching and resurrection of Jesus Christ, has already won in the cosmic confrontation with Satan.[14] Our choice now is whether we will make ourselves available as construction workers to the victorious Christ as he builds the reign of God in this sinful world—or whether we will continue to serve the Domination System, the architects of which, after two millennia have passed, still believe that power is more important that justice, compassion, and peace.[15]

NOTES

1. The CPT Mandate as printed in the organization's brochure is as follows:

    1. We believe the mandate to proclaim the gospel of repentance, salvation and reconciliation includes a strengthened Biblical peace witness.

    2. We believe that faithfulness to what Jesus taught and modelled calls us to more active peacemaking.

    3. We believe a renewed commitment to the gospel of peace calls us to new forms of public witness which may include nonviolent direct action.

    4. We believe the establishment of Christian Peacemaker Teams is an important new dimension for our ongoing peace and justice ministries.

    "To be authentic, such peacemaking should be rooted in and supported by congregations and church-wide agencies. We will begin."

2. I specifically cited the *Toledo Blade*'s Pulitzer Prize-winning series about the Tiger Force unit of the 101st Airborne division, "Buried Secrets, Brutal Truths," first published October 22, 2003, now accessible at www.toledoblade.com/apps/pbcs.dll/section?Category=/SRTIGERFORCE. Viewed December 7, 2007.

3. Kathleen Kern, "The Rest of the Story," *The Mennonite* (February 17, 2004), 16-17

4. From Theologian Walter Wink's *Engaging the Powers* (Minneapolis: Augsburg Fortress Press 1992): "Institutions have an actual spiritual ethos.... In the ancient world view, a seer or prophet was able to sense the diseased spirituality of an institution.... I speak of 'demons' as the actual spirituality of systems and structures that have betrayed their divine vocations. I use the expression 'the Domination System' to indicate what happens when an entire network of powers becomes integrated around idolatrous values" (6-9).

5. See the argument in J. Denny Weaver, "Atonement and the Gospel of Peace," in *Seeking Cultures of Peace: A Peace Church Conversation*, ed. Fernando Enns, Scott Holland, and Ann Riggs (Telford, Pa.: Cascadia Publishing House; copublished World Council of Churches Publications and Herald Press, 2004), 109-23.

6. Ibid. I have adapted Weaver's list of examples.
7. CPTnet news release issued May 24, 2005. Available at www.cpt.org/archives/2005/may05/0036.html. Viewed December 7, 2007.
8. Since I wrote the first draft of this article, four of my colleagues were kidnapped and one, Tom Fox, murdered in Baghdad. CPTer Jim Loney and CPT delegation members Norman Kember and Harmeet Singh Sooden, when called to testify against their kidnapers, held a press conference in London on December 8, 2006 during which they read the following statement:

> We three, members of a Christian Peacemaker Teams (CPT) delegation to Iraq, were kidnapped on November 26, 2005 and held for 118 days before being freed by British and American forces on March 23, 2006. Our friend and colleague, Tom Fox, an American citizen and full-time member of the CPT team working in Baghdad at the time, was kidnapped with us and murdered on March 9, 2006.
>
> We are immensely sad that he is not sitting with us here today.
>
> On behalf of our families and CPT, we thank you for attending this press conference today.
>
> It was on this day a year ago that our captors threatened to execute us unless their demands were met. This ultimatum, unknown to us at the time, was a source of extreme distress for our families, friends and colleagues.
>
> The deadline was extended by two days to December 10, which is International Human Rights Day. On this day, people all over the world will commemorate the adoption of the Universal Declaration of Human Rights by the UN General Assembly in 1948 by speaking out for all those whose human dignity is being violated by torture, arbitrary imprisonment, poverty, racism, oppression or war.
>
> We understand a number of men alleged to be our captors have been apprehended, charged with kidnapping, and are facing trial in the Central Criminal Court of Iraq. We have been asked by the police in our respective countries to testify in the trial. After much reflection upon our traditions, both Sikh and Christian, we are issuing this statement today.
>
> We unconditionally forgive our captors for abducting and holding us. We have no desire to punish them. Punishment can never restore what was taken from us.
>
> What our captors did was wrong. They caused us, our families and our friends great suffering. Yet, we bear no malice towards them and have no wish for retribution. Should those who have been charged with holding us hostage be brought to trial and convicted, we ask that they be granted all possible leniency. We categorically lay aside any rights we may have over them.

In our view, the catastrophic levels of violence and the lack of effective protection of human rights in Iraq is inextricably linked to the U.S.-led invasion and occupation. As for many others, the actions of our kidnappers were part of a cycle of violence they themselves experienced. While this is no way justifies what the men charged with our kidnapping are alleged to have done, we feel this must be considered in any potential judgment.

Forgiveness is an essential part of Sikh, Christian and Muslim teaching. Guru Nanak Dev Ji, the first of the Sikh Gurus said, "'Forgiveness' is my mother . . ." and, "Where there is forgiveness, there is God." Jesus said, "For if you forgive those who sin against you, your heavenly Father will also forgive you." And of Prophet Mohammed (Peace Be Upon Him) it is told that once, while preaching in the city of Ta'if, he was abused, stoned and driven out of the city. An angel appeared to him and offered to crush the city between the two surrounding mountains if he ordered him to do so, whereupon the prophet (or Mohammed PBUH) said, "No. Maybe from them or their offspring will come good deeds."

Through the power of forgiveness, it is our hope that good deeds will come from the lives of our captors, and that we will all learn to reject the use of violence. We believe those who use violence against others are themselves harmed by the use of violence.

Kidnapping is a capital offence in Iraq and we understand that some of our captors could be sentenced to death. The death penalty is an irrevocable judgment. It erases all possibility that those who have harmed others, even seriously, can yet turn to good. We categorically oppose the death penalty.

By this commitment to forgiveness, we hope to plant a seed that one day will bear the fruits of healing and reconciliation for us, our captors, the peoples of Canada, New Zealand, the United Kingdom, the United States, and most of all, Iraq. We look forward to the day when the Universal Declaration of Human Rights is respected by all the world's people. (www.cpt.org/archives/2006/dec06/0008.html)

9. Ched Myers, *"Say to this Mountain": Mark's Story of Discipleship* (Maryknoll, N.Y.: Orbis Books, 1996).

10. The phrase, "as it was already late, he went out to Bethany with the twelve," begs the question, Too late for what? Mark answers the question three verses later.

11. One example of Crossan's tendency to impose these paradigms is his claim that in Jesus' day, 95-97 percent of the Jewish state (and therefore, probably Jesus) was illiterate. Given that no one was conducting literacy censuses at the time, the claim is suspect.—John Dominic Crossan, *Jesus: A Revolutionary Biography* (San Francisco: HarperSanFrancisco, 1994). Crossan's moving

portrait of the Woman at Bethany in Mark 14 may be found in *The Historical Jesus: The Life of a Mediterranean Jewish Peasant* (San Francisco: HarperCollins, 1991).

12. Weaver has also noted the dangers of abstraction in theology: "We have also observed that the abstract and ahistorical character of the classic formulas of atonement and Christology mean that they do not challenge injustice in the social order."—J. Denny Weaver, "Violence in Christian Theology," *Cross Currents* 51/2 (Summer 2001): 150-76.

A concrete example of Weaver's disdain for theological abstraction occurred during my college years when Bluffton College hosted the Intercollegiate Peace Fellowship Conference (an annual gathering of peace organizations from Mennonite-related schools). The Bluffton College Peace Club asked our Student Christian Association to lead prayers for morning worship. The designated leader made a point of telling the assembly that internal "peace with Christ" is what "it" was all about. Weaver, as Peace Club's faculty advisor, told us that this theology had no business being a part of the IPF conference. The function of the IPF conference was to stand in opposition to that type of theology.

13. Aside from Christian Zionists and very right-wing Jews who believe that renewing animal sacrifices on the Temple Mount in Jerusalem would be a sign of progress.

14. Weaver, "Violence in Christian Theology."

15. Some personal reflections about J. Denny Weaver are in order here. My first course with Denny was the freshman seminar for honors students I took the fall of 1980 on American civil religion. I had grown up in a very white, conservative town largely run by three fundamentalist churches. In that environment I had accepted the doctrine that patriotism was a high ideal. My course with Denny made me realize that perhaps the patriotism with which my northwest Ohio town had indoctrinated me ran counter to the gospel, and that allegiance to Jesus Christ came before allegiance to my country. While paradigm shifts most often cause discomfort, this one lifted a burden. I felt I had more solid ground to support my deep belief that killing people was wrong. Weaver helped me to see that American civil religion is a disease, one of whose symptoms is to justify violence.

Other paradigm shifts Denny introduced to his classes made me less comfortable—but he also taught me that comfort did not by itself have merit, and that just because a belief was shocking did not mean it was untrue. For example, he asserted that schisms in Mennonite church history were not necessarily bad, because they demonstrated that people felt deeply enough about something to act on their beliefs. I was troubled by his assertion that Jews use the Holocaust to justify Israeli persecution of Palestinians until I began working in Palestine/Israel and was told and heard the same thing from Israelis active in the peace and human rights movements. I think because of Denny I use words like "heresy" and "blasphemy" more than I might have otherwise.

Weaver served as faculty advisor for the Bluffton College Peace Club, during a "Camelot" phase when we were active organizing around Central American and nuclear weapons issues. He took the heat from an unsympathetic administrator when the Peace Club held a campus-wide vote to declare Bluffton College a nuclear-free zone. (I had approached the administrator several times to get his approval for the venture and he kept canceling the meetings. Ultimately, he told an AP journalist that the effort did not have the support of the administration.)

Probably Weaver's influence also factored into the long e-mail debate I had with L., although I suspect I pursued it with less relish than he has his own theological debates with partisans of substitutionary atonement, Catholic theology, and televangelists.

Finally, the fact that I scrutinized the first draft of this article for every usage of passive voice and form of the verb "to be," and eliminated all unquoted usages of, "There is," "It is," and "This is" has its roots in the profusion of Denny's red ink on the papers of the students in that freshman honors seminar, who, until we took the class, had thought we wrote well.

BIBLIOGRAPHY OF THE WORKS OF J. DENNY WEAVER

Below, as of autumn 2007, is a comprehensive listing of J. Denny Weaver's published scholarly articles, essays for the popular press, book reviews, and occasional comment—writings that primarily address issues in Anabaptist-Mennonite history and the dynamics of a nonviolent theology but that also range far and wide into other areas. Given Weaver's predilection to collecting, we have decided to keep the bibliography as comprehensive as possible, including letters to *Newsweek* and articles in Bluffton University's *Witmarsum* newspaper alongside more typical entries in a scholarly vita.

I. BOOKS

Becoming Anabaptist: The Origin and Significance of Sixteenth-Century Anabaptism, 2nd. ed. Scottdale, Pa.: Herald Press (1987) 2005.

Edited (with Gerald Biesecker-Mast). *Teaching Peace: Nonviolence and the Liberal Arts*. Lanham, Md.: Rowman and Littlefield, 2003.

The Nonviolent Atonement. Grand Rapids, Mich.: Wm. B. Eerdmans, 2001.

Anabaptist Theology in Face of Postmodernity: A Proposal for the Third Millennium. With a foreword by Glen Stassen. The C. Henry Smith Series, vol. 2. Telford, Pa.: Pandora Press U.S.; copublished with Herald Press, 2000.

Keeping Salvation Ethical: Mennonite and Amish Atonement Theology in the Late Nineteenth Century. Studies in Anabaptist and Mennonite History, vol 35. Scottdale, Pa.: Herald Press, 1997.

II. EDITORSHIP

Editor, The C. Henry Smith Series, 2000-present

Vol. 8: Earl Zimmerman, *Practicing the Politics of Jesus: The Origin and Significance of John Howard Yoder's Social Ethics.* "Series Editor's Foreword," 15-17.

Vol. 7: Raylene Hinz-Penner, *Searching for Sacred Ground: the Journey of Chief Lawrence Hart, Mennonite.* "Series Editor's Foreword," 12-14.

Vol. 6: Gerald Biesecker-Mast, *Separation and the Sword in Anabaptist Persuasion: Radical Confessional Rhetoric from Schleitheim to Dordrecht.* "Series Editor's Foreword," 15-17.

Vol. 5: Jeff Gundy, *Walker in the Fog: On Mennonite Writing.* "Series Editor's Foreword," 13-14.

Vol. 4: Julia Kasdorf, *Fixing Tradition: Joseph W. Yoder, Amish American.* "Series Editor's Preface," 11-12.

Vol. 3: Michael A. King, *Fractured Dance: Gadamer and a Mennonite Conflict over Homosexuality.* "Series Editor's Foreword," 17-19.

Vol. 2: J. Denny Weaver, *Anabaptist Theology in Face of Postmodernity: A Proposal for the Third Millennium*

Vol. 1: Susan Biesecker-Mast and Gerald Biesecker-Mast, *Anabaptists and Postmodernity.* "Foreword," 12-14.

III. ESSAYS IN BOOKS

"The Nonviolent Atonement: Human Violence, Discipleship and God." In *Stricken by God? Nonviolent Identification and the Victory of Christ*, ed. Brad Jersak and Michael Hardin, 316-355. Grand Rapids, Mich.: Wm. B. Eerdmans, 2007.

" Living in the Reign of God in the 'Real World': Getting Beyond Two-Kingdom Theology." In *Exiles in the Empire: Believers Church Perspectives on Politics*, ed. Nathan E. Yoder and Carol A. Scheppard, 173-93. Kitchener, Ont.: Pandora Press, 2006.

" Narrative Christus Victor: the Answer to Anselmian Atonement Violence." In *Atonement and Violence: a Theological Conversation*, ed. John Sanders, 1-29. Nashville: Abingdon, Press, 2006.

"Response to Hans Boersma." In *Atonement and Violence*, 73-79.

"Response to Thomas Finger." In *Atonement and Violence*, 115-17.

"Response to T. Scott Daniels." In *Atonement and Violence*, 151-53.

"Violence in Christian Theology." In *Cross Examinations: Readings on the Meaning of the Cross Today*, ed. Marit Trelstad, 225-39. Minneapolis: Augsburg Fortress, 2006.

"Assumptions in Biblical Interpretation." In *Telling Our Stories: Personal Accounts of Engagement with Scripture*, ed. Ray Gingerich and Earl Zimmerman, 243-44. Telford, Pa.: Cascadia Publishing House; copublished Scottdale, Pa.: Herald Press, 2006.

"From Nonresistance to Engaged Nonviolence." In *Telling Our Stories: Personal Accounts of Engagement with Scripture*, ed. Ray Gingerich and Earl Zimmerman, 207-220. Telford, Pa.: Cascadia Publishing House; copublished Scottdale, Pa.: Herald Press, 2006.

"Justice, Spirituality, and the Church: The Atonement Connection." In *Vital Christianity: Spirituality, Justice, and Christian Practice*, ed. David L. Weaver-Zercher and William H. Willimon, 49-58. New York: T & T Clark International, 2005.

"Jesus' Death and the Non-Violent Victory of God." In *Consuming Passion: Why the Killing of Jesus Really Matters*, ed. Simon Barrow and Jonathan Bartley, 47-60. London: Darton, Longman and Todd, 2005.

"Why the 'Almost' is Still Important: A Response to 'Just Policing: How War Could Cease to Be a Church-Dividing Issue.'" In *Just Policing: Mennonite-Catholic Theological Colloquium, 2002*, ed. Ivan J. Kauffman, 89-99. The Bridgefolk Series. Kitchener, Ont.: Pandora Press, 2004.

"Atonement and the Gospel of Peace." In *Seeking Cultures of Peace: A Peace Church Conversation*, ed. Fernando Enns, Scott Holland, and Ann Riggs, 109-23. Telford, Pa.: Cascadia Publishing House; copublished World Council of Churches Publications and Herald Press, 2004.

"Violence in Christian Theology." In *Teaching Peace: Nonviolence and the Liberal Arts*, eds. J. Denny Weaver and Gerald Biesecker-Mast, 39-52. Lanham, Md.: Rowman & Littlefield, 2003.

"Following Jesus in the Face of Terror." In *Where Was God on Sept. 11? Seeds of Faith and Hope*, ed. Donald B. Kraybill and Linda Gehman Peachey, 112-15. Scottdale, Pa.: Herald Press, 2002.

"Nicaea, Womanist Theology, and Anabaptist Particularity." In *Anabaptists and Postmodernity*, ed. Susan Biesecker-Mast and Gerald Biesecker-Mast, 251-79. The C. Henry Smith Series, vol. 1. Telford, Pa.: Pandora Press U.S.; copublished with Herald Press, 2000.

"Reading the Past, Present, and Future in Revelation." In *Apocalypticism and Millennialism: Shaping a Believers Church Eschatology for the 21st Century*, ed. Loren L. Johns, 97-112. Studies in the Believers Church Tradition, no. 2. Kitchner, Ont.: Pandora Press Canada; copublished Scottdale, Pa.: Herald Press, 2000.

"Making Yahweh's Rule Visible." In *Peace and Justice Shall Embrace: Power and Theopolitics in the Bible: Essays in Honor of Millard Lind*, ed. Ted

Grimsrud and Loren L. Johns, 34-48. Telford, Pa.: Pandora Press U.S.; copublished Scottdale, Pa.: Herald Press, 1999. Reprinted as pamphlet and distributed by Christian Peacemaker Teams.

"Theology in the Mirror of the Martyred and Oppressed: Reflections on the Intersections of Yoder and Cone." In *The Wisdom of the Cross: Essays in Honor of John Howard Yoder*, ed. Stanley Hauerwas, Chris K. Huebner, Harry J. Huebner, and Mark Thiessen Nation, 409-429. Grand Rapids, Mich.: Eerdmans, 1999.

"Teaching for Peace." In *Mennonite Education in a Post-Christian World: Essays Presented at the Consultation on Higher Education, Winnipeg, June 1997*, ed. Harry Huebner, 67-80. Winnipeg, Man.: CMBC Publications, 1998.

"Christus Victor, Nonviolence, and Other Religions." In *Mennonite Theology in Face of Modernity: Essays in Honor of Gordon D. Kaufman*, ed. Alain Epp Weaver, 179-203. North Newton, Kan.: Bethel College, 1996.

"Understandings of Salvation: The Church, Pietistic Experience, and Nonresistance." In *Anabaptist Currents: History in Conversation with the Present*, ed. Carl F. Bowman and Stephen L. Longenecker, 27-39. Bridgewater, Va.: Forum for Religious Studies, Bridgewater College, 1995.

"The Socially Active Community: An Alternative Ecclesiology." In *The Limits of Perfectionism: Conversations with J. Lawrence Burkholder*, ed. Rodney J. Sawatsky and Scott Holland, 70-94. Waterloo, Ont.: Institute of Anabaptist-Mennonite Studies, Conrad Grebel College, and Kitchener, Ont.: Pandora Press, 1993.

"The Academic Disciplines and Mennonite Higher Education—Religion." In *Mennonite Higher Education: Experience and Vision: A Symposium on Mennonite Higher Education*, ed. Ken Hawkley, 199-206. Council on Higher Education of the General Conference Mennonite Church, 1992.

[Response to Walter Klaassen]. In *Anabaptist-Mennonite Identities in Ferment*, eds. Leo Driedger and Leland Harder, 27-31. Occasional Papers, no. 14. Elkhart, In.: Institute of Mennonite Studies, 1990.

"Challenges, Conflicts, and Consequences" [response paper]. In *Servants of the Word: Ministry in the Believers' Church*, ed. David B. Eller, 133-40. Elgin, Ill.: Brethren Press, 1990.

"Christology in historical Perspective." In *Jesus Christ and the Mission of the Church: Contemporary Anabaptist Perspectives*, ed. Erland Waltner, 83-105. Newton, Kan..: Faith and Life, 1990. First appeared as "Christology in Historical Perspective." In *Jesus Christ and the Mission of the Church: Contemporary Anabaptist Perspectives*, by George Brunk III, Harry Huebner, and J. Denny Weaver, 49-72. Papers for the Study Conference on Christology, Normal, Ill. 4-6 August 1989. Newton, Kan.: General Conference Mennonite Church, 1989.

"Mennonite Theological Self-Understanding: A Response to A. James Reimer." In *Mennonite Identity: Historical and Contemporary Perspectives*, ed. Calvin Wall Redekop and Samuel J. Steiner, 39-61. Lanham, Md.: University Press of America, 1988.

"Perspectives on a Mennonite Theology." In *Explorations of Systematic Theology From Mennonite Perspectives*, ed. Willard Swartley, 17-36. Occasional Papers, No. 7, Elkhart, Ind.: Institute of Mennonite Studies, 1984.

IV. SCHOLARLY ARTICLES

"In der 'Geschichte Jesu' Leben." *Mennonitische Geschichtsblätter* 63 (2006), 51-72.

"Response to Snyder's 'The Birth and Evolution of Swiss Anabaptism.'" *Mennonite Quarterly Review* 80/4 (Oct. 2006): 685-90.

"Identifying Anabaptist Theology: A response to 'True Evangelical Faith: The Anabaptists and Christian Confession.'" *Mennonite Life* 60.3 (September 2005). www.bethelks.edu/mennonitelife/2005Sept/weaver%20response.php. (15 Nov. 2005).

"Parsing Anabaptist Theology: A Review Essay of Thomas N. Finger's *A Contemporary Anabaptist Theology*." *Direction* 34/2 (Fall 2005): 241-63.

"How My Mind Has Changed." *Mennonite Life* 60/2 (June 2005). www.bethelks.edu/mennonitelife/2005June/weaver.php (1 Aug 2005).

Comment in "Forum with John Milbank: Radical Orthodoxy and the Radical Reformation: What is Radical about Radical Orthodoxy?" *Conrad Grebel Review* 23/2 (Spring 2005): 53.

"The Violence of Satisfaction and the Satisfaction of Violence." *Mennonite Life* 59/2 (June 2004). www.bethelks.edu/mennonitelife/2004 June/weaver.php (8 July 2004).

"Renewing Theology: The Way of John Howard Yoder (Musings from Nicea to September 11)." *Fides et Historia* 35/2 (Summer/Fall 2003): 85-103.

"The John Howard Yoder Legacy: Whither the Second Generation?" *Mennonite Quarterly Review* 77/3 (July 2003): 451-71.

"The Biblical Basis of Nonviolence." *Preservings* 21 (Dec. 2002): 29-32.

"Responding to September 11—and October 7 and January 29: Which Religion Shall We Follow?" *Conrad Grebel Review* 20/2 (Spring 2002): 79-100.

"American Civil Religion, Christ-centered Theology and September 11." *Preservings* 20 (June 2002): 40-45.

"Anabaptist Theology in Face of Postmodernity: Why Theology Matters." *Preservings* no. 19 (Dec. 2001): 3-18.

"Violence in Christian Theology." *CrossCurrents* 51/2 (Summer 2001): 150-76.

"The United States Shape of Mennonite Theologizing: Some Preliminary Observations." *Mennonite Quarterly Review* 73/3 (July 1999): 631-44.

"The General versus the Particular: Exploring Assumptions in Twentieth-Century Mennonite Theologizing." *Conrad Grebel Review* 17/2 (Spring 1999): 28-51.

"The Ambiguity of Ecclesiology in 'The Anabaptist Vision': Implications for a Peace-Church Theology." *Faith and Freedom: A Journal of Christian Ethics* 6/2 (Aug. 1998): 3-11.

"Confessing Jesus Christ from the 'Margins.'" *Direction* 27/1 (Spring 1998): 28-40.

"Reading Sixteenth-Century Anabaptism Theologically: Implications for Modern Mennonites as a Peace Church." *Conrad Grebel Review* 16/1 (Winter 1998): 37-51.

"Peace-Shaped Theology." *Faith and Freedom: A Journal of Christian Ethics* 5/1-2 (June 1996): 22-28.

"Amish and Mennonite Soteriology: Revivalism and Free Church Theologizing in the Nineteenth Century." *Fides et Historia* 27/1 (Winter/Spring 1995): 30-52.

"The Anabaptist Vision: a Historical or a Theological Future? *Conrad Grebel Review* 13/1 (Winter 1995): 69-86.

"Narrative Theology in an Anabaptist-Mennonite Context." *Conrad Grebel Review* 12/2 (Spring 1994): 171-88.

"Some Theological Implications of Christus Victor." *Mennonite Quarterly Review* 68/4 (Oct. 1994): 483-499.

"Christus Victor, Ecclesiology, and Christology." *Mennonite Quarterly Review* 68/3 (July 1994): 277-90.

"Tribute to John S. Oyer." *Mennonite Quarterly Review* 67/4 (Oct. 1993): 392-93.

"Hubmaier versus Hut on the Work of Christ: The Fifth Nicolsburg Article." *Archiv für Reformationsgeschichte* 82 (1991): 171-92.

"Is the Anabaptist Vision Still Relevant?" *Pennsylvania Mennonite Heritage* 14/1 (Jan. 1991): 2-12.

"Atonement for the NonConstantinian Church." *Modern Theology* 6/4 (July 1990): 307-23.

"A Peace of Religion or a Religion of Peace." *Mennonite Life* 44/1 (March 1989): 10-14.

[Response to A. James Reimer and Thomas Finger]. *Conrad Grebel Review* 7/1 (Winter 1989): 74-79.

"Mennonites: Theology, Peace, and Identity." *Conrad Grebel Review* 6/2 (Spring 1988): 119-45.

"The Quickening of Soteriology: Atonement from Christian Burkholder to Daniel Kauffman." *Mennonite Quarterly Review* 61/1 (Jan 1987): 5-45.

"Becoming Anabaptist-Mennonite: The Contemporary Relevance of Sixteenth-Century Anabaptism." *Journal of Mennonite Studies* 4 (1986): 162-82.

[Response letter]. *Conrad Grebel Review* 4/2 (Spring 1986): 164-65.

"Pacifism and Soteriology: A Mennonite Experience." *Christian Scholar's Review* 15/1 (1985): 42-54.

"Further Reflections on 'Perspectives on a Mennonite Theology.'" *Conrad Grebel Review* 3/2 (Spring 1985): 189-93.

"The Work of Christ: On the Difficulty of Identifying an Anabaptist Perspective." *Mennonite Quarterly Review* 59/2 (April 1985): 107-29.

"Perspectives on a Mennonite Theology." *Conrad Grebel Review* 2/3 (Fall 1984): 189-210.

"A Believers' Church Christology." *Mennonite Quarterly Review* 57/2 (April 1983): 112-131.

"The Anabaptist Vision: From Recovery to Reform." *Mennonite Life* 37.3 (Sept 1982): 14-16.

"Discipleship Redefined: Four Sixteenth Century Anabaptists." *Mennonite Quarterly Review* 54/4 (July 1980): 255-79.

"Conrad Grebel's Developing Sense of Deity." *Mennonite Quarterly Review* 52/3 (July 1978): 199-213.

V. ARTICLES IN HANDBOOKS, DICTIONARIES, AND ENCYCLOPEDIAS

"Anabaptism," "Pacifism," "Wenger, John Christian," "Zwickau Prophets." In *Evangelical Dictionary of Theology*, 2nd ed., ed. Walter A. Elwell. Grand Rapids: Baker Book House, 2001.

"Pacifism." In *The Oxford Encyclopedia of the Reformation*, I-IV, ed. Hans J. Hillerbrand. New York: Oxford University, 1996.

"Holdeman, John," "Jansen, Cornelius," "Sudermann, Leonhard," "Toews, David," "Unruh, Tobias A.," "Wedel, Cornelius H." In *Dictionary of Christianity in America*, ed. Daniel G. Reid. Downers Grove, Ill.: InterVarsity, 1990.

"Hartzler, John Ellsworth," "Religious Studies." In *Mennonite Encyclopedia* V, ed. Cornelius J. Dyck and Dennis D. Martin. Scottdale, Pa.: Herald Press, 1990.

"The Search for a Mennonite Theology." In *Mennonite World Handbook*, ed. Diether Götz Lichdi, 143-52. Carol Stream, Ill.: Mennonite World Conference, 1990.

"Pacifism," "Radical Reformation," "Zwickau Prophets." *Evangelical Dictionary of Theology*, ed. Walter A. Elwell. Grand Rapids: Baker Book House, 1984.

VI. ARTICLES IN DENOMINATIONAL PERIODICALS

"The Politics of Revelation." *Mennonite Weekly Review*, 9 Aug. 2004, 6.

"Worthy is the Lamb: Revelation 5:9b-10." *The Mennonite*, 16 Dec. 2003, 16-17.

(with Brad Schantz). "Men as Women's Allies in the Church." *Women's Concerns Report* 169, Sept-Oct. 2003, 14-16.

"Following Jesus in the Face of Terror: A Peace Church Response to Terrorism." *The Mennonite*, 25 Sept. 2001, 10-11.

(with Gerald Biesecker-Mast). "Nonviolent World View Shapes the Curriculum." *Mennonite Weekly Review*, 29 March 2001, 10.

"A New (Kind of) Sister Congregation Relationship." *The Central District Reporter*, May-June 2000, 4, 7.

"The Reign of God Made Visible in Jesus. Part 2: Black Theology." *The Mennonite*, 7 Sept. 1999, 6-7.

"The Theology of Jesus Christ in the Margins. Part 1: Mennonite Theology." *The Mennonite*, 31 Aug. 1999, 4-5.

(with Gerald Biesecker-Mast). "The Church Needs to Present an Alternative to Military Solutions." *The Mennonite*, 27 Oct. 1998, 14-15.

"The Mythical Society." *The Mennonite*, 23 June 1998, 12-13.

"IsIt Lawful to Do Good on the Sabbath?" *Gospel Herald*, 10 June 1997, 1-3, 8.

"Military Personnel as Peace Church Members: Making Sure Which Game We Are Playing." *Gospel Herald*, 21 May 1996, 1-3, 6-7.

"Which Way for Mennonite Theology?" *Gospel Herald*, 23 Jan. 1996, 1-4, 8.

"Haiti: Signs of Hope, Words of Caution." *Gospel Herald*, 26 Dec. 1995, 7-8.

"A Hopeful Haiti Faces Challenges." *The Mennonite*, 14 Nov. 1995, 15-16.

"Pacifism, Starvation, and Somalia: We Must Continue to Reject Just War Thinking." *Gospel Herald*, 27 April 1993, 6-8.

"Violence Does Not Bring Peace." *The Mennonite*, 13 April 1993, 12.

(with Harry Huebner). "We Dare Not Restructure Along National

Boundaries." *Gospel Herald,* 22 Oct. 1991, 8-10; "Don't Stop at the Border." *The Mennonite* 106/20, 22 Oct. 1991, 468-69.

"Keeping Church and State Separate." *Gospel Herald,* 3 July 1990, 457-60.

"The Pledge and the Nicolaitans." *Gospel Herald,* 27 March 1990, 214-15; *The Mennonite* 105/13, 10 July 1990, 309-10.

"Rapture Predictions Fail Because Revelation Doesn't Foretell Future." *Mennonite Weekly Review,* 7 Sept. 1989, 7.

"The Coming Together of the Mennonites." *The Mennonite* 104/6, 28 March 1989, 123-25; *Gospel Herald,* 17 Jan. 1989, 36-37.

"Starting in the Middle." *The Mennonite* 103/8, 26 April 1988, 172-75.

"A Response." *Gospel Herald,* 27 Oct. 1987, 753-54.

"The Borrowers." *Gospel Herald,* 20 Oct. 1987, 729-31.

"Can the Church Regain Its Soul?" *Gospel Herald,* 21 April 1987, 265-67.

"To Love Jesus Is to Follow Him." *Gospel Herald,* 21 Oct. 1986, 710-11.

"Why Bother with Menno?" *Gospel Herald,* 28 Jan. 1986, 49-51.

"Jesus (Foundations for Our Faith—4)." *The Mennonite* 100/22, 26 Nov. 1985, 560-61.

"Anabaptists, Catholics and Mennonites." *With,* June 1985, 5-9.

"American Millennialism: A Dangerous Perspective." *Gospel Herald* (23 Oct. 1984), 734-35.

"I Came Home with Hope." *Gospel Herald,* 4 Sept. 1984, 622-23.

"Whither the Anabaptist Vision?" *Gospel Herald,* 22 Nov. 1983, 816-17; also appeared as "Anabaptists and Ongoing Reformation," *The Mennonite* 99/22, 23 Oct. 1984, 505-507.

"To Catholics from a 'Separated Brother.'" *Gospel Herald,* 13 July 1982, 478-79.

"Can Peacemakers Compete?" *With,* Jan. 1981, 6-9.

"Cut and Run or Do It All." *Gospel Herald,* 30 Sept. 1980, 772-73; also appeared as "Sit and Wait or Get With It," *The Mennonite* 96/30, 25 Aug. 1981, 470-71.

"Two Anabaptist Themes for the Twentieth Century." *Gospel Herald,* 10 June 1980, 473-76; also appeared as "Deux Thêmes Anabaptistes pour le XXe Siècle." *Christ Seul* no. 1, 1981, 9-13.

"Facing the Issues of the '80s." *Gospel Herald,* 16 Sept. 1980, 729-31.

"The Church in Mennonite Tradition." *The Mennonite* 95/27, 8 July 1980, 424-25.

"Christian Faith and Mennonite Tradition." *The Mennonite* 95/26, 24 June 1980, 406-407.

"Revelation and Eschatology." *The Mennonite* 95/16, 15 April 1980, 248-49.

"Ninety-Five Theses on the Church." *The Mennonite* 93/38, 24 Oct. 1978, 609-611, 622; and *Gospel Herald*, 31 Oct. 1978, 837-40.

"John Calvin: A Man Called to Geneva." *Gospel Herald*, 21 Feb. 1978, 152-54.

"A Down-to-Earth View of the Book of Revelation." *Gospel Herald*, 1 Nov. 1977, 810-811.

"Protestant-Catholic Dialogue?" *Gospel Herald*, 6 Aug. 1966, 707-708.

VII. BOOK REVIEWS AND BOOK NOTES

Confessions of Faith in the Anabaptist Tradition, ed. and intro. by Karl Koop. *Journal of Mennonite Studies* 25 (2007): 270-72.

History and Ideology: American Mennonite History and Definition Through History, by Rodney James Sawatsky. *Journal of Mennonite Studies* 24 (2006): 267-68.

Must Christianity Be Violent? Reflections on History, Practice, and Theology, ed. by Kenneth R. Chase and Alan Jacobs. *Conrad Grebel Review* 23/2 (Spring 2005): 104-105.

Writing Peace: The Unheard Voices of Great War Mennonite Objectors, by Melanie Springer Mock. *Theology Today* 60/4 (January 2004): 612-13.

Only the Sword of the Spirit, by Jacob A. Loewen and Wesley J. Prieb. *Preservings* 18 (June 2001): 140-41.

Creative Crusader: Edmund G. Kaufman and Mennonite Community, by James C. Juhnke. *Church History* 66/1 (March 1997): 211.

Nonviolent America: History through the Eyes of Peace, ed. by Louise Hawkley and James C. Juhnke. *Fides et Historia* 27/1 (Winter/Spring 1995): 104-106.

God Our Savior: Theology in a Christological Mode, by C. Norman Kraus. *Mennonite Life* 48/3 (Sept 1993): 34-35.

The Swiss Anabaptists: A Brief Summary of Their History and Beliefs, by Clair R. Weaver. *Pennsylvania Mennonite Heritage* 15/4 (Oct. 1992): 47-48.

Vision, Doctrine, War: Mennonite Identity and Organization in America, 1890-1930, by James C. Juhnke. *Church History* 61/1 (March 1992): 116-17.

The Anabaptists Are Back: Making Peace in a Dangerous World, by Duane Ruth-Heffelbower. *Festival Quarterly* 18/2, Summer 1991, 29.

The Brethren in Christ in Canada: Two Hundred Years of Tradition and Change, by E. Morris Sider. *Fides et Historia* 22/1 (Winter/Spring 1990): 85-87.

Jesus Christ Our Lord: Christology from a Disciple's Perspective, by C. Norman Kraus. *Mennonite Life* 44/1 (March 1989): 35-37.

The Schwenkfelders in Silesia, by Horst Weigelt. *Mennonite Quarterly Review* 63/1 (Jan 1989): 97-99.

Why I Am a Mennonite, ed. by Harry Loewen. *Festival Quarterly* 15/3, Fall 1988, 28.

Tennessee John Stoltzfus: Amish Church-Related Documents and Family Letters, ed. by Paton Yoder. Mennonite Sources and Documents, no.á1. *Pennsylvania History* 55/3 (July 1988): 226-28.

Melchior Hoffman: Social Unrest and Apocalyptic Visions in the Age of Reformation, by Klaus Deppermann. *Religious Studies Review* 14/4 (Oct. 1988): 385.

Dialogue with a Heritage: Cornelius H. Wedel and the Beginnings of Bethel College, by James C. Juhnke. *Mennonite Life* 42/2 (June 1987): 27-28.

Christian Peacemaking and International Conflict: A Realist Pacifist Perspective, by Duane K. Friesen. *Conrad Grebel Review* 5/2 (Spring 1987): 177-81.

Understanding the Atonement for the Mission of the Church, by John Driver. *Conrad Grebel Review* 4/3 (Fall 1986): 259-62.

The Theology of Martin Luther: Five Contemporary Canadian Interpretations, ed. by Egil Grislis. *Mennonite Quarterly Review* 60/4 (Oct. 1986): 583-84.

Land, Piety, Peoplehood: The Establishment of Mennonite Communities in America, 1683-1790, by Richard K. MacMaster. The Mennonite Experience in America, vol. 1. *Pennsylvania History* 533 (July 1986): 231-32.

Christologie Anabaptiste: Pilgram Marpeck et l'humanite du Christ, by Neal Blough. *Mennonite Quarterly Review* 60/3 (July 1986): 475-77.

The Sources of Swiss Anabaptism: The Grebel Letters and Related Documents, ed. by Leland Harder. Classics of the Radical Reformation, vol. 4. *Religious Studies Review* 12/2 (April 1986): 169-70.

Land, Piety, Peoplehood: The Establishment of Mennonite Communities in America, 1683-1790, by Richard K. MacMaster. The Mennonite Experience in America, vol. 1. *Religious Studies Review* 11/4 (Oct. 1985): 417-18.

Believers Baptism for Children of the Church, by Marlin Jeschke. *Religious Studies Review* 11/4 (Oct. 1985): 388.

Maintaining the Right Fellowship: A Narrative Account of Life in the Oldest Mennonite Community in North America, by John L. Ruth. Studies in Anabaptist and Mennonite History, no. 26. *Religious Studies Review* 11/3 (July 1985): 315.

The Nature of Doctrine: Religion and Theology in a Postliberal Age, by George A. Lindbeck. *Conrad Grebel Review* 3/2 (Spring 1985): 221-24.

Anabaptist Portraits, by John Allen Moore. *Mennonite Quarterly Review* 59/2 (April 1985): 194-95.

Continuity and Discontinuity in Church History. Essays Presented to George Huntston Williams on the Occasion of his 65th Birthday, ed. by F. Forrester Church and Timothy George. *Mennonite Quarterly Review* 58/4 (Oct. 1984): 539-41.

The Vision and the Reality, by Lois Barrett. *Religious Studies Review* 10/2 (April 1984): 195.

Pilgrimage of a Congregation, by Naomi Lehman. *Religious Studies Review* 9/4 (Oct. 1983): 394.

Mennonite Women, by Elaine Sommers Rich. *Religious Studies Review* 9/4 (Oct. 1983): 393.

Preacher of the People, by S. G. Shetler. *Religious Studies Review* 9/3 (July 1983): 293-94.

Catholicism, by Richard P. McBrien. *Mennonite Quarterly Review* 57/2 (April 1983): 173-74.

An Introduction to Mennonite History, 2nd. ed., ed. by C.J. Dyck. *Religious Studies Review* 8/4 (Oct. 1982): 381.

Europe in the Reformation, by Peter J. Klassen. *Mennonite Quarterly Review* 56/2 (April 1982): 215-16.

The Mennonite Story, and *The Mennonite Story: Leader's Guide*, by Rudy Baergen. *Mennonite Life* (March 1982): 31.

VIII. MISCELLANEOUS PUBLICATIONS

"Chalk: A Story of an American Abroad." *DreamSeeker Magazine*, Autumn 2007, 23-26.

Interviewed for "Swords into Ploughshares: Seeking the Non-violent God," on Australian radio program *Encounter*," broadcast on ABC Radio National, 22 April 2007. Transcript at www.abc.net.au/rn/relig/enc/default.htm (24 April 2007).

Interviewed and quoted in John Blake, "Can Box of Bones Jolt Faith in Jesus?" *The Atlanta Journal-Constitution,* 4 April 2007. www.ajc.com/living/content/printedition/2007/04/08/sleaster0408a.htm (13 April 2007).

"The Parable of the Forgiving Father." Daily reflection for website of Every Church A Peace Church (24 Nov. 2006. www.ecapc.org/articles/article-11324.htm (27 Nov. 2006).

Back cover endorsement of *Saved from Sacrifice: A Theology of the Cross*, by S. Mark Heim (Eerdmans, 2006).

"Teaching Pacifism." [Letter to the editor], *The Mennonite*, 10 Jan. 2006, 5.

"Why the Cold Shoulder?" [Letter to the editor], *The Mennonite,* 21 June 2005, 5.

"Nationalistic Name." [Letter to the editor], *Mennonite Weekly Review,* 12 July 2004, 4.

"Christ the Victor." Sermon at Second Congregational Church, Rockford, Illinois, 4 April 2004. www.secondcon.com/april42004.html (26 April 2004).

"Take, This Is My Body: Sharing in a Different Kind of Power." *Dream-Seeker Magazine,* Spring 2004, 9-13.

"Dragons of Empire." Peace and Justice Support Network of Mennonite Church USA. 2003. http://peace.mennolink.org/resources/cc-sunday03/chrrelresp.html (9 June 2003).

"An Unjust War." [Letter to the editor], *Mennonite Weekly Review* (7 April 2003), 4.

"Old Material Passed Off as Intelligence." [Letter to the editor], *The Toledo Blade* (23 Feb. 2003), B4.

"Remembering the Future: September 11 and War with Iraq." *Dream-Seeker Magazine,* Winter 2003, 34-37.

Three sidebars, in *Peace Office Newsletter* 31/4, Oct.-Dec. 2001, 2, 6, 10.

Contributed idea to "Pluggers" syndicated cartoon, 9 April 2000.

"Broken and Blessed." First Mennonite Church bulletin, 19 March 2000.

"A Report: One People, Many Stories." *Mennonite Historical Society Newsletter* 5/1 (Feb. 1999): 1.

"What I Learned from John Howard Yoder." *Mennonite Life* 53/1 (March 1998): 12.

Contributed idea to "Pluggers" syndicated cartoon, 13 March 1998.

[Letter to the editor], *U.S. News and World Report,* 12 Jan. 1998, 4.

[Letter to the editor], *Gospel Herald,* 2 Sept. 1997, 5.

[Letter to the editor], *Newsweek,* 15 Sept. 1997, 18.

"The Real Story in the Middle East." [Letter to the editor], *The Mennonite,* 10 Dec 1996, 10.

[Letter to the editor], *Sports Illustrated,* 2 Sept. 1996, 8.

"Do We Need to Give Up a Personal God?" *Mennonot* 2, Spring 1994, 14-15.

"Christian Peacemaker Teams in Haiti." *Central District Reporter* 37/1, July-Aug. 1993, 2.

"BC hosts Church Leaders Conference." *Central District Reporter* 37/1, Jan-Feb 1993, 5.

"Two Parts of the Good News." *Women's Concerns Report* no. 106, Jan.-Feb. 1993, 2-3.

[Letter to the editor], *Newsweek,* 3 Aug. 1992, 12.

Back cover endorsement of *Confessions and Catechism of the Reformation,* ed. Mark A. Noll (Baker, 1991).

"Visitor Feels at Home in Ccommunity." *Mennonite Reporter,* 24 June 1991, B4.

"The Mythical War." *CMBC Alumni Bulletin* 29/2 (Spring 1991): 6-8.

"Who Are We?" *Lancaster Conference News* 11/3, 10 Feb 1991, 7-8. [Excerpts from *PMH* 14/1 (Jan 1991): 2-12.]

[Response to Walter Klaassen]. In *Conrad Grebel Review* 8/1 (Winter 1990): 77-81.

"Today Christians...," *Salt,* July/August 1990, 19. [Excerpts from *Gospel Herald,* 27 March 1990, 214-15.]

"Choosing My Own History: Conrad Grebel or Paul Revere," *Festival Quarterly,* Fall 1985, 11-14.

"Mennonite Symbol Statements." SHUN no. 11 (Fall 1983): 28.

"Where Mennonites are Headed in the 1980s." *Christianity Today,* 20 May 1983, 74.

"A Kingdom Sampler" [Bulletin cover], from Mennonite Publishing House, 9 September 1979.

IX. BLUFFTON UNIVERSITY PUBLICATIONS

"How Can We Be Peacemakers in Today's World?" *Bluffton,* Winter 2005, 6.

"Letter to the Editor." *The Witmarsum,* 20 February 2004, 7.

"Christian Faith and Athletics: Or Can a True Mennonite Enjoy Football?" *Bluffton,* Summer 2003, 12.

"Following Jesus in the Face of Terror: A Peace Church Response to Terrorism." *The Witmarsum,* 28 September 2001, 7, 12. Reprinted from *The Mennonite,* 25 September 2001.

"Thoughts on Religion." *The Witmarsum* 85/11, 18 Dec. 1998, 3.

"On Forgiveness, Reconciliation and Healing." *The Witmarsum* 85/5, 16 Oct. 1998, 3.

"Identifying Marbeck (Center)." *The Witmarsum* 84/21, 24 April 1998, 1, 4

"Thoughts on Christians and the Status Quo." *The Witmarsum* 84/20, 17 April 1998, 2.

"Letter: Cross-Cultural Experience Important." *The Witmarsum* 83/10, 17 January 1997, 2-3.

"On Why Working for Peace Is Not Being Nice." *The Witmarsum* 81/6, 28 Oct. 1994, 2.

"Weaver's Year-Long Canadian Escapade." *The Witmarsum* 78/1, 27 Sept. 1991, 4, 5.

Oral B. Amusante [J. Denny Weaver]. "No Junior Orals Doomed Class of '77." *The Witmarsum*, 1 April 1990, 10.

"Weaver responds." *The Witmarsum* 76/3, 5 Oct. 1989, 2.

"Faculty Speak Out on Junior Oral Reform." *The Witmarsum* 75/21, 20 April 1989, 1, 2.

"The Split Infinitive and Other Threats to Civilization as We Know It." *The Witmarsum* 75/14, 26 Jan. 1989, 4.

"Dialog with a Poet." *Newsletter* of English/Speech/Communication/ Foreign Language, May 1987, 2

"Thinking Critically." *Bluffton College Scope*, Nov. 1986, 3-4.

"Research in the Small College." *Cross-Discipline*, Feb. 1986, 9-13.

"The Pros and Cons of Junior Orals: Con." *The Witmarsum* 72/15, 6 Feb. 1986, 4.

"*What* Proposes New Calendar." *The Whatmarsum*, 1 April 1985, 11.

"Sane Alternatives to the Inanity of Society." *The Whatmarsum*, 1 April 1985, 13, 14.

"TP in BARS Group Opposes Anti-Prayer Laws." *The Whatmarsum*, 1 April 1985, 14.

(with Darryl Nester). "Test your BC Knowledge with This Simple (?) Quiz." *The Witmarsum* 72/3, 10 Oct. 1985, 5.

"Garbage Digs Reveal Much About BC Faculty." *The Witmarsum* 71/13, 17 Jan. 1985, 5, 7.

"The Hoosier-Buckeye Collegiate Conference: Athletics in an Academic Context." In Bluffton College football program for game of 8 September 1984.

"The Freezeniks, or Who's Nuts?" *The Witmarsum* 70/29, 18 May 1984, 2.

"Letter to the Editor." *The Witmarsum* 70/29, 18 May 1984, 5.

Good E. Trachschuhs [J. Denny Weaver]. "An Opinion: Plodding for Jesus." *The Whatmarsum* 70/28, 11 May 1984, 2.

"The Hoosier-Buckeye Collegiate Conference: Academic Excellence and Athletic Achievement." In Bluffton College football program for game of 10 September 1983.

"War and the Trash Bag." *Bluffton College Scope*, July 1983, 7.

"Faculty Column: The Ethnic Question." *The Witmarsum*, 18 Feb. 1983, 2.

"Letter to the Editor." *The Witmarsum*, 18 Feb. 1983, 2.

"Rare Diseases Surface in Bluffton." *The Witmarsum*, 4 Dec. 1981, 4.

"Will the Real Mormons Stand Up." *The Witmarsum*, 24 April 1981, 3.

J. Penny Loafers [J. Denny Weaver]. "'Wit' Reporter Investigates College Bowl." *The Witmarsum*, 13 March 1981.

Jean de Tisserant [J. Denny Weaver]. "Bookstore Christmas Sale." *The Witmarsum*, 12 Dec. 1980, 6.

"BC Students Riot!" *The Witmarsum*, 17 Oct. 1980, 2.

"Mascot Contest." *The Half Wit*, 1 April 1980, 1-2.

"Dean's Search." *The Half Wit*, 1 April 1980, 3-4.

"Another Calendar: A Proposal." *The Half Wit*, 1 April 1980, 6-7.

"New Course Description." *The Half Wit*, 1 April 1980, 8.

(with Lisa Weaver). "Kid Lit." *The Half Wit*, 1 April 1980, 8-9.

"Quiet Thoughts for the Day." *The Half Wit*, 1 April 1980, 9.

(co-authored). "Random Thoughts." *The Witmarsum*, 7 March 1980, 7-8.

"On Teaching, Scholarship, and the Academic Community." *Cross-Discipline*, Dec. 1979, pp. 4-5.

"A New Course Description." *The Witmarsum*, 16 Nov. 1979, 5

"Mug Update." *The Witmarsum*, 16 Nov. 1979, 6.

"Plea for a Lost Mug." *The Witmarsum*. 26 Oct. 1979, 3.

"Boring Forums: Some Helpful Suggestions." *The Witmarsum*, 26 Oct. 1979, 10-11.

"Energy Conservation: A Proposal." *The Witmarsum*, 21 Sept. 1979, 13-15.

"A Research Project." *The Witmarsum*, 8 Sept. 1979, 7-8.

Answers to quiz in "Answers to Research Project," *The Witmarsum* 14 Sept. 1979, 11.

"Professors and Daughters Devise Language Exam." *The Witmarsum*, 12 Jan. 1979, 2-3.

"Religion Professor Attends Colloquium." *The Witmarsum*, 8 Dec. 1978, 3-4.

"Guest Editorial." *The Witmarsum*, 28 Oct. 1977, 9-10.

The Index

A
Abelard, 11, 133
Abraham, 85-86, 94, 99
Adam and Eve, 89
Aesthetics, 231
African American women, 270-272
Afrikaners, 315
a Lasco John, 175, 179-182
Alexander, 258
Algeria, 26
  Lycée Al-Salam, 24
Al Jazeera, 386
Al-Qaeda, 395
Ancient Near East, 351-352
Anabaptist, 48, 50, 163-166, 174-176, 186, 192-193, 196-212, 363, 366
  Atonement, 332
  Authority, 205
  Canon, 199, 203-205, 209, 211
  Central focus, 11
  Church, 154
  Communal Ecclesiology, 195
  Community, 326
  Convictions, 324
  Definition, 15
  Dutch, 175-177, 186
  Early, 331
  Faith, 10, 179
  Historic, 150
  Historiography, 193-194
  History, 11, 163-164
  Mission, 209
  Movement, 198, 206, 211
  Peacemaking, 285
  Perspectives, 13, 29, 326
  Research, 191
  Sixteenth-century, 38, 42, 43, 48, 192, 194, 196, 198-203, 205-209, 211, 272
  Social Movement, 196,
  Sources, 30
  Structures, 195
  Texts and practices, 15
  Theology, 14, 16, 30, 31, 162, 325, 329, 345
  Vision, 199, 205, 328-329
  Writings, 11
  Youth Ministry, 327, 329-330
Anabaptist Theology in Face of Postmodernity, 26, 174, 371
"Anabaptist Vision, The," 191
Anderson, Gary, 130-131
Anderson, Kristin, 390
Anderson, Paul, 74
Anselm of Canterbury, 237-240, 247, 254, 274, 276, 331
Apartheid, 391
Aporia, 38
Apostles' Creed, 331
Aquinas, Thomas, 178
Archiv für Reformationsgeschichte, 27
Arendt, Hannah, 201
Argentine Mennonite Church, 23
Aristotle, 45, 178
Arius, 258
Armani, Aziz, 319-320
Assemblies of God, 314
Associate Mennonite Biblical Seminary, 277
Asymmetrical reciprocity, 232
Atonement, 10, 11, 12, 13, 15, 30, 32, 75, 115-116, 124-125, 129, 133, 135, 138, 156-157, 159-162, 164, 225-229, 231-232, 234-238, 240-242, 247, 263-264, 272-273, 275, 277, 283-285, 287, 346, 389
  Anabaptist, 332
  Anselmian Substitutionary atonement, 22, 38, 115, 125, 129, 133-135, 138, 155, 161, 187, 207, 228, 263, 331, 395
  Biblical, 226
  Classical, 189, 270-271, 273
  Nonviolent, 247, 282, 285, 288, 290-291
  Sacrificial, 288
  Satisfaction, 67-68, 71, 107, 237, 239-240, 247, 274, 277
  Violent, 284
Augustine, 347, 361
Aulén, Gustaf, 124, 239
Aune, David, 127, 130-131
Ausbund, 41, 54
Auschwitz, 347
Ayres, Lewis, 255, 258

B
Babylonians/ Babylon, 338-341
Baker-Fletcher, Karen, 116
Baptism, 110, 184-185
Barnes, Michel, 256
Barth, Karl, 187-188, 236, 252, 311-312, 317
Bartolomé de las Casas, 387
Bauckham, Richard, 127-128, 132

418 INDEX

Beale, Gregory, 134
Bechtel, Trevor, 16
Becoming Anabaptist, 21, 26
Bedminister, Pennsylvania, 328
Bee (*Las Abejas*), 392
Beker, J. Christiaan, 68-70, 107-108
Bellah, Robert, 252
Ben-Daniel, John and Gloria, 133
Bender, Harold S., 11, 191-194, 212
Berkhof, Hendrik, 248-249, 254-257, 260
Berry, Malinda, 16
Bethel College, 21, 22
Bethel Mennonite Church (West Liberty, OH), 328
Belgium, 26
Bible, 64-65, 209, 359
  Androcentric, 267
  Gospel of John, 242
  Hebrew, 82, 84
  Law, 95-99, 108
  Narrative, 88
  Scripture, 257-260
  Text, 84, 87, 91, 92
Biesecker, Sue, 14
Blanke, Fritz, 192
Blake, William, 250
Blaurock, Georg, 197
Blenkinsopp, 360
Blueprint For Congregational Youth Ministry, 325
Bluffton College/University, 24-26, 283, 337, 345-346, 371
  Colleagues, 27
  Faculty, 26
  Marbeck Center, 382
  Mennonite Learning, 24
  NCAA, 25
  Riley Creek, 382
  Shoker Science Center, 382

The Witmarsum, 25
Bluffton, Ohio, 174, 312
Boehme, Jacob, 382
Bogomiles, 175
Bonhoeffer, Dietrich, 233
Boyd, Stephen, 363, 365-366
Brandt, Garth, 331
Bredin, Marc, 132
Bredin, Mark R., 136-137
Breton, Stanislas, 226
Bright, Bill, 330
Britton, Sally, 390
Burkholder, J. Lawrence, 12

C

Cain, 90
Campus Crusade for Christ, 330
Campus Life, 328
Canada, 28
Canadian Mennonite Bible College, 24, 345
Cannon, Katie, 116
Carey, Greg, 137-138
Carlson Brown, Joanne, 116, 237
Carnal generality, 347
Carnegie, David, 133
Cathas, 175
Chaldean Catholic, 314
Champaign County, 328
Charles, R. H., 127
Chiapas, Mexico, 392
Chomsky, Noam, 387
Chopp, Rebecca, 265-266, 273
Christ and the Powers, 249, 255
Christ, Carol, 265
Christ en de Machten: 248
Christian/ Christianity, 374
  Congregations, 301
  Constantinianism, 150
  Evangelical, 186-187
  Growth, 25

Life, 258
Meaning, 33
Mission, 312
Nonviolence, 76
Pacifism, 237-238, 310-311, 320
Peacemakers, 238
Teachings, 33
Theology, 247, 250
Tradition, 266, 273-274, 286
Worship, 341
Christian Peacemaking Teams, 17, 24-25, 318, 386-395
  Operation Dove, 390
Christian Reform Church, 177
Christology, 12, 32, 150-152, 163, 174, 182, 186, 206, 264, 285, 331, 372, 389
  Celestial flesh, 174-177, 186
  Chalcedonian, 181-182, 186
  Classical, 149, 159, 162-165
  Jesuology, 206
Church of the Brethren, 325
Church, 196, 199, 207-208, 233, 289-290, 311-312
  catholicity, 33
  Incarnational, 207
  Mission, 320
  North American, 201, 283, 288
  Post-Constantinian, 75
  Witness, 23, 28, 32, 292
Classen, Claus-Peter, 192
"Clear Refutation, A," 365
Coles, Romand, 229
Collins, John, 88
Community, 11, 334
Congregation, 42
Conrad Grebel Review, the, 26

INDEX

"Contemplation at the Bar R Ranch," 377-378
Coptic Orthodox Church, 313-314
Corporeal sensibility, 347
Council of Chalcedon, 181
Countess Anna of Oldenburg, 179
Cousar, Charles, 111, 117-118
Corpus Christianum, 199, 201
Creation, 44-45, 346, 350, 353-355, 360-361, 364
  Babylonian, 80
  Genesis, 80
  God, 92
  Idea of order, 354
Creeds,
  Ecumenical, 32-33
Cross, 50, 79, 208, 232, 239
  Cross-resurrection, 231-232
  Truth of, 55-54
Crystal City Mennonite Church, 233
Cultivation, 51, 54-55

D

Dean, Kenda Creasy, 325-326
Death, 110, 235, 289
  Jesus Christ, 68-70, 107-111, 115, 124-129, 139, 235, 239
Deep Run Mennonite Church (Bedminister, PA), 328
Deleuze, Gilles, 254
Denck, Hans, 286
Depperman, Klaus, 192
Derrida, Jacques, 348-349
Desacralization, 209
Desert, 351
Descartes, 41
Deutsche Christen, 249
Dillard, Annie, 379
Discipleship, 11, 117, 335

Ethics, 231
  Making disciples, 334
  Pacifism, 232
Disciple-Making Pastor, The, 331
Divinity, 258
Domination System, 388-396
Dominic Crossan, John, 394
Duff, Paul, 137
Duke University, 24, 28, 255
Dula, Peter, 254
Dunamis, 255-258

E

Ecclesia, 229
Ecclesiology, 16
Egyptians, 83
Egypt, 313
Einstein, Albert, 250
Elijah, 89
Ellens, J. Harold, 77
El Salvador, 387
Embodiment, 362
Empire, 201, 204-205, 210-211
Emuna Elish, 80
English Franciscans, 251
Ephesians, 10
Epistle to Martin Micron, 180
Eucharistic Feast, 232-233
Ezekiel, 93, 359-361, 366

F

Faith, 155
Fall of Interpretation: Philosophical Foundations for a Creational Hermeneutics, The, 347
Farrer, Austin, 133
Fearless Speech, 34, 41- 45
Feminist, 267, 272
  Atonement, 274
  Hermeneutic, 278
  Perspective, 277
  Theology, 26, 115-116, 264-268, 273, 275, 277, 287
  Writers, 16
Finamore, Stephen, 136
Finger, Tom, 15, 177
Finlan, Stephen, 127
Fiorenza, 130
"Fire From Heaven: the Hermeneutics of Heresy," 347
Foucault, Michael, 34-43, 254
Foundations of Christian Doctrine, 183
Four Spiritual Laws, 330, 332-333
Four Spiritual Truths of a Peacemaking God, 332
St. Francis, 375
Frankenhausen, 363-364
Freedom, 293
Friedmann, Robert, 48, 54, 150
Friesen, Abraham, 176
Funk, John, 176

G

Gadamer, 348
Gallop and Barna, 186
Gary, 23
Gelassenheit, 48-51, 54-55
General Conference, 23
General Conference Mennonite Church, 325
German Mysticism, 361
Gese, 356
Gingerich, Ray C., 15-16, 289
Girard, René, 135-136
Gnostics, 75
God,
  Back, 358-359
  Body, 349-350, 354-357, 359, 366
  Creation, 92
  Divinity, 258
  Father, 155-160, 258
  Gifts, 43, 49

420 INDEX

of truth, 50, 53
Grace, 12
Humanity, 360-361
Jesus, 80, 89, 93
Justice, 294-296
Restorative, 296-297
Kingdom, 288, 332, 337, 340-341
Law, 95-97, 99
Love, 292-296, 299-301
Mercy, 100
Mission, 296
Reconciling mission, 301
Modus operandi, 98
Name, 355-358, 366
Nonviolence, 13, 75, 77-81, 85, 137, 208, 285, 300-301
Old Testament, 82
Peace, 97, 100, 297
Power, 112, 158, 251, 253, 258-559
Reconciliation, 12, 227-228, 284, 317
Redeeming, 110, 226, 235
Reign, 32, 36, 51-52, 55, 107-108, 127, 135, 195, 201, 247, 286-287, 289-290, 297, 300, 332-335, 389, 396
Rejection of violence, 33
Restoration, 297
Resurrection of Christ, 108
Revelation, 354, 358
Sacrifice, 14
Self-Disclosure, 361
Self-Revelation, 346
Shalom, 282, 286-287, 290-301
Sovereignty, 12
Strength, 161
Submission, 55
Trinity, 229
Triumph, 117

Truth, 15, 51, 158
Victory, 341
Violence, 75-78, 81-94, 99, 284, 299
Word, 361
Yahweh, 82-86, 91
Gorgias, 46
Goshen Biblical Seminary, 24
Goshen College, 24-27
Gospel Herald, The, 26
"Gospel of All Creatures, The," 346, 362-367
Gospel, 109
Good News, 12, 14
John's, 78
Matthew's, 13
Of Jesus, 23
Government, 163-164
Grace, 11
Grebal, Conrad, 197
Gregory of Nyssa, 255, 258-260
Greeks, 34, 36, 41-42, 45
Hellenistic philosophy, 257, 352
Greenberg, 360
Grimsrud, Ted, 136
Grislis, Egil, 182, 186
Groome, Thomas, 333
Group, 325
Guatemala, 387
Guattari, Felix, 254
Gundy, Jeff, 17

H

Habermas, 348
Habits of the Heart, 252
Hagar, 268-270
Haiti, 25, 392
Hamilton, Jack, 328
Hardin, Michael, 67
Hardt, Michael, 254
Hauerwas, 233
Hays, Richard, 255
Heartland Collegiate Athletic Conference, 25
Hebrews, 78
Hebron, 391, 393

Heidegger, 348-349
Heilsgeschichte, 13
Heisenberg's Uncertainty Principle, 250
Hellenistic Philosophy, 257
Hell, 292-295, 298
Hermeneutics, 42, 267-268, 273, 278, 347-348
Strategies, 85-89
Hermsen, Terry, 383
Herodotus, 255
Hesiod, 255
Hesston College, 23, 27
Hiebert, Ted, 351
Hilary of Poiters, 178
Hildegard of Bingen, 276, 362
Hill, Charles E., 135
Hippocratic Corpus, 255-256
Historical Reconstruction, 63-66, 70-71
History of Sexuality, 34
History vs. Nature dichotomy, 351-352
Hoffman, Melchior, 175
Holy Communion, 231-234
Holy Land Trust, 318
Holy Saturday, 296
Holy Spirit, 42
Homer, 255
Hope, 113-114, 299
Hopkins, Julie, 116
"How the Boy Jesus Resisted taking Out the Trash," 372-373
Hubmaier, Balthasar, 15, 151-165
Huebner, Harry, 11, 15-16, 358-359, 367
Hull, Bill, 331-332
Husserl, 349
Hut, Hans, 151-152, 197-198, 208, 361-365
Hutterites, 157
Hütter, Richard, 310-311

INDEX

I

Idolatry, 202-203
Incarnation, 11, 179-185, 207, 240-241
Incorruptible Seed, 184-185
In One Body through the Cross: The Princeton Proposal for Christian Unity, 310
Integrated Congregational Youth Ministry Council, 325
International Solidarity Movement, 218
Interpretation, 346-348, 354-355, 362
Introducing Redemption in Christian Reminism, 274
Iraq, 312, 386-387, 395
Israeli Zochrot Association, 317
Israel, 83-86, 90-96, 99-100, 130, 339, 353
Israel, (nation) 315-316, 391
  Election, 316
  Military, 318-319
  Police, 390
  Soldiers, 390-391
Israel/Palestine, 16, 312, 317, 320, 391
  Conflict, 313, 316
James' epistle, 309-310
Jawiyya, 390-391
Jeremiah, 93
Jerusalem, 312, 393
Jesus, 75, 80, 89, 95, 100, 111, 211, 394
Body of Christ, 183, 186-188, 207, 231, 236
Christ, 97-98, 115, 228, 230, 231, 240, 287
  Christ Event, 109-110, 227, 232, 282
  Message of, 10
  Crucifixion, 116-117, 388
Death, 68-70, 107-111, 115, 124-129, 132-139, 161, 235, 239, 284
Disciples, 331
Divided/Undivided, 181-183, 185
Divine and Human nature, 159, 162, 258
Faith, 330
Flesh, 176, 178, 179, 183, 187-188
Forgiveness, 11
God's revelation, 22, 283
Historical Jesus, 65-67
Interpretive lens, 30, 94
Jesus-event, 211
Lamb, 132
Life/death/resurrection, 286-287, 294
Lordship, 208, 310-311, 316, 332
Ministry, 160
Nonviolence, 14-15, 27, 31, 66, 78-79, 208, 210, 288, 329-330
Nonviolent politics, 32, 37
Of Nazareth, 23
Reconciliation, 15
Restoration, 16
Resurrection, 13, 108-111, 115, 117, 126, 128, 139, 156, 159, 164, 200, 210, 235, 290, 297
Doctrine, 12
Power, 298
Risen, 152-153, 299-300,
Salvific value, 271
Son, 155-158, 258
Suffering, 106-107, 111, 115-118, 296
Teaching, 12, 373, 392
Truth, 33
Unity, 374
Victory: 338, 340

J

Job, 366
Johns, Loren, 15
Johnson, Janeen Bertsche, 16
Johnson, Torrey, 327-328
Jones, 136
Jordan, 313
Joris, David, 180
Josephus, 257
Jubilee (Los Angeles), 327
Judaism, 97
Jews, 338-340
"Judgment and Decision," 365
Judgment, 12, 84
  Divine, 86
Julian of Norwich, 16, 276-277, 294
Justice, 79, 208, 320
  God, 294-295
  Nonviolence-with-justice, 197
  Nonviolence-peace-with-justice, 197
  Justice-with-peace, 196
  Just-peace, 204
  Restorative, 296-297
  Shalom justice, 296

K

Kairos, 47, 52
Kallenberg, Brad, 333
Kansas City, Kansas, 23
Kant, Immanuel, 251
Kaufman, Gordon, 349, 357-359
Keeney, William, 177-178, 183
Keeping Salvation Ethical, 26, 31, 371
Kern, Kathy, 17, 24
Khirbata, 319-320
King, Martin Luther Jr., 117
Kinukawa, Hisako, 66
Kirche und Kaiser, 249
Klassen, Randy, 298
Koivisto, 348

422 INDEX

Kovacs, Judith, 136
Kraybill, Donald, 48
Kraybill, J. Nelson, 330, 332

L
Lacan, Jacques, 234
LaCocque, André, 356-357
Lamott, Anne, 379
Laws, Sophie, 132
Le Fevre, 362
Levinas, Emmanuel, 347-349
Levine, Julia, 380
Liddell, 136
Linn, Matthew, Dennis and Sheila Fabricant, 289, 296
Lints, 348
Lisa, 27
Logan County, 328
"Long Showings," 276
Lord's Supper, 183
Lossky, Vladimir, 239
Luke, 250
Luther, 206-207
Lyonett, Stanislas, 127

M
Madison, Wisconsin, 27
Mantz, Felix, 197-198
Ma'on, 390-391
Marcion, 75, 175
Marduk, 80
Marines, 28
Marion, 349
Marpeck, Pilgram, 42-43, 361-363, 365-366
Marshall, Christopher, 11, 15
Martin, Clarice, 116
Martin, Dale, 127
Martin, Dennis, 187
Martyr, 127-128
Martyr, Justin, 165
Martyr's Mirror, The, 39-40, 48, 55
  Simon, 39-40
Marx, Emmanuel, 351

Mary (mother of Jesus), 49, 175-181, 184-185
Mast, Gerald, 15, 26
McAvoy, Jane, 273-278
MCC Peace Sections, 212
MCC Washington Offices, 212
McDonald, Patricia M., 82, 90
McEntire, Mark, 86
McFague, Sallie, 349-350, 359
Meaning of the Cross, The, 11
Mechtild of Magdeburg, 276
Mennonites, 25, 54-55, 176-177, 201, 205, 310, 313-315, 358-359
  American Mennonite, 206
  Anabaptist-Mennonite, 21-25, 28, 285
  Church, 28, 191, 199, 325, 327
  Communion, 233
  Dutch, 176
  History, 192
  Identity, 283
  Literature, 372
  Nonviolence, 325
  Old Mennonite Church, 23
  Ohio Mennonite Churches, 25
  Peacemaking, 285
  Politics, 374
  Theologians, 331
  Theology, 31, 175, 230, 260, 263-264, 268, 272, 277,
  Women, 265
  Youth For Christ, 328
  Youth Ministry, 325
  Mennonite Board of Missions/ Mennonite Mission Network and Eastern

Mennonite Missions, 313
Mennonite Central Committee, 268, 283, 312-318, 320
  Teachers Abroad Program, 24
Mennonite Quarterly Review, The, 26
Mennonite, The, 26, 386-388
Merleau-Ponty, 347
Merton, Thomas, 375, 378-379
Mexican government, 392
Michelle, 27
Micron, Martin, 175, 178-181
Middle East, 313-315
Milbank, John, 229-232
Milgrom, Jacob, 130
Milton, John, 250-253
Mirror of the Martyr's, The, 387
Monogenesis vs. polygenesis debate, 194
Moses, 99, 355-360, 366
Moyer, Jason, 14
Mulholland, James, 288
Münster, 175, 197-198
Müntzer, Thomas, 197, 361-365
Muslims, 313
Myers, Ched, 393

N
Nakba (catastrophe) of 1948, 318
Narrative Christus Victor, 16-17, 31-32, 64-65, 67-68, 108, 118, 124-125, 138, 150, 156-160, 163-165, 228-229, 237, 247, 251, 263, 287-291, 297-298, 332-334, 345, 389, 394-395
Negri, Antonio, 254

Nel, Malan, 326
Nelson-Pallmeyer, 87-88
Nelson's New Illustrated Bible Dictionary, 134
New York Times, 387
Newton, Isaac, Sir, 133
Nicene-Chalcedonian, 21-23, 32, 310-311
Nicaragua, 387
Nicene, 257-259
Nicholas of Cusa, 362
Niditch, Susan, 83
Niehbur, 14
Nietzsche, Friedrich, 252
Nikolsburg, 197
  Articles, 151
Noah, 90
Noll, Mark, 33
Nominalist Theology, 251-253
Nonviolent Atonement, The, 26, 31, 65, 106, 115, 124, 248, 263, 271, 287, 324
Nonviolence, 65-66, 77, 92, 197-201, 210-211, 237-238, 311, 318-330, 371
  Atonement, 247 282, 285, 288, 290, 299
  Christianity, 76
  Divine Peace, 285
  Eschatology, 12, 291-292, 298-300
  God, 13, 75, 77-81, 85, 137, 203, 285, 300-301
  Gospel, 312
  Jesus, 14-15, 27, 31, 66, 78-79, 208, 210, 288, 329-330
  Justice, 197
  Nonviolence in liberal arts, 26
  Obedience, 240
  Peace and nonviolence, 22, 24
  Peacemaking, 25-26
  Resistance, 139, 212
  Speech, 354
Norris, Kathleen, 379
North Newton, 22, 312
Obedience, 118, 231-232
  Command-obedience, 231
  Nonviolent, 240

O

O'Connor, Flannery, 382
Old Order Amish, 48
On "Not Three Gods": To Ablabius, 259
"On the 12:50 Out of Fairfield," 380-381
On the Holy Trinity, 255
Oosterban, J. A., 187
Origen, 87

P

Pacifism, 77, 240
  Christian, 237-238, 310-311, 320
  Discipleship, 232
Packull, Werner, 192
Pahl, Jon, 329
Palestinian Badil Center for Residency and Refugee Rights, 317
Palestinian Center For Rapprochement between Peoples, 318
Palestinian, 390-393
  Christians, 315-316
  Nonviolence, 318-319
  Struggle, 318
Pannenberg, Wolfhart, 348
Parker, Rebecca, 116
Parminides, 255
Parson, Ray, 15
Paul, 10, 15, 25, 33, 42, 49-50, 67-70, 78-79, 93-100, 106, 109-118, 126, 210, 228, 231, 249, 291, 297
  Apocalyptic outlook, 107, 109
  "Christ hymn," 114
  "New Perspective," 94
  Pauline text, 15, 106
Peace, 80, 182
  Nonviolent-peace-with-justice, 197
  Justice-with-peace, 196
Peachey, Paul, 192
Pentagon, 395
Plato, 45, 257
Paradise Lost, 250, 252
Parrhesia, 34-43, 45, 48, 55
Pedersen, Johannes 133
Plaskow, Judith, 265
Philadelphia, Pennsylvania, 328
Philip, the Landgraf of Hesse, 157, 363
Philips, Dirk, 175
Philo, 257
Pindar, 255
Pippin, Tina, 137-138
Poetry, 378, 380-381
Politics of Jesus, The, 31, 255, 311
Postmodern, 43
Poulakos, John, 46
Power, 201
  Dunamis, 255-258
Powers, the, 50-52, 253-257, 388
Prepon, 47-48, 52
Price of Peace, 14
Prior, Michael, Fr., 315
Protagoras, 45-46
Pullman, Philip, 250

Q

Q, 65

R

Radner, Ephraim, 310
Rainbow Mennonite Church, 23
Raymond of Sabunde, 362
Rebirth of Images, 133
Reconciliation, 108, 286, 294-295, 320
  Universal, 286
Redemption, 12, 272, 275,

354
Reformed soteriology, 181
Reno, R. R., 310
Reply to False Accusations, 185
Reply to Micron, 176, 180
Republic, The, 257
Resistance, 339
Resurrection, 107, 200, 210-211, 275, Jesus, 13, 108-111, 115, 117, 126, 128, 139, 156, 159, 164, 200, 210, 235, 290
Reublin, Wilhelm, 197
Revelation (book of), 12, 15, 65, 67, 71, 124-126, 128-138, 337, 339-341
  "Christian War Scroll, 126
  John (author), 126-128, 130, 132-133, 135-137, 340
  Lamb, 131-133, 138
Rhetoric, 45-47
  Sophistic, 48
  Stewardship rhetoric, 51-55
Ricoeur, Paul, 352-356, 367
Riedemann, Peter, 15, 151, 157-166
Roeschley, Jane, 16
Roman Catholic, 313-314
Roth, John, 374
Rowland, Christopher, 136
Royalty, Robert Jr., 137
Ruether, Rosemary Radford, 274-275
Ruiz, Jean-Pierre, 129

S

Sabeel Ecumenical Liberation Theology Center, 317
Sacrifice, 129, 130-132, 135-136, 228, 232

Self-sacrifice, 231, 237
Salvation, 30, 38, 49, 184, 271, 295, 331-332
Satan, 252-253, 391-392
Satisfaction, 277
Sattler, Michael, 11, 198
Saving Work: Feminist Practices of Theological Education, 265
Say to This Mountain, 393
Scandal of the Evangelical Conscience, The, 186
Scapegoat, 136-137
Schiemer Leonhart, 361, 363-364
Schlaffer Hans, 361-364
Schleitheim confession, 11, 201
Schmitt, Carl, 254
Schüssler Fiorenza, Elisabeth, 129, 266-268, 273, 278
Schwager, Raymund, 79, 91, 107-108, 136, 295
Schwenckfeld, Caspar, 175
Scott, 136
Scripture, 257-260, 267, 284
September 11, 2001 (9/11), 288-289, 395
Sermon on the Mount, 154, 199
Servant, 110
Shalom, 293, 299
  Biblical, 285
  God, 282, 286-287, 290-301
  Justice, 295
Showalter, Elaine, 265
Showings, 276
Sider, Alex, 16
Sider, Ron, 186
Simons, Menno, 173-188, 197-198
Sin, 97, 99, 108, 110, 128, 160-161, 235. 238-239, 292, 298
Sinful nature of hu-

manity, 178-179
Sin offering, 130-131
Singspiration (Kansas City), 327
Sisters in the Wilderness: The Challenge of Womanist God-talk, 268
Smith, C. Henry, 25, 372
Smith, James K.A., 346-349, 354, 366-367
Smith, Jonathan K., 130
Snyder, Arnold, 150, 194
Sonia, 21, 22, 27
Sophists, 45-48, 51- 52
Soteriology, 272, 277, 352
South Africa, 315, 320, 391
Southern Baptist mission board, 314
Sown, 351
Speech and Theology, 348
Spiritualism, 366
Spirituality, 204
Sports Illustrated, 27
St. Anselm, 11
Stayer, James, 192, 194
Steinmetz, David, 24
Stewardship, 44, 51-55
Submission, 49-51, 55-56
Suffering, 106-107, 112, 116-118, 364, 366-367
  Christ's suffering, 106-107, 111, 115-116, 118
  Redemptive, 271
Sweet, Leonard, 333
Syria, 313
Syrian Orthodox Church, 313-314

T

Talbott, Thomas, 293-294
Tanner, Kathryn, 253
Tauler, 362
Teaching Peace, 26
Televangelists,
  Oral Roberts, 27
Teller, Edward, 22

Terrell, JoAnne Marie, 116
Tertullian, 56
Theologia Deutsch, 362-364
"Theological Problem of the Old Testament Doctrine of Creation, The," 350
Theologische Hoschschule, 24
Theology, 81, 153, 226, 246, 265, 283, 347, 378
 "Already, yet not yet," 338
 Black, 270
 Christian, 247, 250
 Contemporary, 310
 Feminist, 26, 115-116, 264-266, 268, 287
 Nominalist Theology, 251-253
 Non-competitive, 259
 Politics, 31
 Powers, 254-255
 Theological construction, 63-64, 71
 Two-dimensional, 358
 Womanist, 26, 115-116, 264, 268, 287
 Youth Ministry, 323-325
Third Reich, 249
Toledo Blade, 27
Torah, 93-97
Trinitarian, 228-230, 247, 255, 258
Troeltsch, Ernst, 14, 252
Truth, 29, 30, 37, 47, 196
 Cross, 53-54
 Divine, 158
 Doxa (human truth), 46
 God's truth, 51, 53-54
 Parrhesia (truth telling), 34-43, 55
 Messianic, 43
Tuckett, Christopher M., 129
Turner, H. E. W., 11

U
United States of America, 315, 387, 386
"Unity of the All," 382
Universalism, 12

V
Valentinus, 175, 178
van Batenburg, Jan, 180
van Braght, Thieleman, 40, 55
Verduin, Leonard, 176
Very Plain and Discreet Answer to Martin Micron, 176
Violence, 31, 80, 82-84, 90, 201, 211, 237, 297, 299, 311, 318, 367
 Atonement, 284, 289
 Biblical text, 86
 Death, 289
 Divine violence, 84, 88, 91-93, 98, 149, 283, 285
 Final Judgment, 75
 Human violence, 91, 99
 God, 75-78, 81-84, 86-94, 99
 Herem, 83
 Myth of Redemptive Violence, 76, 289
 Natural, 346
 Redemptive, 92, 284, 288
 Rejection of, 32, 326-329, 335
 Sacred, 92
 Salvific, 86
 Sin, 89
Voice of Christian Youth (Detroit), 327
von Rad, Gerhard, 350-352, 354
Voolstra, Sjouke, 183-184, 186

W
Walker in the Fog: On Mennonite Writing, 372
Ward, Pete, 323
War, 83-84, 139, 160
 "Christian War Scroll," 126
Waterlanders, 176
Weakness, 112-113, 161
Weaver, Alain Epp, 14, 16
Weaver, J. Denny, 254, 257, 260, 264, 295, 310-311, 345-346
 Anabaptist Understanding, 37
 Anselm's Satisfaction theory, 237
 Career, 24-25
 Challenge, 13
 Education, 23-24
 Narrative Christus Victor, 165, 287-288, 291, 332-334, 345, 389, 394-395
 Nonviolence, 374
 Perspective, 14
 Rhetoric, 14
 Style, 29, 30, 33, 36
 Teachings, 11, 13
 Theology, 10, 17, 29-31, 40, 150, 246, 248, 346
 "A-theology," 31, 36-39
 Atonement, 32, 37, 107, 115-118, 165, 324, 331
 "Bluffton school" of theology, 174
 "non-Constantinian," 247
 Nonviolent Atonement, 282
 Thought, 10
 Truth Telling, 43
 Two Lists, 149-150
 Work and Writings 16, 26-27, 174, 371
Weber, Max, 252
Welty, Lavon, 325-326
Wenger, Mary, 26
Wenger, J. C. and Ruth, 26,

176
West Bank, 313, 319, 389-391, 393
West Liberty, Ohio, 328
"Where Water Finds and Edge," 384
Whitman, 376
Why God Became Human, 274
Wi'am Center for Conflict Resolution, 318
Williams, Delores, 116, 268-274
Williams, Rowan, 251-252
Wink, Walter, 65, 76, 80, 248, 254, 318, 388
Winona Bible Conference, 327
Winona Lake, Indiana, 327
Wisdom of Solomon, 136-137
Wittgenstein, Ludwig, 225-226, 251
Woman at Bethany, 393-394
Womanist,
  Theology, 26, 115-116, 264, 268, 271-273, 277, 287
  Writers, 16
Word of Life organization (New York), 327
"Word of Life Youth Rally," 328
Word, the, 152-153, 157-159, 161
World, 348
World Trade Center, 395
Worship, 130, 138, 338, 341
Wound of Knowledge, The, 251
Wright, James, 379
Wyrtzen, Jack, 327-328
Wyschogrod, Edith, 347

Y
Yahwistic Faith, 351

Yielding, 49, 51, 54
Yoder, Cynthia, 379
Yoder, Bob, 325,
Yoder, John Howard, 11, 31, 42, 50-51, 65, 77, 206, 225-226, 254-255, 260, 310-312, 331
Yoder, Willie, 328
Youth For Christ, 327-329
Youth ministry, 16, 326,
  Anabaptist, 326, 329-330
  Mennonite, 325, 328
  Theology, 323-325
  Youth for Christ, 329
Youth Specialties, 325
Youthworker Journal, 325

Z
Zapatistas, 392
Zimmerli, 360
Zionist, 316
  Christian, 391
Zizek, Slavoj, 234, 236
Zuck, Roy, 134
Zwinglian, 180

The Contributors

Trevor George Hunsberger Bechtel is Assistant Professor of Religion at Bluffton University. He has been named the Pathways Civic Engagement Theme Scholar for 2007-2008 at Bluffton University. In this role he will begin work researching, writing and creating material for a Contemporary Anabaptist Bestiary Project. Through sermons, songs, visual art, and popular science, this project will explore God's self-revelation in the pattern of life of a variety of animals from cherubim to cats.

Malinda Elizabeth Berry is a Ph.D. candidate at Union Theological Seminary in the City of New York. She is currently a dissertation fellow at Goshen College, where she graduated from in 1996 with a B.A. She also holds an M.A. in Peace Studies from Associated Mennonite Biblical Seminary. Her dissertation in systematic theology is a comparative study of Reinhold Niebuhr and Martin Luther King Jr. and their understandings of love and justice. She co-edited *Wrestling with the Text: Young Adult Perspectives on Scripture* (Cascadia, 2007).

Susan L. Biesecker is a lecturer in the English Department at the University of Dayton (Oh.) and is author of numerous academic articles on ancient Greek, twentieth-century feminist, and radical Anabaptist rhetorics. She co-edited *Anabaptists and Postmodernity* and is currently completing a manuscript on the visual rhetorics of tourism in Amish Country.

Laura L. Brenneman is Assistant Professor of Religion at Bluffton University. She holds a Ph.D. in biblical studies from the University of Durham (England). Her forthcoming book, *Corporate Discipline and the People of God*, presents a Pauline theology of community discipline and restoration with a focus on the Corinthian correspondence.

Thomas Finger devotes his time to writing on Anabaptist theology, history, and spirituality; and to ecumenical and interfaith relations, representing Mennonite churches. Presently, this includes dialogue with Iranian religious and political leaders. He also teaches world religions part-time. He is the author of *A Contemporary Anabaptist Theology* (InterVarsity, 2004); *Self, Earth and Society* (InterVarsity, 1997); and *Christian Theology: An Eschatological Approach* (2 vols., Herald, 1985 and 1989). More recently, both he and Denny Weaver contributed essays to John Sanders, ed., *Atonement and Violence* (Abingdon, 2006).

Ray C. Gingerich is Professor of Theology and Ethics, Emeritus, at Eastern Mennonite University and currently serves as director of the Anabaptist Center for Religion and Society. In addition to numerous scholarly articles in the fields of theology, ethics, and Anabaptist history, he has co-edited *Telling Our Stories: Personal Accounts of Engagement with Scripture* (Cascadia, 2006) and *Transforming the Powers: Peace, Justice, and the Domination System* (Fortress, 2006).

Jeff Gundy is Professor of English at Bluffton University. His poetry collections include *Deerflies*, *Rhapsody with Dark Matter*, and, most recently, *Spoken among the Trees*. He is the author of *Walker in the Fog: On Mennonite Writing* (Cascadia, 2006), *Scattering Point: The World in a Mennonite Eye* (SUNY, 2003), and *A Community of Memory: My Days with George and Clara* (Illinois, 1996).

Harry Huebner is Professor of Philosophy and Theology at Canadian Mennonite University in Winnipeg, Canada. He is a graduate of the University of St. Michael's College in Toronto with a PhD (1982) in theology. He is co-author of *Church as Parable: Whatever Happened to Ethics?* (1993), and author of *Echoes of the Word: Theological Ethics as Rhetorical Practice* (2005). He has edited several books and contributed several articles in books and journals on the subject of Christian ethics. His research interests are in philosophical theology and ethics.

Loren L. Johns is Associate Professor of New Testament at the Associated Mennonite Biblical Seminary. Johns has written numerous academic books and articles, including *The Lamb Christology and the Apocalypse of John* (2003). He has edited several books, most recently *Even the Demons Submit: Continuing Jesus' Ministry of Deliverance* (2006), and *Dead Sea Scrolls: Hebrew, Aramaic, and Greek Texts with English Translations. Volume 3: Damascus Document Fragments, the Torah, and Related Documents* (2006).

Janeen Bertsche Johnson is a 1986 graduate of Bluffton University, where she worked three years as J. Denny Weaver's research assistant and took nine of the ten classes he taught. She graduated from

Associated Mennonite Biblical Seminary in 1989, served as a pastor in Wichita, Kansas from 1989-1995, and has been Campus Pastor at AMBS since 1995. She is a member of the Mennonite Church USA Executive Board and has served on numerous other denominational, conference, and congregational committees and boards.

Randy Keeler is Assistant Professor of Religion at Bluffton University and directs the youth ministry undergraduate program. Keeler, who holds a Master of Divinity from Eastern Mennonite Seminary, served for many years as the campus pastor at Bluffton. Before coming to Bluffton, Keeler served as a congregational youth pastor and also was a conference youth minister for Eastern District and Franconia conferences. He is currently a Doctor of Ministry candidate at Fuller Theological Seminary.

Kathleen Kern has worked for Christian Peacemaker Teams since 1993, serving on assignments in Haiti, Washington, D.C., West Bank, Chiapas, Colombia, South Dakota and Democratic Republic of Congo. She is the author of *We Are the Pharisees* (Herald Press 1995) and the novel, *Where Such Unmaking Reigns* (2003). She is working on a general history of CPT from 1986 to 2006 and *As Resident Aliens: CPT's work in the West Bank 1995-2005*, both of which will be published by Wipf and Stock Press. Kern also writes regular reflections for the Mennonite press.

Chris Marshall is the St. John's Associate Professor of Christian Theology at Victoria University of Wellington, New Zealand. He was first exposed to Anabaptism during doctoral studies in the United Kingdom. Since returning to his native New Zealand in 1986, he has maintained close contacts with Mennonites in the U.S and elsewhere. Among his numerous publications are *Faith as a Theme in Mark's Narrative* (Cambridge University Press, 1989), *Kingdom Come: The Kingdom of God in the Teaching of Jesus* (Impetus Publications, 1993), *Beyond Retribution: A New Testament Vision for Justice, Crime and Punishment* (Eerdmans, 2001), *Crowned with Glory and Honor: Human Rights in the Biblical Tradition* (Pandora Press U.S./Herald Press, 2001), and *The Little Book of Biblical Justice* (Good Books, 2005).

Gerald J. Mast is Professor of Communication at Bluffton University. He recently wrote *Separation and the Sword in Anabaptist Persuasion* (Cascadia, 2006). Together with J. Denny Weaver, he edited *Teaching Peace: Nonviolence and the Liberal Arts* (2003), and co-edited *Anabaptists and Postmodernity* (2000). Mast has published articles in such journals as *Rhetoric and Public Affairs, The Mennonite Quarterly Review,* and *Fides et Historia*.

Jason R. Moyer is currently a graduate student at the University of Iowa, where he studies rhetoric and public advocacy in the communication studies department. He completed his B.A. from Bluffton University and his M.A from Bowling Green State University.

Raymond F. Person Jr. is Professor of Religion at Ohio Northern University. A member of First Mennonite Church in Bluffton, Ohio, Person has published numerous books in the field of Hebrew Bible studies, including *The Deuteronomic School* (2002), *Structure and Meaning in Conversation and Literature* (1999), *The Kings/Isaiah and Kings/Jeremiah Recensions* (1997), and *Conversations with Jonah: Conversation Analysis, Literary Criticism, and the Book of Jonah* (1996).

Jane Roeschley holds an MA in Christian Formation from Associated Mennonite Biblical Seminary. She currently serves as the Associate Pastor of the Mennonite Church of Normal, Illinois, with a focus on worship and lay ministry development.

J. Alexander Sider is Assistant Professor of Religion at Bluffton University. He received his doctorate in theology and ethics from Duke University, and has authored numerous scholarly articles. He is co-editor of the Polyglossia Series with Herald Press.

Alain Epp Weaver served with Mennonite Central Committee in the Middle East for eleven years, most recently as the representative for Palestine, Jordan, and Iraq. He is the author of *States of Exile: Visions of Diaspora, Witness, and Return* (Herald Press, 2008). He also edited *Under Vine and Fig Tree: Biblical Theologies of Land and the Palestinian-Israeli Conflict* (2007) and, with Peter Dula, *Borders and Bridges: Mennonite Witness in a Religiously Diverse World* (2007), both published by Cascadia.

www.ingramcontent.com/pod-product-compliance
Ingram Content Group UK Ltd.
Pitfield, Milton Keynes, MK11 3LW, UK
UKHW021315180426
11947UKWH00015B/1238